COWLES FOUNDATION FOR RESEARCH IN ECONOMICS
AT YALE UNIVERSITY

Monograph 27

COWLES FOUNDATION

FOR RESEARCH IN ECONOMICS AT YALE UNIVERSITY

The Cowles Foundation for Research in Economics at Yale University, established as an activity of the Department of Economics in 1955, has as its purpose the conduct and encouragement of research in economics and related social sciences with particular emphasis on the development and application of logical, mathematical, and statistical methods of analysis. The professional research staff have, as a rule, a departmental appointment and some teaching responsibility.

The Cowles Foundation continues the work of the Cowles Commission for Research in Economics founded in 1932 by Alfred Cowles at Colorado Springs, Colorado. The Commission moved to Chicago in 1939 and was affiliated with the University of Chicago until 1955. In 1955 the profesional research staff of the Commission accepted appointments at Yale and, along with other members of the Yale Department of Economics, formed the research staff of the newly established Cowles Fundation.

A list of Cowles Foundation Monographs appears at the end of this volume.

Disequilibrium Dynamics

A Theoretical Analysis of Inflation and Unemployment

KATSUHITO IWAI

New Haven and London, Yale University Press

Designed by James J. Johnson
and set in Monophoto Times New Roman by
Asco Trade Typesetting Ltd., Hong Kong.
Printed in the United States of America by
Edwards Brothers, Inc., Ann Arbor, Mich.

Library of Congress Cataloging in Publication Data

Iwai, Katsuhito, 1947–
    Disequilibrium dynamics.

    (Monograph—Cowles Foundation for Research in
Economics at Yale University; 27)
    Bibliography: p.
    Includes index.
    1. Equilibrium (Economics)   2. Keynesian economics.
3. Inflation (Finance)—Mathematical models.
4. Unemployment—Mathematical models.   I. Title.
II. Series: Cowles Foundation for Research in Economics
at Yale University. Monograph; 27.
HB145.I92 339.5′0724 80–26445
ISBN 0–300–02556–4

HB
145
·I 92
1981

10   9   8   7   6   5   4   3   2   1

TO M. M.

Contents

Figures

xiii

Preface

In *The General Theory of Employment, Interest and Money*, John Maynard Keynes attacked "the celebrated *optimism* of traditional economic theory, which has led to economists being looked upon as Candides, who . . . teach that all is for the best in the best of all possible worlds provided we will let well alone." He challenged the orthodox doctrine that an unguided market economy has "a natural tendency towards optimum employment of resources." The Keynesian revolution prevailed for thirty or forty years. But now it falters. A counter-revolution, under the banners of monetarism, natural unemployment, rational expectations, and so forth, threatens to turn economics back to the Panglossian *ancien régime*.

The present book raises Keynes's challenge once again. The current crisis in economics compels certain of its basic assumptions to be reexamined critically. My focus is the central assumption of the orthodox theory that prices and wages are determined in perfectly competitive markets by the impersonal force of the law of demand and supply. In its stead, I propose a model of a monopolistically competitive economy in which the numerous interdependent firms set their own prices and fix their own wage offers without ever knowing what demands and supplies will be forthcoming. On this foundation I have tried to build a structure that explains the evolution of prices, wages, employment, and output for the economy as a whole, not as a smooth trajectory of equilibrium positions, but as a causal process that is moved by the complex pattern of dynamic interactions among firms. My main object is to establish a method of dynamic analysis which breaks away from the rigid framework of traditional theory that has been preoccupied with describing equilibrium and asserting a natural tendency toward it.

Keynes's initial challenge was less than sweeping. As a student of Alfred Marshall, he retained the assumption of perfect competition and failed to criticize the orthodox analysis of the manner in which prices are formed in a market economy. Naturally, counter-revolutionaries have attacked this unguarded spot in his theory. Marx once wrote that history repeats itself twice— the first time as tragedy, the second as farce. It is hoped that the postulate of monopolistic competition I have chosen as the new point of departure will save this second challenge from turning into a farce.

The book consists of three parts. Part I reformulates the theory of cumulative process of Knut Wicksell. It shows that if, in a monetary economy, prices and wages are flexible, a deviation from equilibrium, however small, inevitably produces errors in firms' expectations and starts a dynamic process that tends to drive prices and wages cumulatively away from equilibrium. Such a process of inflation or deflation breeds, in the course of its own development, both accelerating and decelerating forces, and whether or not it will eventually return to equilibrium is decided only by the relative strength of these conflicting forces. With flexible prices and wages there is no a priori ground for a belief in the self-adjusting character of the economic system. On the contrary, it is argued in part II, inflexibility rather than flexibility of money wages is what stabilizes a monetary economy. With sticky money wages, the system normally approaches a Keynesian equilibrium where employment is determined by effective demand. (There are, of course, no natural market forces that fix the effective demand at the level just sufficient for the maintenance of full or natural employment.) It is only in response to a macroeconomic disturbance large enough to break the inflexibility of money wages that the system abandons Keynesian equilibrium and sets off a cumulative process of inflation or deflation. A Keynesian principle of effective demand is thus integrated with a Wicksellian theory of cumulative process. Part III then undertakes a long-run analysis of inflation and unemployment. It demonstrates that a monetary economy never outlives its monetary history no matter how long it is run. In particular, if money wages rise more readily than they fall, the Phillips curve never turns vertical. The economy we happen to live in therefore never lives up to the idealized portrait of orthodox economics even in its never-never land of the long run. Part III concludes with an analysis of the problem of wage-push stagflation, showing how this can be approached by the method developed in the book.

The whole argument is set out, as far as possible, with a view to minimizing the use of nonelementary mathematics. I have therefore gathered in the mathematical appendix most of the technical discussions that demand knowledge beyond calculus and basic probability concepts or that require more than three lines of equations. The main text is, of course, self-contained.

Since this is not a book in the detective story genre, this outline of its main "plot" has not, I hope, destroyed the interest of the reader.

When I began to work on the monograph more than seven years ago, I naively supposed that all I had to do was to "complicate" the orthodox theory by introducing various forms of imperfections, frictions, or market failures into its equilibrium models. After some preliminary studies, however, I found myself in a position analogous to that of the meteorologist who first defined atmosphere as an imperfect vacuum and then tried to explain its nature and motions. I had to start all over again. Hence, the book has had an embarrassingly long gestation period. I am, therefore, very grateful to many friends and colleagues who have given me generous encouragement and helpful advice during these years. In particular, I am indebted to Masahiko Aoki, William Brainard, Takenori Inoki, Gerald Jaynes, Meir Kohn, Kazuo Sato, John Sutton, James Tobin, and Ross Zucker, who have taken the trouble to read various sections of the earlier versions of the book and have suggested many valuable improvements; to George Akerlof, who kindly served as a referee and gave me most fruitful comments and penetrating criticisms; and to many students whose reactions to this material in classrooms have led me to modify its presentation substantially. Computer programs for the numerical results in chapters 6 and 7 were written with amazing efficiency by Tim Kehoe. I wish to thank him as well as Hiroshi Yoshikawa, Kazumi Asako, Ken Ariga, and Kiyohiko Nishimura for their assistance.

The Cowles Foundation for Research in Economics, with which I have been affiliated for the last seven years, has provided an excellent environment for my work. In addition to thanking its stimulating research staff, I should like to express appreciation to Lydia Zimmerman, Mary Hawley, Dori Clifton, and the late Althea Strauss for their extensive administrative assistance and Glena Ames for her skillful typing.

Finally, I would like to thank the National Science Foundation for its generous support.

New Haven
May 1980

PART I

Wicksellian Disequilibrium Dynamics

CHAPTER 1

Dynamic Theory of the Monopolistically and Monopsonistically Competitive Firm

1. *Introduction: Wicksell's Theory of Cumulative Process*

Neoclassical economics is divided into two separate disciplines—(a) the theory of value and (b) the quantity theory of money. The theory of value is concerned primarily with the determination of the system of relative or real prices that equate demand and supply for every commodity, thereby guaranteeing the full employment of every scarce resource. The task of the quantity theory of money is then to fix the general level of nominal prices by an equilibrium relation between the demand and supply of money.

Knut Wicksell first challenged the real–monetary dichotomy of neoclassical economics and provided the key to the synthesis of these two theories. His theory of cumulative process, first presented in *Interest and Prices* (1898) and restated in *Lectures on Political Economy: Volume II* (1906), was an attempt to explain the general movement of nominal prices from the perspective of the formation of individual prices, that is, from the perspective of the theory of value (Wicksell 1935, 1936).[1] As is often the case in revolutionary ideas, the core of Wicksell's theory is remarkably simple, indeed deceptively trivial. One of the most innovative architects of neoclassical economics, Wicksell found it quite natural to choose as his point of departure the well-known law of demand and supply: price will rise if demand exceeds supply, and price will fall if supply exceeds demand. He states that "every rise or fall in the price of a particular commodity presupposes a disturbance of the equilibrium between the supply of and the demand for that commodity, whether the disturbance has actually taken place or is merely prospective." By a surprising turn of argument and without having fallen victim to the fallacy of composition, Wicksell applied this law of microeconomics to the explanation of changes in the general price level

---

Section 15, "On Markup Pricing Theory," may be regarded as optional reading.

1. Two of Wicksell's articles (1907, 1958) give brief summaries of his theory of cumulative process. The following account of Wicksell's theory owes much to Myrdal (1939).

of all commodities. "What is true in this respect of each commodity separately must doubtless be true of all commodities collectively." "A general rise in prices," he continues, "is therefore only conceivable on the supposition that the general demand has for some reason become or is expected to become greater than the supply" (Wicksell 1935, p. 159). Similarly, a general fall in prices is conceivable only on the supposition that the general demand has become or is expected to become smaller than the supply.

Wicksell was well aware that this simple idea was a step into the world of heresy. For, by tracing the fundamental cause of general rise or fall in prices to disturbance in the equilibrium relation between the general demand and supply of commodities, his theory undermined the very foundation of classical and neoclassical economics—Say's law of markets, the law that alleges that "supply creates its own demand" and hence the general demand and general supply are always and necessarily equal. He said, "This may sound paradoxical, because we have accustomed ourselves, with J. B. Say, to regard goods themselves as reciprocally constituting and limiting the demand for each other" (1935, p. 159). Wicksell, perhaps still nostalgic for the old quantity theory of money, apologetically remarked that the general demand and general supply *ultimately* coincide, but he nonetheless made the following assertion:

> We are concerned with precisely what occurs, *in the first place* with the middle link in the final exchange of one good against another which is formed by the demand of money for goods and the supply of goods against money. Any theory of money worthy of the name must be able to show how and why the monetary or pecuniary demand for goods exceeds or falls short of the supply of goods in given conditions.
>
> The advocates of the Quantity Theory have perhaps not sufficiently considered this point. They usually make the mistake of postulating their [conclusions] instead of clearly proving them. That a large and a small quantity of money *can* serve the same purposes of turnover if commodity prices rise or fall proportionately to the quantity is one thing. It is another thing to show why such a change of price must always follow a change in the quantity of money and to describe what happens [1935, p. 160]

In working out the theory of cumulative process—the theory of the movement of nominal prices in "the middle link in the final exchange of one good against another"—Wicksell came to a view that is antithetical to the doctrine of neoclassical economics. He found that the effects of a disequilibrium between general demand and supply on monetary prices are not temporal but *cumulative*: any deviation from an equilibrium sets off a dynamic process that continually leads the system away from the equilibrium. If, for any reason, the general demand is set and maintained above the general supply, no matter how small the gap, "prices will rise and will go on rising; or if they are already in the process of falling, they will fall more slowly and eventually begin to rise." If, on the other hand, the general demand is maintained below the general supply, "prices will fall continuously and without limit" (1936, p. 120).[2] Wicksell then had to conclude that "the movement and equilibrium of actual money prices represent a fundamentally different phenomenon . . . from those of *relative* prices (1936, p. 100).

> The latter might perhaps be compared with a mechanical system which satisfies the conditions of *stable* equilibrium, for instance a pendulm. Every movement away from the position of equilibrium sets forces into operation—on a scale that increases with the extent of the movement— which tend to restore the system to its original position, and actually succeed in doing so, though some oscillations may intervene.
>
> The analogous picture for *money* prices should rather be some easily movable object, such as a cylinder, which rests on a horizontal plane in so-called *neutral* equilibrium. The plane is somewhat rough and a certain force is required to set the price-cylinder in motion and to keep it in motion. But so long as this force . . . remains in operation, the cylinder continues to move in the same direction. Indeed it will, after a time, start "rolling": the motion is an accelerated one up to a certain point, and it continues for a time even when the force has ceased to operate. Once the cylinder has come to rest, there is no tendency for it to be restored to its original position. It simply remains where it is so long as no opposite forces come into operation to push it back. [1936, p. 101]

That free competition in markets produces not chaos but order has been the chief tenet of orthodox economics since the days of the Physiocrats, and it found its most arresting expression in the image of the Invisible Hand in Adam Smith's *Wealth of Nations*. In neoclassical economics, this faith in the self-regulating nature of the market system lends a teleological character to the notion of equilibrium. It is not that neoclassical theory has been indifferent to the study of disequilibrium states—the analysis of causal processes that are out of equilibrium—but that the object of its analysis of causal processes has been to reveal the existence of a tendency toward equilibrium, a tendency that underlies apparently disorderly sequences of cause and effect. Only the position of equilibrium has virtual reality; a deviation from it is merely evanescent.

---

2. Wicksell, as a student of Böhm-Bawerk, naturally sought the difference between the rate of interest determined in the credit market (i.e., the market rate of interest) and the expected yield on the newly produced capital (i.e., the normal or natural rate of interest) as the chief determinant of the level of general demand for commodities in relation to the level of general supply. This alternative characterization of the equilibrium condition in Wicksell's theory is, however, a side issue for the problems we are concerned with. It would, of course, become important as soon as we attempt to study the problem of investment and longer-run dynamic processes.

Suppose, however, that the equilibrium between general demand and supply does not have a self-regulating tendency—that any disturbance causes nominal prices to move cumulatively away from equilibrium. Then equilibrium can no longer be assured the privileged status of virtual reality. Any causal process of economic events is no less "real" than the position of equilibrium. If there is anything special about equilibrium, it is as a point of reference in the study of observed sequences of economic events, which may help us to grasp some regularities in the very dispersion of phenomena.

Wicksell's vision was an emancipation. He broke the spell of the Invisible Hand, that faith in the self-adjusting nature of the price mechanism in the market system. Economics could become, then, a "science of process" without a teleology.

Wicksell's theory of cumulative process eventually provided the new foundation of monetary theory and macroeconomics in his home country, Sweden, and was developed further by Erik Lindahl (1939), Gunner Myrdal (1939), Bertil Ohlin (1937), and others of the Stockholm school (see also Hansen 1951). It soon penetrated the Austrian school and became the basis of the trade-cycle theories of L. von Mises (1934) and Friedrich A. Hayek (1931, 1933). Its invasion into the Anglo-American community of economists came considerably later, but we see its impact in D. H. Robertson's work on monetary theory (1940) and in J. M. Keynes's *Treatise on Money* (1930).[3]

The eventual fate of the Wicksellian tradition was, however, not a happy one. Its impact on economists was soon eclipsed by the "Keynesian revolution," triggered in 1936 by the publication of Keynes's *General Theory*.[4] Its trace was then washed away, together with the economics of Keynes, in the quiet counter-revolution of neoclassical economics.[5] The recent revival of the quantity theory of money and the frictional/voluntary theory of unemployment, under the banner of monetarism and natural rate, threaten to return economics to the pre-Wicksellian era.

One of the primary objects of part I is to reconstruct a model of inflation and other disequilibrium phenomena from the Wicksellian perspective, that is, from the perspective of the microeconomic process of price formation, and to reexamine, in a critical manner, the classical and neoclassical belief of the

---

3. Keynes remained Wicksellian in his analysis of inflation even after the publication of *The General Theory* (see Keynes 1940).

4. Just after the publication of *The General Theory* there was a heated controversy between Keynes (1937a, b) and Ohlin (1937). Part II of this book is concerned with this controversy.

5. See Hicks (1946, pp. 251–54) and Patinkin (1965, note E), as examples of attempts at interpreting Wicksell's theory of cumulative process within the framework of neoclassical equilibrium theory. Naturally, they found a certain inconsistency in Wicksell's theory.

self-adjusting nature of the laissez-faire market economy. It is, in fact, a search
for a theory of process without a teleology, which has been long lost.

2. How Are Prices Formed?

How are prices formed in markets? By the law of demand and supply (so we
are told by Wicksell). Price rises when demand exceeds supply and falls when
supply exceeds demand. But "whose behavior is thereby expressed? And how
is that behavior motivated?" (Koopmans 1957, p. 179). For if, as is supposed
by the principle of perfect competition in neoclassical economics, each individual
participant in the economy takes prices as given and determines purchases and
sales accordingly, "there is no one left over whose job it is to make a decision
on price" (Arrow 1959, p. 43). There is thus a logical difficulty in the formulation
of the law of demand and supply, which was the springboard of Wicksell's
theory of cumulative process. Hence, to develop a comprehensive theory of
disequilibrium processes from the Wicksellian perspective, it is no longer possible to use Wicksell's own theory; it is necessary to go deeper than he did and
to analyze the process of price formation from the ground up.

  We have to start from scratch.

3. Price Formation in Markets without Walrasian Auctioneers

Walras, one of the founders of the neoclassical school, attempted to avoid the
logical difficulty pertaining to the law of demand and supply by superimposing
on his general equilibrium theory a peculiar model of auction process. He looked
upon "the whole world . . . as a vast general market made up of diverse markets
where social wealth is bought and sold" and then supposed that it has a well-
organized structure in which "purchases and sales are made by auction, through
the instrumentality of stockbrokers, commercial brokers or criers acting as
agents who centralize transactions in such a way that the terms of every exchange are openly announced . . ." (Walras 1954, p. 84).[6]

  At the beginning of every market day, the criers, or auctioneers, cry the
prices of commodities at random, register both demands and supplies offered
at these prices, raise the prices of those commodities for which the demand
exceeds the supply and lower the prices of those commodities for which the
supply exceeds the demand, and keep crying new prices until the demand and

---

  6. When Walras introduced the problem of production into his system, he had
to imagine two markets instead of one—one being the market of factor services and
the other the market of products. When he enlarged his system to include the problem
of capital formation, he added the market of capital goods. In those cases, the same
auction process as envisaged in the pure exchange case was supposed to work in each
market. See Walras (1954, pp. 41, 42).

supply of each and every commodity are equal. Walras's auctioneers will allow transactions of commodities among buyers and sellers to take place effectively at the established equilibrium prices and will then happily retire until the opening of the next market day (1954, pp. 40–41, 169–72, 242, 282).

The irony is that when it came to the point of explaining the formation of prices, which were supposed to act as the Invisible Hand, coordinating the "decentralized" decisions of market participants, Walras had to rely upon the instrumentality of auctioneers, whose job it was to "centralize" the formation of prices and the exchange of commodities. And the job Walras assigned his auctioneers was merely to solve "practically" the problem to which his general equilibrium theory had already given a "theoretical" solution in the form of a set of algebraic equations (1954, pp. 106, 162, 169, 241, 242). This guaranteed that the only possible state of affairs in his economy was the one characterized by the simultaneous equilibrium of demand and supply of all existing commodities. But this is solely because any other state of affairs was prevented by the very manner in which the process of price formation was conceived, that is, by the prohibition of any actual transactions at disequilibrium prices. Here, market is forced to imitate theory.

Walras's model of auction process was no more than a reiteration of the preconception of neoclassical economics. It did not get us any closer to resolving the fundamental question: Is the price mechanism really self-regulating in a decentralized economy? It was indeed a false start.

We start our critical investigation of the performance of the Invisible Hand by banishing Walrasian auctioneers from our model of the market economy. There are, after all, no auctioneers in our modern capitalistic economy (except perhaps in the Paris Bourse) who centralize the process of price formation and coordinate decentralized decisions of individual participants. No sooner do we banish the Walrasian auctioneers than we find ourselves unable to operate comfortably within the basic postulates of neoclassical economics. In particular, the hypothesis of perfect competition, which states that all sellers and buyers take prices as given, has to be abandoned once and for all. If prices are ever to be changed in the absence of auctioneers, a real economic agent who is actually buying and selling in markets must be responsible for changing them.[7]

In markets without Walrasian demons, every seller becomes a potential monopolist and every buyer becomes a potential monopsonist.[8] However, *who*

---

7. Thus, we shall not follow the counsel of conservative procedure by Clower and Leijonhufvud (1975), who prefer, at least temporarily, to "continue working with models that postulate the existence of a central coordinator of trading activity" in spite of their acknowledgment that the Walrasian model is "unsuitable for analysis and *virtual* disequilibria."

8. See the pioneering work of Arrow (1959) on this issue. Leijonhufvud (1968, especially sec. II-2) also makes an important contribution.

actually exercises the potential price-setting power and *how* that power is put to use is another matter. This is an empirical problem, which can be settled only by examining such factors as (a) the degree of standardization of the commodity traded, (b) the extent and efficiency of the information network among sellers and buyers, and (c) the numbers of buyers and sellers and their relative balance. In general, it is determined by the particular structure of market organization.[9]

The form of market organization in which approximately equal numbers (which may be just one) of buyers and sellers communicate with each other and negotiate prices may be called a "negotiated-price market."[10] In this form of market, the price-setting power is equally shared and equally exercised by buyers and sellers. Since no one in the market supplies complete information concerning possible transaction opportunities open to market participants, relevant information must be acquired through each participant's own search activity, which requires his or her own economic resources. Costs of obtaining the perfect information about possible trading opportunities (e.g., locations of buyers and sellers, their bids and offers, characteristics of commodities, trading partners' negotiating skills, etc.) are of course prohibitive. Hence, each participant must be content with imperfect information when deciding whether to trade with such and such a person at such and such a price. The term of transaction (i.e., the price) often varies from one seller to another, from one buyer to another, and from one transaction to another. If, however, the number of buyers and sellers is quite large and the information network among them is quite efficient, the average price emerging in it may not be so far away from the equilibrium price identified by the neoclassical economics. Indeed, the negotiated-price market form resembles Alfred Marshall's "corn market in a country town," which may have been the dominant form in England in the late nineteenth century when Marshall was writing (see Hicks 1965, p. 56). But its days have largely passed. Today, the negotiated-price market form is not the rule but the exception; it is found only in such well-organized markets as those for securities, raw commodities, and certain agricultural products such as corn in a country town.

To negotiate price is in itself a costly economic activity. It requires both the seller and the buyer to have detailed information about each other; it is

---

9. See Dunlop (1944, chap. 2) for an illuminating study of various structures of market organization. See also Arrow (1959).

10. Dunlop (1944) called this type of market a "bourse" when it involves many buyers and sellers and reserved the name "negotiated-price market" for the case in which the number of effective buyers and sellers is reduced to one. In this book, however, we lump these two cases together and call them summarily "negotiated-price market," to avoid possible confusion between this type of market organization and the Walras auction market, the latter of which may have been modeled after the Paris Bourse.

frustrating and time-consuming, and its outcome is uncertain. If a seller must deal separately with a large number of prospective customers, or if a buyer must purchase separately from a large number of sellers, the total of negotiation costs may become absurdly high relative to the profit to be gained from the resulting transactions. Thus, as the relative balance of numbers between buyers and sellers is tipped to one side or the other, the negotiated-price market form disappears and an entirely different form of market organization is likely to evolve. Under such circumstances we can reasonably expect that a seller or a buyer in the concentrated side of the market starts quoting a price unilaterally, asking prospective buyers or sellers to "take it or leave it." A seller or a buyer is then able to save a good deal of negotiation costs, possibly at the expense of some surpluses that could be squeezed out if discriminatory prices were charged to different buyers or sellers by separate negotiations. This form of market organization, in which one side of the market quotes a price on a take-it-or-leave-it basis, is called a "quoted-price market" (see Dunlop 1944, p. 11).

If one side of the market has adopted a take-it-or-leave-it pricing policy, those on the other side of the market have little choice but to take the quoted price as given. Thus, even traders on the clustered side of the market who are potential monopolists or monopsonists are now forced to behave as mere price takers. They can influence price formation only indirectly, through their search for the most advantageous sellers or buyers in the market.

It goes without saying that in our modern industrial economy, firms are, almost by definition, economic agents larger in size than households. They are almost invariably located on the concentrated side of the product market and sell their products to a large number of customers. They often differentiate their products from those of their rivals by changing a product's physical character-istics, by offering special services to customers, by exploiting the privileges allowed by patent and trademark, and by relying on their reputations or on differences in geographical location.[11] We can expect, therefore, that in a modern capitalistic economy it is usually firms who quote prices on a take-it-or-leave-it basis.

---

11. Recent literature on the economics of imperfect information has shown that unless very stringent assumptions are imposed as to firms' behavior out of equilibrium, the market with imperfectly informed buyers tends to approach an equilibrium in which sellers retain some price-setting power. See, for example, Rothschild (1975). It should, however, be pointed out that the differentiation of products caused by customers' imperfect information is almost always associated with other causes of product dif-ferentiation. In this book we sidestep the problem of imperfect information on the part of buyers and simply assume that the products sold by the firms are for some reason differentiated from each other. This will allow us to concentrate on the problems of imperfect information on the part of firms, which arises from their adoption of a take-it-or-leave-it pricing policy.

Nonunionized and even certain unionized labor markets also fall into the category of quoted-price markets. In this case it is employers (again, firms) who are located in the concentrated side of most of the labor market. Two employers who offer the same money wage rate are almost always differentiated by workers on the basis of varying nonpecuniary working conditions. Here again, it is firms that usually quote money wages to potential employees on a take-it-or-leave-it basis.

For our purposes we shall suppose that in the product market every price quoted by a firm is on a take-it-or-leave-it basis and that in the labor market every money wage quoted by a firm is also on a take-it-or-leave-it basis. This appears a trivial assumption to make, but its implications are far-reaching.

4. Informational Implications of Decentralized Market Organization

It is well known that in neoclassical economics, competitive equilibrium prices play two fundamental informational roles.[12] First, they signal correctly, quickly, and free of charge the relative scarcity of goods and services to all market participants. They are indeed necessary and sufficient information, in the sense that in order to decide demands and supplies, all that market participants need to know are the equilibrium prices. We may call this function of price the "signaling function." Second, the competitive equilibrium prices provide market participants with enough incentives to reveal their true preferences in the forms of purchase orders or sales offers. As no room for price negotiations is allowed, market participants do not have to fear the loss of tactical advantage by revealing their true preferences.[13] This function of prices may be called the "incentive function."

It is easy to see that in a negotiated-price market, prices cease to play any incentive function and lose, at least partially, their signaling function. For if prices are to be decided by negotiation, it is clearly advantageous that both the seller and the buyer not reveal their true preferences. Even if a negotiation is successfully concluded, each settled price acts merely as a term of the transaction, reflecting the particular circumstances related to each negotiating process. Of course, the negotiated prices convey some information about the opportunities of transactions to other market participants, but their usefulness is often very limited. It must also be noted that in a decentralized market form such as this, it is not generally costless for market participants to be informed of the prices settled in transactions in which they are not directly involved.

---

12. The classical analysis of this problem is that of Hayek (1945). A more modern treatment can be found, for instance, in Hurwicz (1960, 1972).

13. Rigorously speaking, this is true only if the number of market participants is very large and the weights of individual actions become negligible. See, for example, Hurwicz (1972) for a related discussion.

However, when the prices and wages are quoted by firms on a take-it-or-leave-it basis, part of the ground lost in regard to their signaling function is recovered, and more fundamentally, their incentive function is fully restored. Here, rather than searching around by themselves, firms allow the quoted prices and wages to disseminate directly to prospective customers and employees information about possible transaction opportunities. Prices and wages cease to be mere terms of transactions and become free and public information signals. Furthermore, because, once quoted, prices and wages are no longer liable to negotiation, it again becomes advantageous for buyers and workers to reveal to firms their ture product demands and true labor supplies.

However, a new informational problem immediately arises for firms operating under these conditions. If the prices and wages are to provide incentives for prospective customers and workers, they must be quoted *prior* to the prospective customers' product demand and prospective employees' labor supply decisions. This means that when the firms make their decisions regarding prices and wages, they are necessarily uncertain about the level of product demand and the level of labor supply which the quoted prices and wages are expected to induce. In other words, the firms must make their price and wage decisions *under inherent uncertainty*. In such circumstances, to make decisions at all, the firms have to form certain *expectations* about the product demand and labor supply schedules they are facing, and they have no choice but to base their decisions on these expectations. Now, expectations are expectations; they are always liable to disappointment. This, in turn, means that the prices and wages decided upon these often erroneous expectations, necessarily become unreliable disseminators of information. We can thus say that although the prices and wages quoted on a take-it-or-leave-it basis do effectively provide incentives for the true revelation of preferences, they nonetheless fail to reflect the true transaction opportunities available in the marketplace.

5. *The World of Competing Monopolists and Monopsonists*

So far, we have discussed only vertical market relations between firms and prospective customers in the product market and between firms and prospective employees in the labor market. There is, however, another dimension of relations that is no less important; that is the horizontal dimension relating to rivalry and interdependence between firms.

If the number of rival firms is small, there emerges an oligopolistic interdependence together with unpredictable variations of cooperative and non-cooperative behavior. For our purposes, therefore, we shall assume that the number of firms in the economy is large and that their oligopolistic interdependence (whose extents may be measured by cross-elasticities of product demands and cross-elasticities of labor supplies) is negligible. Note, however, that this by no means implies that the firms do not base their decisions on their

expectations of their rivals' actions. On the contrary, their decisions have to be guided by these expectations. What we do ignore here is firms' recognition of the impact of their own actions on their rivals' actions.

Our neglect of oligopolistic interdependence among firms is not as serious as it appears. First, it is the very behavioral assumption adopted by Cournot and Nash's noncooperative oligopoly theory, which postulates that oligopolistic firms behave as if their own price and/or output decisions had no impact on those of their rivals (see Cournot 1897 and Nash 1950). Second, even if, for example, the automobile and tobacco industries both have oligopolistic market structures, it is hard to believe that the pricing policy of General Motors takes account of its impact upon the pricing policy of Reynolds Tobacco, and vice versa.

Thus, the economic picture we are presenting here as a workable alternative to the neoclassical equilibrium theory is closely akin to that of the theory of monopolistic and monopsonistic competition, developed by Piero Sraffa (1926), Joan Robinson (1933), and E. H. Chamberlin (1933), among others, in the late 1920s and early 1930s.[14] Our main concern is not to rework this established theory, but simply to renovate its theoretical framework to make it an important building block of disequilibrium dynamics. In retrospect, the so-called monopolistic competition "revolution" has failed to live up to the enthusiasm it received at birth, and the *ancien régime* of competitive equilibrium theory has quietly succeeded in a counterrevolution. What is more disappointing and even surprising is that with the notable exception of Michal Kalecki (1938, 1939, 1954), this revolution seldom interacted with the Keynesian "revolution," which was triggered off just a few years later. Why this should have been so is an intriguing question that would require careful doctrine-historical analysis, but it can at least be said that one of the major reasons relates to the fact that the conventional method of monopolistic and monopsonistic competition theory was so rigidly static in its nature that its potentially rich informational and hence dynamic implications have never been thoroughly explored.

The aim of chapter 1 is to recast the theory of the monopolistically and monopsonistically competitive firm along flowing historical time and to prepare the ground for the construction of macroeconomic dynamics in later chapters.

6. *Period Analysis*

Time flows continuously, but human decisions are made more or less periodically. Following the tradition of the Stockholm school approach to economic

---

14. See Triffin (1940) for an attempt to remove the partial equilibrium nature of monopolistic competition. See also Negishi (1961) for a rigorous treatment of the general equilibrium analysis of the monopolistic competition theory.

dynamics (in particular, see Myrdal 1939), we shall use the method of "period analysis." Accordingly, we divide the continuous flow of time into a sequence of periods with equal length and label them by the integer index t. In general, a unit period may correspond to a week, a month, a quarter, or a year, depending on the nature of the problem at hand. We then assume that only at the junction of two adjacent periods are changes in expectations and plans allowed. At the beginning of every period, firms review their market experiences in the preceding period, revise their expectations, and make their plans for that period on the basis of the new expectations they have just formed. At the end of the period, they observe realized market outcomes and execute their plans accordingly. Within a unit period, therefore, all expectations and all plans are kept frozen.

In many respects, period analysis requires much more simplification than is needed when using continuous-time analysis. But it has the advantage of crystalizing the causal chain that links one economic position to the next. Furthermore, because of the public information nature of quoted prices and wages in our monopolistically-cum-monopsonistically competitive economy, there is necessarily a lag between the time when firms announce their prices and wages and the time when customers express their demands and workers offer their labor supplies. Also, to enhance the effectiveness of prices and wages as public signals, it is usually advantageous to fix them for some time period. (In chapter 6 we study the determination of the optimal time period between successive changes in money wages, by explicitly incorporating the cost of wage change.) Consequently, the postulate of period analysis is more apt to handle these informational characteristics of quoted-price markets.

7. The Basic Story

Imagine a world with many monopolistically and monopsonistically competitive firms. Firms are labeled by an index i running from 1 to I. We have already assumed that the number of firms in the economy is large, so that the oligopolistic interdependence between firms can be safely ignored. We shall ignore the entry and exit of firms and treat I as fixed. We shall also ignore any international trade.

Each firm is assumed to hire homogeneous workers in the labor market and sell a single differentiated product in the product market. Let us now describe how a firm, say the ith firm, behaves in our economy. Since the behavior of the firm is inherently dynamic, we must give a dynamic account of it.

At the beginning of period t, the firm announces a money wage rate $w_t(i)$ to be maintained in the rest of that period and makes a plan for labor employment. Workers in the labor market compare this money wage with money wages offered by other employers and decide whether they should apply for a job with this employer. Toward the end of the period, the firm can count the number of workers willing to work at the announced wage. Let us denote this

by $l_t(i)$ and call it the labor supply in period t. Of course, the firm does not have to hire all the labor supply. Let $h_t(i)$ represent the maximum number of workers the firm is willing to hire in period t and call it the effective demand for labor. (We give a more precise characterization of this notion in section 14.) Next, let $n_t(i)$ be the number of workers actually employed in period t. It is then natural to suppose that this actual labor employment is determined at the end of period t by the "short" side of the available labor supply $l_t(i)$ and the effective labor demand $h_t(i)$, so that we have

$$(1-1) \qquad\qquad n_t(i) = \min \left[l_t(i), h_t(i) \right].$$

(We, in fact, deduce this form of labor employment policy as an optimal solution in section 14.) When the actual labor supply falls short of the effective demand, the firm is unable to fill all the vacancies. On the other hand, if the actual labor supply turns out to be greater than the effective labor demand, a certain fraction of workers willing to work at the money wage offered become unemployed in that period. For our purposes, it is not necessary to specify how the firm distributes the limited employment among job seekers in the excess-supply situation. It may be decided on the basis of first come, first served, on the basis of seniority, or simply by casting lots. We shall, however, rule out the uniform reduction of working hours below an institutionally fixed standard hours. It is the common practice in labor markets to ration the number of workers rather than to ration the working hours of each job seeker in such circumstances.

The production activity is started at the end of period t. Production of course takes time. In the present monograph, we shall assume that a unit production cycle takes τ (≥ 1) periods and that it requires labor input only at the start of the operation. The production process is, in other words, a point input/point output process with a production period equal to τ. Output thus appears in period $(t + \tau)$. Let $q_{t+\tau}(i)$ represent the firm's output in period $(t + \tau)$. For convenience, the product is assumed to be nonstorable, so that the firm holds no final inventories. It is like Marshall's "corn," or better, "fish," in his very short-run model. But all services, as well as such products as fashion clothes and automobiles, which change their styles every season or every year and thus quickly depreciate the values of their secondhand models, also fall into this category of products. It is widely believed that the rigidity of prices has a great deal to do with the storability of products. This, however, does not seem to be borne out by facts. Products such as raw commodities and agricultural products, and of course securities, whose prices are most flexible, are often the most durable commodities, whereas prices of labor services, which are far more perishable than "fish," are associated with one of the most rigid prices in the entire economy. The durability of product is merely one of many factors that determine the structure of market organization, which is the ultimate determinant of the extent of price flexibility.

In general, inventories in the form of final stocks perform at least two distinct functions. First, they function as an absorber of volatile short-run changes in demand conditions. Second, an unexpected change in final inventories signals the firm that a revision of its expectations regarding the demand condition is desirable. It should be borne in mind, however, that our assumption of product perishability eliminates only the first of these functions; the second is retained. Even if the product is not durable, the mere observation of an abnormal excess demand or supply warns the firm to revise its expectation regarding demand conditions. In this sense, our neglect of final inventories is not as serious as it first appears.

(But, of course, it is still very serious.)

The firm has to sell its output $q_{t+\tau}(i)$ during period $(t + \tau)$. At the beginning of that period, the firm announces a price $p_{t+\tau}(i)$ and makes a plan for the sale of its product. Buyers in the product market compare this price with prices simultaneously announced by other firms and decide how many orders they should send this particular firm. By the close of the period the firm can count the number of orders for its product. Let us denote this by $x_{t+\tau}(i)$ and call it the product demand in period $(t + \tau)$. If this current demand falls short of a given product supply $q_{t+\tau}(i)$, the firm must leave the excess supply in its warehouse to rot or become outmoded. If, on the other hand, demand exceeds supply, the firm may either ration the orders, or leave unfilled orders to be filled in the next period, thus risking their cancellation. For simplicity, we assume that the cancellation rate of unfilled orders is 100 percent, so that the carrying of unfilled orders is equivalent to the rationing of orders. It is then obvious that the product sale in period $(t + \tau)$, represented by $y_{t+\tau}(i)$, is determined by the short side of current demand and supply: that is,

$$(1-2) \qquad\qquad y_{t+\tau}(i) = \min\left[x_{t+\tau}(i), q_{t+\tau}(i)\right].$$

This completes our description of a basic cycle in the firm's short-run market activity, which constitutes a succession of the stages of money wage determination, labor employment decision, production activity, price formation, and product sale. The excess of sales revenue over wage cost, given by $p_{t+\tau}(i)y_{t+\tau}(i) - w_t(i)n_t(i)$, defines the gross profit accrued to the ith firm from this activity cycle. (In this definition of gross profit, we have ignored the existence of a time discount rate.) Since the study of a firm's investment decisions is beyond the scope of this book, we ignore the existence of overhead and user costs in the following analysis.

8. *An Overview of the Model of the Firm*

To ensure its continued existence as an organization, a firm must start a new activity cycle in each period and follow up the sequence of different phases in each cylce. The firm as an organization is thus characterized by the coexistence of different phases of successively renewed short-run activity cycles. Figure 1–1 illustrates this synchronic-cum-diachronic nature of a firm's market activities.

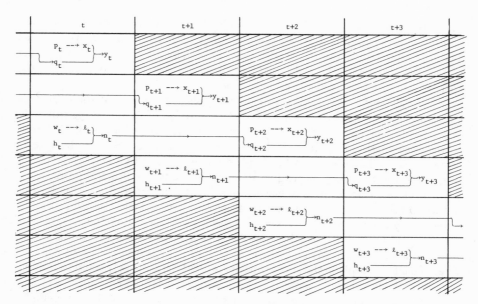

FIGURE 1–1. The Synchronic-cum-Diachronic Nature of the Firm's Short-Run
Market Activities. In this diagram, the production lag τ is assumed
to be two periods.

With the help of figure 1–1, it is possible, even at this earlier stage, to
present a brief overview of the nature of an individual firm's decision process.
It may not be fully comprehensible, but it should help the reader understand
the more rigorous analysis that will ensure.

At the beginning of each period, the firm has to make decisions simultaneously as to different phases of different activity cycles. To be specific, at the
beginning of period t, the firm has to decide the price of its product $p_t(i)$ in the
product market, and the rate of money wage $w_t(i)$ and the level of effective labor
demand $h_t(i)$ in the labor market.

When the firm contemplates the pricing policy it should take, it already
knows the amount of output $q_t(i)$ coming from the production process started
τ periods before, but it does not have complete knowledge of the number of
orders it will receive from buyers. The firm's pricing policy is therefore guided
by the amount of output it has to sell as well as by its *expectations* regarding
the briskness of the current product market. The former is likely to exert downward pressure on the level of price, and the latter, upward pressure.

In the labor market, the firm has to determine the level of effective labor
demand $h_t(i)$, the maximum number of workers it is willing to hire in a period.
The purpose of labor employment is, of course, to produce output that will be
sold in the future product market. To determine the level of effective labor
demand, the firm must therefore compare the prospective sales revenue in the
future with the wage cost associated with current employment. The former

depends upon the briskness of demand conditions in the future product market, and the latter is governed by the rate of money wage the firm pays its workers. The firm thus tends to raise its effective labor demand if the state of product demand is expected to be more prosperous in the future, but to lower it if the current rate of money wage becomes higher.

The rate of money wage $w_t(i)$ is also a policy variable that the firm must determine at the beginning of period t. The purpose of money wage policy is, of course, for the employment of workers, the purpose of which is, as we know, to produce salable output in the future product market. Hence, the rate of money wage is, like the level of effective demand, guided by the firm's expectations as to the briskness of product demand in the future. Furthermore, when the firm decides on its money wage policy, it also has incomplete knowledge of the supply of labor that its money wage rate will attract. The firm's money wage policy thus depends also on its expectations regarding the tightness of labor supply in the current labor market. The firm will bid up its money wage when either the future product demand is expected to become more brisk or when the labor supply in the short run (the present period) is expected to tighten.

Once the firm has chosen product price, effective labor demand, and money wage at the beginning of period t, no real decisions in markets remain to be made during the rest of the period. The firm has only to sit back and observe the demand for its product and the supply of labor. Toward the end of period t, the firm compares the realized demand for its product $x_t(i)$ in the product market with the available supply $q_t(i)$ and sets the sales level $y_t(i)$ equal to their short side; and the firm compares the realized labor supply $l_t(i)$ in the labor market with the effective labor demand $h_t(i)$ and sets the actual employment level $n_t(i)$ equal to their short side. In either case, all the firm has to do is to execute its plans in accordance to the realized market outcomes.

As the next period opens up, the firm reviews all the market experiences it had in the previous period and, if necessary, revises expectations about the current as well as the future market environment. It will then make a new round of simultaneous decisions on product price, effective labor demand, and money wage in the light of newly revised expectations, and wait until the end of the period to execute its employment and sales plans. The firm will repeat this decision process period by period from then on.

The basic story is as simple as this. What remains to be done in this chapter is to work out the details and make the analysis more rigorous and at the same time, more intelligible. Toward this end, we have to sacrifice certain mathematical generality. Specifically, we introduce simplifying assumptions as to (a) the representation of the firm's incomplete knowledge about market environment, (b) the setting up of its objective function, (c) the specification of its production process, (d) the specification of its product demand schedule, and (e) the specification of its labor supply schedule. The model consequent on these assumptions will be, of course, a very special one. We believe, however, that it will incorporate at least those elements that are indispensable for a meaningful description of the behavior of a modern manufacturing firm when making decisions involving time and uncertainty. We hope that the generality of the theory will be judged not by the generality of the mathematical apparatus used but by the generality of implications that are generated. We start by specifying our model.

9. On the Maximization Hypothesis in a World of Uncertainty

In the hypothetical world of complete certainty, we would have no problem formulating a firm's decision-making considerations. Any knowledge could be easily quantified and any decision process could be reduced to the simple mathematical problem of optimizing a well-defined objective function. In a world of uncertainty, however, the best a firm can do is to represent its own imperfect knowledge by suitable subjective probability distributions and to make its decisions on the basis of these distributions, no matter how difficult the task might be.

There is a great deal of controversy as to whether uncertain knowledge about the future can be represented by such a concept as a subjective probability distribution. It is sometimes argued that the search for defects in neoclassical economic theory should center on its use of the calculus of probability, which is "capable of reducing uncertainty to the same calculable status as that of certainty itself" (Keynes 1937a). However, in the treatment of *dynamic* questions pertaining to disequilibria in a monetary economy, it is of the utmost importance to separate this question—whether or not each firm (or more generally each economic agent) makes its decision on the basis of subjective probability distributions—from the more fundamental question of whether firms are ever capable of forming correct probability distributions regarding their market environment. The first question is essentially empirical, whereas the second can be dealt with within the realm of economic logic. Here, we sidestep the first question and devote ourselves entirely to the second. Indeed, in chapter 3 we demonstrate that in a monetary economy the subjective probability distributions of a majority of firms are *bound* to be falsified by the very aggregate outcome of their own market decisions. Needless to say, the force of our thesis would be greatly strengthened if each firm did not even bother to form subjective probability distributions when judging uncertain futures. In this sense, our assumption about the formation of subjective probability distributions is merely "strategic."

Even if we had ignored deep philosophical issues pertaining to the notion of subjective probabilities, we still have to face another equally embarrassing problem. In the world of uncertainty, there is considerable doubt about the explanatory power of the conventional "maximization hypothesis." The "satisficing principle" advocated by the behavioral school of economists is indeed a powerful hypothesis as to the description of a firm's behavior under uncertainty (Simon 1955). Here, however, we shall stick to the conventional wisdom. (However, the model of money wage adjustment we develop in chapter 6 has exactly the same behavioral structure as that of a satisficing decision maker. This model of money wage adjustment is derived by maximization of the long-run average profit with an explicit introduction of the costs of decision making.) We have several reasons for doing this.

Having assumed away the oligopolistic interdependence between firms, we have eliminated from our model game-theoretic uncertainty, whose existence is often singled out as the chief cause of the difficulty of setting up a sensible objective function for the firm. Another reason is operational: The maximization hypothesis would enable us to keep track of the connection between the firm's (or its manager's) inner perception of the surrounding market environment and its actual actions we can observe in the markets. This hypothesis, at least, is not a black box. Indeed, without this transparency, it would become almost impossible to develop a comprehensive dynamic theory that could deal with the interaction between individual firms' coping with their uncertain market environment on the basis of their expectations and the market environment itself, which is in turn at least partially comprised of the collectivity of the individual firms' behaviors. But the major reason is strategic: we would like to demonstrate that even if the firm were assumed to be a maximizer, the dynamic workings of the decentralized market economy are fundamentally different from those described by neoclassical equilibrium theory.

Hereafter, we assume that our firm makes its decisions so as to maximize the subjective expectation of its gross profit. Because of several simplifying assumptions made so far, our firm does not have to look beyond a single production period for its decisions. For convenience, we also suppose that the firm is neutral toward risk, although it would not be difficult to introduce risk aversion.

10. *The Short-Run Production Function*

Our firm is assumed to produce a single differentiated product with inputs of homogeneous labor and heterogeneous capital goods. (Raw materials and intermediate products will be ignored; but see footnote 17 in chapter 3.) In a short period of time, the stock of capital goods can be regarded as fixed, and only the input of labor time regulates the current rate of output. This short-run technological relation between the rate of output and the required level of labor input can be summarized by a short-run production function. For mathematical convenience in the following analysis, we adopt the simplest specification of short-run production function, a first-order approximation to the more general functional form. We have already assumed that the production process is a point input/point output process with a production period τ (≥ 1).

(It is also assumed that the production period τ is uniform across firms.) If it is assumed further that the degree of returns to labor input, denoted by $\gamma(i)$, is constant, the ith firm's short-run production function can be represented by the following multiplicative form:

$$(1\text{--}3) \qquad\qquad q_{t+\tau}(i) = j_t(i)n_t(i)^{\gamma(i)}, \qquad i = 1, 2, \ldots, I,$$

$q_{t+\tau}(i)$ being the rate of output in period $(t + \tau)$, $n_t(i)$ the level of labor input (measured by the number of workers) employed at the end of the tth period, and $j_t(i)$ a given index of productivity during the tth period. This short-run production function is subject to increasing, constant, or decreasing returns to labor input, as the parameter $\gamma(i)$ is greater than, equal to, or less than unity. There is overwhelming empirical evidence suggesting that the short-run production functions of most manufacturing firms are subject to constant or increasing returns to labor input, at least up to a point corresponding to a given production capacity of the stock of capital goods (see, e.g., Johnston 1960).[15] It is important to note that this model of the firm allows not only decreasing but also constant and, to a certain extent, increasing returns to labor input. To simplify the exposition, we assume in what follows that the productive capacity of the stock of capital goods is seldom reached even in booms, as a result of the availability of abundant reserve capacities. This does not, however, imply that each firm can expand output indefinitely; it implies only that the sole bottleneck of each firm's productive capacity is the availability of workers in the present labor market.

Note that the time-consuming nature of the production process introduces, in addition to the uncertainty injected by the signaling function of the take-it-or-leave-it price and wage policy, yet another source of uncertainty. (As a matter of fact, the very fact that production processes are organized by capitalistic firms in the capitalistic economy has stemmed precisely from the "capitalistic" nature of production—the fact that production takes time.) Output from today's input will appear in the product market only in a certain future period. But the future is, of course, unknowable. The firms have thus no choice but to base today's decisions regarding wage and labor employment upon their expectations about the state of product demand in the future. In other words, when production takes time, wage and employment decisions necessarily involve an element of speculation. Clearly, the longer the production period, the

---

15. Kuh (1965), Neild (1963), and many others have found the pro-cyclical movement of labor productivity in manufacturing industries. Within the framework of this book, this phenomenon can be explained either as a reflection of the existence of increasing returns to labor input in the short run, or as a reflection of the existence of indirect workers who are not directly engaged in production and whose employment level is insensitive to short-run business fluctuations. The second explanation is, of course, close to the idea of labor hoarding studied by Solow (1968) and Fair (1969).

harder it becomes for firms to form reliable expectations about relevant future market conditions.

11. *The Product Demand Schedule*

In the product market, households, firms, and governments spend their money on various products offered by a number of firms. It is often convenient to lump these different decision units together and simply call them "spenders" in the product market. They constitute the demand side of the market. Let us denote by $P_t X_t$ the total nominal value of all the purchase orders sent to firms during period t. And let us interpret P_t as representing an index of the general price level in period t. [The formal definition of P_t is given by (A1–1) in appendix 1–a.] Then, the total *real* value of spenders' purchase orders in period t is given by X_t. This X_t is nothing but Keynesian effective demand and is called the total product demand in period t. It is not necessary at this stage to elucidate the mechanism through which X_t is determined in the economy.

Firms in the product market are competing with each other for a given level of total product demand. We denote as $p_t(i)$ the price the ith firm quotes in period t and as $x_t(i)$ the demand for its product in period t. Their product, $p_t(i)x_t(i)$, represents the value of the demand for the ith firm's product. It is then evident that the total sum of these values across firms must add up to the nominal value of total product demand in each period; that is, we have the following "adding-up equation":

$$(1–4) \qquad \sum_{i=1}^{I} p_t(i)x_t(i) = P_t X_t.$$

To complete the picture of the product market, we have to explain the factors that determine how a given level of total product demand is divided across various products offered by various firms, while maintaining the adding-up condition. In other words, we have to specify the system of product demand schedules. Spenders' needs, tastes, and goodwill are, of course, the major factors influencing the allocation of their total product demand. They are, however, rather long-run determinants and are taken here to be fixed. In the short run, it is primilarily the system of *relative* prices that governs the division of total product demand among firms. It is one of the most basic principles in economics that spenders, as long as they are free from money illusion, determine their purchases of a particular product not on the basis of the nominal price per se but on the basis of its relation to the prices of other products. Since the index of general price P_t aggregates all the prices quoted in the product market, we can represent the relative price of the ith firm's product by $p_t(i)/P_t$. (That an individual firm can control only the nominal value of its price, even though the demand for its product is regulated by its relation to the other firms' pricing decisions, will become a key fact in our theory of cumulative inflation process in chapter 3.) All the other factors (except, of course, the level of total product demand) are lumped together and relegated to the rather peripheral position of random disturbance. Let this random disturbance in period t be denoted by $\alpha_t(i)$. We shall then suppose that the demand for the ith firm's product in period t is determined by the following constant-elasticity schedule:

$$(1-5) \qquad x_t(i) = \left[\frac{p_t(i)}{P_t}\right]^{-\eta(i)} X_t^{\xi(i)} \alpha_t(i); \qquad i = 1, 2, \ldots, I.$$

This is perhaps the simplest specification of product demand schedules that is capable of incorporating our view of the product market as a world of many competing monopolists. It might be regarded as a first-order approximation to the more general system of product demand schedules.

The price elasticity $\eta(i)$ in the schedule above is assumed to be a constant greater than unity. Its reciprocal, $1/\eta(i)$, is sometimes called the "degree of monopoly," for it measures the power of each firm to raise its own price relative to its rivals' prices. One can expect that in the long run the degree of monopoly reflects not only the spenders' tastes for, needs of, and goodwill to a particular firm's product, but also the "process of concentration" in the whole economy (or in a particular industry group) (see Kalecki 1954, chap. 1). In the short run, it is essentially a given datum both to an individual firm and to the economy as a whole. The total-demand elasticity, $\xi(i) > 0$, on the other hand, measures the responsiveness of the demand for product i to a change in the level of total product demand X_t. (We may say that the product is a necessity if it is less than unity, and a luxury if it is greater than unity.)

In appendix 1–a, we demonstrate that the system of product demand schedules (1–5) is, under an appropriate definition of the general price level P_t, consistent with the adding-up equation (1–4). We also discuss there some of the important properties possessed by this product demand system.

Notice that the notion of product demand employed here is different from that of planned or ex ante demand for product. Ours is the spenders' binding offer of purchase (or binding order) of a certain amount of given product. In a world of uncertainty, a spender must take into account the possibility that a shortage of supply may render the firm unable to fulfill all of his or her orders. He or she has therefore to form a certain subjective probability distribution of the possible purchase in order to decide the magnitude of his or her purchase order. The notion of ex ante demand may then be defined as the expected value of the uncertain amount of actual purchase. Obviously, it should be smaller than the product demand the spender actually signals to the firm.

12. *The Labor Supply Schedule*

In the labor market, workers supply their labor power to various firms. Let us recall that we have represented by $l_t(i)$ the number of workers willing to work with the ith firm in period t. Let us then denote by L_t the sum total of all the labor supplies in period t, which is defined by the following adding-up equation:

$$(1-6) \qquad \sum_{i=1}^{I} l_t(i) = L_t.$$

We shall call L_t the total labor supply in period t. Standard textbooks tell us that the level of total labor supply is determined by such economic factors as (a) average real wage rate, (b) anticipated rate of change in real wages, (c) aggregate rate of unemployment, and so on. However, little harm would be done even if we would regard it as a fixed datum in a short period of time.

Our monopsonistic firms compete with each other for a given level of total labor supply. For convenience, we shall assume that each worker can apply only to a single employer in each period, although we could modify this assumption at the expense of analytical simplicity.[16] Abstracting from many empirically important factors, we shall again single out the system of relative money wages as the main factor determining how a given level of total labor supply is distributed among various employers. All the other factors except the level of total labor supply will be treated as random disturbances. Let $w_t(i)$, W_t, and $\beta_t(i)$ represent, respectively, the money wage rate of the ith employer, the general money wage level [defined by (A1–3) in appendix 1–b], and the random disturbance summarizing all the other factors. We shall then specify the labor supply schedule to the ith employer as follows:

$$(1-7) \qquad l_t(i) = \left[\frac{w_t(i)}{W_t} \right]^{\varepsilon(i)} L_t^{\lambda(i)} \beta_t(i), \qquad i = 1, 2, \ldots, I.$$

This can be once again regarded as a first-order approximation to the more general functional form.

The wage elasticity $\varepsilon(i)$ is assumed to be a constant positive number. The reciprocal of the wage elasticity $1/\varepsilon(i)$, sometimes called the "degree of monopsony," measures the ith employer's power to raise its own money wage relative to the competing firms' money wages in the labor market. In the long run it will reflect not only workers' preferences for a particular firm's working condition but also the "process of concentration" in the whole economy. But in

---

16. We have thus eliminated the possibility of the workers, unsuccessful in finding jobs in their first application, rushing to other firms whose gates are still open, *within a unit period*. We have also ignored the similar possibility for the spenders in product markets. We do not believe, however, that the main themes of this book would be affected by introducing these complications into our model. Recent works by Barro and Grossman (1971), Bennasy (1975), Younes (1976), Grandmont and Laroque (1976), Drèze (1975), and Malinvaud (1977) are mainly concerned with the notion of within-period equilibrium for such search behaviors of market participants.

the short run it can be regarded as a given datum. On the other hand, the total-labor-supply elasticity $\lambda(i)$ measures the proportional sensitivity of labor supply to firm i to a change in the total labor force. Finally, the random disturbance $\beta_t(i)$ is exogenous to the system of labor supply schedules.

In appendix 1–b, we specify the formula for the index of general money wage W_t, which makes the system of labor supply schedules (1–7) consistent with the adding-up equation (1–6).

The reader may have already recognized that by having supposed that workers respond only to actual, rather than estimated, relative wages, we eliminated the possibility of workers' voluntary unemployment caused by their misconception of the distribution of actual money wages available in the labor market. We believe that, in spite of the great theoretical emphasis being put on this cause of voluntary unemployment in the recent "search theory of unemployment," it is empirically rather a minor cause of unemployment compared with the magnitude of involuntary unemployment with which we are concerned.[17]

13. The Optimal Pricing Policy

We are now in a position to embark upon a detailed analysis of how the firm will cope with an uncertain market environment and make decisions on money wage, labor employment, and product price. For convenience, we begin with an analysis of its pricing policy in the product market, postponing to later sections a study of its employment and money wage policy. Since in what follows we deal only with the behavior of a single firm, we shall omit the firm-specific index i from the present section (until the beginning of chapter 3, where we begin an analysis of the economy as a whole).

At the beginning of period t, the firm has to decide the level of product price, p_t, that it will quote in the product market on a take-it-or-leave-it basis. The amount of output, q_t, that the firm wishes to sell in the same period is already given by the labor employment decision made τ periods earlier. On the other hand, when the firm contemplates what pricing policy to use, it has only an imperfect knowledge of the demand for its product. By the imperfection

---

17. See Phelps, Mortensen, Alchian, and Lucas and Rapping, in Phelps et al. (1970), for the search-theoretic explanation of voluntary unemployment. Note that our model still has room for search-theoretic voluntary unemployment, for the level of total labor supply L_t may depend upon workers' anticipations of general price level and general money wage level, and their misapprehension of these aggregate variables may cause their voluntary withdrawal from employment and hence voluntary unemployment. In fact, the theory of voluntary unemployment by Friedman (1968) is based on this mechanism. We do not, however, consider this problem further. See Clark and Summers (1979) for an interesting empirical criticism of the search-theoretic explanation of unemployment.

of knowledge we mean two things. First, the firm does not know the true structure of the product demand schedule (1–5). Its properties must be perceived through its past experience in the product market in addition to its a priori knowledge. Sometimes the product demand schedule perceived is very inaccurate and has no resemblance to the true schedule. Sometimes it is very accurate. But for our purposes it does not seem unreasonable to suppose that the firm has succeeded in constructing the following reasonable subjective demand schedule:

$$(1\text{–}8) \qquad\qquad x_t = \left(\frac{p_t}{P_t}\right)^{-\hat{\eta}} X_t^{\hat{\xi}} \alpha_t.$$

Here, $\hat{\eta} > 1$ and $\hat{\xi} > 0$ are the firm's subjective estimates of the price elasticity and the total-demand elasticity, respectively. We suppose that the firm behaves as if their values were known with certainty. (In what follows a caret above a symbol indicates that it is a subjective parameter.) Thus, the only mistake we have allowed for our firm in its subjective specification of the demand schedule is an under or overestimation of η and ξ.

To simplify the notation, let us amalgamate the general price level, the total product demand, and the random disturbance into a single variable a_t:

$$(1\text{–}9) \qquad\qquad a_t \equiv P_t^{\hat{\eta}} X_t^{\hat{\xi}} \alpha_t.$$

We shall call this new variable the "state of product demand" in period t. It summarizes the extent of the briskness of business conditions in the product market in period t. Then the subjective product demand schedule (1–8) can be rewritten as

$$(1\text{–}8') \qquad\qquad x_t = p_t^{-\hat{\eta}} a_t.$$

This is no more than a constant-elasticity demand function with a single multiplicative shift parameter a_t.

The second meaning of the imperfection of knowledge is that when the firm decides its product price at the beginning of period t, it is impossible to know the true value of the state of product demand a_t. The general price level, the level of total product demand, and the value of random disturbance, all of which are amalgamated into it, are all beyond the direct control of an individual firm. The best the firm can do is to form a certain subjective probability distribution of a_t and then make decisions on its basis. Now, we need to introduce some new notations, in order to represent the firm's subjective probability distribution of a_t in a formal manner. First, we denote by δ_t the set of data available to the firm at the beginning of period t. Since the firm reviews all the past experiences only at the beginning of each period, this represents all the data on the basis of which decisions in period t have to be made. We denote by $\hat{E}(a_t : \delta_t)$ the firm's subjective expectation of the state of product demand a_t, evaluated on the basis of the available data δ_t. Since the firm keeps accumulating new information from its period-to-period activities, the state of information, or δ_t, has to be specified explicitly lest we lose track of the *evolving* flow of information and its dynamic impact upon the firm's expectation-formation process. But the discussion of how this subjective expectation is formed over time will be postponed until chapter 2. For the time being, we shall treat it as a given datum. (This should *not* be confused with the often-made assumption of static expectation.)

Unlike the neoclassical world of perfect competition in which every market participant has to guess only *the* equilibrium price, there is no way of replacing uncertainty with precise, certainty-equivalent expectations in our dynamic theory of the monopolistic-cum-monopsonistic firm. In the truly dynamic (and thus uncertain) market environment, no expectations are exact and all expectations are subject to surprises—and all the surprises have certain effects on the firm's actions in the future. The firm, therefore, has to take into account the inexactitude of its own expectation when it decides on price. Let us define the surprise concerning the firm's expectation of the state of product demand by the proportionate gap between the actual and the expected value of the state of product demand, that is, by $[a_t - \hat{E}(a_t : \delta_t)]/\hat{E}(a_t : \delta_t)$. If this turns out to be zero at the end of period t, the firm's subjective expectation has hit the mark; and if this turns out to be positive (negative), its subjective expectation has been proved a bit too pessimistic (optimistic). (By definition, the subjective expectation of the surprise is equal to zero.) The firm has therefore to assign a subjective probability distribution to the magnitude of this surprise. Now, if the firm believes that all the systematic determinants of a_t have already been incorporated into its calculation of $\hat{E}(a_t : \delta_t)$, it is natural to treat its own surprise as a purely random event beyond its control. Accordingly, we shall assume that the firm *believes* that its surprise in regard to the subjective expectation of the state of product demand is a random variable independently drawn from a given time-invariant subjective probability distribution $\hat{A}(\cdot)$. [Note that $\hat{A}(\cdot)$ has to be a probability distribution defined over $[-1, \infty)$ and that the expected value of the surprise is by definition equal to zero. Fortunately, our model does not require any specification of the functional form of this subjective probability distribution.] $\hat{E}(a_t : \delta_t)$ and $\hat{A}(\cdot)$ completely summarize the firm's subjective probability distribution of the state of product demand.

Given the foregoing specification of the firm's inner perception of the structure and conditions of the product market and given the amount of output to be thrown into the market, we are now able to deduce the firm's optimal pricing policy, which maximizes the firm's subjective expectation of the gross profit:

$$\hat{E}(p_t y_t - w_{t-\tau} n_{t-\tau} : \delta_t) = \hat{E}(p_t y_t : \delta_t) - w_{t-\tau} n_{t-\tau}.$$

Since the wage cost, which was already incurred τ periods before, is a sunk cost, the firm in fact has only to choose the level of product price that maximizes the expected sales revenue.

The formal derivation of the optimal pricing policy is cumbersome and is relegated to appendix 1–c. Here we are content to summarize the results obtained therein.

To begin with, we have to introduce a mysterious parameter, $\hat{g}^*$, which will be called the "subjective-normal ratio of product demand to supply." It is a constant whose value is defined by the following rather awkward-looking equation:

$$(1\text{–}10) \qquad 1 - \hat{A}(1/\hat{g}^* - 1) - (\hat{\eta} - 1)\hat{g}^* \int_{-1}^{1/\hat{g}^*-1} (1 + z)\,d\hat{A}(z) = 0.$$

[We shall assume that this equation has a unique solution. It is shown in appendix 1–d that this is true under reasonable conditions as to the nature of the subjective probability distribution $\hat{A}(\cdot)$: for instance, an exponential distribution and a uniform distribution, for which it is very easy to solve the value of $\hat{g}^*$, satisfying such conditions.] Why this constant is called the subjective-normal ratio of product demand to supply will become evident in a moment. What is important about this mysterious constant is not that it is determined by the weird equation (1–10), to which it is hard to give an interpretation, but that its value is determined solely by the perceived price elasticity $\hat{\eta}$ and the subjective probability distribution $\hat{A}(\cdot)$, which represent the firm's perception of the real characteristics of the product market. In this notation, we can now state the optimal condition for the pricing policy in the following simple form:

> Proposition 1–1. *The optimal product price p_t^* is an increasing function of the firm's subjective expectation of the state of product demand $\hat{E}(a_t : \delta_t)$ and a decreasing function of the amount of available product supply q_t. Indeed, its value can be computed explicitly by the formula*
>
> $$(1\text{–}11) \qquad p_t^* = \left[\frac{\hat{E}(a_t : \delta_t)}{\hat{g}^* q_t} \right]^{1/\hat{\eta}}.$$
>
> *Alternatively, the same optimal pricing policy can be characterized as the condition that the firm should choose the level of price so as to equate the expected value of the ratio of product demand to supply with the constant subjective-normal ratio $\hat{g}^*$, that is, so as to maintain the following equation at the beginning of every period:*
>
> $$(1\text{–}12) \qquad \hat{E}\left(\frac{x_t}{q_t} : \delta_t \right) = \hat{g}^*.$$

We have thus established two equivalent characterizations of the firm's optimal pricing policy: one is an explicit formula that enables the firm to calculate the level of product price on the basis of its own expectation of the state of product demand and the amount of product supply at hand; the other is an implicit formula that tells us about the firm's intention with respect to the effect of its pricing decision. [The equivalence of these two alternative characterizations can be easily checked by substituting the subjective product demand schedule (1–8′) into the implicit form (1–12) and solving the latter with respect to p_t. We would then obtain the explicit formula (1–11).]

The explicit formula (1–11) for the optimal price says that, other things being equal, the firm raises (lowers) its product price when it expects the state of product demand to become more (less) brisk or when the product supply becomes less (more) abundant. (This is as it should be.)[18] The response elasticity of this optimal price equation is nothing but the reciprocal of the subjective price elasticity $1/\hat{\eta}$, which measures the firm's subjective evaluation of its own price administrative power in the product market and is sometimes called the "subjective degree of monopoly."

Now, let us interpret the implicit form of the optimal pricing policy (1–12). The subjective-normal ratio $\hat{g}^*$ is the "target" proportion between demand and supply which the firm wishes to achieve in the product market by adjusting the level of product price p_t. Ex ante (i.e., at the beginning of period t) the firm "intends" to realize this subjective-normal ratio, the target. It is, however, only by accident that the firm's subjective expectation proves exactly correct. Ex post (i.e., at the end of period t) the realized ratio of demand to supply, x_t/q_t, may exceed or fall short of $\hat{g}^*$, depending upon a particular realization of the state of product demand a_t.

The important feature about the optimal pricing policy described above is that the subjective-normal ratio $\hat{g}^*$ is a constant number whose value is dependent neither upon a change in the firm's subjective expectation of the state of product demand nor upon a change in the supply of product. This will help tremendously to simplify our exposition. (Although this appealing feature of the optimal pricing policy is not robust to some modification of the simplifying assumptions, it should be emphasized that all the propositions in this book would be qualitatively immune to the specific assumptions adopted in this feature.) If the firm sets its price too high (relative to the expected state of product demand), it earns a high per unit revenue from its sale while risking a part of its output to perish in the warehouse. If, on the other hand, the firm sets its price too low, it does not have to worry too much about the possible deficiency of demands (although it may have to ration some customers) but

---

18. In view of the definition (1–9) of a_t, the explicit formula (1–11) can be rewritten as

$$p_t^* = \left[\frac{\hat{E}(P_t^{\hat{\eta}} X_t^{\hat{\xi}} \alpha_t : \delta_t)}{\hat{g}^* q_t} \right]^{1/\hat{\eta}}.$$

This implies that the firm raises its product price when the general price level P_t or the total product demand X_t is expected to increase in period t. Note that, other things being equal, an expected rise in P_t tends to push up p_t^* by the equal magnitude.

has to be content with a lower per unit sales revenue. The subjective-normal ratio of product demand to supply $\hat{g}^*$ is therefore the outcome of the firm's balancing of the expected benefits/costs between the situations of excess supply and demand. Since *no* symmetry exists between these two situations with respect to cost/benefit structure, there is no a priori reason to believe that $\hat{g}^*$ is equal or even close to unity. Its value may be greater or less than unity, depending upon the value of $\hat{\eta}$ and the shape of $\hat{A}(\cdot)$. (We are, however, able to show in appendix 1–d that an increase in $\hat{\eta}$, or equivalently a decrease in the subjective degree of monopoly $1/\hat{\eta}$, raises the value of $\hat{g}^*$. This means, of course, that the stronger the competitive threat felt by the firm, the lower the excess product supply it is willing to accept. Competition tends to reduce excess supply, whereas weakening competition tends to increase it.)

14. *The Optimal Employment Policy*

The firm employs workers for the purpose of production activity, which, in turn, is conducted for the purpose of ultimately selling output in the product market. Production takes time; output will appear only after the elapse of τ periods. Thus, at the beginning of period t, when the firm contemplates the labor employment policy it should use, its decision must be guided by its own expectation of how brisk the product demand will be at the time when the output from that labor employment is ready for sale. According to the notation we have adopted herein, the firm's subjective expectation of the state of product demand in period $t + \tau$, formed on the basis of the data available during period t, is represented by $\hat{E}(a_{t+\tau} : \delta_t)$. The proportionate deviation of the actual value of $a_{t+\tau}$ from this, that is, $[a_{t+\tau} - \hat{E}(a_{t+\tau} : \delta_t)]/\hat{E}(a_{t+\tau} : \delta_t)$, again represents the firm's surprise with respect to this expectation. We shall then assume, as before, that the firm believes this surprise to be a purely random variable, independently drawn from a given time-invariant subjective probability distribution $\hat{A}^{(\tau)}(\cdot)$. [$\hat{A}^{(\tau)}(\cdot)$ is a probability distribution with mean zero and the support of $[-1, \infty)$.] With this assumption, it is possible to compute the value of gross profit the firm is expected to earn from a given level of labor employment n_t to be hired at the end of period t. In fact, a little calculation (see appendix 1–e) leads to the following formula:

$$(1\text{–}13) \qquad \hat{\phi}\hat{\chi}\left[\frac{\hat{E}(a_{t+\tau} : \delta_t)}{\hat{g}^*}\right]^{1/\hat{\eta}} (j_t n_t^\gamma)^{(\hat{\eta}-1)/\hat{\eta}} - w_t n_t,$$

with $\hat{\phi}$ and $\hat{\chi}$ being constants defined by (A1–11) and (A1–12), respectively.

The firm, however, cannot choose the level of employment at will, for the principle of voluntary exchange prevents it from employing more workers than are supplied to it. The firm need not, of course, employ all the willing workers. (For our purposes, all the problems associated with labor hoarding are ignored.) Its optimal labor employment policy must therefore take account of the existence of the following labor supply constraint:

(1–14) $n_t \leqslant l_t.$

However, to present the structure of the firm's optimal employment policy in the most transparent manner, it is convenient to ignore the existence of this inequality for the time being (and only for the time being). It is then evident that without this constraint our firm would determine its labor employment merely by maximizing the prospective gross profit (1–13). It is not hard to see that unless the short-run production function is subject to strong increasing returns to labor input, or more specifically, as long as

(1–15) $\gamma < \dfrac{\hat{\eta}}{\hat{\eta} - 1},$

there exists a unique level of labor employment that would equate the marginal expected revenue with the marginal cost and thereby maximize the prospective gross profit (1–13). In fact, a little calculus is enough to deduce the following explicit formula for this critical level of employment:

$$(1\text{–}16) \qquad h_t \equiv \left\{ \left[\frac{\gamma(\hat{\eta} - 1)\hat{\phi}\hat{\chi}}{\hat{\eta}} \right]^{\hat{\eta}} j_t^{(\hat{\eta}-1)} \left[\frac{\hat{E}(a_{t+\tau} : \delta_t)}{\hat{g}^*} \right] w_t^{-\hat{\eta}} \right\}^{1/[\hat{\eta} - \gamma(\hat{\eta} - 1)]}.$$

(See appendix 1–e for the derivation.) This is of course nothing other than the effective labor demand, which we introduced in section 7. (The reason it is so named will soon become evident.) Formula (1–16) says, among other things, that when the firm expects an increase in the state of product demand τ periods later, it raises the effective labor demand today. For the firm's production activity requires τ periods for its completion, and thus the resulting output will be sold only during period $(t + \tau)$. This effective labor demand links the labor employment today with the demand for product in the future (or, more precisely, the expectation of it formed today) and will play a key role in our theory of disequilibrium dynamics.[19] Formula (1–16) also says that an increase in the productivity index also raises the effective demand for labor, but an increase in the firm's own money wage rate fixed at the beginning of period t tends to lower it.

Let us now reconsider the labor market inequality (1–14). If a given labor supply l_t to be observed at the end of period t turns out to be greater than the effective labor demand h_t, it is obvious that our firm should employ workers only up to the level of effective labor demand. For at this level of employment

---

19. We can rewrite the formula of the effective labor demand as follows:

$$h_t = \left\{ \left[\frac{\gamma(\hat{\eta} - 1)\hat{\phi}\hat{\chi}}{\hat{\eta}} \right]^{\hat{\eta}} j_t^{(\hat{\eta}-1)} \left[\frac{\hat{E}(P_{t+\tau}^{\hat{\eta}} X_{t+\tau}^{\hat{\varepsilon}} \alpha_{t+\tau} : \delta_t)}{\hat{g}^*} \right] w_t^{-\hat{\eta}} \right\}^{1/[\hat{\eta} - \gamma(\hat{\eta} - 1)]}$$

The firm thus increases its effective demand if the total product demand $X_{t+\tau}$ or the general price level $P_{t+\tau}$ is expected to increase in the future, in relation to the rate of current money wage w_t. Note that an expected increase in $P_{t+\tau}$ and an actual decrease in w_t have approximately the same impact upon the firm's h_t.

the firm is in fact maximizing the expected gross profit, and a further increase in employment would only reduce the expected gross profit. In this situation, a fraction of workers who are willing to work at the going money wage are involuntarily unemployed. Owing to the low productivity or the expected deficiency of future product demand, or the too-high money wage it quoted at the beginning of period t, the firm in this situation has no incentive to absorb these unfortunate workers in the present period. If, on the other hand, a given labor supply l_t is short of the effective demand for labor h_t, it is obvious that the firm should hire all the willing workers. In this case, a labor supply shortage prevents it from exploiting as much potential gross profit as it wishes. Summing up, we can state the optimal employment policy as follows:

> Proposition 1–2. *The optimal employment is determined by the short side of the effective labor demand and a given labor supply: that is,*

$$(1-17) \qquad\qquad n_t = \min(h_t, l_t).$$

This justifies the ad hoc rule (1–1) that we introduced in section 7.

In essence, the phenomenon of involuntary unemployment in deficient effective demand situations arises from the fact that, in a decentralized labor market without the omnipotent Walrasian auctioneer, each firm quotes its own money wage on a take-it-or-leave-it basis. Since the quoted money wage functions as a chief conveyor of the information concerning the pecuniary working condition, it must be announced beforehand in order to induce the revelation of the true labor supply preferences by workers. In consequence, the firm's money wage decision has to be guided by its anticipation about the present labor supply condition as well as about the future product market condition. Of course, anticipations are always liable to disappointment. When the actual labor supply turns out to be unexpectedly large relative to the effective labor demand, the burden of the firm's expectation error falls on the shoulders of unfortunate workers. They will be unemployed, involuntarily.

This is, however, only a microscopic and short-run explanation of involuntary unemployment. Why and how involuntary unemployment spreads over the whole economy and why and how it persists, even in the long run, are entirely different problems which demand entirely different solutions. An elucidation of the mechanisms that cause involuntary unemployment as a macroscopic phenomenon is presented in chapters 3 to 5; an explanation of the persistence of involuntary unemployment in the long run is given in chapter 7.

15. On Markup Pricing Theory

Let us digress for a moment and consider "markup pricing theory." Since the content of this section has little bearing on the main thread of our argument, the reader may skip it at the first reading.

Markup pricing theory, first formulated by Michal Kalecki (1938, 1954), maintains that a manufacturing firm operating below the point of practical capacity fixes a price as a constant markup on the unit prime cost, the rate of markup being determined by the degree of monopoly enjoyed by the firm in the product market.[20] The theory of the firm we have developed so far predicts precisely this markup pricing in an ex ante sense. Indeed, in appendix 1–f, we show that in the situation of less-than-full employment, the expected value of the product price to be announced in period $(t + \tau)$, predicted on the basis of the data available at the beginning of period t, is given by

$$(1-18) \qquad \hat{E}(p_{t+\tau} : \delta_t) = \frac{\hat{\eta}}{\gamma(\hat{\eta} - 1)\hat{\phi}} \left(\frac{w_t n_t}{q_{t+\tau}} \right) \qquad \text{when } n_t = h_t < l_t.$$

In words, the product price in the underemployment situation is *expected* to be set as a constant markup on the unit wage cost, the markup ratio being $\hat{\eta}/\gamma(\hat{\eta} - 1)\hat{\phi}$. Since the effective labor demand h_t is the level of employment that equates marginal expected revenue with marginal wage cost, this result is hardly surprising under the assumption of constant price elasticity and constant degree of returns to labor input. The constant markup ratio $\hat{\eta}/\gamma(\hat{\eta} - 1)\hat{\phi}$ in this formula is pegged by the degree of returns to labor input γ and by the subjective degree of monopoly $1/\hat{\eta}$. [The constant number $\hat{\phi}$, defined by (A1–11), is an increasing function of $\hat{g}^*$, which in turn is a decreasing function of $1/\hat{\eta}$ as long as the optimal price is unique.] We can thus unambiguously assert that, other things being equal, an increase in the returns to labor input lowers the markup ratio, whereas an increase in the subjective degree of monopoly raises it.

We have, however, no intention of claiming that our model is the sole explanation of the markup pricing theory. Far from it, we wish to emphasize that many important rationales for the markup pricing behavior advanced by various economists—as a device for coordinating pricing behaviors among oligopolists, as a consequence of satisficing behavior of the firm, as a device for maintaining goodwill of customers, as an effective form of limit pricing, as a rule to ensure sound financial positions in the long run, as a way to finance investments—are entirely absent from our model.[21] What we have claimed is merely that, unlike the neoclassical model of the firm, our very simplified model is not inconsistent with the empirically robust markup pricing hypothesis.

It should also be borne in mind that our markup formula applies only to the relation between the unit wage cost and the level of price the firm expects itself to quote in the future product market. If, during the course of production,

---

20. See Godley and Nordhaus (1972) for a recent study of the markup pricing theory.

21. See Scherer (1970, chap. 5) for an excellent discussion on various rationales for the markup pricing hypothesis.

the firm acquires new information about market conditions and updates its expectation of the state of product demand, the price actually quoted in the product market necessarily diverges from the marked-up level. The markup formula is realized only when the firm's expectation has remained the same while the output has been moving in the pipeline.[22]

Kalecki was careful enough to point out that his markup pricing theory holds true only in the situation of incomplete resource utilization. When the bottleneck of a certain resource is reached, the markup pricing rule becomes "defunct" and a further rise in demand will cause a price increase beyond the level indicated by the markup rule. The price then becomes "demand-determined" (Kalecki 1954). This is again precisely what our theory of the firm suggests. When the effective demand for labor exceeds a given labor supply at the end of period t, the firm hires all the willing workers in that period. At the beginning of period $(t + \tau)$, the firm then sets the price at the level that is expected to equate the ratio of demand to *full-employment supply* with the subjective-normal ratio $\hat{g}^*$. Just as in the perfectly competitive market, the price in this situation is determined by an interaction between demand and full-employment productive capacity, and its level becomes higher than the level indicated by the ex ante markup formula (1–18) given above. More formally, we can express the ex ante price-formation formula for this case as follows:

$$(1\text{-}19) \qquad \hat{E}(p^*_{t+\tau} : \delta_t) = \frac{\hat{\eta}}{\gamma(\hat{\eta} - 1)\hat{\phi}}\left(\frac{w_t n_t}{q_{t+\tau}}\right)\left(\frac{h_t}{n_t}\right)^{[\hat{\eta} - \gamma(\hat{\eta} - 1)]/\hat{\eta}}$$

$$\geqslant \frac{\hat{\eta}}{\gamma(\hat{\eta} - 1)\hat{\phi}}\left(\frac{w_t n_t}{q_{t+\tau}}\right) \qquad \text{for } n_t = l_t \leqslant h_t.$$

(See appendix 1–f for the derivation.)

That the price-fixing firm's ex ante price-formation process is very different between full-employment and underemployment situations has often been

---

22. More formally, we can obtain the following equation for the actual price level in the less-than-full-employment situation:

$$p^*_{t+\tau} = \left[\frac{\hat{E}(a_{t+\tau} : \delta_{t+\tau})}{\hat{g}^*(j_t h_t^\gamma)}\right]^{1/\hat{\eta}}$$

$$= \left[\frac{\hat{E}(a_{t+\tau} : \delta_t)}{\hat{g}^*(j_t h_t^\gamma)}\right]^{1/\eta}\left[\frac{\hat{E}(a_{t+\tau} : \delta_{t+\tau})}{\hat{E}(a_{t+}{}^\tau : \delta_t)}\right]^{1/\eta}$$

$$= \left\{\left[\frac{\hat{\eta}}{\gamma(\hat{\eta} - 1)\hat{\phi}}\right]\left(\frac{w_t h_t}{j_t h_t^\gamma}\right)\right\}\left\{\left[\frac{\hat{E}(a_{t+\tau} : \delta_{t+\tau})}{\hat{E}(a_{t+\tau} : \delta_t)}\right]^{1/\hat{\eta}} \bigg/ \hat{\chi}\right\} \qquad \text{by (A1–12).}$$

Thus, if the expected state of product demand has been revised optimistically (pessimistically), the actual price in the less-than-full-employment situation is set higher (lower) than the markup level $[\hat{\eta}/\gamma(\hat{\eta} - 1)\hat{\phi}](w_t h_t/j_t h_t^\gamma)$.

forgotten in recent literature on markup pricing theory. It will, however, provide a key to the precise understanding of the often-contradictory forces working for the determination of income distribution in the short and long run.[23]

Before leaving this section, it may be of some help to the reader to give a brief graphical exposition of the two different price-formation schemes in Marshallian price–quantity diagrams. This is a straightforward extension into the world of uncertainty of the standard marginal revenue = marginal cost analysis. In each of the diagrams shown on the next few pages, we draw two sets of *isoelastic* curves. The first set consists of the average cost (a.c.) curve, depicting $w_t n_t / q_{t+\tau}$; the marginal cost (m.c.) curve, depicting $(1/\gamma)(w_t n_t / q_{t+\tau})$; and the marked-up average cost (m.u.a.c.) curve, depicting $[\hat{\eta}/\gamma(\hat{\eta} - 1)\hat{\phi}](w_t n_t / q_{t+\tau})$. [Note that $q_{t+\tau} = j_t n_t^\gamma$, or $n_t = (q_{t+\tau}/j_t)^{1/\gamma}$.] All these curves have the common elasticity $(1 - \gamma)/\gamma$ up to the point of full-employment capacity (f.e.c.), given by $j_t l_t^\gamma$, and suddenly become vertical at the point. (Of course, if overtime or other flexible working arrangements were allowed in our model, these cost curves would not jump but only start rising progressively at full-employment capacity.) The second set of isoelastic curves consists of the expected price (e.p.) curve and the expected marginal revenue (e.m.r.) curve. The former traces the formula for the expected price: $\hat{E}(p_{t+\tau} : \delta_t) = \hat{\chi}[\hat{E}(a_{t+\tau} : \delta_t)/\hat{g}^* q_{t+\tau}]^{1/\hat{\eta}}$, and the latter traces the relation

$$\partial \hat{E}(p_{t+\tau} y_{t+\tau} : \delta_t)/\partial q_{t+\tau} = [(\hat{\eta} - 1)\hat{\phi}\hat{\chi}/\hat{\eta}][\hat{E}(a_{t+\tau} : \delta_t)/\hat{g}^* q_{t+\tau}]^{1/\hat{\eta}}.$$

Their elasticities are equal to $1/\hat{\eta}$, and the former is an expansion of the latter by the proportion of $(\hat{\eta} - 1)\hat{\phi}/\hat{\eta}$. If we superimpose these two sets of isoelastic curves on the same price–quantity diagram, it is not hard to see that the expected price curve crosses the marked-up average curve (or its extension beyond the full-employment capacity) at the output level equal to $j_t h_t^\gamma$. At this level of output (the effective demand output, or e.d.o.) the expected marginal revenue curve must also meet the marginal cost curve (or its extension beyond the full-employment capacity); this is, of course, the graphical presentation of the very definition of effective labor demand given in the preceding section.

The first two diagrams examine the case of constant returns to labor input. This is what Kalecki had in mind in his markup theory of pricing. In this case, the average and marginal cost curves coincide with each other and become horizontal up to the full-employment capacity. If the effective labor demand falls short of the labor supply, as is the case in figure 1–2, the expected price is determined as a constant markup on the average wage cost. But if the effective

---

23. It can be argued, for instance, that Kalecki's theory of income distribution is confined to underemployment situations, whereas Kaldor's theory of income distribution (1956, 1961) is concerned exclusively with full-employment situations.

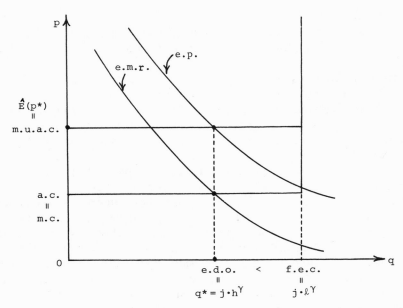

FIGURE 1–2. Determination of the Expected Price in an Underemployment
Situation—The Case of Constant Returns to Labor Input

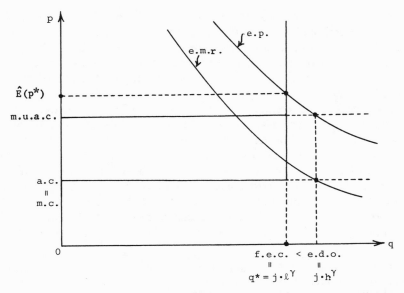

FIGURE 1–3. Determination of the Expected Price in a Full-Employment Situation
—The Case of Constant Returns to Labor Input

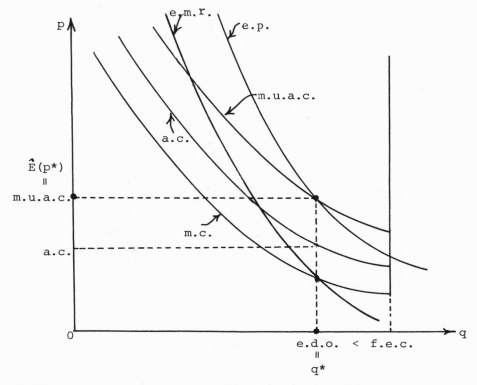

FIGURE 1–4. Determination of the Expected Price in an Underemployment
Situation—The Case of Increasing Returns to Labor Input

labor demand exceeds the labor supply, as is the case in figure 1–3, the expected price becomes higher than the marked-up average cost in order to absorb the anticipated higher demand for product. Figures 1–4 and 1–5 consider the case of increasing returns to labor input, where the marginal wage cost curve always lies below the average wage cost curve. Figures 1–6 and 1–7 take up the case of decreasing returns to labor input, where the marginal cost curve lies above the average cost curve. The processes of price determination in these cases are analogous to the case of constant returns and thus require no further explanation.

16. *The Optimal Money Wage Policy*

At the beginning of period t, the firm must also make a decision on the rate of money wage w_t to be announced in the labor market. This act sets off a new short-run activity cycle which will be concluded at the end of period $(t + \tau)$.

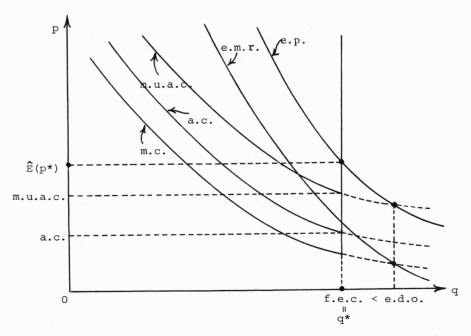

FIGURE 1–5. Determination of the Expected Price in a Full-Employment Situation
—The Case of Increasing Returns to Labor Input

In our discussion of the optimal pricing policy in section 13, we implicitly
supposed that the firm can adjust its price at the beginning of every period
without incurring any adjustment cost. (Note that at the same time we pro-
hibited the firm from readjusting the price for the rest of the period. Adjustment
costs for a price change are infinite except at the junction of two adjacent
periods.) This does not appear an unreasonable assumption as long as we
confine ourselves to the analysis of the monopolistically competitive firm,
although it might become serious once we introduce oligopolistic interdependence between firms. In the case of money wage determination, however,
the assumption concerning its adjustment costs becomes critical for any serious
attempt at describing the economy's disequilibrium situations. The labor market
is much more prone to various imperfections and frictions than are most
product markets. For our purposes, therefore, we shall distinguish two kinds
of economies according to the particular assumption concerning the nature
of money wage adjustment costs. The economy in which the firm is free to
adjust its money wage without incurring any costs will be called the *Wicksellian
economy.* As we see in chapter 3, this type of economy possesses features that
are strikingly similar to the ones brought to light by Knut Wicksell and the

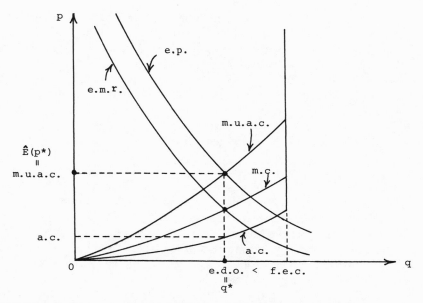

FIGURE 1–6. Determination of the Expected Price in an Underemployment Situation—The Case of Decreasing Returns to Labor Input

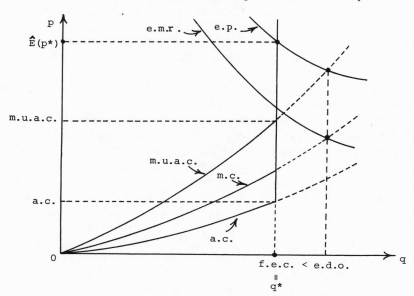

FIGURE 1–7. Determination of the Expected Price in a Full-Employment Situation —The Case of Decreasing Returns to Labor Input

Stockholm school economists. On the other hand, the more frictional economy, in which the firm can adjust its money wage only by incurring certain informational, administrative, sociological, political, and economic costs, will be called the *Keynesian economy*. As we see in parts II and III, this type of economy engenders more Keynesian features than Keynes himself imagined. Mere frictions in the labor market have permanent influences on the dynamic workings of the economy, and they alter the whole nature of its equilibrium as well as its disequilibrium. In part I, however, we study only the behavior of the Wicksellian economy. Study of the more general Keynesian economy will not be undertaken until part II.

There are basically three reasons why we have an independent interest in the Wicksellian economy, which is, after all, a special case of the Keynesian economy. The first reason is that the assumption of a flexible money wage is a reasonable approximation to reality as long as we limit our analysis to the economy's inflationary phase. Money wages are in general much more flexible upward than downward. The second reason is that the assumption of flexible money wages will enable us to look afresh at the money wage problem—a thought experiment of Keynes (1936, chap. 19) which examined whether or not the hypothetical downward flexibility of money wage would add stability to the monetary economy. But whereas Keynes devoted one whole chapter (chap. 19) of *The General Theory* to the money wage problem, we can spare only two sections (section 20 of chapter 3 and section 15 of chapter 5). The final reason is that by studying the Wicksellian economy separately we are able to throw some light on the relationship between Keynes's effective demand principle in *The General Theory* and the Stockholm school's ex ante and ex post approach.

As demonstrated in chapter 3, within the confines of the flexible-wage Wicksellian economy, the Keynesian effective demand principle is incapable of standing on its own feet, whereas the Stockholm ex ante approach is an effective method for analyzing its dynamic nature. In chapters 4 and 5, however, we show that once we enter the territory of the inflexible-wage Keynesian economy, the Keynesian effective demand principle gains effectiveness as an analytical method and that the two approaches become complementary as methods for analyzing equilibria and disequilibria of the economy. We believe that these results will help to disentangle some confusions in the present state of macroeconomic theory.

At the beginning of period t, the firm must determine its money wage policy. The firm is, however, necessarily uncertain about how many workers it can attract during the period. First, it does not know the true functional form of the labor supply schedule (1–7) and has to base its decision on the subjective estimate of the labor supply schedule. We shall assume, as in the case of the subjective product demand schedule, that the firm has succeeded in constructing the following reasonable subjective labor supply schedule:

$$(1\text{–}20) \qquad\qquad l_t = \left(\frac{w_t}{W_t}\right)^{\hat{\varepsilon}} L_t^{\hat{\lambda}}\beta_t,$$

where $\hat{\varepsilon}$ and $\hat{\lambda}$ are the subjective estimate of the wage elasticity ε and that of the total-labor-supply elasticity λ, respectively. We shall assume that the firm behaves as if the values of $\hat{\varepsilon}$ and $\hat{\lambda}$ are known. Second, the firm is simply unable to know in advance the value of the general money wage W_t, the level of total labor supply L_t, or the random disturbance β_t. The firm thus has no choice but to represent its uncertainty about these variables by suitable subjective probability distributions. To formalize this, let us first represent by b_t a composite random variable defined by

$$(1\text{–}21) \qquad\qquad b_t \equiv W_t^{\hat{\varepsilon}} L_t^{-\lambda}\beta_t^{-1},$$

and rewrite the subjective labor supply schedule $(1\text{–}20)$ as follows:

$$(1\text{–}20') \qquad\qquad l_t = w_t^{\hat{\varepsilon}} b_t^{-1}.$$

The composite random variable b_t will be called the state of labor supply in period t. It represents the extent of the tightness of the labor supply in period t. The firm's subjective expectation of this composite variable, conditional upon the data δ_t available at the beginning of period t, can be expressed as $\hat{E}(b_t : \delta_t)$. A discussion of how such subjective expectation is formed is postponed until chapter 2. For the time being, we regard it as given. Just as in the product price determination, the firm must take account of an almost inevitable surprise pertaining to its expectation in order to determine its money wage. Let us once again define the surprise in regard to the expectation of the present state of labor supply by the proportionate gap between the true value of b_t and its subjective expectation $\hat{E}(b_t : \delta_t)$, that is, by $[b_t - \hat{E}(b_t : \delta_t)]/\hat{E}(b_t : \delta_t)$, and assume that the firm views this surprise as a purely random variable independently drawn from a given stationary subjective probability distribution $\hat{B}(\cdot)$. [$\hat{B}(\cdot)$ is defined over $[-1, \infty)$. The expected value of the surprise is, by definition, equal to zero.]

The firm's choice of the rate of money wage is for the purpose of attracting workers for its production activity. But the firm's employment of workers is for the purpose of ultimating selling output in the future product market. In determining its money wage rate at the start of period t, the firm has little choice but to be guided not only by its subjective expectation of the state of labor supply in the same period, but also by its subjective expectation of the state of product demand in period $(t + \tau)$ when the resulting output will appear in the product market. The firm's computation of the expected gross profit and its determination of the optimal money wage (which maximizes it) have to take this into account.

Fortunately, in appendix 1–g we are able to characterize an optimal wage policy whose structure is almost as simple as that of the optimal pricing policy. Relegating all the necessary calculations to that appendix, let us summarize the result obtained therein.

As in the characterization of the optimal pricing policy in section 13, it is necessary at the outset to introduce a constant, $\hat{f}^*$. We shall call this the subjective-normal ratio of labor demand to supply, and define it as the solution to the following rather unattractive equation:

$$(1-22) \qquad \hat{B}\left(\frac{1}{\hat{f}^*} - 1\right) - \hat{\varepsilon} \int_{1/\hat{f}^*-1}^{\infty} [\hat{f}^*(1+z)]^{-\gamma(\hat{\eta}-1)/\hat{\eta}} \, d\hat{B}(z)$$

$$+ (1+\hat{\varepsilon}) \int_{1/\hat{f}^*-1}^{\infty} [\hat{f}^*(1+z)]^{-1} \, d\hat{B}(z) = 0,$$

which the reader is *not* expected to memorize. [We shall assume henceforth that this equation has a unique solution. This is guaranteed, as shown in appendix 1–h, when, for instance, $\hat{B}(\cdot)$ is a uniform probability distribution or an exponential probability distribution.] What is again crucial for our theory is not that this subjective-normal ratio is defined by such an evil-looking equation, but that its constant value is determined solely by the subjective elasticities $\hat{\eta}$ and $\hat{\varepsilon}$, the degree of returns γ, and the subjective probability distribution $\hat{B}(\cdot)$. In this notation, we can characterize the nature of the optimal money wage policy in the form:

Proposition 1–3. *In the Wicksellian economy, the optimal money wage in period t is an increasing function of the firm's subjective expectation of the state of product demand in period $(t + \tau)$, of the firm's subjective expectation of the state of labor supply in period t, and of the index of productivity in period t. Its value can be computed explicitly by the formula*

$$(1-23) \qquad w_t^* = \left\{ \frac{\gamma(\hat{\eta}-1)\hat{\phi}\hat{\chi}}{\hat{\eta}} \left[\frac{\hat{E}(a_{t+\tau}:\delta_t)}{\hat{g}^*} \right]^{1/\hat{\eta}} \right.$$

$$\left. \times \left[\frac{\hat{E}(b_t:\delta_t)}{\hat{f}^*} \right]^{[\hat{\eta}-\gamma(\hat{\eta}-1)]/\hat{\eta}} j_t^{(\hat{\eta}-1)/\hat{\eta}} \right\}^{\hat{\eta}/[\hat{\eta}+\hat{\varepsilon}\hat{\eta}(1-\gamma)+\hat{\varepsilon}\gamma]}$$

Furthermore, *to quote the rate of money wage according to* (1–23) *is tantamount to adjusting the money wage to the level that equates the expected ratio of labor demand to supply with the constant subjective-normal ratio* $\hat{f}^*$:

(1–24)
$$\hat{E}\left(\frac{h_t}{l_t} : \delta_t\right) = \hat{f}*$$

We have thus established two equivalent characterizations of the optimal money wage policy. [Their equivalence can be established by substituting (1–16) and (1–20′) into (1–24) and solving it with respect to w_t.]

The explicit formula for the optimal money wage (1–23) says that the firm in the Wicksellian economy raises the rate of money wage when it expects the product demand to become more brisk in the future period, when it expects the labor supply to tighten in the present period, or when the index of productivity increases.[24] The response elasticities of this optimal money wage equation depend upon the degree of returns to labor input γ and the subjective elasticities $\hat{\eta}$ and $\hat{\varepsilon}$, which specify the firm's perception of the structure of its market environment.

The implicit formula for the optimal money wage (1–24) says, on the other hand, that in the Wicksellian economy the firm adjusts its money wage at the beginning of every period so that the proportion between labor demand and supply might be *on average* equal to the subjective-normal ratio. Ex post, however, the realized ratio of demand to supply may exceed or come short of the subjective-normal ratio.

There is again no a priori reason to believe that $\hat{f}*$ is equal to or even close to unity. Its value may be greater or less than unity, depending upon the relative magnitudes of the structural parameters $\hat{\varepsilon}$, $\hat{\eta}$, γ, and $\hat{B}(\cdot)$. [However, we can show that, as long as the optimal money wage policy is unique, an increase in $1/\hat{\varepsilon}$, the subjective degree of monopsony, raises (other things being equal) the value of the subjective-normal ratio $\hat{f}*$ (see appendix 1–h). That is, an increase in the firm's confidence on its own wage-setting power vis-à-vis other firms in the labor market tends to reduce the money wage and is thus expected to raise its effective labor demand and lower the labor supply at the same time. We can also show that, other things being equal, an increase in

---

24. In view of the definitions of $a_{t+\tau}$ and b_t, the optimal money wage equation (1–23) can be rewritten as

$$w_t^* = \left\{ \frac{\gamma(\hat{\eta}-1)\hat{\phi}\hat{\chi}}{\hat{\eta}} \left[\frac{E(P_{t+\tau}^{\hat{\eta}} X_{t+\tau}^{\hat{\varepsilon}} \alpha_{t+\tau} : \delta_t)}{\hat{g}*} \right]^{1/\hat{\eta}} \right.$$
$$\left. \times \left[\frac{\hat{E}(W_t^{\hat{\varepsilon}} L_t^{-\hat{\lambda}} \beta_t^{-1} : \delta_t)}{\hat{f}*} \right]^{[\hat{\eta}-\gamma(\hat{\eta}-1)]/\hat{\eta}} j_t^{(\hat{\eta}-1)/\hat{\eta}} \right\}^{\hat{\eta}/[\hat{\eta}+\hat{\varepsilon}\hat{\eta}(1-\gamma)+\hat{\varepsilon}\gamma]}$$

The firm thus raises its current money wage rate if the total product demand $X_{t+\tau}$ or the general price level $P_{t+\tau}$ is expected to increase in the future, or if the general money wage level W_t is expected to increase or the total labor supply L_t is expected to decrease in the present period.

$1/\hat{\eta}$, the subjective degree of monopoly, lowers $\hat{f}^*$, but an increase in γ, the degree of returns to labor, raises $\hat{f}^*$.]

Before leaving the present section, it would be useful for later discussions to record an immediate corollary to proposition 1–3. To this end, let u_t represent the rate of involuntary unemployment among workers willing to work in our firm, and define it by

$$(1\text{--}25) \qquad u_t \equiv \frac{l_t - n_t}{l_t} = \max\left(1 - \frac{h_t}{l_t}, 0\right);$$

and let v_t represent the rate of unfilled vacancies, and define it by

$$(1\text{--}26) \qquad v_t \equiv \frac{h_t - n_t}{n_t} = \max\left(\frac{h_t}{l_t} - 1, 0\right).$$

It is easy to show that the difference between the rate of unfilled vacancies and the rate of involuntary unemployment we have just introduced is identically equal to the rate of excess demand for labor (i.e., the ratio of labor demand to supply minus 1):

$$(1\text{--}27) \qquad v_t - u_t \equiv \max\left(\frac{h_t}{l_t} - 1, 0\right) - \max\left(1 - \frac{h_t}{l_t}, 0\right) \equiv \frac{h_t}{l_t} - 1.$$

Thus, once the rate of excess labor demand is given, the rate of unfilled vacancies becomes a mirror image of the rate of involuntary unemployment. Hence, we shall restrict our attention to the rate of involuntary unemployment and refer to the rate of unfilled vacancies only when the need arises.

In appendix 1–i, we are able to compute the expected value of the rate of involuntary unemployment and obtain the following expression:

$$(1\text{--}28) \qquad \hat{E}(u_t : \delta_t) = \hat{B}\left[\frac{1}{\hat{E}(h_t/l_t : \delta_t)} - 1\right]$$
$$- \hat{E}\left(\frac{h_t}{l_t} : \delta_t\right) \int_{-1}^{1/\hat{E}(h_t/l_t : \delta_t) - 1} (1 + z)\, d\hat{B}(z).$$

The expected rate of involuntary unemployment is therefore a function only of the expected ratio of labor demand to supply, and its functional form is determined solely by the shape of the subjective probability distribution $\hat{B}(\cdot)$. [It is very easy to show that $\hat{E}(u_t : \delta_t)$ is a nonnegative, nonincreasing, and convex function of $\hat{E}(h_t/l_t : \delta_t)$ (see appendix 1–i).] Consequently, once the expected value of the ratio of labor demand to supply is given, the expected rate of involuntary unemployment can be determined uniquely by this function. Accordingly, we can define a constant number $\hat{u}^*$ as the value of the expected rate of involuntary unemployment that corresponds uniquely to the subjective-normal ratio of labor demand to supply $\hat{f}^*$:

$$(1-29) \qquad \hat{u}^* \equiv \hat{B}\left(\frac{1}{\hat{f}^*} - 1\right) - \hat{f}^* \int_{-1}^{1/\hat{f}^* - 1} (1 + z)\, d\hat{B}(z).$$

This constant number will be called the subjective-normal rate of involuntary unemployment. Its value is determined exclusively by the parameters $\hat{\eta}$, $\hat{\varepsilon}$, γ, and $\hat{B}(\cdot)$. As a mirror image, the subjective-normal rate of unfilled vacancies, denoted by $\hat{v}^*$, can be defined by

$$(1-30) \qquad\qquad \hat{v}^* \equiv \hat{u}^* + \hat{f}^* - 1.$$

Our corollary now becomes obvious.

> Corollary to Proposition 1–3. *The optimal money wage policy in the Wicksellian economy can be given the alternative characterization that the firm's subjective expected rate of involuntary unemployment should coincide with its constant subjective-normal rate* $\hat{u}^*$:
>
> $$(1-31) \qquad\qquad \hat{E}(u_t : \delta_t) = \hat{u}^*,$$
>
> *or equivalently, that the firm's subjective expected rate of unfilled vacancies should coincide with its constant subjective-normal rate* $\hat{v}^*$:
>
> $$(1-32) \qquad\qquad \hat{E}(v_t : \delta_t) = \hat{v}^*.$$

17. *The Firm's Short-Run Market Activities Recapitulated*

In this chapter we have investigated the dynamic behavior of a firm in a monopolistically and monopsonistically competitive economy. The firm produces a single differentiated product by employing homogeneous and variable labor services. Production is a point input/point output process with a fixed gestation period. The firm quotes a price on a take-it-or-leave-it basis and sells its product in the product market. It also quotes a money wage on a take-it-or-leave-it basis and hires workers in the labor market. The demand for the firm's product is a function of the firm's announced price *relative to* other prices, of the level of total demand (determined by the consumers' consumption-saving choices, the firms' investment decisions, and the government's public expenditures), and of a random disturbance. Similarly, the supply of labor to the firm is a function of its wage offer *relative to* that of other firms, of the level of total labor supply (determined by the workers' decisions on participation in the labor force), and of the random disturbance. It is clear, however, that when the firm announces its product price, it cannot have complete knowledge of the prices of other firms, the level of total demand, or the realized value of random disturbance. By the same token, when the firm announces its own wage, it necessarily has incomplete knowledge of the wage offers of other firms, the level of total labor supply, and the actual value of the random disturbance. (Nor does it have complete knowledge of the state of product demand that will prevail at the time when its output has to be sold.) Hence, the firm is faced with inherent uncertainty and has to determine its price and wage on the basis of its subjective probability distributions of these incompletely known variables. Moreover, since the firm's announcement of wage, determination of labor employment, engagement in production, announcement of price, and sale of product are made at different points in time, the firm's decisions have to take account of changing information structure and hence must be made sequentially.

We can now recapitulate how the firm makes such sequential decisions in changing and uncertain markets.

1. At the beginning of every period, the firm sets its money wage rate with the intention of equating the ratio of effective labor demand to labor supply with a given constant called the subjective-normal ratio of labor demand to supply. The value of this constant is determined solely by the degree of returns to labor input, the perceived price and wage elasticities, and the subjective probability distributions of the surprises.

2. The optimal wage, thus characterized, increases as the firm's subjective expectation of the briskness of product demand *in the future*, the firm's subjective expectation of the tightness of labor supply in the current period, or a given index of labor productivity increases.

3. In each period there is a level of labor employment that is expected to equate the marginal revenue with the marginal cost were it not for the labor supply constraint. This level of employment is called the effective labor demand. Its value is an increasing function of the firm's subjective expectation of the briskness of product demand in the future, an increasing function of a given index of productivity, and a decreasing function of a given money wage of its own determined at the beginning of the period.

4. The actual employment level is determined by the short side of the actual labor supply and the effective labor demand. Therefore, when the effective labor demand falls short of a given labor supply, some workers who are willing to supply their labor services to the firm at the announced wage are going to be unemployed.

5. Once the employment is determined, the firm immediately starts engaging in production activity. After the elapse of a production period, output appears in the product market, and the firm has to quote a price for it.

6. The level of price set by the firm at the beginning of the period is determined in such a way that the subjective expected ratio of product demand to supply should be equal to a given constant called the subjective-normal ratio of product demand to supply. The value of this subjective-normal ratio is determined solely by the perceived price elasticity of product demand and the subjective probability distribution of the surprise about the state of product demand.

7. The optimal price, thus characterized, turns out to be an increasing

function of the firm's subjective expectation of the briskness of product demand and a decreasing function of the level of product supply at its hands.

8. Finally, at the end of the period, the sales volume is determined by the short side of the actual product demand and the given product supply. The firm will then happily harvest its profit.

The above, however, describes only the process of decisions in a single activity cycle of the firm. As was illustrated in figure 1–1, to ensure its existence as an organization, the firm has to embark anew upon a similar activity cycle at the beginning of every period and to conclude the old one at the close of every period. The firm as an organization is characterized by the simultaneous operation of various phases of various activity cycles embarked upon at various points in time.

CHAPTER 2

The Process of Expectation Formation

1. Basic Theory of Expectation Formation

It is one thing to show how the firm's decisions in a dynamic and thus uncertain world are guided by expectations, but it is another to examine how expectations themselves are formed in an ever-changing world. Any dynamic economic theory worthy of the name must be a synthesis of these two theoretical explorations. Let us pass on to this problem of expectation formation.[1]

The study of the process of expectation formation by an individual can hardly be undertaken unless we study at the same time how an individual acquires knowledge about the environment in which he or she is living. The process of expectation formation and the process of acquiring knowledge (i.e., learning) are merely different sides of the same coin.

Once we enter into an ever-changing, uncertain world, it is essential to distinguish *conceptually* between the *objective* world in which an individual is situated and the *subjective* model of the world which an individual perceives and upon which decisions have to be based. The failure to draw a clear-cut conceptual line between them is the source of much confusion in the existing (or nonexisting) state of the theory of expectation formation in economics.

At the outset, let us emphasize that the subjective model perceived by an individual should be regarded neither as an abstraction nor as a mere deduction of the real world. It has an independent structure of its own, which may be

---

Sections 3, 4, and 5 may be regarded as optional reading.

1. The theory of expectation formation we develop in this chapter is in many ways similar to Jean Piaget's ideas of developmental psychology and genetic epistemology. See, for instance, Piaget (1957, 1967, 1972). The ideas, which accord in their essence with Piaget's, are independently advanced by many contemporary scientists and thinkers in surprisingly diverse fields, except in economics. In the field of economics, as far as we know, the closest to our idea is found only in Simon (1959). The neoclassical economics has been from its birth deeply immersed in the doctrine of empiricism. This has had an unfortunate consequence on the development of the theory of expectation formation.

fantastically different from the true structure of reality, the large part of which, being unconscious, remains unknown even to the individual. It must be quickly added, however, that saying that the subjective model is conceptually distinct from the objective world by no means implies that they are totally unrelated to each other. On the contrary, they are interrelated, and they do interact with each other. In fact, the process of human learning consists precisely of the mechanism through which the subjective model of an individual is continually adapting to the objective structure of the real world. It is this microscopic mechanism that we are primarily concerned with in this chapter. (However, how the objective world itself is adapted to the subjective models perceived by individuals is a more subtle problem that requires a careful macroscopic analysis. The whole discussion of chapter 3 in effect amounts to an elucidation of this macroeconomic mechanism.)

Nothing is further from the truth than the naive empiricistic view that the process of learning is, like taking a photograph of scenery, a passive copying of reality. It is, instead, a far more complicated process which involves a considerable conscious and unconscious activity on the part of the subject. In fact, the process of human learning can be regarded as a continual interaction of two different levels of internal activities—one working in the short run and the other operating through the long-run course of events.

In the short run, an individual behaves as if the subjective model of the world were given once and for all. An individual has no choice but to use this a priori scheme of the subjective world as an "invariant" system of reference for gathering, processing, and analyzing the information he or she receives from the surrounding world. The process of learning in the short run is, in other words, an attempt at "assimilating" the objective world into the already existing subjective model.[2] We, as mortal beings who cannot inspect the world from outside, are destined to draw its perspective only by projecting our own map of the world (i.e., our Gestalt) onto the outside. We do not learn about the world by copying it; we merely copy what we already know. For instance, it is now a common belief in perceptual psychology that the phenomenon of visual illusion that we experience in our daily life is rooted precisely in this general human nature (see, e.g., Gombrich 1960).

If the process of learning in the short run consists of the assimilation of past reality data into the existing subjective model, the process of expectation formation in the short run might be regarded as the assimilation of the still uncertain future world into the existing subjective model. After having incorporated all the relevant information from the past into the subjective model, an individual has no choice but to anticipate the future events by extrapolating the existing subjective model into the future. To learn about the past is to

---

2. The terminology "assimilating" is borrowed from Piaget.

prepare for the future. We keep acquiring new knowledge about our environment by no other reason than that we are living in the world in which the future is always unknowable.

In the long run, however, the subjective model itself is subject to change. To anticipate the future is to confront the subjective model with the hard reality it is supposed to explain. The subjective model is only a working hypothesis for an individual, and the act of anticipation inevitably involves an element of testing that working hypothesis. If expectations formed on the basis of a given subjective model have persistently disappointed the learning individual, he or she is likely to search for a better model than the present one for assimilating the past data in a satisfactory way. Eventually, an individual will construct a new subjective model of the world and repeat the same assimilating activity as before by regarding it henceforth as a given invariant scheme of cognition. The process of learning in the long run therefore consists of the attempt to "accommodate" the subjective model to the demand of reality.[3]

It should be noted, however, that such a "Gestalt change" (i.e., a transition of the subjective model from one to another) is seldom the smooth process that conventional empiricistic learning models have taught us to believe. It is, in general, a discontinuous process that is almost always preceded by a period of cognitive crisis. By cognitive crisis, we mean an uncertain state of mind in which several alternative subjective models of the world are competing with each other, and yet one has been unable to settle one's mind on any of them. A transition is often made at a stroke in the middle of a crisis. And once the transition is made, the crisis comes to an end and a smooth short-run learning process begins. A Gestalt change is thus a miniature of the Copernican revolution.

Surprise is the source of human knowledge. An individual has something to learn from the objective world as long as reality data persistently upset expectations that have been formed on the basis of the existing subjective model. A person stops learning only when the reality data no longer surprise him or her. If such a hypothetical state of "no surprise" were possible and actually attained, there would remain no compelling reason to seek any further revision of the existing subjective model of the world. It is a state in which the subjective model is fully accommodated to the objective world, and thus the objective world is consistently assimilated into the subjective model. It is, in other words, a state of mind in which all the major tensions between the subjective model and the objective world have disappeared. It is nothing but a state of *equilibrium* in regard to an individual's learning process. It is, at the same time, also a state of equilibrium in regard to an individual's expectation-formation process. In

---

3. The terminology "accommodating" is also borrowed from Piaget.

what follows, we call this hypothetical state of mind an individual's "expectational equilibrium," for short. In this expectational equilibrium there remains no incentive for the individual to change the existing routine pattern of forming expectations about the future.

The important feature of this notion of expectational equilibrium is that there is no way to ascertain in advance whether or not one is actually in a state of expectational equilibrium. All one can do is to sustain the hypothesis by examining the past performance of one's own expectations. It is essentially an intertemporal concept which involves a retrospective comparison of different points of time.

Once we defined the notion of expectational equilibrium, we can reinterpret an individual's learning and expectation-formation process as an attempt at establishing an expectational equilibrium over time. As long as there remains a major tension between the objective world and the subjective model, the process of learning and expectation formation is in disequilibrium, and equilibriating attempts continue on the part of the individual. The tension or disequilibrium is the motive force to the process of learning and expectation formation, and this disequilibrium creates within itself the very dynamic force that works to alleviate it.

Although tempting, it would be a fatal mistake to jump to the conclusion that an expectational equilibrium is always logically possible and is stable. The very fact that an individual's learning and expectation-formation process consists of a continuous tension between the subjective model and the objective world means nothing more than that the existence and stability of expectational equilibrium depends not only on the "rationality" of the individual (whatever it means) but also on the dynamic structure of the objective world. Here, the social sciences have to part company with individual psychology. If by the "objective world" we mean only the physical and biological environment of an isolated individual, as in the case of Robinson Crusoe, there is little problem in supposing that individual's learning and expectation-formation process will in the course of time approach, by trial and error, a state of equilibrium. For the structure of such objective world is given independently of the learning activity of the individual and waits passively to be learned. As soon as the individual has been situated in a society consisting of multiple members, however, the nature of the objective world surrounding him or her undergoes a fundamental change from that of the objective world surrounding an isolated individual. It now becomes, at least partly, a product of a great many individuals' separate actions, which in turn are taken on the basis of their subjective models of the objective world. Hence, the objective world loses its fixity; it interacts dynamically with the subjective models of individuals. In consequence, as soon as we begin to study social phenomena, we are no longer able to take for granted the stability of or even the existence of an expectational equilibrium.

We then have to study closely the way in which the structure of the objective world itself interacts with changes in the subjective models of multiple individuals acting in it. This is indeed one of the major tasks of chapter 3.

2. The Theory of Expectation Formation within the Formal Theory of the Firm

Within the framework of our formal theory of the firm, the subjective model of the world that the firm perceives may be represented by a system of econometric equations that contain several parameters. The firm believes that its econometric model can explain the dynamic motions of such variables as the general price level, the general wage level, the total demand, and the total labor supply, which are expected to effect the demand for its product and the supply of labor to its factory. In the short run, the firm regards the parametric specification of its own model as fixed, and estimates the value of the unknown parameters by incorporating all relevant past data. The estimated model can then be used to calculate unbiased estimates of the unknown variables a_t, $a_{t+\tau}$, and b_t. These unbiased estimates are nothing but the subjective expectations we represented by $\hat{E}(a_t : \delta_t)$, $\hat{E}(a_{t+\tau} : \delta_t)$, and $\hat{E}(b_t : \delta_t)$ in chapter 1. Also, the firm's subjective probability distributions of its own surprises, represented by $\hat{A}(\cdot)$, $\hat{A}^{(\tau)}(\cdot)$, and $\hat{B}(\cdot)$, can be regarded as summaries of the statistical properties of these unbiased estimators. Their specification is determined solely by the stochastic specification of its own econometric model of the world.

As time goes on, our firm acquires new data from its own market activities. It revises the estimates of unknown parameters in the light of newly acquired data on the basis of the existing specification and then recomputes the subjective expectations of the relevant variables following the routine procedure. In short, the firm in our model behaves like a lazy econometrician in the short run.

3. A Simple Example of the Short-Run Expectation-Formation Process

In order to present a concrete example of the firm's short-run expectation-formation process, let us digress for a moment and consider an extremely simple specification of its subjective model. To minimize possible misunderstanding, let us hasten to emphasize here that the whole purpose of this section is to provide the reader with an example of a short-run expectation process that has a mathematically tractable structure. None of the propositions we shall establish in the book are dependent upon the particular example given here.

Since the following three sections are in the nature of mathematical exercises, the reader may skip them at first reading.

To begin with, let us rerecord the definitions of the state of product demand a_t and the state of labor supply b_t we gave in chapter 1:

$$(2\text{--}1) \qquad\qquad a_t \equiv P_t^{\hat{\eta}} X_t^{\hat{\varepsilon}} \alpha_t$$

and

(2-2) $$b_t \equiv W_t^{\hat{\varepsilon}} L_t^{-\hat{\lambda}} \beta_t^{-1},$$

where P_t, X_t, W_t, and L_t are the general price level, the total product demand, the general money wage level, and the total labor supply, respectively, in period t; $\hat{\eta}$, $\hat{\xi}$, $\hat{\varepsilon}$, and $\hat{\lambda}$ are the firm's subjective estimates of the elasticities in its product demand and labor supply schedules; and α_t and β_t are random disturbances. Hence, to form expectations of a_t and b_t, the firm has to construct a model of the economy which is intended to explain the dynamic movements of P_t, X_t, W_t, and L_t.

Suppose, then, that the firm believes that the aggregate variables P_t, X_t, W_t, and L_t move from one period to the next according to the following multiplicative random-walk equations:

(2-3) $$P_{t+1} = P_t(1 + \zeta_{P_t}), \qquad W_{t+1} = W_t(1 + \zeta_{W_t})$$

and

(2-4) $$X_{t+1} = X_t(1 + \zeta_{X_t}), \qquad L_{t+1} = L_t(1 + \zeta_{L_t}),$$

where

$$\zeta_{P_t}, \zeta_{W_t}, \zeta_{X_t}, \text{ and } \zeta_{L_t}$$

are long-normally distributed random variables with means equal to $\hat{\mu}_P$, $\hat{\mu}_W$, $\hat{\mu}_X$, and $\hat{\mu}_L$, respectively. One can interpret $\hat{\mu}_P$, $\hat{\mu}_X$, $\hat{\mu}_W$, and $\hat{\mu}_L$ as the average growth rates of P_t, X_t, W_t, and L_t, respectively. In the present example, they are all assumed to be constant. For convenience, let us further assume that

$$\zeta_{P_t}, \zeta_{X_t}, \zeta_{W_t}, \text{ and } \zeta_{L_t}$$

are mutually independent, although this "unrealistic" assumption can easily be relaxed. It should again be emphasized that the particular subjective model given above has nothing to do with our own view of the performance of the aggregate economy. It was chosen solely on the basis of its simplicity, that is, on the basis of its very "unreality."

In order to form expectations, the firm has to gather data about these aggregate variables from markets. It seems reasonable to suppose that although it is easy to obtain accurate information about prices and wages (which are, in fact, "announced" in the markets), information about the quantity variables (except the ones the firm directly deals with) is hard to acquire. In this example we go to the extreme and assume that the firm can observe P_t and W_t accurately at the end of every period but cannot directly observe X_t and L_t *even* at the end of the period. The latter assumption does not, however, mean that the firm is completely in the dark about X_t and L_t. On the contrary, there is still a way for the firm to infer their realized values from other observable variables.

To see this, let us rewrite the subjective product demand and labor supply schedules, (1–8) and (1–20), in the following manner:

(2–5) $(x_t p_t^{\hat{\eta}} P_t^{-\hat{\eta}})^{1/\hat{\xi}} = X_t(\alpha_t^{1/\hat{\xi}})$

and

(2–6) $(l_t w_t^{-\hat{\varepsilon}} W_t^{\hat{\varepsilon}})^{1/\hat{\lambda}} = L_t(\beta_t^{-1/\hat{\lambda}}).$

In both equations, all the variables on the left-hand sides are *observable* at the end of period t. (p_t and w_t are, of course, known even at the beginning of the period.) Hence, we can interpret the composite variables, $(x_t p_t^{\hat{\eta}} P_t^{-\hat{\eta}})^{1/\hat{\xi}}$ and $(l_t w_t^{-\hat{\varepsilon}} W_t^{\hat{\varepsilon}})^{1/\hat{\lambda}}$, as observations of the unobservable variables, X_t and L_t, with multiplicative observation errors, $\alpha_t^{1/\hat{\xi}}$ and $\beta_t^{-1/\hat{\lambda}}$, respectively. Any student of econometrics can now identify (2–5) and (2–6) as multiplicative forms of the "observational error equation" (see, e.g., Theil 1971). For convenience, we suppose that (the firm believes that) both of the observation errors, $\alpha_t^{1/\hat{\xi}}$ and $\beta_t^{-1/\hat{\lambda}}$, are log-normally distributed independent random variables with mean equal to unity.

In the present simple example, the firm's subjective model thus consists of (a) the system of multiplicative random-walk models, (2–3) and (2–4); (b) the system of multiplicative observational error equations, (2–5) and (2–6); and (c) the stochastic specification of the random disturbances. This can be regarded as a variant of the well-known errors-in-variables model of econometrics. It is therefore possible to compute the unbiased estimators of P_t, W_t, X_t, and L_t, and hence those of the composite variables, $a_t \equiv P_t^{\hat{\eta}} X_t^{\hat{\xi}} \alpha_t$, $b_t \equiv W_t^{\hat{\varepsilon}} L_t^{-\hat{\lambda}} \beta_t^{-1}$, and $a_{t+\tau} \equiv P_{t+\tau}^{\hat{\eta}} X_{t+\tau}^{\hat{\xi}} \alpha_{t+\tau}$, as an exercise in econometric theory. Indeed, those unbiased estimators are nothing but the firm's subjective expectations of a_t, b_t, and $a_{t+\tau}$, which we denoted by $\hat{E}(a_t : \delta_t)$, $\hat{E}(b_t : \delta_t)$, and $\hat{E}(a_{t+\tau} : \delta_t)$ in chapter 1.

In appendix 2, we have done such an econometric exercise and obtained the following (approximate) formulas for the computation of the firm's subjective expectations. If we denote the time difference $(z_{t+1} - z_t)$ by Δz_t, they are written

(2–7) $\dfrac{\Delta \hat{E}(a_t : \delta_t)}{\hat{E}(a_t : \delta_t)} \triangleq \hat{\xi} \hat{\mu}_X + \hat{\eta}\left[(1 - \hat{\theta}_X)\dfrac{\Delta P_{t-1}}{P_{t-1}} + \hat{\theta}_X \hat{\mu}_P\right] + \hat{\theta}_X\left[\dfrac{a_t}{\hat{E}(a_t : \delta_t)} - 1\right],$

(2–8) $\dfrac{\Delta \hat{E}(b_t : \delta_t)}{\hat{E}(b_t : \delta_t)} \triangleq -\hat{\lambda} \hat{\mu}_L + \hat{\varepsilon}\left[(1 - \hat{\theta}_L)\dfrac{\Delta W_{t-1}}{W_{t-1}} + \hat{\theta}_L \hat{\mu}_W\right]$

$\qquad\qquad\qquad + \hat{\theta}_L\left[\dfrac{b_t}{\hat{E}(b_t : \delta_t)} - 1\right],$

and

(2–9) $\dfrac{\Delta \hat{E}(a_{t+\tau} : \delta_t)}{\hat{E}(a_{t+\tau} : \delta_t)} \triangleq \dfrac{\Delta \hat{E}(a_t : \delta_t)}{\hat{E}(a_t : \delta_t)},$

with $(0 \leqslant \hat{\theta}_X \leqslant 1)$ and $(0 \leqslant \hat{\theta}_L \leqslant 1)$ being constants whose values are defined by (A2–8) and (A2–13).

The first two formulas are variants of the all-too-familiar adaptive expectation rules. Equation (2–7), for instance, says that in order to compute $\hat{E}(a_{t+1} : \delta_{t+1})$ at the beginning of period $(t + 1)$, the firm first extrapolates $\hat{E}(a_t : \delta_t)$ formed in the perceding period by the rate equal to $\hat{\xi}\hat{\mu}_X + \hat{\eta}[(1 - \hat{\theta}_X)\Delta P_{t-1}/P_{t-1} + \hat{\theta}_X\hat{\mu}_P]$ and then adjusts the consequent estimate upward or downward in proportion to the magnitude of surprise, $a_t/\hat{E}(a_t : \delta_t) - 1$. Here $\hat{\mu}_X$ is the expected growth rate of X_t, and $(1 - \hat{\theta}_X)\Delta P_{t-1}/P_{t-1} + \hat{\theta}_X\hat{\mu}_P$ is the weighted average of the observed and the expected growth rate of P_t. The adaptive coefficient $\hat{\theta}_X$ of the surprise term in (2–7) is a constant whose value is determined by the extent of volatility of the disturbance ζ_X of the random-walk equation (2–4) in relation to that of the error term $\alpha^{1/\xi}$ in the observational error equation (2–5). Indeed, its definition (A2–8) says that the value of $\hat{\theta}_X$ increases as the variance of ζ_X increases but decreases as the variance of $\alpha^{1/\xi}$ increases. This means that as the firm's confidence in the tightness of the correlation between the true but unobservable X_t and its observation $(x_t p_t^{\hat{\eta}} P_t^{-\hat{\eta}})^{1/\xi}$ declines relative to the volatility of the dynamic motion of X_t, the firm becomes less sensitive to the observed surprise, $a_t/\hat{E}(a_t : \delta_t) - 1$, in its revision of the subjective expectation of a_{t+1}. This is as one might expect it to be. The interpretation of the second adaptive expectation rule (2–8) is analogous. Equation (2–9), on the other hand, says that to compute the expected value of $a_{t+\tau+1}$ at the beginning of period $(t + 1)$, the firm has no choice but to extrapolate the newly computed estimate of a_{t+1} further into the future.

A question remains: How can the firm observe its own surprises, $a_t/\hat{E}(a_t : \delta_t) - 1$ and $b_t/\hat{E}(b_t : \delta_t) - 1$, in the market? The answer is provided immediately, once we rewrite them in the following manner:

$$\frac{a_t}{\hat{E}(a_t : \delta_t)} - 1 = \frac{p_t^{-\hat{\eta}}a_t/q_t}{p_t^{-\hat{\eta}}\hat{E}(a_t : \delta_t)/q_t} - 1 = \frac{x_t/q_t}{\hat{E}(x_t/q_t : \delta_t)} - 1,$$

and

$$\frac{b_t}{\hat{E}(b_t : \delta_t)} - 1 = \frac{h_t/w_t^{\hat{\xi}}b_t^{-1}}{h_t\hat{E}(b_t : \delta_t)/w_t^{\hat{\xi}}} - 1 = \frac{h_t/l_t}{\hat{E}(h_t/l_t : \delta_t)} - 1.$$

Since the optimal pricing policy and the optimal money wage policy established in propositions 1–1 and 1–3 require that $\hat{E}(x_t/q_t : \delta_t)$ and $\hat{E}(h_t/l_t : \delta_t)$ be set equal to $\hat{g}^*$ and $\hat{f}^*$, respectively, these two equations are resolved into

(2–10)
$$\frac{a_t}{\hat{E}(a_t : \delta_t)} - 1 = \left[\frac{x_t}{q_t} - \hat{g}^*\right] \Big/ \hat{g}^*$$

and

(2-11)
$$\frac{b_t}{\hat{E}(b_t : \delta_t)} - 1 = \left[\frac{h_t}{l_t} - \hat{f}*\right]\Bigg/\hat{f}*.$$

Consequently, we can now identify the surprise in regard to the present state of product demand with the gap between the actual and the subjective-normal ratio of product demand to supply and the surprise in regard to the present state of labor supply with the gap between the actual and the subjective normal ratio of labor supply to demand. Since the firm in this Wicksellian economy fixes the product price and money wage in such a way as to bring the ratio of product demand to supply and the ratio of labor supply to demand to be on average equal to their corresponding subjective normal ratio, this result should surprise no one. Substituting (2–10) and (2–11), we can rewrite the expectation-formation equations (2–7) and (2–8) as follows:

(2-12)
$$\frac{\Delta\hat{E}(a_t : \delta_t)}{\hat{E}(a_t : \delta_t)} \triangleq \hat{\theta}_X \left[\frac{x_t}{q_t} - \hat{g}*\right]\Bigg/\hat{g}* + \hat{\xi}\hat{\mu}_X + \hat{\eta}\left[(1 - \hat{\theta}_X)\frac{\Delta P_{t-1}}{P_{t-1}} + \hat{\theta}_X\hat{\mu}_P\right]$$

and

(2-13)
$$\frac{\Delta\hat{E}(b_t : \delta_t)}{\hat{E}(b_t : \delta_t)} \triangleq \hat{\theta}_L \left[\frac{h_t}{l_t} - \hat{f}*\right]\Bigg/\hat{f}* + \hat{\lambda}\hat{\mu}_L + \hat{\varepsilon}\left[(1 - \hat{\theta}_L)\frac{\Delta W_{t-1}}{W_{t-1}} + \hat{\theta}_L\hat{\mu}_W\right],$$

which require little explanation.

It goes without saying that we have been able to deduce the foregoing simple short-run expectation-formation formulas only because we have considered the simplest possible specification of the firm's subjective model of the world—a system of multiplicative random-walk equations with multiplicative observational-error equations. Obviously, as the subjective model becomes more sophisticated, expectation-formation equations will be more complicated. But no matter how complicated they become, the following principle will remain true: that the firm adjusts its subjective expectations of relevant random variables at least partially in response to its surprises at the market outcomes, which are registered in the forms of the gap between the observed and the subjective-normal ratio of product demand to supply and of the gap between the observed and subjective-normal ratio of labor demand to supply.

4. *A Price Adjustment Equation, or an Example of a Personified Law of Demand and Supply*

In chapter 1 we examined how the firm's optimal product price and money wage in the Wicksellian economy are guided by its own expectations about the present as well as future market conditions. In section 3 of this chapter, we were able to formalize, by means of a very special example, how the firm updates its expectations in response to its past experience in the market. If we mix these two results (and shake a bit), price and wage *adjustment* equations will result.

Rewriting the explicit form of the optimal pricing policy (1–11) in logarithmic form and taking its time difference, we have

$$(2\text{–}14) \qquad \Delta \ln p_t = \frac{1}{\hat{\eta}} \Delta \ln \hat{E}(a_t : \delta_t) - \frac{1}{\hat{\eta}} \Delta \ln q_t.$$

Using the approximation $\Delta \ln Z \underset{\Delta}{=} \Delta Z / Z$, we get

$$(2\text{–}14') \qquad \frac{\Delta p_t}{p_t} \underset{\Delta}{=} \frac{1}{\hat{\eta}} \frac{\Delta \hat{E}(a_t : \delta_t)}{\hat{E}(a_t : \delta_t)} - \frac{1}{\hat{\eta}} \frac{\Delta q_t}{q_t},$$

If we substitute the adaptive expectation rule (2–12) into this, we finally obtain the firm's price adjustment equation in the form

$$(2\text{–}15) \qquad \frac{\Delta p_t}{p_t} \underset{\Delta}{=} \frac{\hat{\theta}_X}{\hat{\eta}} \left(\frac{x_t}{q_t} - \hat{g}^* \right) \Big/ \hat{g}^* + \left[(1 - \hat{\theta}_X) \frac{\Delta P_t}{P_t} + \hat{\theta}_X \hat{\mu}_P \right] + \frac{1}{\hat{\eta}} \left(\hat{\xi} \hat{\mu}_X - \frac{\Delta q_t}{q_t} \right).$$

This price adjustment equation says that, other things being equal, the firm raises the product price when the realized ratio of product demand to supply exceeds the subjective-normal ratio and lowers it when the realized ratio is short of the subjective-normal ratio. The product price responds to the gap between the realized and the subjective-normal ratio for no other reason than that it represents the firm's surprise in regard to its expectation of the present state of product demand. When the gap is positive, for instance, it is a signal to the firm that it has underestimated the vigor of the demand for its product. The firm will then revise upward its expectation of the state of product demand and raise the level of product price to exploit the favorable market condition. The response coefficient of this price adjustment equation is the product of the subjective degree of monopoly $1/\hat{\eta}$ and the adaptive coefficient $\hat{\theta}_X$. This means that, other things being equal, the more competitive the product market is, less responsive is the product price to the gap between the realized and the subjective-normal ratio of product demand to supply. As the competitiveness increases more and more, the product price of an individual firm becomes more market-determined, and finally, in the limit case of perfect competition (i.e., when $1/\hat{\eta} = 0$), the product price becomes totally insensitive to changes in the demand condition for *its own* product.[4] This result clearly conforms to the conventional notion of perfect competition. The reason why the response coefficient is also proportional to the adaptive coefficient is obvious.

We have thus succeeded in establishing a *personified* law of demand and

---

4. This conclusion accords with the empirical findings of Eckstein and Wyss (1972).

supply in our monopolistically competitive economy. The *impersonal* law of demand and supply in neoclassical economics has been mathematically formulated by Paul Samuelson (1949) as $\Delta p_t / p_t = F(x_t/q_t - 1)$, where $F(0) = 0$ and $F'(x_t/q_t - 1) > 0$. But this is no more than an ad hoc theoretical construction, purported to represent the miraculous working of the Invisible Hand in a perfectly competitive market or the act of the fictitious Walrasian auctioneers. In contrast, our price-adjustment equation is a true behavioral equation of a real participant of the market—the firm—whose hands should be clearly visible, even to economists.

In the recent theoretical and empirical literature on price determination, the role of the anticipated general price level in the price-formation process is very much emphasized. In particular, the proponents of the normal rate theory of unemployment claim that it is not the absolute price level per se but its *relation* to the expected price level that responds to the gap between demand and supply (see, e.g., Phelps 1970; Friedman 1968, 1970; and Lucas 1972a, b, 1975). Our price adjustment equation (2–15) is, at least formally, consistent with this view, for the second term in it is the weighted average of the observed and the expected rate of change in the general price level; moreover its response coefficient is equal to unity. Hence, if the actual rate of price inflation was in line with its expected rate, this implies that the gap between the observed and the subjective-normal ratio of demand to supply will advance or retard the rate of price change only in relation to the expected rate of change in the general price level. This property of the price adjustment equation is due to the fact that, given the level of total demand, the demand schedule for individual product is homogeneous of degree zero with respect to all prices. This is, in other words, the reflection of the absence of money illusion among spenders in the product market. It should be noted, however, that since the level of total demand is in general negatively correlated with the level of general price, the careless regression of the rate of change in product price on the expected rate of change in the general price level would generate a regression coefficient far smaller than unity.

It should be borne in mind here that in spite of the formal similarity between the price adjustment equation advocated by the normal rate theorists and our price adjustment equation given above, the underlying causal relations are almost opposite. Whereas the former claims that it is an unanticipated price change which causes the actual demand-supply ratio to deviate from the subjective-normal ratio, the latter implies that it is a deviation of the actual demand-supply ratio from its subjective-normal value which causes, through the firm's revision of the expectation of the state of product demand, the product price to rise or fall relatively to the expected rate of price inflation. This reversal of causal direction will have important implications for the theoretical understanding of the nature of inflation and related disequilibrium phenomena.

It is, however, still premature to draw any conclusion at this stage of our investigation.

Our price adjustment equation also says that the firm raises its product price when the rate of change in product supply fails to keep up with the expected rate of change in total demand multiplied by the total-demand elasticity. When this occurs, the firm attempts to choke off some of the demand for its product and bring the ratio of demand to supply in line with the subjective-normal ratio by raising the price. The response coefficient to this term is the subjective degree of monopoly, so that as the competitiveness of the product market increases, the sensitivity of the price to this term will diminish.

Invariably, empirical studies of the process of price determination have shown that unit labor cost, either actual or standardized, is at least partially passed on to the level of product price (see, e.g., Eckstein and Wyss 1972 and Gordley and Nordhaus 1972). Some readers may have been puzzled by the apparent absence of the variable representing the rate of change in the money wage rate in our price adjustment equation. The answer is simple. The rate of change in the money wage rate has not gone away, but is concealed in the term $\Delta q_t / q_t$, the rate of change in product supply. If one recalls the discussion of markup pricing theory in section 15 of chapter 1, this becomes self-evident. When the effective labor demand is continuously smaller than or equal to the labor supply, we can substitute $j_{t-\tau} h^y_{t-\tau}$ for q_t and, upon further substitution of the definition (1–16) of h_t and the expectation-formation equation (2–12), we can rewrite the price adjustment equation as follows:

$$(2\text{–}16) \qquad \frac{\Delta p_t}{p_t} \triangleq \frac{\hat{\eta}(1-\gamma)}{\gamma + \hat{\eta}(1-\gamma)} \left[(1 - \hat{\theta}_x)\frac{\Delta P_{t-1}}{P_{t-1}} + \hat{\theta}_x \hat{\mu}_P \right]$$

$$+ \frac{\hat{\theta}_x}{\hat{\eta}\hat{g}^*}\left[\left(\frac{x_t}{q_t} - \frac{x_{t-\tau}}{q_{t-\tau}}\right) + \frac{\hat{\eta}(1-\gamma)}{\gamma + \hat{\eta}(1-\gamma)}\left(\frac{x_{t-\tau}}{q_{t-\tau}} - \hat{g}^*\right) \right]$$

$$+ \frac{\gamma}{\gamma + \hat{\eta}(1-\gamma)}\left(\frac{\Delta w_{t-\tau}}{w_{t-\tau}} - \frac{\Delta j_{t-\tau}}{j_{t-\tau}}\right) + \frac{\hat{\eta}(1-\gamma)}{\gamma + \hat{\eta}(1-\gamma)}\left(\xi\hat{\mu}_x - \frac{\Delta j_{t-\tau}}{j_{t-\tau}}\right).$$

In particular, if the degree of returns to labor input γ is equal to unity, this can be simplified to

$$(2\text{–}16') \qquad \frac{\Delta p_t}{p_t} \triangleq \frac{\hat{\theta}_x}{\hat{\eta}\hat{g}^*}\left(\frac{x_t}{q_t} - \frac{x_{t-\tau}}{q_{t-\tau}}\right) + \left(\frac{\Delta w_{t-\tau}}{w_{t-\tau}} - \frac{\Delta j_{t-\tau}}{j_{t-\tau}}\right).$$

In words, in the case of constant returns to labor input, the rate of price change depends, when labor is continuously oversupplied, upon the change in the ratio of product demand to supply from period $t - \tau$ to period t and upon the rate of change in money wage in terms of efficiency unit in period $t - \tau$. That the response coefficient of the latter equals unity implies a complete forward pass-through of unit wage cost, as is easily expected from the validity of the markup pricing formula in this underemployment situation. Notice also in (2–16′) the *change* of and not the level of the ratio of product demand to supply appears as an explanatory variable. This fact may be important to empirical testing of the price adjustment equation. Now, if we drop the assumption of constant returns to labor input, this simple result must be somewhat modified. As equation (2–16) indicates, the rate of price change now becomes dependent also on the expected rate of change in the general price level and the gap between the expected rate of change in total demand and the rate of change in productivity index. Their response coefficients are positive if the degree of returns to labor γ is less than unity, and negative if γ is greater than unity. This general price adjustment equation also says that, in general, the rate of change in the product price in this underemployment situation depends not only on the change in the ratio of product demand to supply from period $t - \tau$ to t but also upon the gap between the realized and the subjective-normal ratio of product demand to supply in period $t - \tau$. The response coefficient of this additional term is again positive if γ is smaller than unity and negative if γ is greater than unity. Finally, this general price adjustment equation says that the response coefficient of the rate of change in money wage in terms of efficiency unit is not in general equal to unity. It is smaller than unity if γ is smaller than unity and greater than unity if γ is greater than unity. Note, however, that even in this general case the *unit labor cost*, not the efficiency money wage rate, is completely passed on to the level of price. [This is not explicit in the foregoing price adjustment equation but becomes immediately obvious once we recall the markup pricing formula (1–18).]

When, on the other hand, the effective labor demand h_t is continuously exceeding the labor supply, we can substitute the full-employment output $j_{t-\tau} l_{t-\tau}^\gamma$ for q_t in (2–15) and obtain the following price adjustment equation:

$$(2\text{–}17) \qquad \frac{\Delta p_t}{p_t} \triangleq \left[(1 - \hat{\theta}_X) \frac{\Delta P_{t-1}}{P_{t-1}} + \hat{\theta}_X \hat{\mu}_P \right] + \frac{\hat{\theta}_X}{\hat{\eta}} \left(\frac{x_t}{q_t} - \hat{g}^* \right) \Big/ \hat{g}^*$$

$$+ \frac{1}{\hat{\eta}} \left[\hat{\xi} \hat{\mu}_X - \left(\frac{\Delta j_{t-\tau}}{j_{t-\tau}} + \gamma \frac{\Delta l_{t-\tau}}{l_{t-\tau}} \right) \right].$$

There is not much difference between this and the original price adjustment equation (2–15). But the important point in this full-employment situation is that the unit labor cost does *not* influence the determination of product price, and that the demand conditions, together with a given full-employment output level $j_{t-\tau} l_{t-\tau}^\gamma$, are the sole determinants of the level of product price. This should again be obvious from the discussion in section 15 of chapter 1. In fact, if we carelessly regress the rate of change in product price on the rate of change in money wage rate in this full-employment situation, the regression coefficient would have a counter intuitive negative sign, because then the positive correlation between money wage and the labor supply would be picked up by the regression.

5. A Money-Wage-Adjustment Equation in the Wicksellian Labor Market

Let us pass on to the money-wage-adjustment equation. Rewriting the explicit form of the optimal money wage policy (1–23) in logarithmic form, taking the time difference, and then approximating it, we obtain

$$(2\text{-}18) \qquad \frac{\Delta w_t}{w_t} \triangleq \frac{1}{\hat{\varepsilon}\hat{\eta}(1-\gamma)+\hat{\varepsilon}\gamma+\hat{\eta}} \left\{ \frac{\Delta\hat{E}(a_{t+\tau}:\delta_t)}{\hat{E}(a_{t+\tau}:\delta_t)} \right.$$

$$\left. + [\hat{\eta}(1-\gamma)+\gamma]\frac{\Delta\hat{E}(b_t:\delta_t)}{\hat{E}(b_t:\delta_t)} + (\hat{\eta}-1)\frac{\Delta j_t}{j_t} \right\}.$$

If we substitute the expectation-formation rules (2–9), (2–12), and (2–13) into this, we obtain the following money-wage-adjustment equation in our Wicksellian labor market:

$$(2\text{-}19) \qquad \frac{\Delta w_t}{w_t} \triangleq \frac{1}{\hat{\varepsilon}\hat{\eta}(1-\gamma)+\hat{\varepsilon}\gamma+\hat{\eta}} \left\{ [\hat{\eta}(1-\gamma)+\gamma]\hat{\theta}_L\left(\frac{h_t}{l_t}-\hat{f}^*\right)\middle/\hat{f}^* \right.$$

$$+ \hat{\theta}_X\left(\frac{x_t}{q_t}-\hat{g}^*\right)\middle/\hat{g}^* + [\hat{\eta}(1-\gamma)+\gamma]\hat{\varepsilon}\left[(1-\hat{\theta}_L)\frac{\Delta W_{t-1}}{W_{t-1}}\right.$$

$$\left. + \hat{\theta}_L\hat{\mu}_W\right] + \hat{\eta}\left[(1-\hat{\theta}_X)\frac{\Delta P_{t-1}}{P_{t-1}}+\hat{\theta}_X\hat{\mu}_P\right] - [\hat{\eta}(1-\gamma)+\gamma]\hat{\lambda}\hat{\mu}_L$$

$$\left. + \hat{\xi}\hat{\mu}_X + (\hat{\eta}-1)\frac{\Delta j_t}{j_t} \right\}.$$

In the first place, the money-wage-adjustment equation we have just derived states that, other things being equal, the firm in the Wicksellian economy raises its money wage when the realized ratio of labor demand to supply exceeds its subjective-normal ratio or when the realized ratio of product demand to supply exceeds its subjective-normal ratio. The gap between the realized and the subjective-normal ratio of labor demand to supply registers the firm's surprise in regard to its expectation of the tightness of labor supply. This gap, when it is positive, signals to the firm that it has overestimated the number of willing workers. The firm will then revise its expected number of willing workers downward; that is, it will revise its expectation of the state of labor supply (an index of the tightness of labor supply) upward. In order to take account of the tight situation in the labor market, the firm then bids up the level of money wage to be offered workers in the next period. The absolute

value of the response coefficient pertaining to this gap depends, in addition
to the adaptive coefficient $\hat{\theta}_L$, positively upon $1/\hat{\varepsilon}$, negatively upon $1/\hat{\eta}$, and
negatively upon γ. On the other hand, a gap between the realized and the
subjective-normal ratio of product demand to supply registers the firm's
surprise in regard to its expectation of the briskness of the future product
demand. This gap, when it is positive, is a signal that the strength of demand
for product, not only at present but also in the futute, has been underestimated.
The firm then tries to step up its production level in anticipation of a future
sales increase by bidding up its money wage rate vis-à-vis other firms. Recall
that when a production process takes time, the firm's labor employment and
money wage decision have to be based upon its expectation about future sales
conditions and thus necessarily contain an element of speculation. The response
coefficient pertaining to this gap depends, in addition to the adaptive coefficient
$\hat{\theta}_X$, positively upon $1/\hat{\varepsilon}$, positively upon γ, but a bit ambiguously on $1/\hat{\eta}$.

We have thus deduced choice-theoretically another law of demand and
supply, which in this case works in the Wicksellian labor market. Unlike the
law of supply and demand in neoclassical economics, however, our law of supply
and demand in the labor market maintains that the rate of change in money
wage is influenced not only by the gap in the labor market but also by the gap
observed in the product market. In other words, in our model, a disturbance
of the product market spills over into the labor market via the induced change
in the expectation of future product market conditions and influences the
firm's money wage adjustment.

In addition, our money-wage-adjustment equation says that the rate of
change in the money wage responds to both the weighted average of the observed
and the expected rate of change in the general money wage level and to the
weighted average of the observed and the expected rate of change in the general
price level. It is important to note that the response coefficients for these two
expectation terms add up to unity. (That is, $\{[\hat{\eta}(1 - \gamma) + \gamma]\hat{\varepsilon} + \hat{\eta}\}/[\hat{\varepsilon}\hat{\eta}(1 - \gamma)$
$+ \hat{\varepsilon}\gamma + \hat{\eta}] = 1$.) This is again a reflection of the homogeneity-of-degree-zero
property of *both* the labor supply and product demand schedules, given certain
levels of total labor supply and total product demand.

Finally, our money-wage-adjustment equation states that the rate of change
in the money wage depends negatively on the expected rate of change in total
labor supply, positively upon the expected rate of change in total product
demand, and positively upon the change in the productivity index.

It should be pointed out here that our money-wage-adjustment equation
was deduced under the assumption of a flexible money wage. It will be abandoned in parts II and III, which deal with the sticky-wage Keynesian economy.
(The price adjustment equation will, however, remain valid even in the
Keynesian economy.)

This section must, however, be concluded by a warning that, in spite of
the formal similarity, the economic implications of our example of price and

wage adjustment equations are very different from those of the Walrasian auction model, which assumes the possibility of recontracting. In our model, changes in prices and wages are followed by actual changes in sales, output, and employment. As long as the firm's expectations about its market environment are subject to surprises, the burden of such quantity adjustments is partly shifted to workers and spenders in the form of involuntary unemployment and unfilled orders. In this sense, it seems more appropriate to interpret our price and wage adjustment equations as an example of the microscopic representation of the short-run Phillips curve.

So much for the discussion of a special example. Let us go back to our more general framework of the theory of the firm.

6. *Formal Definition of Expectational Equilibrium*

In the long run, persistent surprises will intermittently induce the firm to change its specification of the subjective model of the world. When, however, its subjective model happens to be informationally compatible with the true structure of the world and hence its expectations about the future will not on the average produce any surprises, the firm is said to have attained a state of expectational equilibrium. To put this more precisely, we say that the firm has achieved a state of expectational equilibrium if its subjective probability distributions of relevant random variables coincide with its objective probability distributions, conditional upon the same set of data available to it. The difference between the subjective and objective probabilities lies in the fact that whereas the former is computed on the basis of the firm's often very distorted subjective model of the world, the latter is computed on the basis of the true structure of the objective world. (There is, of course, a certain conceptual difficulty as to the notion of objective probability, because the objective world itself includes the firm in question, whose actions are guided by its subjective view of the objective world. This "circularity" is indeed the very logical foundation for the propositions we derive in chapter 3.) In what follows, we represent by $\Pr\{Z:\delta\}$ and $\hat{\Pr}\{Z:\delta\}$ respectively, the objective and the subjective probabilities of an event Z conditional upon a set of data δ; and by $E(z:\delta)$ and $\hat{E}(z:\delta)$, respectively, the objective and the subjective expectation of a random variable z conditional upon δ.

Within our theoretical framework, the market environment relevant to the firm's decisions consists of (a) the product demand and labor supply schedules and (b) the probability distributions pertaining to the state of product demand and the state of labor supply. The former can be summarized by the values of the elasticities η, ξ, ε, and λ. The latter can be represented by their objective expected values, $E(a_t:\delta_t)$, $E(b_t:\delta_t)$, and $E(a_{t+\tau}:\delta_t)$, and the objective probability distributions, $A(\cdot)$, $B(\cdot)$, and $A^{(\tau)}(\cdot)$, which describe statistically how the true values of a_t, b_t, and $a_{t+\tau}$ deviate from their expected values. In terms of these notations, we can finally redefine the expectational equilibrium of the firm as a state in which the following three sets of conditions are satisfied. First, the firm's subjective estimates of the elasticities coincide with their true values:

(2–20) $\hat{\eta} = \eta, \quad \hat{\xi} = \xi, \quad \hat{\varepsilon} = \varepsilon, \quad \text{and} \quad \hat{\lambda} = \lambda.$

Second, the subjective probability distributions of the surprise coincide, for the same set of information, with their true probability distributions:

(2–21) $\hat{A}(z) = A(z), \quad \hat{B}(z) = B(z), \quad \text{and} \quad \hat{A}^{(\tau)}(z) = A^{(\tau)}(z).$

Third, the subjective expectations of the relevant random variables coincide, for the same set of information, with their objective expected values:

(2–22) $$\hat{E}(a_t : \delta_t) = E(a_t : \delta_t),$$
$$\hat{E}(b_t : \delta_t) = E(b_t : \delta_t),$$
$$\hat{E}(a_{t+\tau} : \delta_t) = E(a_{t+\tau} : \delta_t).$$

7. The Rational Expectations Hypothesis

In his model of price movement in a competitive market, John F. Muth (1961) proposed a hypothesis "that expectations, since they are informed predictions of future events, are essentially the same as the predictions of the relevant economic theory," which he called the "rational expectation hypothesis." One can regard this hypothesis as an extension of the good-old assumption of perfect foresight into the world of uncertainty. The hypothesis of rational expectations as stated by Muth is vague. In particular, it is not perfectly clear from the foregoing definition alone whether by "the relevant economic theory" he meant the decision maker's subjective model of the world or the neoclassical economic theory presented as a true copy of the real world. If by "the relevant economic theory" he meant the former, his hypothesis would be compatible with our theory of expectational formation advanced in previous sections. For, then, it would merely mean rather tautologically that an individual *intends to* be rational and uses his or her subjective model of the world as efficiently as possible in forming expectations about future events. However, since he restated his hypothesis as: "expectations of firms (or, more generally, the subjective probability distribution of outcomes) tend to be distributed, for the same information set, about the prediction of the theory (or the 'objective' probability distribution of outcomes)," we know that he meant the latter when he used the term "the relevant economic theory." This rational expectation hypothesis is thus formally equivalent to the conditions for expectational equilibrium introduced in section 6. It is, however, essential to keep in mind that whereas we introduced these conditions as the mere *defining characteristic* of a state of expectational equilibrium, without having prejudged either its existence or stability, the concept of rational expectations was posited as a behavioral hypothesis as to a rational economic man's expectation-formation activity. In fact, the hypothesis of rational expectations can be interpreted as a hypothesis about the strong *stability* (and, of course, the *existence*) of an expectational equilibrium, imposed quite independently of the macroscopic structure of the economy in which the rational economic man is situated. Trivial though it might appear at first glance, this conceptual difference is of fundamental importance, and produces views poles apart on the essence of disequilibrium in the economy.

8. *Normal Rate Theory of Unemployment*

In the recent controversy over the theoretical explanation of the Phillips curve —a negative correlation between the inflation rate and unemployment rate detected by A. W. Phillips (1958; Lipsey 1960; see also Fisher 1926)—some proponents of the "normal rate theory of unemployment" have forcefully build their case against the existence of the downward-sloping long-run Phillips curve upon the behavioral hypothesis of rational expectations.[5] The normal rate theory of unemployment claims that there exists only one rate of unemployment that is consistent with equilibrium in the structure of real wage rates. This rate, whose magnitude is totally independent of any systematic time patterns of nominal variables such as prices, money wages, and money stock, is called the normal rate of unemployment. Real wage rates are said to be in equilibrium if actual and anticipated changes in prices (and other relevant variables) are on average equal, that is, if all the participants in the labor market are in expectational equilibrium. The actual rate of unemployment, of course, deviates temporarily from the normal rate whenever real wage rates are thrown out of equilibrium by a sudden and unforeseen change in prices. Thus, there is a trade-off between unemployment and unanticipated inflation in the short run. But, assert the normal rate theorists, the "rational" public will sooner or later learn from their past mistakes and become capable of forming correct expectations about the new time pattern of price changes. Real wage rates will then return to their equilibrium structure and the normal rate of unemployment will be restored. Milton Friedman, the leader of the normal rate theorists, maintains that "there is a *short-run* 'trade-off' between inflation and unemployment, but no *long-run* 'trade-off,'" because "as Abraham Lincoln said, 'you can fool all of the people some of the time, but you can't fool all of the people all of the time'" (1975, p. 21). Another advocate of the normal rate theory, Robert

---

5. These proponents include Phelps (1970), Friedman (1968, 1970), Lucas (1972a, 1972b, 1975), and Sargent (1973, 1975, 1976). In this book we call their theory the normal rate theory of unemployment instead of the more commonly used name, "natural rate theory of unemployment."

Lucas, asserted in a similar vein that "rational expectations are equivalent to the existence of a [normal rate of unemployment]" (1972b, p. 54).

Let us introduce the notion of "normal" rates and "normal" ratios into our own theoretical framework. Let g^*, f^*, u^*, and v^*, be, respectively, the values of the subjective-normal ratios and rates $\hat{g}^*$, $\hat{f}^*$, $\hat{u}^*$, and $\hat{v}^*$ when all the subjective parameters, $\hat{\eta}$, $\hat{\varepsilon}$, $\hat{A}(\cdot)$, and $\hat{B}(\cdot)$, in their definitions (1–10), (1–20), (1–27), and (1–28), are replaced by the corresponding objective parameters, η, ε, $A(\cdot)$, and $B(\cdot)$. Formally, we define g^*, f^*, u^*, and v^* as follows:

$$(2\text{–}23) \qquad 1 - A(1/g^* - 1) - (\eta - 1)g^* \int_{-1}^{1/g^*-1} (1 + z)dA(z) \equiv 0,$$

$$(2\text{–}24) \qquad B(1/f^* - 1) - \varepsilon \int_{1/f^*-1}^{\infty} [f^*(1 + z)]^{-\gamma(\eta-1)/\eta} dB(z)$$

$$+ (1 + \varepsilon) \int_{1/f^*-1}^{\infty} [f^*(1 + z)]^{-1} dB(z) \equiv 0,$$

$$(2\text{–}25) \qquad u^* \equiv B(1/f^* - 1) - f^* \int_{-1}^{1/f^*-1} (1 + z) dB(z),$$

$$(2\text{–}26) \qquad v^* \equiv u^* + f^* - 1.$$

We shall call these objective parameters the normal ratio of product demand to supply, the normal ratio of labor demand to supply, the normal rate of involuntary unemployment, and the normal rate of unfilled vacancies, respectively. It is clear that these normal ratios and rates are constants whose values are fixed by the objective characteristics of the market environment and are totally independent of any systematic time pattern of nominal variables in the economy. They are truly "normal" values.

The introduction of the notions of normal rates and normal ratios immediately allows us to obtain a set of propositions that are *formally* congruent with the normal rate theory of unemployment. We can, in fact, show:

Proposition 2–1. When the firm is in a state of expectational equilibrium, the ratio of product demand to supply is on the average equal to its constant normal ratio:

$$(2\text{–}27) \qquad E\left(\frac{x_t}{q_t} : \delta_t\right) = g^*.$$

Proposition 2–2. In the Wicksellian economy, when the firm is in a state of expectational equilibrium, the ratio of labor demand to supply and the rate of involuntary unemployment are on average equal to the corresponding constant normal ratio and rate:

$$(2\text{–}28) \qquad E\left(\frac{h_t}{l_t} : \delta_t\right) = f^*$$

and

$$(2\text{--}29) \qquad\qquad E(u_t : \delta_t) = u^*.$$

The proof of proposition 2–1 is trivial. By proposition 1–1 we know that the firm sets its price in such a way that the subjective expectation $\hat{E}(x_t/q_t : \delta_t)$ should be equal to the subjective normal ratio $\hat{g}^*$. If the firm is in a state of expectational equilibrium, the first two conditions for it, given by (2–20) and (2–21), imply that the subjective-normal ratio $\hat{g}^*$ should be identical to the corresponding normal ratio g^*. Moreover, the third condition, given by (2–22), asserts that the subjective expectation $\hat{E}(x_t/q_t : \delta_t)$ should coincide with the objective expectation $E(x_t/q_t : \delta_t)$, conditional upon the same information set δ_t. As a result, $E(x_t/q_t : \delta_t)$ must be equal to g^* in a state of expectational equilibrium (Q. E. D.). Proposition 2–2 can be proved in a similar manner.

We have thus demonstrated that the conditions for expectational equilibrium, which are formally equivalent to the statement of the hypothesis of rational expectations, imply the normality of the rate of unemployment in the Wicksellian labor market. Thus, the deductive logic of the normal rate theory of unemployment has been confirmed even within our theoretical framework. Does this mean that the normal rate theory should now be enthroned to the glory of an unrefutable truth? Our answer is emphatically negative.

Propositions 2–1 and 2–2 by no means confirmed the validity of the normal rate theory per se. Rather, they crystalized the fact that the normal rate theory stands or falls together with the assumptions upon which it is built. In chapter 6 we show that in the Keynesian economy, in which money wages are not perfectly flexible even at the beginning of period, the aggregate rate of involuntary unemployment will be permanently above the constant normal rate, and if money wages are relatively inflexible downward, the aggregate rate of involuntary unemployment remains negatively correlated with the rate of inflation, even in the long run. The normal rate theory thus hinges critically on the assumption of the perfect flexibility of money wages. Equally fundamentally we can claim that even within the boundary of the Wicksellian economy, the very axiom of the normal rate theory of unemployment—the hypothesis of rational expectations—depends tacitly upon Say's laws of markets, which are never satisfied in the monetary economy we happen to live in. Chapter 3 may be considered to be an explanation of such a hastily voiced claim.

9. Summary

The process of expectation formation is best understood as a continual interaction of two different levels of internal activities—one working in the short run and the other operating through the long-run course of events. In the short run, a person behaves as if his or her subjective model of the world were given once and for all, and tries to assimilate the objective world into it. His or her expectations of the future are thus no more than a projection of the existing subjective model into the still unknown future world. In the long run, however, the person tries to accommodate the subjective model to the objective world. If actual observations of the reality have persistently upset the expectations, the person starts searching for another subjective model that would better accommodate to the demand of reality. After a period of cognitive crisis, a new subjective model will emerge, and a new short-run process of expectation formation on its basis will begin at that point. In this chapter we have applied this general idea to the analysis of the expectation-formation process of an individual firm.

In the short run, the firm is supposed to have a subjective econometric model representing the economy surrounding it. The firm treats the specification of the econometric model as *given* and endeavors to estimate its structural parameters by employing the past data and predicts the future values of the relevant variables by projecting the estimated model into the future. Thus, once we are given a specification of the firm's econometric model of the surrounding world, the analysis of its expectation-formation process in the short run becomes a classroom exercise in econometrics.

[In optional sections, we have studied in detail a special example in which the firm's subjective econometric model consists of a set of multiplicative random-walk equations and multiplicative observational error equations. It is easy to show that in this case (and only in this special case) the firm's short-run expectation-formation process can be represented by a set of familiar adaptive-expectation formulas. Then, an example of a price adjustment equation can be obtained by combining these adaptive-expectation formulas with the optimal price equation. It can be shown that the rate of price change is correlated with the gap between the observed ratio of product demand to supply and the corresponding subjective-normal ratio. This explanatory variable registers the firm's surprise or expectation error in regard to its subjective expectation of the state of product demand, the existence of which invites the firm to revise its subjective expectation and hence to adjust its product price. This relation might be interpreted as a *personified* law of demand and supply. An example of a wage adjustment equation in the Wicksellian labor market can be obtained in the same manner.]

In the long run, the firm's subjective econometric model itself is subject to change. If the firm has been persistently disappointed at the performances of its own subjective expectations, the firm is forced to revise the specification of its own subjective econometric model. We say that the firm is in a state of expectational equilibrium if its subjective probability distributions of all the relevant random variables coincide, for the same set of information available to it, with their objective probability distributions. This is a hypothetical state in which the firm's subjective model is informationally compatible with the true structure of the economy surrounding it, and hence the firm's subjective expectations are on average confirmed by the realized market outcomes. Our definition of expectational equilibrium is, of course, formally identical with the hypothesis of rational expectations. However, although we introduced it merely as a defining characteristic of a state of expectational equilibrium, the hypothesis of rational expectations introduces the same notion as a behavioral hypothesis about a rational agent's expectation-formation process. This seemingly slight difference will lead to quite divergent views of the nature of the economy's disequilibrium.

Within the framework of our simple theory of the firm under uncertainty, it is easy to prove that if the firm is in a state of expectational equilibrium, the rate of involuntary unemployment (among workers supplying their labor services to it) is on average equal to a given constant called the normal rate of involuntary unemployment. The magnitude of this normal rate is determined solely by the real characteristics of the market and is totally independent of any systematic time pattern of the inflation rate and of other nominal variables. This proposition thus confirms the validity of the deductive logic of the normal rate theory of unemployment. But it by no means confirms the validity of the normal rate theory itself. Rather, it crystalizes the fact that the normal rate theory of unemployment stands or falls together with its critical assumptions: namely, the hypothesis of rational expectations and the supposition of the complete flexibility of money wages. Indeed, these two assumptions will be subject to close scrutiny in the rest of the book.

CHAPTER 3

The Cumulative Inflation Process and Say's Laws of Markets

1. *On Macroeconomic Dynamics*

In chapter 1 we saw how an individual firm determines price, wage, employment, and production on the basis of its expectations about the dynamic and uncertain market environment.

In chapter 2 we turned our attention to the problem of how these expectations are formed and reformed over time as the firm acquires new information from its market activity. We then found that it is surprises that work as the main motive force of the firm's dynamic behavior. For if the firm is persistently surprised by the discrepancy between its expectations and the realized market outcomes, it will sooner or later alter its expectations and then change its price, wage, employment, and output in order to adapt them to newly revised expectations. If we are concerned solely with the analysis of the dynamic behavior of a *single* firm, that is, with microeconomic dynamics, this is the end of the story. For we have succeeded in working out the implications of a disturbance of the market environment, which to a single firm is a "fact" given exogenously.

However, our goal is to construct a theoretical framework for macroeconomic dynamics. We have set up a model of the individual firm for no other reason than to provide its building blocks.

The task of macroeconomic dynamics, then, is to show how the aggregate variables, such as general price level, general money wage level, total labor employment, and total product supply, are determined in each period, and to exhibit a causal process by which they are moved from one position to another. These aggregate variables are, of course, aggregate outcomes of simultaneous but separate decisions of different firms as to their own price, wage, employment, output policies, which are formed on the basis of their expectations about market conditions. But these market conditions, in turn, involve not only factors exogenous to markets but also the very aggregate outcomes of firms' own decisions in markets. (There is a trace of a bootstrap mechanism here.) From the macroscopic standpoint, therefore, the market environment surrounding the firms cannot be regarded merely as an exogenously determined fact. In our macroeconomic dynamics, it is thus no longer sufficient to study how each firm separately reacts to a given change in its market environment. It is necessary to work out in detail how simultaneous but separate decisions of different firms interfere with each other and how their interaction alters the very market environment they are in and thereby produces an outcome that may prove contradictory to their original intentions. It is, in other words, necessary to consider the possibility of an endogenous disturbance of the market environment.

For economists there is no graver sin than to commit the "fallacy of composition"—a fallacy in which what is true of a part is, on that account alone, alleged to be true of the whole. In this chapter we develop a theoretical framework that will keep us from falling victim to this fallacy.

2. A Simplifying Assumption

Before we proceed, let us introduce a simplifying assumption which will be sustained throughout the rest of the book.

It is our assumption that firms' subjective estimates of the elasticities, $\hat{\eta}(i)$, $\hat{\xi}(i)$, $\hat{\varepsilon}(i)$, and $\hat{\lambda}(i)$, happen to be equal to the corresponding objective elasticities, $\eta(i)$, $\xi(i)$, $\varepsilon(i)$, and $\lambda(i)$, and that firms' subjective probability distributions of surprises, $\hat{A}_i(\cdot)$, $\hat{A}_i^{(\tau)}(\cdot)$, and $\hat{B}_i(\cdot)$, coincide with the corresponding objective probability distributions, $A_i(\cdot)$, $A_i^{(\tau)}(\cdot)$, and $B_i(\cdot)$. That is, we shall assume in what follows that both the first and second conditions for expectational equilibrium, (2–20) and (2–21), are to be satisfied for all firms in the economy. (But we shall *not* assume its third set of conditions.) Then all the subjective-normal ratios and rates, $\hat{g}^*(i)$, $\hat{f}^*(i)$, $\hat{u}^*(i)$, and $\hat{v}^*(i)$, coincide with the corresponding normal ratios and rates, $g^*(i)$, $f^*(i)$, $u^*(i)$, and $v^*(i)$, respectively. [It also follows that the subjective constants, $\hat{\phi}(i)$ and $\hat{\chi}(i)$, which was defined by (A1–7) and (A1–8), should be replaced by their objective counterparts, $\phi(i)$ and $\chi(i)$, the definitions of which are obvious.] It must be emphasized, however, that this assumption has been introduced solely for the simplification of the exposition; it could be dispensed with if we were willing to endure a heavy notational burden. Besides, the conceptual distinction between subjective and objective parameters will still remain in spite of their assumed quantitative equality.

3. The Definition of Aggregate Variables

In chapter 1 we defined the notions of total product demand and total labor supply and denoted them by X_t and L_t, respectively. The former is the aggregate real value of all the purchase orders (or demands) for products the spenders sent to firms. It is, in other words, the real value of the sum total of households' purchase orders for consumption goods, firms' purchase orders for investment goods, and the local and central governments' purchase orders for both. The latter, on the other hand, represents the sum total of labor supply offers by all workers in the economy. It is true that the volume of total product demand and the level of total labor supply at a point in time are influenced by such aggregate variables as the general price level, the general money wage level, the level of total labor employment, and the amount of total product supply, which are, in turn, the very outcomes of firms' market activities in the past as well as at present. It is, however, important to bear in mind that in spite of the existence of such influences, the decisions of the spenders on their product demand and the decisions of the workers on their labor supply are made independently of the decisions of the firms on their price, wage, employment, and output; there is no nexus uniting their separate decisions in any automatic fashion.

The total product demand and the total labor supply must be divided across firms. It was argued in chapter 1 that, given the volume of total product demand X_t, the chief determinant of the level of product demand to the ith firm $x_t(i)$ is the quoted price $p_t(i)$ in relation to the general price level P_t, and that, given the level of total labor supply L_t, the chief determinant of the labor supply to the ith firm $l_t(i)$ is the money wage $w_t(i)$ in relation to the general money wage level W_t. The particular specification of product demand and labor supply schedules we have chosen to use is the following constant-elasticity form:

$$(3\text{--}1) \qquad x_t(i) = \left[\frac{p_t(i)}{P_t}\right]^{-\eta(i)} X_t^{\xi(i)} \alpha_t(i), \qquad i = 1, 2, \ldots, I,$$

$$(3\text{--}2) \qquad l_t(i) = \left[\frac{w_t(i)}{W_t}\right]^{\varepsilon(i)} L_t^{\lambda(i)} \beta_t(i), \qquad i = 1, 2, \ldots, I,$$

where $\alpha_t(i)$ and $\beta_t(i)$ are unsystematic random disturbances, $\eta(i)$ and $\varepsilon(i)$ the price and the wage elasticity, and $\xi(i)$ and $\lambda(i)$ the total-demand and the total-labor-supply elasticity.

It is demonstrated in appendixes 1–a and 1–b that, under appropriate definitions of the general price level P_t and the general money wage level W_t, both the system of product demand schedules (3–1) and the system of labor supply schedules (3–2) satisfy the following adding-up equations in every period:

$$(3\text{--}3) \qquad \sum_{i=1}^{I} p_t(i) x_t(i) = P_t X_t$$

and

$$(3\text{--}4) \qquad \sum_{i=1}^{I} l_t(i) = L_t.$$

That is, the values of product demand, distributed across firms, have to add up to the original value of total product demand, and the numbers of labor supply, distributed across firms, have to add up to the total labor supply. These adding-up conditions guarantee us that the foregoing systems of product demand and labor supply schedules have perfectly consistent micro and macro structures, so that the murky aggregation problem, the well-known stumbling block to any attempt at integrating micro- and macroeconomics, will not obscure our subsequent investigation.

Since, in view of the adding-up equation (3–3), the total product demand X_t can be rewritten as $\sum p_t(i)x_t(i)/P_t$, it is natural to define the total product supply and the total sales volume (or the total income), respectively, by the following aggregation formulas:

$$(3\text{–}5) \qquad Q_t \equiv \sum_{i=1}^{I} \frac{p_t(i)q_t(i)}{P_t}$$

and

$$(3\text{–}6) \qquad Y_t \equiv \sum_{i=1}^{I} \frac{p_t(i)y_t(i)}{P_t}.$$

By the same token, in view of the adding-up equation (3–4) of total labor supply, it is natural to define the total (effective) labor demand and the total labor employment, respectively, by

$$(3\text{–}7) \qquad H_t \equiv \sum_{i=1}^{I} h_t(i)$$

and

$$(3\text{–}8) \qquad N_t \equiv \sum_{i=1}^{I} n_t(i).$$

We can also define the aggregate rate of involuntary unemployment and the aggregate rate of unfilled job vacancies, respectively, as

$$(3\text{–}9) \qquad U_t \equiv \frac{L_t - N_t}{L_t} = \sum_{i=1}^{I} \left[\frac{l_t(i)}{L_t} \right] u_t(i)$$

and

$$(3\text{–}10) \qquad V_t \equiv \frac{H_t - N_t}{L_t} = \sum_{i=1}^{I} \left[\frac{l_t(i)}{L_t} \right] v_t(i)$$

Finally, we define the aggregate normal ratio of product demand to supply and the aggregate normal ratio of labor demand to supply, respectively, as

$$(3\text{--}11) \qquad G^* \equiv \sum_{i=1}^{I} \left[\frac{p_t(i) q_t(i)}{P_t Q_t} \right] g^*(i)$$

and

$$(3\text{--}12) \qquad F^* \equiv \sum_{i=1}^{I} \left[\frac{l_t(i)}{L_t} \right] f^*(i).$$

In general, these aggregate normal ratios fluctuate slightly over time, as their weights may change from period to period (except in the case where individual normal ratios are uniform across firms). But in what follows we will treat them as given constants.

4. *The Fundamental Equation of the Product Market*

Let us now introduce a macroeconomic notion that will play a key role in the development of our macroeconomic dynamics. Define the product market gap as $(X_t/Q_t - G^*)/G^*$, that is, as the proportionate gap between the ratio of total product demand to supply and the aggregate normal ratio of product demand to supply. The value of this gap is thus determined by the relative balance between the volume of total product demand X_t, which aggregates spenders' purchase orders in the current product market, and the volume of total product supply Q_t, which is fixed by firms' employment decisions τ periods earlier. It becomes positive or negative according as X_t deviates from Q_t proportionally more or less than the given G^*. It becomes zero only when X_t happens to exceed Q_t by the proportion exactly equal to G^*.

The existence of a positive or negative product market gap represents an imbalance in macroscopic conditions of the product market. We shall now argue that the emergence of a nonzero product market gap indeed renders the intentions of the firms in the product market mutually incompatible and necessarily upsets the expectations of at least one of them. To elucidate this fundamental mechanism, let us first rewrite the expression for the product market gap in the following manner:

$$(3\text{--}13) \qquad \left(\frac{X_t}{Q_t} - G^* \right) \Big/ G^* = \frac{\Sigma p_t(i) x_t(i)}{G^* P_t Q_t} - \frac{\Sigma p_t(i) q_t(i) g^*(i)}{G^* P_t Q_t}$$

by (3–3) and (3–11)

$$\equiv \sum_{i=1}^{I} \left[\frac{g^*(i) p_t(i) q_t(i)}{G^* P_t Q_t} \right] \left[\frac{x_t(i)}{q_t(i)} - g^*(i) \right] \Big/ g^*(i),$$

which states merely that the proportional gaps between the ratio of product demand to supply and its constant normal ratio, that is, $[x_t(i)/q_t(i) - g^*(i)]/g^*(i)$, across firms have to add up to the existing size of the product market gap,

$(X_t/Q_t - G^*)/G^*$. This new adding-up equation is no more than a simple transformation of the original adding-up condition (3–3), which constrains spenders' demand schedules in the product market. Its immediate implication is that if the product market gap is positive, the ratios of product demand to supply of some firms inevitably exceed their normal ratios, and that if the product market gap is negative, the ratios of product demand to supply of some firms inevitably fall short of their normal ratios. This is no more than an arithmetic truism. But as soon as we recall the nature of the firm's optimal pricing policy studied in chapter 1, we reach a fundamental conclusion.

Now, the optimal pricing policy, established in proposition 1–1, states that at the beginning of every period, the firm quotes the price at the level that is expected to bring the ratio of product demand to supply equal to the given subjective-normal ratio:

$$(3\text{–}14) \qquad \hat{E}\left[\frac{x_t(i)}{q_t(i)} : \delta_t(i)\right] - g^*(i) = 0.$$

Ex ante, therefore, each firm "intends" to realize the subjective-normal ratio of product demand to supply. There would be little problem if only a single firm tried to realize its intention. *The whole is, however, not the mere sum of its parts. What is possible for a single firm is not necessarily possible for all the firms simultaneously.* Indeed, it is now plain from the new adding-up equation (3–13) that unless the product market gap happens to be zero, the intentions of all the firms are mutually incompatible. For if the product market gap is positive, the realized ratio of product demand to supply of at least one firm (and often a majority of the firms) becomes necessarily greater than the given normal ratio, thereby contradicting its expectation, and if it is negative, the realized ratio of product demand to supply of at least one firm becomes necessarily smaller than the normal ratio, again upsetting its expectation. In other words, the existence of a nonzero product market gap implies the existence of a surprise (or an expectation error) on the part of at least one firm in the product market.

We can summarize the foregoing observation in a more formal manner. Rewriting the optimal pricing policy (3–14) as

$$\hat{E}\left[p_t(i)^{-\eta(i)} a_t(i)/q_t(i) : \delta_t(i)\right] - g^*(i)$$
$$= x_t(i)\hat{E}\left[a_t(i) : \delta_t(i)\right]/a_t(i)q_t(i) - g^*(i) = 0,$$

and rearranging terms, we obtain

$$(3\text{–}15) \qquad \frac{a_t(i)}{\hat{E}\left[a_t(i) : \delta_t(i)\right]} - 1 = \left[\frac{x_t(i)}{q_t(i)} - g^*(i)\right]\Big/ g^*(i).$$

[This relation was derived as equation (2–10). It says that a firm's surprise with respect to its subjective expectation of $a_t(i)$ is registered in the market in the form of a discrepancy between the realized and the subjective-normal ratio of product demand to supply.] Substituting this into the new adding-up equation (3–13), we immediately obtain the following equation:

$$(3\text{–}16) \quad \sum_{i=1}^{I} \left[\frac{g^*(i)p_t(i)q_t(i)}{G^* P_t Q_t} \right] \left[\frac{a_t(i)}{\hat{E}\left[a_t(i):\delta_t(i)\right]} - 1 \right] = \left(\frac{X_t}{Q_t} - G^* \right) \Big/ G^*.$$

We call this equation the "fundamental equation of the product market." Its right-hand side is, of course, the product market gap in period t. The left-hand side is, on the other hand, simply the weighted average of individual firms' surprise in regard to their expectations of the present state of product demand. [It is easy to see from (3–11) that the weights add up to unity.] It will be called the average surprise in regard to the present state of product demand in period t. We have thus established a one-to-one correspondence between the size of the product market gap and the average surprise. If either one of them is zero, the other must be zero; and if either one of them is positive (negative), the other becomes positive (negative) as well. Therefore, surprises the firms as a whole are allowed to entertain in the product market are completely determined by the existing size of the product market gap.

To avoid possible confusion, let us make it clear that the fundamental equation of the product market (3–16) is not a definitional relation, substituting one symbol for another. It is an "equation" that was deduced from the condition (3–14) of the firm's optimal pricing policy and from the new adding-up equation (3–13), which imposes a certain macroscopic constraint upon firms' simultaneous but separate pricing decisions in the product market. It is a relation between two completely different things—on the one side, the product market gap whose value is determined by the aggregative relative balance between the spenders' demands for product and the firms' supplies of product, and on the other side, the average of surprises on the part of firms that have to quote product prices under uncertainty. Indeed, the theory of cumulative inflation process we develop in section 13 is no more than the working out of the causal process implied by this fundamental equation of the product market. There, we present the process of inflation as a metamorphosis of the firms' mutually incompatible attempts at raising their relative prices simultaneously into an unexpected rise in the general level of nominal prices.

Some reader might have noticed a striking similarity between our fundamental equation of the product market and the famous (second) fundamental equation of Keynes in his *Treatise on Money* (1930, chap. 10). Keynes' (second) fundamental equation maintains that the difference between the value of new investment and that of savings equals the total "windfall" profit of all the firms in the economy. Of course, the former can be, under suitable definition of savings, made equal to the difference between total product demand and total product supply, and the latter can be interpreted as an aggregate index of the surprises on the part of firms in the economy. This is not a fortuitous coincidence. The essence of the ideas behind these two fundamental equations is in fact the same. (By the way, his fundamental equation is not a definitional equation either, even though many critics of his theory have so claimed.) Keynes's derivation of the fundamental equation was based upon a rather peculiar assumption as to the determination of the prices of consumption and investment goods. He (implicitly) supposed that firms decide in advance how much to produce of consumption goods and that the output of consumption goods is thrown into the market at whatever price consumers are willing to take; whereas, as for investment goods, he (explicitly) supposed that their prices are determined by the excess of "bearishness" on the part of the holders of the existing assets as well as by the behavior of banking system, quite independently of the demand and supply conditions in the markets for *new* investment goods. In contrast, our fundamental equation of the product market was deduced from explicit consideration of firms' optimal pricing decisions. In spite of this difference, both Keynes's fundamental equation and our fundamental equation are based upon the common idea that the prices (the prices of new investment goods in the case of Keynes) do not clear the product market instantaneously, so that the participants in market transactions have to base their decisions upon the prevailing *disequilibrium* prices.

Since the implication of our fundamental equation is of the paramount importance in our subsequent analysis, we would like to record it in the following form:

Proposition 3–1. *If the product market gap is positive, the firms as an aggregate necessarily underestimate the current state of product demand. And if the product market gap is negative, the firms as an aggregate necessarily overestimate the current state of product demand. It is if and only if the product market gap is equal to zero that firms' expectations are on average confirmed by the realized market outcomes.*

We can put forward this argument a little further. In chapter 2 we introduced the notion of expectational equilibrium. We said that a firm is in expectational equilibrium if its expectations are not persistently upset by the realized market outcomes. The condition for this equilibrium notion is of course stronger than the mere absence of a surprise on the part of the firm. But we can at least argue from proposition 3–1 that, if the product market gap deviates from zero, it is unlikely that the surprises which are endogenously produced are consistent with firms' expectational equilibria. Indeed, if the number of firms is large, unsystematic surprises of different firms tend, by the law of large numbers, to cancel each other, and, as a result, if all firms were to be simultaneously in their expectational equilibrium, little room would remain for the average surprise to deviate from zero. In appendixes A3–a and b, we are indeed able to turn this intuitive argument into the following form:

Proposition 3–1'. *In the economy with a very large number of firms, if the product market gap is either positive or negative, not all firms are simultaneously capable of attaining their expectational equilibrium concerning the present state of product demand, with probability 1.*

Clearly, this proposition strengthens the implication of proposition 3–1 and establishes a logical connection between the seemingly "individualistic" notion of expectational equilibrium and the "macroscopic" market condition, represented by the notion of the product market gap. (The qualification "with probability 1" in proposition 3–1' will not affect the main line of the argument and will be ignored.)

5. The Fundamental Equation of the Labor Market

Let the labor market gap in period t be defined by the proportionate gap between the ratio of total labor demand to supply and the aggregate normal ratio of labor demand to supply, $(H_t/L_t - F^*)/F^*$. Its value is therefore determined by the relative balance between the level of total labor demand H_t, which aggregates firms' effective demands for labor, and the level of total labor supply L_t, which aggregates workers' labor supply offers. It becomes positive or negative according to whether the former exceeds the latter proportionally more or less than the given aggregate normal ratio F^*. And it becomes zero only if H_t happens to deviate from L_t by a proportion exactly equal to F^*.

As in the case of the product market gap, the existence of a positive or negative labor market gap represents a macroeconomic imbalance in the current labor market. Indeed, by combining the optimal money wage policy (1–24) with the adding-up constraint (3–4) of the labor supply schedules, it is possible to deduce the following equation, which will be called the "fundamental equation of the labor market":

$$(3\text{–}17) \qquad \sum_{i=1}^{I} \left[\frac{f^*(i)l_t(i)}{F^*L_t} \right] \left[\frac{b_t(i)}{\hat{E}[b_t(i):\delta_t(i)]} - 1 \right] = \left(\frac{H_t}{L_t} - F^* \right) \Big/ F^*.$$

The derivation of this second fundamental equation is analogous to that of the first fundamental equation (3–16).

The right-hand side of the fundamental equation of the labor market is nothing but the labor market gap we defined already. The left-hand side is, on the other hand, the weighted average of individual firms' surprises concerning their expectations of the state of labor supply which represents the tightness of labor supply. We shall call this the average surprise in regard to the extent of tightness of labor supply. We have thus shown that surprises the firms on average have to experience in the labor market are completely determined by the existing size of the labor market gap.

Summarizing, we have established:

Proposition 3–2. *If there is a positive labor market gap, the firms in the Wicksellian labor market as an aggregate inevitably underestimate the tightness of labor supply. And if there is a negative labor market gap, they as an aggregate inevitably overestimate the tightness of labor supply. It is if and only if the labor market gap equals zero that their expectations become, on average, consistent with the actual market outcomes.*

If the number of firms is very large, this proposition can be strengthened in the following manner:

Proposition 3–2'. *If the labor market gap is nonzero, not all firms in the Wicksellian economy are capable of attaining their expectational equilibrium concerning the present state of labor supply, with probability 1.*

The proof of this stronger proposition is similar to that of proposition 3–1'.

Note in passing that the fundamental equation of the labor market (3–17) was deduced under the assumption of flexible money wages. It becomes defunct, at least in the present form, as soon as we introduce the inflexibility of money wages into our picture of the economy. In chapter 5, which deals with the short-run behavior of the sticky-wage Keynesian economy, we replace it by a more general formula, "the generalized fundamental equation of the labor market."

To explore further the implications of our fundamental equations, we have to digress for a while and take up one of the most old-fashioned topics in the history of economics—Say's law of markets.

6. Say's Laws

In a barter economy, a sale of a product is necessarily a purchase of another product of equal value. The total value of all products demanded is therefore always and necessarily equal to the total value of all products supplied. Say's law, that "supply creates its own demand," is indeed a tautology in a barter economy.

In a monetary economy, however, we all know that there is no place for Say's law. Money is a medium of exchange. In principle, any marketable commodity or asset can serve as a medium of exchange if the condition for double coincidence of wants is satisfied. But money is a particular medium of exchange by delivery of which any contractual obligation can be discharged without further ado. Money is also a store of value. Of course, any marketable commodity or asset is a store of value as long as it is storable. But money distinguishes itself from other stores of value in that, because of its privileged function as the most effective medium of exchange, it is salable without notice and without loss at any point in the future. It is, in other words, the most liquid store of value and is held by the public as such. Money as a liquid store of value then splits up the identity between the sale and purchase of a barter exchange into two independent acts separated in time and in space. A seller of a product receives money, but there is no necessity for him or her to spend all of it immediately on other products; the seller can hoard part or all of it. Moreover, as long as the seller has already hoarded a certain amount of money, he or she can spend it on products that cost more than his or her current sales revenue. Money hoarded is only a potentiality of spending on an unspecified product at an unspecified time. (This is precisely what "liquidity" means.) Hence, in a monetary economy, supply does not necessarily create its own demand, and the total product demand is no longer identically equal to the total product supply.[1]

In fact, in a monetary economy, not only do the total values of products demanded and supplied lose their identity, but they are also deprived of any other form of necessary relation that unites them. Total product demand and total product supply are, respectively, an aggregate outcome of spenders' spending decisions and an aggregate outcome of producers' output decisions, which are made independently of each other. It then follows that the product market gap, $(X_t/Q_t - G^*)/G^*$, may be positive, negative, or zero, depending upon the relative strength of these two independent sets of decisions. Without the help of a central coordinating agency, such as Walras's auctioneers, it can become zero only by accident.

For our purposes, therefore, it is reasonable to call the assertion that the product market gap is always and necessarily equal to zero, that is, the assertion that

$$\left(\frac{X_t}{Q_t} - G^*\right)\bigg/ G^* \equiv 0,$$

"Say's law of the product market."[2]

---

1. It is not without some interest to give a quotation of the famous passage of J. B. Say:

> It is worthwhile to remark that a product is sooner created, than it, from that instant, affords a market for other products to the full extent of its own value. When the producer has put the finishing hand to his product, he is most anxious to sell it immediately, lest its value should vanish in his hands. Nor is he less anxious to dispose of the money he may get for it; *for the value of money is also perishable.* But the only way of getting rid of money is in the purchase of some product or other. Thus, the mere circumstance of the creation of one product immediately opens a vent for other products. [Italics ours; Say 1921, vol. 1, p. 167]

Note the peculiar statement in the italics, which seems to imply that people have no preferences for money as liquidity and try to dispose of it as soon as they acquire it. Thus, the foundation of Say's law collapses, at least in the sense adopted by Say, as soon as money enters into the sphere of commodity exchanges and is being held by the public as the most liquid store value.

2. In his influential article in 1965, Clower called the aggregate budget identity (that the value of demands and the value of supplies of all commodities and assets,

In a noncapitalistic agrarian or artisan economy in which everyone employs oneself, there is no distinction between supply of and demand for labor. But the advent of the wage system within the monetary economy causes a split between the act of labor supply and the act of labor demand. The total supply of and the total demand for labor in the monetary economy are, respectively, an aggregate outcome of workers' labor supply decisions and an aggregate outcome of employers' labor demand decisions, which are made at each point independently of each other. In the monetary economy, therefore, not only do total labor supply and total labor demand lose their identity, but they are deprived of any automatic relation in the short run, unless being coordinated by a highly authoritative central job-allocating agency (or by Walras's auctioneers). It follows that the labor market gap, $(H_t/L_t - F^*)/F^*$, may be positive or negative or zero, depending upon the relative intensity of workers' labor supplies and employers' labor demands. It becomes zero again only by chance.

Therefore, it is not unreasonable for us to call the assertion that the labor market gap is always and necessarily equal to zero, that is, the assertion that

$$\left(\frac{H_t}{L_t} - F^*\right)\bigg/ F^* \equiv 0,$$

"Say's law of the labor market."

Our definitions of the foregoing two Say's laws are somewhat unconventional. But they at least seem to caputre the spirit of the "law of markets" advocated by J. B. Say, which has constituted the fundamental principle, often tacit but sometimes explicit, of classical and neoclassical economics since his time.

7. To Assume Rational Expectations as a Behavioral Hypothesis Is to Assume Say's Laws

The hypothesis of rational expectations, explained in chapter 2, maintains that *since* economic agents forming expectations are rational, we should postulate that their expectations are always in equilibrium. This has been introduced

---

inclusive of money, are equal) "Say's principle," and called the postulate that the value of effective demands and that of effective supplies are equal, "Walras's law." The same terminology was followed by Leijonhufvud (1968). Unfortunately, the meaning of Say's law employed in the present book fits neither into their Say's principle nor into their Walras's law. Our definition is much closer to what J. B. Say meant in the passage quoted in the previous footnote and what Keynes tried to express in *The General Theory*. It is, in other words, Say's law in the sense of Lange (1942) that postulates that the total values of products demanded and supplied, *exclusive of money*, are identically equal to each other.

Note that, in our model, since spenders are not allowed to shop around when their orders are not fulfilled in their first attempts, we do not have to distinguish, as Clower did, between the concept of notional demands and supplies and that of effective demands and supplies. In fact, all demands and supplies are effective in our model of the economy.

into economics *as a behavioral hypothesis* concerning the expectation-formation
activity of rational individuals, *without regard to* macroscopic conditions of the
economy. It has thus been suspected of committing the fallacy of composition.

Such a suspicion is now upheld. In the monetary economy where Say's
laws break down, there is always a possibility that either the product market
gap or the labor market gap becomes positive or negative. But propositions
3–1' and 3–2' have demonstrated to us that if *for whatever reason* the product
market gap or the labor market gap deviates from zero, it becomes *impossible*
that all the firms are simultaneously in their expectational equilibrium. It then
follows that in order to postulate, as the hypothesis of rational expectations
did, that all firms are always in expectational equilibrium, it is necessary to
assume that both the product market gap and the labor market gap are always
and necessarily equal to zero; that is, it is necessary to assume both Say's law
of the product market and Say's law of the labor market.

It is doubtful that proponents of the hypothesis of rational expectations
really believe in Say's laws. But they at least tacitly assume them to be true.
Needless to say, to assume the truth of Say's laws is to assume *away* all the
essential characteristics of the monetary economy we now live in.

About forty years ago, Keynes made the following remark: "I doubt if
many modern economists really accept Say's law that supply creates its own
demand. But they have not been aware that they are tacitly assuming it"
(1937a, p. 223). Sadly enough, the same remark applies equally well to today's
economists.

8. *Causal Analysis in Macroeconomic Dynamics*

In neoclassical economics, faith in human rationality is the guiding principle
of theoretical investigation. The normal rate theory of unemployment has
followed this tradition and placed the hypothesis of rational expectations in
its central position. If the rate of unemployment deviates from its normal level,
it is due to a misperception of market conditions on the part of workers (in
the case of the search theory of unemployment) or of the firms (in the case of
our model of the firm in chapter 1). But according to the hypothesis of rational
expectations, an error of expectations is merely a temporal aberration. It will
be soon rectified by the rationality of those who have committed it, and as a
result the deviation of the rate of unemployment from its normal level will
soon correct itself. Within the framework of the normal rate theory of unemployment, it is thus the power of human rationality that countervails a loss of
equilibrium and governs the real determination of market conditions. It is
indeed unnecessary for economists to trace out the precise causal mechanism
through which the position of equilibrium will be restored.

However, as soon as Say's laws have been removed from our picture of
the economy—and this amounts to taking explicit account of the essential

nature of the monetary economy—it is no longer possible to posit the hypothesis of rational expectations as a behavioral postulate. And as soon as the hypothesis of rational expectations has been disposed of, it becomes necessary to treat the firm's expectation formation as a process in time—a process that involves a mutual interaction between the firm's subjective model and the objective structure of the market environment. Rationality is then no longer the sole guiding principle; a mere appeal to human rationality will lead us nowhere. Instead, we have to analyze causal sequences of economic events step by step, without prejudgment of their final destiny, their telos.

Our fundamental equation of the product market (3–16) demonstrated that whenever the product market gap is nonzero, some firms' expectations about the state of the product market are necessarily upset. Surprises, or errors in expectations, are thus an inevitable result of an imbalance in macroscopic conditions of the product market. Similarly, our fundamental equation of the labor market (3–17) established that whenever the labor market gap diverges from zero, some firms' expectations about the tightness of the labor market are necessarily upset. Their surprises are again an inevitable result of an imbalance in macroscopic conditions of the labor market.

Surprises are the fuel of the economy. Surprises, once having come into existence, will sooner or later get firms to revise their expectations about market conditions and then cause them to adjust their prices, wages, outputs, and employments in markets. These induced changes in prices, wages, outputs, and employments will, in turn, create new market conditions, thereby preparing a new round of economic changes in subsequent periods.

The significance of our two fundamental equations, therefore, lies in the fact that they have located the primary cause of the firms' surprises within the system of economic relations, not in such external factors as human folly, ecological uncertainty, or unpredictability of monetary policy. We are thus given an endogenous explanation of the emergence of surprises in the economy. And we are now able to use it as a critical link in our attempt at tracing out causal chains of economic events in our Wicksellian economy.

9. Expectational Equilibrium versus Wicksellian Equilibrium

That we cannot assume as a behavioral hypothesis that all firms are simultaneously in expectational equilibrium does not prevent us from conceiving a *state of the economy* in which all the firms happen to be in expectational equilibrium. On the contrary, such a state will serve as an important benchmark in our subsequent macroeconomic dynamics. Henceforth, we shall call this hypothetical state of the economy a state of "Expectational equilibrium," with a capital E.

We need, however, another notion of equilibrium in our macroeconomic dynamics. We say that the Wicksellian economy is in a state of "Wicksellian equilibrium" if both the product and labor market gaps are equal to zero.

Let us elucidate the logical relationship between these two notions of equilibrium. In the case of an isolated individual like Robinson Crusoe (before his encounter with Friday), the notion of equilibrium is simple enough. All his conscious decisions at a point in time are necessarily compatible with each other. (Here we have abstracted from the problem of bounded or limited rationality, which is taken up in parts II and III.) If there is any incompatibility, it is only with respect to the decisions made at different points in time. Such an intertemporal incompatibility has to be due to a change in his knowledge about the environment and hence to a change in his expectations about future events, which leads him to revise his original plans. Consequently, in the case of Robinson Crusoe, the only relevant notion of equilibrium is that of expectational equilibrium—the coincidence between the subjective and the objective probabilities of future events.

The nature of equilibrium undergoes a radical change when we pass from the world consisting only of Robinson Crusoe to a society consisting of multiple individuals.[3] In a society where its members' activities are interdependent, the outcome of a decision in general depends upon what other individuals do. If different individuals make decisions simultaneously but separately, then in order for *all* of them to realize their intended outcomes, it is necessary that a mutual compatibility of their decisions be assured at the outset. If for whatever reason their decisions were mutually incompatible, it is inevitable that their realized outcomes would prove disappointing and in consequence some persons would find themselves out of their expectational equilibrium.

Therefore, as soon as we have left behind the world of Robinson Crusoe, we have to distinguish two different notions of equilibrium—the one concerned with expectational equilibrium of all of its members, and the other representing the mutual compatibility of their simultaneous decisions. The latter synchronic equilibrium notion is, in fact, logically prior to the former diachronic one, in the sense that a breakdown of the latter inevitably disrupts the former.

In our Wicksellian economy, we call a state in which all firms are simultaneously in their expectational equilibria a state of Expectational equilibrium. And the notion of Wicksellian equilibrium, which is defined as a state in which neither the product nor the labor market gap is open, represents nothing more

---

3. The following discussion owes a debt to an important article of Hayek (1937). Hayek, however, did not pursue sufficiently the implications of his analysis of the notion of equilibrium in social processes. He rightly pointed out the importance of the problem of mutual compatibility of actions made independently by a number of people, but then turned away from it and addressed himself to the different problem of how markets are capable of harmonizing the division of knowledge among different individuals. To be more specific, Hayek noted the possibility of the breakdown of Wicksellian equilibrium but investigated only those situations where the conditions for Wicksellian equilibrium are somehow satisfied—situations that we call secondary disequilibrium (see section 10).

then the condition for mutual compatibility of simultaneous decisions of all firms. Indeed, propositions 3–1' and 3–2' have shown that whenever either of the market gaps are open, that is, whenever the condition for Wicksellian equilibrium is disturbed, at least one firm will inevitably be thrown out of its expectational equilibrium, thereby disrupting Expectational equilibrium of the economy *as a whole*. The condition for Wicksellian equilibrium is, in other words, a necessary precondition for the existence of a state of Expectational equilibrium.[4]

It is now possible to reinterpret Say's laws of product and labor markets as an assertion that the economy is always and necessarily in Wicksellian equilibrium. They are, in other words, assertions that firms' simultaneous decisions can *never* be mutually incompatible. Thus, our critique of the hypothesis of rational expectations given in section 7 can be restated as follows. The hypothesis of rational expectations has missed the fundamental difference between the nature of equilibrium within a society that consists of multiple individuals and the nature of equilibrium of an isolated individual like Robinson Crusoe. As soon as we leave a laboratory of individual psychology or a literary laboratory of Daniel Defoe, we have to check the mutual compatibility of individuals' simultaneous decisions before we can speak of their expectational equilibria. In the monetary economy, where Say's laws fail, such mutual compatibility generally breaks down and firms' expectation formations are unable to attain their equilibria simultaneously, thereby making the hypothesis of rational expectations logically untenable.

10. *Wicksellian Disequilibrium versus Secondary Disequilibrium*

If there is anything useful about notions of equilibrium, it is their role as analytical norms in our classification of possible states of the economy.

The fact that the existence of Expectational equilibrium requires a prior fulfillment of the conditions for Wicksellian equilibrium suggests immediately that *two* different forms of disequilibrium can be distinguished in our Wicksellian

---

4. Our definition of Wicksellian equilibrium is close to the notion of monetary equilibrium of Bent Hansen (1951), the modern representative of the Stockholm school. He generalized the concept of monetary equilibrium of Wicksell, Lindhal, and Myrdal by distinguishing between the product market and the factor market. It should be noted, however, that while our Wicksellian equilibrium is merely the precondition for the realization of Expectational equilibrium of the economy as a whole, Hansen identified his notion of monetary equilibrium with neoclassical general equilibrium. This difference is due to the fact that in describing the economy's disequilibria, Hansen had to rely upon the story of Walrasian market auctioneer. See, however, recent works of Akerlof (1969, 1976), who removed the Walrasian auctioneer from Hansen's system and succeeded in presenting very interesting models of inflation. In fact, our Wicksellian theory of cumulative inflation, developed later in the chapter, is akin to Akerlof's models of inflation.

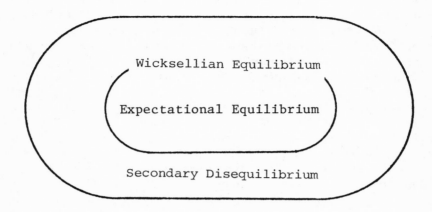

FIGURE 3–1. Hierarchical Relations among Equilibria and Disequilibria in the
Wicksellian Economy

economy. The first form will be called "Wicksellian disequilibrium." It represents
a set of disequilibrium situations that are caused by a disturbance of the condition of Wicksellian equilibrium, that is, by the emergence of either a product
market gap or a labor market gap or both. The second and indeed secondary
form of disequilibrium will be called "secondary disequilibrium." It refers to a
set of disequilibrium situations in which, although both product and labor
market gaps are closed, some firm's expectations are nonetheless out of
equilibrium.

When the economy is in Wicksellian disequilibrium, some firm's expectations are necessarily out of its expectational equilibrium, and in consequence
the conditions for Expectational equilibrium of the economy as a whole are
automatically disrupted. Surprises of the firm are thus an inevitable result of
the existing imbalance in macroeconomic conditions. They are, in other words,
merely symptoms of the more fundamental cause of disequilibrium. In contrast,
in the case of secondary disequilibrium, there is no logical necessity for the
emergence of errors in firms' expectations. Here surprises are the very "cause"
of the economy's disequilibrium.

Figure 3–1 illustrates rather schematically the hierarchical relationship
between equilibria and disequilibria in the Wicksellian economy. From the
vantage point of a surveyor, this is an incredibly distorted map, for the set of
states of Expectational equilibrium, in effect, ought to occupy a negligible
portion (i.e., a subset of measure zero) of the whole set of Wicksellian equilibria,

which in turn occupies a negligible subset of the whole collection of possible states of the economy.

The following analysis will proceed from the particular to the general. First, we examine the characteristics of a state of Expectational equilibrium in the Wicksellian economy; next, we study the self-adjusting nature of secondary disequilibrium; finally, we investigate endogenous macroeconomic dynamics in the domain of Wicksellian disequilibrium.

11. *Expectational Equilibrium of the Economy as a Whole*

In the Wicksellian economy, a state of Expectational equilibrium is the home ground of the normal rate theory of unemployment. Since all firms in it are by definition in their expectational equilibrium, the ratio of product demand to supply, the ratio of labor demand to supply, the rate of involuntary unemployment, and the rate of unfilled vacancies are all on average equal to the corresponding normal ratios and rates, whose constant values are determined by given market and technological characteristics. (Recall propositions 2–1 and 2–2.) They are, in other words, independent of the time pattern of changes in any monetary variables in the economy. In this sense, we can say that money is on average "neutral" in an Expectational equilibrium state. It should be emphasized, however, that this long-run neutrality of money is only a characteristic feature of the state of Expectational equilibrium in our Wicksellian economy, which would break down whenever either the product market gap or the labor market gap were broken open even by a small change in market variables. (We shall, however, return to this subject in part III and demonstrate that in case nominal wages are sticky, money is no longer neutral, even in a state of Expectational equilibrium.)

Other than the long-run neutrality of money, we can say very little about the nature of the state of Expectational equilibrium of our Wicksellian economy unless we introduce a detailed specification of the total demand and total labor supply schedules as well as certain assumptions concerning the government's monetary and fiscal policy. Since this is the territory of orthodox economic theory (although perfect competition is almost always assumed there) and our marginal productivity seems next to nothing in this territory, we shall not pursue the analysis of the nature of Expectational equilibrium further in this chapter, except for one remark.

In a state of Expectational equilibrium we now know that the average demand/supply ratio of, say, the ith firm's product is equal to its constant normal ratio. It then follows that unless this normal ratio happens to be 1, demand is not on average equal to its supply but diverges permanently from the latter. Does this not imply, some readers will undoubtedly ask, a perpetual disequilibrium on the part of spenders in a state of Expectational equilibrium?

This puzzle is resolved as soon as we recall the definition of the notion of product demand. It is defined herein as the magnitude of purchase orders sent by the spenders to the supplying firm. It is then clear that, in determining purchase orders, each spender has to take account of the possibility that some of them may not be honored by the supplier, so that he or she has to inflate the magnitude of the orders in accordance with the anticipated probability of rejection. Hence, if the ratio of product demand to supply of the ith firm is on average equal to $g^*(i)$, and if the firm rations its product either uniformly or purely randomly in the case of excess demand, it is plausible to suppose that spenders will come to expect it over the long period of time and inflate the magnitudes of their purchase orders by the factor equal to $g^*(i)$ above the expected level of product supply. This seems to imply that a state of Expectational equilibrium in our Wicksellian economy is likely to be consistent with the conditions of expectational equilibrium on the part of spenders as well. (A similar story can be told in the case of the labor supply decisions of workers.)

12. *Secondary Disequilibrium and the Invisible Hand*

Even when neither the product nor the labor market gap is open, the Wicksellian economy may still be out of Expectational equilibrium. For we, mortal beings, can never be free of errors. We have already given the name "secondary disequilibrium" to this situation in which some firms fail to achieve expectational equilibrium, even though neither the product nor the labor market gap exists and hence there is no necessity on the part of the firms to commit expectation errors.

In the product market this secondary disequilibrium manifests itself as a deviation of the system of relative prices from that of equilibrium; in the labor market it manifests itself as a deviation of the system of relative wages from that of equilibrium. We now claim that the secondary disequilibrium has an automatic tendency to correct itself and smoothly approach Expectational equilibrium.

Suppose that the economy has been in a happy state of Expectational equilibrium until the ith firm suddenly becomes optimistic and raises its expectation of the state of product demand. All the other firms, however, keep their expectations as they were. Suppose also that for some reason both the product and the labor market gap remain zero even after this sudden disruption of the ith firm's expectational equilibrium. The economy now enters the domain of secondary disequilibrium.

The ith firm, which now has a higher expectation of the state of product demand, sets its price higher than the previous equilibrium level, whereas all the other firms set their price at the same level as before. Evidently, the system of relative prices deviates from its equilibrium configuration; the relative price of the ith firm's product is now higher than the equilibrium value, whereas the relative prices of all the other products become on average lower than their equilibrium values. It is the system of relative prices that governs the allocation of total product demand among firms, and such distortion of the system of relative prices tends to shift the spenders' demand from the ith product to the others. Since the product market gap is assumed to be zero, this implies that the ith firm is now likely to face a subnormal ratio of demand to supply of its product, while all the other firms on average experience supernormal ratios of demand to supply. [Recall the adding-up equation (3–13).]

For some time, the ith firm may regard the glut of the demand for its product as an evanescent phenomenon; but as the subnormal ratio of demand to supply persists, it will eventually come to attribute this to its own over-estimation of the state of the product demand. The firm will then revise its too-optimistic expectation downward and roll back the price of its product. Other things being equal, such downward revision of the expectation will tend to restore the ith firm's expectational equilibrium, and such rolling back of the level of price will move its relative price in the direction of reestablishing the equilibrium configuration of relative prices. This is what we call the *direct* self-adjusting mechanism of secondary disequilibrium, which involves only the adjustment activity of the ith firm, the culprit of this secondary disequilibrium.

There is, however, another route through which a secondary disequilibrium will correct itself. It is through the reactions of the other firms, a majority of which have had to face supernormal ratios of demand to supply as a consequence not of their own faults, but of the ith firm's unwarranted switch to optimism. For some time, these firms will probably regard the supernormality of the demand/supply ratio merely as transient; but gradually they will come to notice the persistence of this excessive influx of product demand. They will then feel it necessary to revise their expectations of the state of product demand upward and will raise the prices of their products accordingly. These induced changes of the other firms' prices will, on the whole, tend to lower the ith firm's relative price further and shift back the swollen demand for their products to the ith product. This will, of course, speed up the ith firm's return to its expectational equilibrium. This is the *indirect* self-adjusting mechanism of secondary disequilibrium, and it will work to reinforce the direct self-adjusting mechanism of secondary disequilibrium.

In fact, we could have reached the same conclusion more mechanically by invoking our fundamental equation of the product market (3–16). For it says that if the product market gap is zero, firms' surprises are on average necessarily equal to zero. Hence, if one firm has for some reason overestimated the state of product demand and overpriced its product, other firms are forced, on the whole, to underestimate the state of product demand with equal intensity. The former's attempt at rectifying its overestimation and the consequent rolling back of its own price, on the one hand, and the latter's attempt at rectifying their (forced) underestimation and the consequent bidding up of their prices, on the other, tend to reinforce each other's effect upon the system of relative prices and aid each other's effort to restore expectational equilibrium.

(To make our argument complete, we must take into account the reactions arising from firms' output supply adjustment. Suffice it to say here, however, that these supply responses are likely to support the self-adjusting mechanism of secondary disequilibrium.)

It should be noted here that our discussion of the self-adjusting nature of secondary disequilibrium has implicitly relied upon the fact that the system of product demand schedules (3–1), as specified here, implies gross substitutability of every pair of products in the product market, in the sense that the demand for a product increases, other things being equal, whenever the price of the other product is raised.[5] If, instead, the product of the ith firm is a gross complement of the product of the, say, kth firm, then the increase in the price of the latter will tend to direct the spenders' demand further away from the latter, and will work in the direction of upsetting the latter's attempt at restoring its expectational equilibrium. Thus, in order for the indirect self-adjusting mechanism of secondary disequilibrium to work in the "correct" direction, the extent of gross complementarity must be sufficiently limited between products.[6]

Since a similar argument can be applied to the labor market as well, we can maintain:

Proposition 3–3. *The secondary disequilibrium has a strong automatic tendency to correct itself as long as the extent of gross complementarity between products in the product market and between working conditions of different employers in the labor market is sufficiently limited.*

In an economy where Say's laws are valid, secondary disequilibrium is the only possible form of disequilibrium. In such an economy, the above observation implies that, as long as the gross substitutability is prevalent, the economy as a whole is more rational than the mere summation of individual rationalities. Here, the Invisible Hand of the price mechanism assists firms' individual attempts to correct their own errors, and is always ready to work its wonder in restoring an orderly state of Expectational equilibrium whenever it is disturbed by an unforeseen shock.

---

5. As shown in Appendix 1–a, the gross cross-elasticity $[\partial x(i)/\partial p(j)]/[x(i)/p(j)]|_{PX=\text{const.}}$, which measures the extent of gross substitutability of product i with respect to product j, equals $[\eta(j)-1]p(j)x(j)/PX$ (>0) in our model. So all the products in our model are gross substitutes of each other, and their strength increases as the price elasticity, $\eta(j)$, increases, Similarly, the gross cross-elasticity $[\partial l(i)/\partial w(j)]/[l(i)/w(j)]|_{WL=\text{const.}}$, which measures the extent of gross substitutability of the working condition of firm i with respect to the working condition of firm j, equals $-\varepsilon(j)l(j)/L$ (<0) in our model. So the working conditions of all the firms in our model are gross substitutes of each other, and their strength increases as the wage elasticity $\varepsilon(j)$ increases.

6. This is, of course, one of the main conclusions in the stability theory of the Walrasian general equilibrium model. See, for instance, Negishi (1962) or Arrow and Hahn (1971).

In a monetary economy, however, secondary disequilibrium is only a secondary form of disequilibrium. Since neither of Say's laws holds true, the product market gap and the labor market gap are in constant danger of being opened up by a sudden change in the macroeconomic environment. And as soon as either one of them is opened up and, as a result, the economy enters Wicksellian disequilibrium, the nature of dynamic adjustment process becomes qualitatively different from that of secondary disequilibrium. Indeed, we now have to abandon the optimistic faith in the working of the Invisible Hand.

13. *Wicksellian Disequilibrium and Cumulative Price Inflation*

Imagine again an economy that has been in a happy state of Expectational equilibrium for a long, long time. Both the product market gap and the labor market gap have been continuously filled up, and all firms' expectations have been on the average continually confirmed by the realized market outcomes. Suppose that in period zero the total demand suddenly increases above the level indicated by the past trend, and then resumes the past trend growth rate (but not the past trend level) from the next period on. (If the economy had not been in Expectational equilibrium prior to this sudden change of total demand, the analysis of a new disequilibrium situation becomes slightly more complicated.) Such a sudden upward drift of the total demand may be due to an upward shift of firms' marginal efficiency schedules of capital; to a decline of consumers' time preferences; a downward shift of asset holders' liquidity preferences; an expansion of government expenditures; a reduction of tax schedules; or an injection of liquidity into financial markets through the central bank's open-market operations. Whatever the cause, it certainly creates a positive gap in the product market for some time after the period. We thus have

$$\left(\frac{X_t}{Q_t} - G^*\right)\bigg/ G^* > 0.$$

A condition for Wicksellian equilibrium has been disrupted.

Now, we know from the new adding-up equation (3–13) that the emergence of a product market gap implies that at least one of the firms, and usually a majority of them, have to face supernormally high ratios of demand to supply of their products. Their reactions will depend upon their expectations as to whether this demand influx will be temporary or permanent. As long as they regard it as temporary, due presumably to a transient increase in the firm-specific random disturbance $\alpha_t(i)$, nothing will happen, at least on the surface of the product market, except for spenders' frustration over their inability to purchase as many products as they wish. The general price level will still keep track of the trend path that has been followed in past happy days. This, however, is only a lull before the storm. Sooner or later, most firms, faced with continual inflow of supernormally large demands, come to realize that the change is not temporary but permanent, caused possibly by an increase in total demand above the past trend path. Eventually, they will revise their expectations of the total demand upward and hence those of the state of product demand upward, to take account of this new change in macroeconomic conditions. The economy will start losing track of the trend path from that instant.

In the product market it is the system of relative prices that regulates the division of a given volume of total product demand among different products. [Recall the product demand schedule (3–1).] Thus, if a firm wishes to eliminate supernormal ratio of demand to supply of its product, the only means available to it in the short run is to raise its price relatively higher than the general price level. The firm has control over its own price, of course, but it has no control over other firms' prices. (There is no price cartel.) In fact, when the firm determines its own price at the beginning of each period, it cannot know the prices of other firms and has to form the best expectation it can as to the level of general price that aggregates them. It then follows that when a supernormal demand/supply ratio persists, the firm tries to choke it off by raising its own price relative to its expectation of the general price level.[7]

Now, if only a single firm experienced a supernormally large demand and raises its price relative to its expectation of the general price level, there would be little problem. The whole is, however, not the mere sum of its parts. When there is a positive product market gap, then, as an arithmetic fact, most firms in the product market must be experiencing supernormally high ratios of demand to supply. [Recall the adding-up equation (3–13).] They therefore *simultaneously* attempt to raise their own prices relative to the level of general price. (That is, they simultaneously raise their own prices relative to their expectations of the general price level.) *This is, of course, a contradiction.* No matter how rational they might be, their intentions are arithmetically incompatible with each other. Their simultaneous attempts at raising their relative prices will *necessarily* (in the eyes of the observing economist) end up nullifying each other's effect. Toward the end of the period they will learn, to their surprise, that the level of general price has gone up above its expected level, as the very aggregate outcome of their simultaneous bidding up of their own prices relative to their expectations of the level of general price. Note that the

---

7. Let us recall the form of the optimal price equation given in footnote 18 of chapter 1:

$$p_t^*(i) = \left[\frac{\hat{E}(P_t^{\eta(i)} X_t^{\xi(i)} \alpha_t(i) : \delta_t(i))}{g^*(i) q_t(i)} \right]^{1/\eta(i)}, \qquad i = 1, 2, \ldots, I.$$

Notice that the exponent of the expectation of the general price level is (roughly) equal to unity. This is, of course, due to the homogeneous-of-degree-zero property of product demand schedule with respect to the system of relative prices. It follows that when the expectation of total product demand is revised upward (downward) the firm increases (decreases) the price proportionally higher (lower) than the expectation of the general price level.

story is essentially the same even if the firms already expected a higher-than-usual increase in the general price level at the time of their price decisions. In that case, the realized level of general price will rise unexpectedly higher than the already expected increase of it.

We have thus succeeded in elucidating the causal mechanism hidden behind the seemingly static fundamental equation of the product market (3–16). This time, we have presented it as a metamorphosis of the internal contradiction involved in firms' simultaneous but separate attempts at raising their relative prices into an unexpected rise in the level of general price.

This is, however, not the end of the story. To repeat, surprises on the part of firms are the fuel of the economy. Firms that have discerned an unexpected increase of the general price level will sooner or later revise their expectations upward. But such revisions of expectations will be of little help. For as long as the product market gap is positive and hence a majority of firms are experiencing supernormal ratios of demand to supply, they will again simultaneously raise their own prices relative to their revised expectations of the general price level.[8] And, of course, their simultaneous bidding up of prices will inevitably betray their intentions of realigning the relative prices, and only the level of general price will increase "unexpectedly." Firms will then find the structure of relative prices as intolerable as before, with the discrepancy between the realized and the expected general price level as wide as before. (The demand for their products will still remain supernormally high.) Further upward revisions of the expected general price level and an equally large increase in the general price level itself will follow the lead.

A cumulative price inflation will thus be triggered off in the product market. The realized and the expected general price level will chase each other at a speed higher than the equilibrium rate. This cumulative price inflation is expected to continue indefinitely as long as a positive product market gap continues to exist in the economy.

Our discussion can be expounded more mechanically by use of our first fundamental equation (3–16), which may, in view of the defination of $a_t(i)$ given by (1–9), be rewritten as

$$\sum_{i=1}^{I} \left[\frac{P_t(i)q_t(i)g^*(i)}{P_t Q_t G^*} \right] \left\{ \frac{P_t^{\eta(i)} X_t^{\xi(i)} \alpha_t(i)}{\hat{E}[P_t^{\eta(i)} X_t^{\xi(i)} \alpha_t(i) : \delta_t(i)]} - 1 \right\}$$
$$= \left(\frac{X_t}{Q_t} - G^* \right) \Big/ G^*.$$

This equation maintains that as long as a positive product market gap exists,

---

8. According to the optimal price equation re-recorded in the preceding footnote, an upward revision of the expectation of the general price level induces, other things being equal, a proportional increase of the individual price.

the average surprise in regard to the expectations of the present state of product supply is necessarily positive. If disappointed firms try to revise their expectations of either the total demand or the general price level or both in the upward direction, it will only lead to a corresponding increase in the actual level of general price and keep the size of the average surprise equal to the size of product market gap, as before.

We have thus established:

> Proposition 3–4. *As long as there exists a positive product market gap in the economy, a cumulative price inflation process, in which the actual and the expected level of general price are chasing each other at a speed higher than the equilibrium rate, will continue indefinitely.*

14. *Wicksellian Disequilibrium and Cumulative Wage Inflation*

Wicksellian disequilibrium will not only disrupt the serenity of the product market but also invade the labor market almost simultaneously. Let us now turn to an analysis of the spillover effects of a sudden upsurge in total demand upon the labor market.

At least at the initial stage of this Wicksellian disequilibrium, a disturbance in the product market will be transmitted into the labor market through a change in expectations about the future state of product demand. For if production takes time, firms' money wage and labor employment decisions have no choice but to be guided by expectations about the state of product demand in the future period in which they will sell their output whose inputs are about to be implemented.

In fact, when firms begin to interpret continual supernormal increases in demand as being caused by a lasting upsurge of total demand, they will update not only their expectations of the total product demand in the present period but also those in future periods. Now, when demands for their products are expected to remain high in the future, firms attempt to increase their outputs by hiring more workers so as not to forgo the better prospective yields in the future. They therefore augment their effective demands for labor, and at the same time start bidding up their money wages. [Recall the effective labor demand equation (1–16) and the optimal money wage equation (1–23). Both are increasing functions of the expectation of the state of product demand in the future.] Total labor demand H_t will increase, and as a result, a positive labor market gap

$$\left(\frac{H_t}{L_t} - F^*\right)\bigg/ F^* > 0$$

will emerge in the economy.

Given the level of total labor supply L_t, workers allocate themselves among firms on the basis of the system of relative wages. [Recall the labor supply schedules (3–2).] It follows that if a firm wishes to suppress a supernormal ratio of labor demand to supply, it must attempt to raise its money wage relative to rivals' money wages. Since the firm cannot know the money wages of the rivals in advance, it has no choice but to raise its wage relative to its expectation of the general money wage level, an aggregation of the money wages of its competitors. Now, if there exists a positive labor market gap in the economy, then, as an arithmetic fact, *most* firms must be experiencing supernormal ratios of labor demand to supply. They will therefore simultaneously bid up their money wages relative to their expectations of the general money wage level. Of course, their intentions of raising their relative wages simultaneously are mutually incompatible. Simultaneous bidding up of money wages by a majority of firms will necessarily cancel, and at the end of the period only the level of general money wage will go up above its expected level, leaving relative wages basically intact. Eventually, most firms will notice their underestimation of the level of general money wage and start revising their expectations upward. But, of course, these revised expectations will inevitably be upset by an unexpected rise in the actual general money wage level, the very aggregate outcome of their own money wage decisions based upon their revised expectations. A cumulative wage inflation will thus be triggered in the labor market. The expected and the realized level of general money wage will chase each other at a speed higher than the equilibrium rate. This cumulative wage inflation process will continue indefinitely as long as a positive labor market gap continued to exist in the economy.

Again, our discussion may be more formally expounded by the fundamental equation of the Wicksellian labor market (3–17), which can, in view of (1–21), be rewritten as

$$\sum_{i=1}^{I} \left[\frac{f^*(i)l_t(i)}{F^*L_t} \right] \left\{ \frac{W_t^{\varepsilon(i)} L_t^{-\lambda(i)} \beta_t(i)^{-1}}{\hat{E}[W_t^{\varepsilon(i)} L_t^{-\lambda(i)} \beta_t(i)^{-1} : \delta_t(i)]} - 1 \right\}$$
$$= \left(\frac{H_t}{L_t} - F^* \right) \bigg/ F^*.$$

In sum, we have:

Proposition 3–5. *As long as a positive labor market gap exists in the Wicksellian economy, a cumulative wage inflation process, in which the expected and the realized level of general money wage are rising at a higher rate than the equilibrium rate, will continue indefinitely.*

15. *The Movement of the Real Wage Rate during the Cumulative Inflation Process*

We have seen above that the initial increase in total product demand will stimulate total labor demand, through firms' optimistic revisions of their expectations of the future state of product demand, and will trigger a cumulative wage inflation process in the labor market. We supposed in the discussion above that before the impact of the initial increase in total product demand spilled over into it, the labor market had been in Expectational equilibrium, in which the aggregate rate of involuntary unemployment had fluctuated around the normal rate u^*. This normal rate of involuntary unemployment is of course a positive constant, so that, unless its value is very small, there still exists a slack in the labor market which employers can squeeze. It then follows that the increase in total labor demand by firms, induced by the initial increase in total product demand, is likely to reduce the aggregate rate of involuntary unemployment and, which amounts to the same thing, enlarge the level of total labor employment. This will, of course, push up the volume of total product supply τ periods later, through the short-run production functions, and will narrow the existing positive gap in the product market. The pace of cumulative price inflation will thus be somewhat moderated by this repercussion. But even if we put aside the possibility that the economy will soon hit the hard wall of full employment and become physically incapable of expanding the total product supply beyond that, we can still argue that the existing product market gap will not completely be eliminated by this induced increase in total product supply. Let's look at the reason for this.

Suppose, for the sake of argument, that the balance between total demand and supply has been completely restored in the product market. Then, cumulative price inflation will be braked, although inertia may keep it going for some time. As a result, cumulatively rising money wages, generated by the existing positive gap in the labor market, will start overtaking the general level of prices, and the aggregate real wage rate will begin to increase. Now, the slowing down of the general rise in prices will break the bullish sentiment of the firms as to the prospective sales revenue in the future product market, whereas the cumulative rise in money wages will multiply their burden of wage costs. Evidently, both effects will work together to discourage firms' effective demands for labor. (In fact, an expected decline in the general price level and an actual rise in the money wage rate have the same negative impact on the effective labor demand.[9]) Therefore, such an increase in the aggregate real wage rate will decrease the level

---

9. Let us recall the form of the effective labor demand recorded in footnote 19 of chapter 1:

$$h_t(i) = \left\{ \left[\frac{\gamma(i)(\eta(i) - 1)\phi(i)\chi(i)}{\eta(i)} \right]^{\eta(i)} j_t(i)^{\eta(i)-1} \right.$$
$$\left. \left[\frac{E(P_{t+\tau}^{\eta(i)} X_{t+\tau}^{\xi(i)} \alpha_{t+\tau}(i) : \delta_t(i))}{g^*(i) w_t(i)^{\eta(i)}} \right] \right\}^{1/[\eta(i) - \gamma(i)(\eta(i)-1)]}$$

Note that the exponent of $P_{t+\tau}$ is approximately $\eta(i)/[\eta(i) - \gamma(i)(\eta(i) - 1)]$ and that of $w_t(i)$ is $-\eta(i)/[\eta(i) - \gamma(i)(\eta(i) - 1)]$.

of total labor demand and narrow the existing positive labor market gap. In consequence, the ongoing cumulative wage inflation will be slowed. At the same time, this decline of total labor demand will check the level of labor employment, which will in turn retard the advance of total supply in the product market. A positive product market gap will then reemerge in the economy and a cumulative inflation process will be rekindled.

It follows that during a cumulative inflation process, both the product market and the labor market tend to keep a positive gap in such a way that the resulting cumulative price and wage inflation maintain a more-or-less stable path regarding the aggregate ratio of price to wage. For, as we have seen, any imbalance between the product and the labor market gap would cause a change in the aggregate real wage rate, and induce a change in the level of total labor demand that would work to correct the imbalance. This is indeed a crucial observation for our analysis of the stability of the Wicksellian economy to be discussed in section 20. For it means that, contrary to the prevalent belief among orthodox economists, an adjustment of the aggregate real wage will itself contribute little to the elimination of the existing disequilibrium in the Wicksellian economy; its function is simply to redistribute the existing disequilibrium between product and labor market.

If, on the other hand, the normal rate of involuntary unemployment is nearly zero and hence little room is left for the expansion of total labor employment beyond its normal level, there will be little fluctuation of real wage rates during the course of a cumulative inflation process.

16. Is Cumulative Inflation a Monetary or a Real Phenomenon?

We have thus fulfilled the promise made at the outset of chapter 1—to develop a theory of inflation and other disequilibrium phenomena from the Wicksellian perspective, that is, from the perspective of the process of price formation.

Our theory of cumulative price-cum-wage inflation is essentially a demand-pull theory of inflation. For it has sought the main cause of inflation in the increase of the volume of total product demand relative to that of total product supply. The wage-push theory of inflation—the rival of the demand-push theory—will be presented in chapter 8, where we develop a simple model of wage determination under trade unionism.

There is hardly any doubt that cumulative inflation is a *monetary* phenomenon. It *is* a disequilibrium process in which the level of general price and the level of general wage, both nominal aggregate variables, are rising cumulatively. One should not, however, jump to the conclusion that cumulative inflation is exclusively a monetary phenomenon and has little to do with the real structure of the economy. On the contrary, it is a *real* phenomenon as well. In fact, the very mechanism of cumulative inflation lies in the inevitable failure of the price mechansim when the conditions for Wicksellian equilibrium are being disturbed. The metamorphosis of firms' frustrated attempts at adjusting *relative* prices and *relative* wages into the realized changes in *nominal* prices and *money* wages is the essence of the cumulative inflation process. The orthodox habit of separating monetary from real forces of the economy could completely blind one with respect to the fundamental nature of inflation.

Note in passing that in a cumulative price-cum-wage inflation process, both the general price level and the general money wage level will grow at rates higher than the rates that had been followed in the previous equilibrium state. But this by no means implies that they will grow at accelerating speeds. The general price level and the general money wage level will grow at accelerating, or decelerating, or steady rates, depending upon the equilibrating forces in firms' expectation-formation processes as well as upon various other adjustment forces working in the entire economy. The term "cumulative" should not be interpreted as "accelerating," as has often been done.

17. *Unfilled Orders and Unfilled Vacancies as Macroscopic Phenomena*

In our discussion of the behavior of an individual firm, we showed that the firm selects its price and wage so that the ratio of product demand to supply and the ratio of labor demand to supply might be on average equal to their corresponding subjective-normal ratios. Therefore, if orders for products are persistently unfilled at a rate higher than the normal rate, the firm should regard it as an indication of its underestimation of the briskness of product demand; and if job vacancies are persistently unfilled at a rate higher than the normal rate, the firm should regard it as an indication of its underestimation of the tightness of labor supply. From the standpoint of an individual firm, there appears no necessity to make mistakes in its expectation formation, and consequently there appears no necessity for the rate of unfilled orders and the rate of unfilled vacancies to be higher than their corresponding normal rates. The firm cannot blame anyone but itself.

From the (transcendental) standpoint of the observing economist, however, the verdict is entirely different. During the process of cumulative inflation the existence of a positive product market gap *necessarily* leads a majority of firms to underestimate the state of product demand and the existence of a positive labor market gap *necessarily* leads a majority of firms to underestimate the tightness of labor supply. Their simultaneous errors in expectations are the inevitable consequences of a macroscopic disturbance that has disrupted the conditions for Wicksellian equilibrium. An individual firm is a mere victim of the forces working at the macroscopic level, which are beyond its control.

During the process of cumulative inflation there are therefore widespread unfilled orders at rates higher than normal in the product market and there are widespread unfilled vacancies at rates higher than normal in the labor market. We have thus succeeded in giving an explanation of unfilled orders and unfilled vacancies not only as microscopic phenomena, but as a macroscopic phenomenon as well.

18. *The Determinants of Total Product Demand*

We have analyzed only the initial phase of Wicksellian disequilibrium. Sooner or later, forces hitherto suppressed will emerge and begin to counteract or reinforce the ongoing cumulative price-cum-wage inflation process. In particular, we have so far proceeded in our analysis as if the movement of total product demand were exogenously given. But we now have to take into consideration the response of total product demand to changes in labor employment, product supply, product price, and money wage, which were of course nothing but firms' reactions to the original change in total product demand itself. Consequently, to give a satisfactory account of the *later phases* of Wicksellian disequilibrium, we have to specify the factors that influence the volume of total product demand.

Most of the macroeconomics literature since *The General Theory* has followed the lead of Keynes and devoted itself to the study of forces that determine the level of total product demand. It is not a gross exaggeration to maintain here that there has been a surprisingly wide consensus among macroeconomists with respect to the factors that determine the volume of total product demand, in spite of frequent disagreements over their relative importance. It may well be argued that most of the controversies in macroeconomics are rooted in sharp differences in viewpoint as to the self-adjusting nature of the economy, not as to the specification of the total product demand schedule. Since the primary object of this book is to develop a theory of economic process and appraise the extent of the economy's self-adjusting nature, we do not attempt to erect yet another model of the determination of total product demand. We even refrain from writing down a mathematical structure of its schedule. Instead, we rely on the standard macroeconomic theory in the following exposition of the determination of total product demand.[10] But our disequilibrium dynamics can be linked, without difficulty, to many other possible theories of total demand determination.

Total product demand is made up of three sources: consumption expenditure, investment demand, and government purchase. Consumption expenditure, in turn, is determined primarily by (a) the level of real disposable income (not only of today but also of the past), (b) the distributional share of income between wage and nonwage earners, (c) real net private wealth, (d) the distribution of

---

10. The orthodox interpretation of the Keynesian theory of total demand determination can be found in Hicks (1937), Modigliani (1944, 1963), A. H. Hansen (1953), and most standard textbooks of macroeconomics. The more heterodox interpretations are given, for instance, in Robinson (1962), Kaldor (1961), Weintraub (1959), and Davidson (1972). But insofar as the determination of total product demand is concerned, the latter are hardly distinguishable from the former, at least in their "formal" structures.

wealth between debtors and creditors, and (e) the real rate of interest. (For simplicity, we aggregate the whole term structure of interest into a single rate and call it the rate of interest.) Investment demand is regulated by (a) the marginal efficiency of capital, which reflects the prospective yields of new investment goods; (b) the real rate of interest as the cost of outside finance of investment; and (c) the accumulated retained profit as a source of internal finance of investment. The magnitude of government purchase, on the other hand, can be taken to be exogenously determined.

The real rate of interest, which influences both consumption expenditure and investment demand, is nothing but the excess of the money rate of interest over the expected rate of inflation. Although little can be said about the precise mechanism through which people's expectation of the rate of inflation is formed, the money rate of interest is liable to a further analysis. The money rate of interest is the opportunity cost of holding wealth in the form of money; it can thus be regarded as the price that equilibrates the asset holders' desire to hold money with the available real supply of money. Since an individual's desire for money, when the money rate of interest is given, varies according to income level (which determines the amount of money balance required for transactions), degree of indebtedness, bullish/bearish sentiment, and so on, not only (a) the real quantity of money created by the banking system, but also such factors as (b) total income level, (c) the distribution of private debts among asset holders, and (d) the relative strength of their bullish/bearish sentiments influence the manner in which the money rate of interest is established in the financial market.

The level of total product demand at each point in time is thus the outcome of the interaction between factors that determine the consumption expenditure, the investment demand, and the government purchase in the product market, and factors that determine the money rate of interest in the financial market. Needless to say, the existing large-scale aggregate econometric models have much richer specifications of the forces that determine the volume of total product demand. But for our primary purpose, the simplified specification given above is more than sufficient.

We are therefore in a position to discuss the later phases of the development of Wicksellian disequilibrium.

19. *The Upward Multiplier Process during Cumulative Inflation*

We have seen in our investigation of the initial stage of cumulative inflation process that an original increase in total product demand will promptly induce an increase in total labor demand (and then create a positive gap in the labor market). Such an increase in total labor demand will evidently raise the level of total labor employment and then the level of total income, unless the wall of full employment has already been reached.

Now, one of the crucial determinants of total product demand is, as we have seen, the level of total income, both at present and in the past. An increase in total income tends to push up the volume of total product demand mainly through an increase in consumption expenditure by consumers and partly through an induced expansion of investment demand by firms. (Moreover, as long as the product market has a positive gap, some spenders' spending plans are continuously frustrated by the shortage of product supplies. If they are not discouraged too much, part of their unspent cash balances will be carried forward and added to their product demands in subsequent periods.)

Thus, at the second stage of cumulative inflation process, the initial upsurge of total product demand will induce an additional rise in the volume of total product demand. This will set moving the Kahn–Keynes multiplier process in the upward direction, in which an induced increase in total labor employment and a further induced increase in total product demand will reinforce each other and amplify the initiating increase in total product demand.[11] It is well known, however, that as long as the marginal propensity to spend is less than unity, this upward multiplier process will gradually work itself out (or else be halted by the thick wall of full-employment productive capacity). Thus, the upward multiplier process during the cumulative inflation is not explosive in itself, although it certainly aggravates the ongoing cumulative inflation by widening the gap in the product market.

20. *The Money Wage Problem*

The salient feature of the cumulative inflation process is that cumulative rises in prices and wages will never cease as long as the fundamental macroeconomic imbalance that has given rise to them continues to exist. That is, they would persist indefinitely, as long as either the product market gap or the labor market gap remains open.

During the cumulative inflation process, the real wage rate will fluctuate relative to whether the gap in the product market is wider or narrower than the gap in the labor market. But as we have seen in section 15, it will only work to stabilize itself and have little impact on the basic imbalance in macroeconomic conditions.

To make the situation worse, the cumulative inflation process is in general accompanied by an upward Kahn–Keynes multiplier process. Its effect is, as we have seen above, only to widen the original imbalance in macroeconomic conditions.

Therefore, the question of the stability of the Wicksellian economy— whether or not the Wicksellian economy will automatically return to a position of Wicksellian equilibrium after it has plunged into a cumulative inflation

---

11. For more on the Kahn–Keynes multiplier process, see Keynes (1936), chapter 10, or any textbook on macroeconomics.

process—can no longer be answered by appealing to the "price mechanism." Indeed, it is the price mechanism itself that causes a cumulative process to develop in Wicksellian disequilibrium. Instead, the answer to this question hinges critically on the answer to a monetary question: whether or not cumulatively rising prices and money wages are by themselves capable of pulling down the initial upsurge of total product demand and thus closing the product and the labor market gap simultaneously. This is in its essential form nothing but the "money wage problem" of J. M. Keynes, although Keynes's chief concern in *The General Theory* was whether or not "hypothetical laissez-faire falls" of prices and money wages would work as an equilibrator of the monetary economy in depressions (1936, chap. 19).

The money wage problem is notoriously complex. In the first place, rising prices will reduce the real purchasing power of the stock of outside money and other public debts. We have learned from Keynes and post-Keynesians that, as long as the economy is out of the liquidity trap and as long as firms' investment decisions are sensitive to changes in interest rates, the depreciation of the real values of monetary assets will raise short-term rates of interest through liquidity preferences, augment long-term rates of interest through the chain reaction of the term structure of interest rates, and finally discourage firms' demands for investment goods (Keynes 1936, chap. 19). We have also learned from Pigou, Scitovsky, Harberler, and Patinkin that the depreciation of the real value of money stock and other nominal public debts held by households may directly depress their demands for current consumption goods (see, e.g., Pigou 1943 and Patinkin 1965). These Keynes and Pigou effects are both stabilizers of the system.

But, of course, if the economy is a "pure inside money economy" as was envisaged by Wicksell, or if the supply of money stock responds with positive conformity to the needs of trade through the mechanism of credit creation by the banking sector, these stabilizers would be nullified, and no hope for the *automatic* tendency for stability would remain in our Wicksellian economy.

The effects of rising prices on the private debt/credit structure in financial markets are no less important. Rising prices, as long as they were not anticipated in advance, have the effect of transferring the real purchasing power from holders of private financial assets to their issuers, by relieving the real indebtedness of the latter, at least in the short run. Since debtors are likely to have a higher propensity to spend out of their wealth than creditors are, this mere redistributional effect of private wealth has a destabilizing tendency and may weaken or even overwhelm the Pigou effect of public wealth. Moreover, the relief of the indebtedness of private debtors effected by rising prices may encourage them to deepen their indebtedness further by issuing more debt or by replacing their short-term debts in maturity by long-term debts. This may, by injecting new liquidity into financial markets, weaken or even overwhelm the

Keynes effect. This debt-inflation process clearly destabilizes the system. (See Irving Fisher 1933).[12]

If, furthermore, the spenders in the economy, being faced with cumulatively rising prices and money wages, have come to expect their continuous rises in the future, the cumulative inflation process will probably worsen. First, expected rises in money wages will stimulate workers' expenditures on current consumption goods by raising their hopes for higher earning streams in the future. Second, expected rises in prices will encourage households and firms to spend more on currently available consumption and investment goods rather than postponing their purchases at the inflated prices expected to prevail in the future. (Expected rising prices will directly reduce the real rate of interest.) These expectation effects will further increase the total demand, and pour additional fuel on the existing cumulative inflation process. They are again destabilizers in our Wicksellian economy. If, moreover, prices and wages are growing at accelerating speeds, spenders may begin to expect aggravating inflation in the future and raise their current demands higher and higher. Therefore, there will always be a danger that a moderate inflation will turn into a galloping inflation, and may lead to an eventual collapse of the public's trust in the stability of the value of money, which is the very foundation of the monetary nature of the existing economic system.[13]

In sum, whether a cumulative inflation process, once started by a sudden upsurge of total demand, will bring itself to a halt depends chiefly upon the *relative balance* between the force of stabilizers and the force of destabilizers in its entire course. In the case of Wicksell's pure credit economy, there is *no* stabilizing force to rely upon. The position of Wicksellian equilibrium is always and necessarily unstable. Even if the economy has outside money—money issued by an agency exogenous to it—there is no a priori reason to believe that the stabilizing forces are decisively stronger. The position of Wicksellian equilibrium may be stable or unstable, depending upon the particular circumstances as well as upon the behavior of the banking sector as to credit creation. Moreover, even if it is stable, the process of automatic equilibriation comes only after,

---

12. Irving Fisher maintained that the debt-deflation process, the reverse of the debt-inflation process defined above, was the chief cause of the Great Depression. His idea was recently taken up by Minsky (1975).

13. On the basis of Keynes's rather obscure discussion of the essential nature of money in *The General Theory* (1936, chap. 17), Lerner (1952) and, more recently, Davidson (1972, chap. 9) and Davidson (1980) convincingly argued that for money to function as a store of value and serve as the basis of a market economy, the public must have sufficient trust in the stability of its purchasing power and that such stability of the purchasing power of money depends essentially upon the inflexibility of wages and prices. We consider this problem more fully in chapter 5, in which the inflexibility of money wages is introduced into our theoretical framework.

and as a result of, a cumulative rise in prices and wages. It must be a long and painful process.[14]

We have thus confirmed Wicksell's thesis that "the movement and equilibrium of actual money prices represent a fundamentally different phenomenon, above all in a fully developed credit system, from those of *relative* prices" (1936, p. 100; see chapter 1). In a barter economy with Say's laws of markets, only the systems of relative prices and relative wages matter to the actions of market participants. In fact, it was shown in section 12 that in such an economy, as long as gross substitution is predominant, the movements of relative prices and relative wages are always assisted by the Invisible Hand, so that "every movement away from the position of equilibrium sets forces into operation which tend to restore the system to its original position" (Wicksell 1936, p. 101). By contrast, in a monetary economy, the effects of gross substitution lose their stabilizing power. Whenever a gap appears in either of the markets, the self-adjusting nature of the systems of relative prices and relative wages is paralyzed, and their frustration is channeled into cumulative changes in nominal prices and money wages. Such cumulative inflation or deflation will, as we have seen, generate in the course of its own development not only stabilizing forces but also strong destabilizing forces. In the absence of Say's laws, there is therefore no Invisible Hand to count upon.

21. *Fixed versus Discretionary Economic Policy*

In the dynamic Walrasian general equilibrium theory in *Value and Capital,* John Hicks (1946) defined equilibrium over time as a state of the economy in which (a) all individuals are reaching their most preferred positions, subject to the constraints by which they are bound, and (b) the expectations on which their decisions are based, in each single period, are consistent with one another and with what actually happened.[15] In many of his writings on the normal rate theory of unemployment, Milton Friedman has regarded the absence of discrepancy between the actual and the anticipated values as the defining characteristic of long-period equilibrium (see, e.g., Friedman 1968, 1970, 1975). There is no doubt that their equilibrium notions are similar to our notion of Expectational equilibrium. Hicks stated that "the degree of disequilibrium marks the extent to which expectations are cheated, and plans go astray," and maintained that "whenever prices are fairly steady, the system is likely to be

14. See Tobin (1975) for the analysis of the stability of monetary economy on the basis of a modified Keynesian model. His conclusion accords well with ours, which has been advanced in a less formal manner in the present section.

15. See also Hicks (1965). To be fair to Hicks, however, it must be noted here that he later repudiated the approach he took in *Value and Capital.* He said in 1975: "Clearly I need to change my name. Let it be understood that *Value and Capital* was the work of J. R. Hicks, a 'neo-classical' economist, now deceased."

quite adequately in equilibrium, and it is chiefly in times of rapid price-movement that acute disequilibrium is likely to occur" (1946, p. 132). In the same manner, Friedman maintained that "the temporary trade-off [between inflation and unemployment] comes not from inflation *per se*, but from unanticipated inflation, which generally means, from a rising rate of inflation" (1970, p. 15). Clearly, both Hicks (in *Value and Capital*) and Friedman regard the slow adaptation of people's expectation formations to rapid changes in prices to be the chief *cause* of disequilibrium. In other words, they both seem to believe that the only possible form of disequilibrium is what we have called secondary disequilibrium, which is caused by incidental and by no means inevitable mistakes in people's expectation-formation processes.

Indeed, in the mathematical version of the normal rate theory of unemployment formulated by R. E. Lucas (1972a, b, 1975), T. Sargent (1973, 1975, 1976), and others, Say's laws are quite explicitly postulated.[16] In fact, these authors simply *assumed* that total product demand equals total product supply and that total labor supply equals total labor demand (thus eliminating the possibility of involuntary unemployment) and then *solved* their models under the hypothesis of rational expectations to generate stochastic equilibrium paths of price, wage, output, employment, and so on. They thus assumed away not only the possibility of Wicksellian disequilibrium but also the possibility of secondary disequilibrium. There is no room for any disequilibrium therein.

Now, if one held the view, either consciously or unconsciously, that secondary disequilibrium is the only possible form of disequilibrium, it would be quite natural to advocate the following policy prescription: "that the monetary and fiscal authority should *not* lean against the wind but stick to a pre-announced policy target as steadily as possible." The rationale for such a fixed policy prescription is obvious. In the first place, since the sole cause of (secondary) disequilibrium lies in the slow adaptation of people's expectation formation to a changing market environment, the more predictable government policy is, the less probable it is that the economy will be thrown out of expectational equilibrium. And—this is an important point—the case for such a fixed policy would be strengthened rather than diminished the less "rational" we human beings are and the longer it takes us to correct our mistakes. Second, since the Invisible Hand of price mechanism works quite effectively (and in fact assists people's error-learning processes quite efficiently) in the economy with Say's laws, the interference of Visible Hands of the government and the central bank may well undermine the inherent stability of the economy. This rea-

---

16. The explicit postulate of Say's law, however, is not special in these mathematical versions of the normal rate theory of unemployment. In fact, in the pure-exchange model of Walrasian general equilibrium, "Walras's law" is equivalent to our Say's law of the product market. In the production model of Walrasian general equilibrium model, on the other hand, Walras's law can be regarded as equivalent to the simultaneous fulfillment of Say's laws of product and labor markets.

soning seem to be the underlying rationale for Milton Friedman's famous policy prescription (1968) that the monetary authority should adopt the policy of achieving a preannounced steady rate of growth in a specified monetary aggregate (which may be M1, or M2, or M13).

In a monetary economy, however, the fundamental cause of disequilibrium lies in the disturbance of Wicksellian equilibrium conditions. In Wicksellian disequilibrium, firms' expectation errors are a necessary consequence of the breakdown of Wicksellian equilibrium conditions, and the resulting cumulative changes in prices and wages are merely symptoms of the underlying disequilibrium. We have seen that these symptoms will generate within the system both stabilizing forces and destabilizing forces, and the stability of Wicksellian equilibrium hinges upon the relative strengths of these competing forces. A priori there is no presumption for the existence of any strong tendency for stability, and the position of Wicksellian equilibrium may indeed be quite unstable. Now, in a dynamic and thus uncertain economy, market gaps are in constant danger of being opened up by sudden changes in the economic and noneconomic environment. In particular, one of the components of total product demand—the demands for investment goods which are governed by firms' fragile long-term expectations (i.e., marginal efficiency of capital)—may collapse or be overheated at any moment of time. Thus, in the Wicksellian economy, it is very likely that discretionary government policy is called for, that the government should whenever possible "lean against the wind" and attempt to maintain the equilibrium relation between total product demand and supply and between total labor demand and supply, by effectively employing both fiscal and monetary policies to counteract major shocks that endanger them.

22. *Other Causes of Cumulative Process*

Until now we have explored only the process of cumulative inflation brought about by a sudden increase in total demand in the product market. Obviously, a similar analysis can be applied, with appropriate changes in "sign," to the process of cumulative deflation brought by a sudden drop of total demand in the product market.

It should be noted that throughout this cumulative deflation process, a majority of firms are bound to overestimate both the briskness of product demand and the tightness of labor supply. So in the product market, most firms have to leave an abnormally large part of their product rotting in their warehouse, and in the labor market an abnormally large fraction of workers are unable to find jobs in spite of their willingness to work at the wages offered. We have thus succeeded in explaining such phenomena as product oversupply and involuntary unemployment not only as microscopic, as in section 14 of chapter 1, but also as macroscopic phenomena whose occurrence is inevitable during the process of cumulative deflation.

However, the assumption of downward flexibility of money wages, upon which our discussion of cumulative deflation process is based, is far more objectionable than the assumption of upward flexibility of money wages. In reality, the full deployment of cumulative wage deflation would certainly be resisted by the downward inflexibility of money wages. A fuller analysis of the impact of a sudden decline of total demand is therefore better postponed until part II, in which the downward inflexibility of money wages will be duly taken into consideration.

Another plausible cause of a cumulative inflation (deflation) process is found in a sudden decline (increase) in the level of the total labor supply. This will first create a positive (negative) labor market gap and then be transmitted into the product market in the form of the induced creation of a positive (negative) product market gap. Its fuller analysis will, however, be left to the interested reader.

23. *The Case of Stagflation*

A different story will emerge if we consider the economy's response to sudden and widespread declines in firms' productivity, $j_t(i)$. Such a change might be brought about by a sudden and widespread destruction of machines and equipments due to a natural disaster; or by a sudden and widespread shortage of raw materials and fuels due to bad harvests, an oil embargo, abnormal speculation on international commodities, new trade barriers, devaluation, and so on.[17]

---

17. If the firm uses raw material and fuels in production, then rises in their market prices caused by a shortage have qualitatively the same impact on the behavior of the firms as a decline of labor productivity index. More specifically, if the short-run production function is represented as $q_{t+\tau} = j_t n_t^\gamma m_t^\theta$, where m_t is the amount of raw materials and θ is a positive constant, it is easy to show that the demand for them is given by

$$m_t = \left\{ \gamma^{\gamma(\eta-1)} \theta^{[\eta-\gamma(\eta-1)]} \left[\frac{(\eta-1)\phi\chi}{\eta} \right]^\eta j_t^{(\eta-1)} \right.$$
$$\left. \times \left[\frac{\hat{E}(a_{t+\tau} : \delta_t)}{g^*} \right] w_t^{-[\eta-\theta(\eta-1)]} v_t^{-\theta(\eta-1)} \right\}^{1/[\eta-(\gamma+\theta)(\eta-1)]},$$

and the effective labor demand is given by

$$h_t = \left\{ \gamma^{[\eta-\theta(\eta-1)]} \theta^{\theta(\eta-1)} \left[\frac{(\eta-1)\phi\chi}{\eta} \right]^\eta j_t^{(\eta-1)} \right.$$
$$\left. \times \left[\frac{\hat{E}(a_{t+\tau} : \delta_t)}{g^*} \right] w_t^{-\gamma(\eta-1)} v_t^{-[\eta-\gamma(\eta-1)]} \right\}^{1/[\eta-(\gamma+\theta)(\eta-1)]},$$

where v_t is a given market price of raw materials in period t. Thus, an increase in v_t lowers both the effective labor demand and the demand for raw materials; a decrease in the demand for raw materials will certainly reduce $q_{t+\tau}$ for a given level of labor employment.

Whatever the cause, the impact of such sudden drops in productivity across firms will show up in the labor market because those firms whose productivity has declined will immediately curtail their effective demands for labor. [Recall formula (1–16) of the effective labor demand, rewritten in footnote 9.] The total labor demand will then decrease, and a negative labor market gap,

$$\left(\frac{H_t}{L_t} - F^*\right)\Big/F^* < 0$$

will emerge in the economy. Sooner or later, a cumulative wage *deflation* process will start in the labor market.

On the other hand, a widespread decline in productivity across firms will also affect the product market. In fact, it will affect the product market through two routes. In the first place, a decline in productivity will proportionally reduce the output level τ periods later for a given level of total labor employment. Second, an induced decline in effective labor demand will decrease the level of labor employment itself, which will, of course, work to reduce the level of output τ periods later. Thus, a positive product market gap larger in size than the negative labor market gap will be created in that period:

$$\left(\frac{X_{t+\tau}}{Q_{t+\tau}} - G^*\right)\Big/G^* > 0.$$

Sooner or later, a sharp cumulative price *inflation* will be started in the product market.

Therefore, a widespread decline of productivity across firms will provoke simultaneously a cumulative wage deflation in the labor market and a cumulative price inflation in the product market. In other words, a "stagflation" situation will emerge in our Wicksellian economy. This explanation of stagflation seems to have captured certain essential features of recent experiences in the advanced capitalist economies, although we have no intention to claim that it is the only explanation for them. (A wage-push theory of stagflation is presented in chapter 8.)

In the Wicksellian economy, in which both prices and money wages are assumed to be flexible at the beginning of every period, such a stagflation situation will give rise to a rapid decline of aggregate real wage. (If, as in the Keynesian economy, money wages are not flexible downward, the decline in the aggregate real wage will be much slower and the involuntary unemployment would spread over the entire economy much more quickly. Notice, however, that even in the Keynesian economy, the aggregate real wage rate has to decline.) Firms will respond to this situation first by slowing down the curtailment of their effective labor demand, and at some point may even start expanding their labor demand. (Workers may cut short part of their labor supply, but in what follows we ignore this possibility.) Eventually, the total labor demand will reach the original level (or the trend path that had been followed before the decline in productivity). Then the negative labor market gap will be closed, and the cumulative wage deflation process will soon lose its momentum. However, the positive product market gap will remain open. For, as was already pointed out, the positive product market gap in this stagflation situation was created not only by the decline of labor employment effected by the initial decline of effective labor demand, but also by the decline of productivity itself. The cumulative price inflation process will thus continue, albeit at a somewhat slower pace. In consequence, even after this point the aggregate real wage rate will keep declining and hence the total labor demand will keep expanding. Soon, a positive labor market gap will emerge, the cumulative wage deflation will stop, and eventually a cumulative wage inflation will be triggered off. Thus, the economy will reach a situation in which a positive product market gap and a positive labor market gap coexist and give rise to cumulative inflation in both markets. This situation is, of course, identical with the familiar situation in which an initial upsurge in the total demand creates a positive product market gap and a positive labor market gap simultaneously and thus triggers off a cumulative price-cum-wage inflation process.

Our account of stagflation has supposed implicitly that the volume of total product demand remains unchanged in spite of changes in total labor employment, total product supply, the rate of price inflation, the rate of wage inflation, and other factors. As soon as reactions of total product demand to these changes and further repercussions are taken into consideration, the description of the economy's dynamic behavior in the stagflation situation becomes an extremely difficult task.

24. *Summary*

Let us recapitulate the main thread of the argument.

There are basically two different approaches to the study of inflation. The first approach regards inflation "always and everywhere a monetary phenomenon in the sense that it is and can be produced only by a more rapid increase in the quantity of money than in output" (Friedman 1970) and tries to understand it by examining the equilibrium relation between the demand for and the supply of the stock of money. The age-old quantity theory of money and its recent revival under the banner of "monetarism" fall into this category.

The second approach was initiated by Knut Wicksell. This approach tries to understand the phenomenon of inflation and other disequilibrium phenomena from the perspective of the process of price formation. It is this second approach that we have followed in part I. However, Wicksell's theory of cumulative inflation had no solid microeconomic foundation. As is now widely recognized, the law of supply and demand, upon which Wicksell based his theory, is at best an ad hoc construct which has no theoretical foundation and is squarely at variance with the assumption of perfect competition of neoclassical economics. It is for this reason that we began from scratch and constructed from the ground up a theory of price formation in markets out of equilibrium. It is upon this microeconomic foundation that the macroeconomic dynamics of the present chapter have been approached.

By aggregating all the firms' optimal price equations, it is possible to obtain an equation, called the fundamental equation of the product market, which states that the weighted average of individual firms' surprise with respect to their expectation of the state of product demand is equal to the product market gap (i.e., the proportionate gap between the ratio of total demand to supply and its average normal ratio). Similarly, an aggregation of all firms' optimal money wage equation in the Wicksellian labor market leads to another equation, called the fundamental equation of the labor market, which states that the weighted average of individual firms' surprise with respect to their expectation of the tightness of labor supply is equal to the labor market gap (i.e., the proportionate gap between the ratio of total labor demand to supply and the average normal ratio). From the first fundamental equation it is only a short step to a proposition that all the firms in the economy are simultaneously capable of attaining expectational equilibrium with respect to the state of product demand only if the product market gap is (almost surely) equal to zero. And from the second fundamental equation it is equally easy to establish an analogous proposition that all the firms in the Wicksellian economy are simultaneously capable of attaining expectational equilibrium with respect to the tightness of the labor market only if the labor market gap is (almost surely) equal to zero.

Therefore, to assume from the beginning, as the hypothesis of rational expectations did, that rational firms should always be in expectational equilibrium is tantamount to assuming that neither the product market gap nor the labor market gap can deviate from zero; that is, it is tantamount to assuming both Say's law of the product market (that the product market gap is identically equal to zero) and Say's law of the labor market (that the labor market gap is identically equal to zero). We can thus conclude that the normal rate theory of unemployment, which is built upon the hypothesis of rational expectations, relies on a tacit assumption of these Say's laws. And, needless to say, to assume Say's laws is to assume away all the essential features of the monetary economy.

Surprises of firms are the fuel of the economy. Firms that have been surprised at the discrepancy between their expectations and the realized market outcomes will sooner or later revise their expectations and then adjust their price, wage, employment, and output on the basis of their new view of the market conditions. Such changes will, in turn, create new market conditions, thereby setting off a new round of economic changes. What our two fundamental equations have demonstrated is that in the monetary economy, surprises (or expectation errors) on the part of firms are inevitable results of the existing macroeconomic situations, which are summarized in our model by the product market gap and the labor market gap. The existence of surprises is thus explained endogenously, and on the basis of this we can work out a causal analysis of macroeconomic changes.

A Wicksellian economy is said to be in a state of Wicksellian equilibrium if both the product market gap and the labor market gap are zero. It is said to be in a state of Expectational equilibrium if all the firms are simultaneously in expectational equilibrium. Evidently, the conditions for Expectational equilibrium presuppose fulfillment of the conditions for Wicksellian equilibrium. For we now know that when either the product market gap or the labor market gap is open, a majority of firms are inevitably thrown out of expectational equilibrium.

We can then distinguish two forms of disequilibrium. The first form is called Wicksellian disequilibrium. It is a form of disequilibrium caused by a disturbance of the conditions for Wicksellian equilibrium. The second form is called secondary disequilibrium. It refers to a situation in which although the economy is in Wicksellian equilibrium, some firms' expectations are for some reason displaced from their equilibrium. In the case of secondary disequilibrium, the disequilibrium *is* the errors in expectations, whereas in the case of Wicksellian disequilibrium, the disequilibrium *causes* errors in expectations. Therefore, the analysis of secondary disequilibrium can be reduced to the analysis of how firms revise their expectations over time and how their adjusted expectations interact with each other. It is not hard to show that as long as most products are gross substitutes in the eyes of spenders, and as long as the working conditions of most firms are gross substitutes in the eyes of workers, the price mechanism works to strengthen each firm's error-learning activity and provides the economy in secondary disequilibrium with a built-in stabilizing tendency. Neoclassical equilibrium theory and, more specifically, normal rate theory of unemployment have confined their analysis to this form of disequilibrium.

The fundamental form of disequilibrium is, of course, that of Wicksellian disequilibrium. When there is a positive product market gap in the economy, a Wicksellian cumulative price inflation process or price–price spiral will be triggered in the product market. Its mechanism can be described as follows. When there is a positive product market gap, a majority of firms must be (as an arithmetic fact) experiencing supernormal excess demand for their products. Their simultaneous attempts at eliminating this by means of raising the prices of their products relative to their expectations regarding the general price level are, however, mutually incompatible. Their simultaneous bidding up of prices will necessarily cancel out each other's "relative" effect and will end up by raising the level of general price "unexpectedly." This unexpected (but inevitable in the eyes of the observing economist) rise in the general price level will sooner or later induce firms to revise upward their expectations of the general price level, and will lead them to raise their prices once more relative to their updated expectations of the general price level. But their second-round attempt at raising their relative prices will again cancel each other out and only contribute to a further unexpected rise in the general price level. And so on. The process of cumulative price inflation, thus explained, will continue indefinitely as long as a positive product market gap continues to exist in the economy. In the same manner, when there is a positive labor market gap, a cumulative wage inflation process or wage–wage spiral will be triggered in the Wicksellian labor market and will persist as long as a positive labor market gap continues to exist in the economy.

During a cumulative inflation process, the Kahn–Keynes multiplier process starts in motion in an upward direction. It will, however, only stimulate the ongoing inflation and never work to stabilize it. During a cumulative inflation process, the real wage rate tends to fluctuate according to the relative balance between the widths of the product and labor market gaps. Contrary to the hope of neoclassical economists, this fluctuation of the real wage rate works only to redistribute the original macro disequilibrium into product and labor markets; it has no power itself to halt the ongoing cumulative inflation process.

Since the cumulative inflation process continues *as long as* either a positive product market gap or a positive labor market gap continues to exist, we can no longer answer the question of the stability of the Wicksellian economy by appealing to the power of price mechanism. Instead, we have to ask a "monetary" question: whether or not cumulative rises of prices and money wages are capable of reducing the volume of total product demand and the level of total effective labor demand and thereby automatically restore the conditions for Wicksellian equilibrium. This is nothing but the well-known money wage problem of Keynes, with reverse signs. It can be then argued that (a) the Keynes effect (i.e., the negative influence on the volume of investment demand of a depreciation of the real value of money stock through an induced increase in the rate of interest in financial markets) and (b) the Pigou effect (i.e., the direct and negative impact on the consumption demand of a decline of the purchasing power of outside money) are the chief stabilizers of the monetary economy; but their effectiveness could be nullified if there were no outside money or if the monetary authority allowed the supply of bank credit to respond in positive conformity to the demand of trades. On the other hand, the chief destabilizers are (a) the consumption effect of the redistribution of private wealth from debtors to creditors, effected by an unanticipated inflation; (b) the debt–inflation process (i.e., the liquidity effect of this redistribution of private wealth in financial markets); and (c) the price-expectation effect. A priori there is no way to ascertain which effects, either stabilizing or destabilizing, are decisively stronger, and there is no presumption for the existence of the Invisible Hand (i.e., an automatic stabilizing tendency) in the Wicksellian economy.

Our Wicksellian macroeconomic dynamics has also been able to explain a stagflation situation in which a positive product market gap and a negative labor market gap coexist in the economy.

25. *The Paradox of Money*

Money is a paradoxical entity. (Its origin is, like that of language, an enigma in the human history.) It has split up the identity of the sale and purchase of direct barter and surmounted all the restrictions on the possibility of exchanges imposed by it. It is not merely a vehicle of exchange but a vehicle of the vast expansion of the sphere of exchanges itself. But the very act of separating the purchase from the sale and the sale from the purchase contains its own negation. For it destroys Say's laws of markets and deprives the economy of its Invisible Hand. The consequent cumulative inflation or deflation process may lead to a collapse of the very monetary foundation of the monetary economy.

"Our desire to hold money as a store of wealth is," according to Keynes, "a barometer of the degree of our distrust of our own calculations and conventions. . . . The possession of actual money lulls our disquietude, and the premium which we require to make us part with money is the measure of the degree of our disquietude" (1937a, p. 217). Yet it is precisely this desire to hold money as a store of wealth that produces the very disquietude of the monetary economy as a whole.

Is there any mechanism in the monetary economy, aside from the possibility of government intervention, which is capable of counterbalancing the system-wide "irrationality" caused by the breakdown of Say's laws? It is the main task of part II to answer this question.

Keynesian Disequilibrium Dynamics in the Short Run

CHAPTER 4

The Keynesian Principle of Effective Demand

1. Introduction: Keynes versus Wicksell

There is little doubt that Keynes regarded the principle of effective demand as one of his most fundamental contributions to economic science—perhaps the most fundamental of all. This principle may be summed up by saying that the scale of output and employment as a whole is determined chiefly by the equilibrium between demand and supply of output as a whole (i.e., by the volume of effective demand).[1] His *General Theory* is indeed "primarily a study of the forces which determine changes in the scale of output and employment as a whole" (Keynes 1936, p. vii). He accused (neo-)classical economists of having tacitly assumed Say's law and thus artificially removed all the obstacles to full employment in their economic system. Keynes then asserted that "if [Say's law] is not the true law relating the aggregate demand and supply functions, there is a vitally important chapter of economic theory which remains to be written and without which all discussions concerning the volume of aggregate employment are futile" (1936, p. 26).

Wicksell's theory of cumulative process, developed about forty years prior to *The General Theory*, already contained a germ of a "theory of the demand and supply of output *as a whole*." For, as noted at the outset of part I, its starting point was the simple idea that if general prices rise, it must be due to an excess demand of *all commodities* relative to their supply. As Keynes was to do later, Wicksell then accused the advocates of the Quantity Theory of Money and of the orthodox neoclassical equilibrium theory of having "not sufficiently considered" the implications of the possible divergence between the demand and supply of all commodities, that is, of the possible breakdown of Say's law, stating that they "usually made the mistake of postulating their [conclusions] instead of clearly proving them" (Wicksell 1935, p. 160).

The Keynesian principle of effective demand and the Wicksellian approach to economic dynamics part company at this point, however.

---

1. See *The General Theory* (1936, chap. 3) or Keynes's own summary (1937a).

Wicksell's theory of output as a whole was inherited and expanded by the Stockholm school economists (as well as by Keynes himself in *Treatise on Money*). The Stockholm school placed the fundamental importance on the divergence between "looking forward" (or ex ante) and "looking backward" (or ex post) and sought the cause for this divergence in the imbalance between total product demand and total product supply or, which becomes equivalent under appropriate definition of saving, between ex ante investment and ex ante saving. This approach is, in other words, primarily a disequilibrium-theoretic one. Bertil Ohlin, one of the representatives of the Stockholm school, summarizes the method of the Wicksellian approach as follows:

> There is no reason why the planned investment plus the planned consumption should be equal to the expected total income for society as a whole. In other words, the planned investment will differ from the planned saving, unless they should happen to be equal by mere chance. Owing to this difference, expectations will not be fulfilled. At the end of the period people will find that their incomes, investment and savings during that period have not been what they expected them to be. Consequently, the expectations, plans and actions with reference to the next period will differ from what they were in the last period. The economic situation will change in a way which can only be explained through a study of how these differences between expectations and the actual course of events during one period influence expectations and actions in the future. [1937a, p. 237]

Ohlin then attacked the methodology of Keynes and denied even the validity of equilibrium analysis. He said, for example:

> Thus, I cannot find that the economic system tends towards a stable equilibrium described by simple reference to the change in the volume of investments. It is highly improbable that the system ever gets to a state where expectations are fulfilled. . . . Nor is there a tendency to move in the direction of some such position. And if the system should happen to get into such a position, this does not mean that it tends to remain there. [1937a, p. 238]

The Keynesian principle of effective demand, on the other hand, is much more orthodox in its methodology than is the Wicksellian approach. It is as equally equilibrium-theoretic as the (neo-)classical economics that Keynes was trying to undermine. Indeed, in a lecture he gave a year after the publication of *The General Theory*, he remarked:

> I'm more classical than the Swedes, for I am still discussing the conditions of short-period equilibrium. Let us suppose identity of *ex post* and *ex ante*, my theory remains. *Ex ante* decisions may be decided by trial and error or by judicious foresight, or (as in fact) by both. [1937b, p. 182]

In the same lecture he even asserted:

> I now feel that if I were writing the book again I should begin by setting forth my theory on the assumption that short-period expectations were always fulfilled; and then have a subsequent chapter showing what difference it makes when short-period expectations are disappointed.
>
> For other economists, I find, lay the whole emphasis, and find the whole explanation in the *differences* between effective demand and income; and they are so convinced that this is the right course that they do not notice that in my treatment this is *not* so. The method of handling has taken several different forms though the underlying thought seems to me much the same in all of them. [p. 181][2]

There is thus a wide gap in methodology between the equilibrium-theoretic Keynesian principle and the disequilibrium-theoretic Wicksellian approach, and both claim to be *the* most fundamental breakthrough in the construction of the theory of output, employment, and prices for the society as a whole.

The analysis given in chapter 3 demonstrated that in a flexible-wage Wicksellian economy, the Keynesian principle of effective demand is not capable of standing on its own feet. The fundamental equation of the product market asserted that as long as there is an imbalance between total product demand and supply in the sense that the product market has a "gap," a majority of firms' expectations about the state of product demand are necessarily upset and these inevitable disappointments and the consequent revisions of expectations bring about a cumulative price inflation or deflation in the product market. Similarly, the fundamental equation of the labor market asserted that, as long as there is an imbalance between total labor demand and supply in the sense that the labor market has a "gap," a majority of firms' expectations about the state of labor supply are necessarily upset, and the similar "endogenous" dynamic force brings about a cumulative wage inflation or deflation in the labor market. It is thus these imbalances or gaps that constitute the chief motive force of the Wicksellian economy. Indeed, it was proved in chapter 3 that "the assumption that short-period expectations are always fulfilled" is in the Wicksellian economy tantamount to assuming Say's laws of the product and labor markets, thereby inviting back the beautiful neoclassical equilibrium theory that Keynes sought to dispel. In the Wicksellian economy, the level of total product demand is relevant only in so far as it determines, together with the given level of total product supply, the value of product market gap (and indirectly influences the value of labor market gap) and thus causes an inevitable divergence between ex ante and ex post. We may thus conclude that, within the confines of the flexible-wage Wicksellian economy, the Wicksellian

---

2. Kregel (1976) contains insightful discussions on this equilibrium-theoretic nature of Keynes's short-run analysis.

approach, which lays the whole emphasis on the *gaps* and the resulting disappointments of expectations in the analysis of the evolution of the economic
process, possesses an overwhelming theoretical supremacy over the Keynesian
principle of effective demand.

Can we salvage the Keynesian principle of effective demand from wreckage?
The answer is affirmative. In Part II, I attempt to "rescue" Keynesian economics.
The starting point of such an endeavor is, not surprisingly, the removal of the
Wicksellian assumption of part I that money wages are perfectly flexible at the
beginning of every period. Instead, we shall now introduce the Keynesian
assumption that money wages are not completely flexible, even at the beginning
of a period.

Indeed, in order to present the Keynesian principle of effective demand
in its purest form and to bring out in full relief the fundamental difference
between the workings of the economy with and without the inflexibility of
money wages, we shall swing the pendulum from one extreme to another and
introduce in chapter 4 (and in that chapter only) an "ultra-Keynesian" assumption that money wages are *absolutely* rigid.

Once the Wicksellian assumption of flexible money wages is replaced by
this ultra-Keynesian assumption of absolute money wage rigidity, the knife-
edge property of the Wicksellian economy will vanish without traces, and an
economy that has an entirely opposed feature will emerge in its place. First,
it will be argued that, whereas any nonzero gap still leads to endogenous
creation of surprises in the product market, the assumed absolute rigidity of
money wages now deprives the labor market gap of the power of causing any
endogenous surprises, no matter how large it might be. Consequently, any
value of labor market gap and hence any level of total labor employment
(below full employment) that is determined by equilibrium between total product demand and supply (in the sense of zero product market gap) becomes
consistent with Expectational equilibrium of the economy as a whole. This is,
of course, nothing more than the restatement of the Keynesian principle of
effective demand within the framework of our disequilibrium economic dynamics. Second, it will be shown in chapter 4 that any imbalance between total
demand and supply in the product market will induce "quantity" variables to
move in a direction that restores their balance. Thus, under the assumption of
absolute money wage rigidity, the economy may find itself in stable equilibrium
at any level of total labor employment, as long as it does not exceed the full-
employment level.

However, such a resurrection of the Keynesian principle in no way de-
precates the importance of the disequilibrium-theoretic method of the Wicksellian approach. The primary object of chapter 5 is, in fact, to provide a
synthesis of the Keynesian principle and the Wicksellian approach. To this
end, we let the pendulum partially swing back and find a balance between the
two extreme positions. More specifically, we abandon the ultra-Keynesian

assumption of the absolute money wage rigidity and suppose more generally that the firm has to incur a certain cost of adjustment every time it changes its money wage. This is our somewhat novel formalization of the notion of money wage inflexibility in the world of monopsonistic competition.

It will then be shown that under this general formulation of money wage inflexibility, there is a band of values of the labor market gap, called the equilibrium band, within which firms' simultaneous wage adjustment activities are mutually compatible but outside which they become incompatible. As a result, as long as the labor market gap remains within this band, the economic system behaves like the one characterized by the Keynesian principle of effective demand. But as soon as the labor market gap strays away from the equilibrium band, firms' expectations about the state of labor supply are inevitably upset by the very aggregate outcome of their money wage adjustments. If it sinks below the lower barrier of this band, the economy will be likely to plunge into a cumulative deflation process or a "crisis," and if it jumps above the upper barrier, it will be likely to set in motion a cumulative inflation process or an "inflationary hysteria." The analysis of these disequilibrium situations is of course the special province of the Wicksellian approach. We are therefore able in chapter 5 to make a happy reconciliation between the Keynesian principle of effective demand and the Wicksellian approach to economic dynamics and show that they are not competitive, but rather complementary methods for analyzing the Keynesian economy—the former being more effective in characterizing its equilibrium and the latter being indispensable for describing the course of events in disequilibrium.

Perhaps what is most fundamental to our inquiry is not this happy marriage of Keynes and Wicksell as such; it is rather the implication it has in our search for the possible "anchor" of the monetary economy, which was shown in part I to lack any inherent stability. For our synthesis implies that it is the inflexibility of money wages that empowers the monetary economy with a stable character by blunting the knife-edge condition for the mutual compatibility of the decisions of firms. And as money wages become more rigid, the more immune the economy becomes from crisis or from inflationary hysteria. This may be characterized as a paradox of rationality. The inflexibility of money wages, which often appears to be the result of the irrationality of workers or employers at the microscopic level, in fact bestows a certain rationality on the dynamic working of the monetary economy as a whole.

But we seem to have anticipated too much of the following story. We better start giving a full account of it.

2. *The Ultra-Keynesian Assumption of the Absolute Rigidity of Money Wages*

Let us start our analysis of the equilibrium and dynamics of the ultra-Keynesian economy. The existence of a nonzero labor market gap represents an overall imbalance between demands and supplies in the labor market. When it is positive, at least one firm, and usually most, experiences a supernormal excess demand for labor; when it is negative, most firms experience a subnormal excess demand for labor. If money wages were flexible, then in order to eliminate such supernormal or subnormal excess labor demands, firms would simultaneously attempt to adjust their relative wages by raising or lowering money wages. It is this simultaneous bidding up or down of money wages that would create surprises endogenously and upset firms' expectational equilibrium in the Wicksellian labor market. But as soon as the assumption of absolute rigidity of money wages is introduced into our theoretical framework, firms are simply deprived of the means of adjusting their relative wages, no matter how supernormal or subnormal their excess labor demands are. They have no alternative but to accept any ratio of labor demand to supply.[3] In consequence, surprises can no longer be created endogenously in the ultra-Keynesian labor market. We can thus maintain that under the assumption of absolute money wage rigidity, any macroscopic imbalance between labor demand and supply, that is, any value of the labor market gap, is consistent with Expectational equilibrium of the economy as a whole. Since the value of the labor market gap is negatively correlated with the aggregate rate of involuntary unemployment and hence positively correlated with the level of total labor employment,[4] this implies that any aggregate rate of involuntary unemployment (as long as it is non-negative) and any level of total labor employment (as long as it is below the level of total labor supply) are consistent with Expectational equilibrium.

On the other hand, since we still retain the assumption of the complete flexibility of product prices at the beginning of every period, the emergence of any nonzero product market gap necessarily renders firms' relative price adjustments mutually incompatible and inevitably disrupts their expectational equilibria. Thus, even in this ultra-Keynesian economy, Expectational equilibrium still requires as its precondition the absence of any gap in the product market.

3. The Keynesian Principle of Effective Demand

The Keynesian principle of effective demand maintains that the scale of total labor employment is determined by the equilibrium relation between total product demand and supply. Keynes asserted in a lecture, quoted earlier, that this principle holds true even when ex post and ex ante coincide with each

---

3. It is true that the firms "can" control their own effective demands for labor. But once money wages are fixed, their levels are determined solely by their expectations of the state of product demand in the future in the short run. Recall that the effective demand for labor was defined as the level of labor employment that would maximize the expected gross revenue were there no labor supply constraint.

4. The relation between the value of labor market gap and the aggregate rate of involuntary unemployment is discussed in detail in chapter 5.

other (1937b, p. 182). We are now in a position to establish the Keynesian principle of effective demand in a state of Expectational equilibrium of our ultra-Keynesian economy.

Any college sophomore knows that, given the schedule of marginal efficiency of investment of producers, the propensity to consume of households, the liquidity preference of asset holders, the central bank's monetary policy, the government taxes and expenditures, and other factors, the volume of total product demand is determined primarily by the current as well as past levels of total income in the hands of spenders in the product market. Since the level of total income is positively correlated with the level of total labor employment, there should also exist a strong positive relationship between the volume of total product demand and the level of total labor employment in the current as well as in past periods. Their relationship, written $X_t = X(N_t, N_{t-1}, N_{t-2}, \ldots)$, can be called the total demand schedule. This corresponds to what Keynes called aggregate demand function in *The General Theory* (1936, p. 25).

On the other hand, at the end of every period, each firm determines its employment by comparing its effective labor demand and a given labor supply, and starts its production activity from that moment. Output appears in the product market after the elapse of a production period τ. The level of total product supply is then the economy-wide aggregate of each firm's output decision and thus the aggregate consequence of each firm's labor employment decision τ periods earlier. Given the technological conditions of production and available stock of capital goods, there is therefore a strong positive relationship between the volume of total product supply Q_t and the level of total labor employment τ period earlier $N_{t-\tau}$. Their relationship, written $Q_t = Q(N_{t-\tau})$, can be called the total supply schedule. This corresponds to Keynes' aggregate supply function in *The General Theory* (1936, p. 25).

We now have both the total demand and the total supply schedule. Our next task is to find an equilibrium between them. Indeed, we already know (see proposition 3–1′) that for the economy to be in Expectational equilibrium, the product market gap has to be zero, so that we have

$$\left(\frac{X_t}{Q_t} - G^*\right)\Big/ G^* = 0 \qquad \text{for } t = 1, 2, \ldots.$$

This is simply the equation that balances demand and supply of output as a whole and hence "clears" the market for it. If we substitute the total demand and the total supply schedule in this market-clearing equation and solve it, we are then able to determine the level of total labor employment, or its trajectory over time, which is capable of sustaining the balance between demand and supply of output as a whole. Since under the assumption of absolute money wage rigidity any level of total labor employment, as long as it does not exceed the level of total labor supply, is consistent with Expectational equilibrium, the level of total labor employment thus "solved" defines an equilibrium position of the economy. We have thus established:

> Proposition 4–1 *Under the assumption of the absolute rigidity of money wages, the total labor employment in a state of Expectational equilibrium is fixed at whatever level is required to balance the total demand and supply schedules in the product market. Its ultimate determinants are thus the marginal efficiency of investment, the propensity to consume, the schedule of liquidity preferences, the supply of cash balance, the government taxes and expenditures, and other factors upon which the shape of the total demand schedule depends, as well as the conditions of technology and the stock of capital goods upon which the shape of the total supply schedule depends. There is no a priori reason to expect that the equilibrium level of employment thus determined is equal to the full-employment level.*

Simple though it is, this is the substance of the Keynesian principle of effective demand within the framework of our disequilibrium dynamics. It is simply the all-too-familiar Marshallian demand and supply analysis applied to the determination of employment and output as a whole. As was emphasized by Keynes himself, his principle of effective demand is a mere elucidation of the conditions of Expectational equilibrium (or short-period equilibrium), in which ex ante and ex post are on average equal to each other. In contrast to the Wicksellian approach which lays the whole emphasis on the differences between total product demand and total product supply and between total labor demand and total labor supply, the Keynesian effective demand principle is based upon the conditions for their equilibrium. Its methodology is thus purely equilibrium-theoretic. Although it has often been misunderstood by his own disciples as well as by his critics, this equilibrium-theoretic nature of the principle is Keynes's main point of emphasis. For having shown that any level of employment is consistent with equilibrium, Keynes could exploit the (neo-) classical equation: equilibrium = normality = reality and assert that a situation with large involuntary unemployment is no less "normal" and no less "real" than the situation of full employment. Indeed, it is rather the situation of full employment that has the quality of unreality in the economic world of Keynes.

4. *The Stability of Keynesian Equilibrium under the Assumption of Absolute Money Wage Rigidity*

In an economy with absolute money wage rigidity, the situation in which no gap exists in the product market and hence no endogenous source of surprises exists in the entire economy may be given the name "Keynesian equilibrium." It is the situation in which the level of employment and output as a whole is determined by the Keynesian principle of effective demand. (Under the more general formulation of the inflexibility of money wages given in chapter 5, we need one supplementary condition to characterize the notion of Keynesian equilibrium.) It is evident that Expectational equilibrium is, by necessity, Keynesian equilibrium. But Keynesian equilibrium is not necessarily Expectational equilibrium, for Keynesian equilibrium is a synchronic equilibrium notion that assures only the mutual compatibility of firms' simultaneous decisions at a point in time.

We now argue that under the assumption of absolute money wage rigidity, the position of Keynesian equilibrium has a stable nature in the sense that any movement away from it sets in motion forces that tend to restore it.

To see this, suppose that the balance between total product demand and supply is upset by a shock and that there emerges a *negative* gap,

$$\left(\frac{X_t}{Q_t} - G^*\right)\bigg/ G^* < 0,$$

in the product market. Then arithmetic, or the adding-up equation (3–13) in the product market, tells us that a majority of the firms now face subnormal ratios of demand to supply. When they start interpreting their failure to sell their products at normal rate not as a temporary phenomenon, but as a permanent one, they revise downward their expectations of the state of product demand and cut their product prices accordingly. This will, as we have seen in chapter 3, set off a cumulative deflation process in the product market.

Furthermore, if firms believe that the state of product demand will remain sluggish even in the future, they have to revise downward their expectation of future sales as well. Firms will then curtail their effective labor demands so as to reduce their product supply in the future. This will result in a decline of their labor employments and after the elapse of a production period reduce the level of total product supply. Evidently, such an induced decline of total product supply contributes to the elimination of the existing negative gap in the product market.

But such "quantity" adjustment may not be sufficiently strong to finish its task.[5] But, fortunately in that case, "price" adjustment would come to help

---

5. According to the schedule of effective labor demand (1–16), a 1 percent decline in the expectation of the future state of product demand tends to reduce effective labor demand by $100/[\gamma + \eta(1 - \gamma)]$ percent. Therefore, if the reduction of effective labor demand were completely transformed into the equal reduction of actual labor employment, the resulting decline of total product supply τ periods later would be roughly by $100\gamma/[\gamma + \eta(1 - \gamma)]$ percent, which exceeds one percent only if the degree of returns to labor input γ is greater than unity. However, in general there are always some firms that have excess demands for labor. For those firms, a reduction of effective demand for labor does not result in an equal reduction of actual labor employment. Thus, unless the degree of returns to labor input is greater than unity *and* most firms have experienced excess supplies of labor before the reduction of effective labor demand, the resulting reduction in the level of total product supply will not completely offset the initial decline in the volume of total product demand. In what follows we ignore the case in which the induced reduction of total product supply exceeds the original decline of total product demand.

it. To see this, suppose that a negative gap still remains in the product market after the induced decline of total product supply. Then a cumulative price deflation will continue, although at a somewhat slower rate. We know that the process of cumulative price deflation consists of the process of the expected level of general price chasing the realized level of general price in the downward direction. It is therefore very likely that during the process of cumulative price deflation, firms also revise their expectations of the future level of general price and hence of the future state of product demand in the downward direction. [Recall that $a_{t+\tau}(i) \equiv P_{t+\tau}^{\hat{\eta}(i)} X_{t+\tau}^{\hat{\xi}(i)} \alpha_{t+\tau}(i)$.] Other things being equal, such an additional pessimistic revision of the future state of product demand will further discourage effective demands for labor and repress actual labor employment. It will then reduce the level of total product supply τ periods later, and eventually close the remaining negative product market gap. The cumulative price deflation will then consummate itself. (If we were in the Wicksellian economy, other things would not be equal. For as we saw in chapter 3, the accompanying cumulative wage deflation would stimulate the effective labor demands and indeed offset the effect of the ongoing cumulative price deflation. But under the assumption of absolute money wage rigidity, the possibility of cumulative wage deflation counterbalancing the stabilizing effect of the cumulative price deflation is by definition foreclosed.)

We have thus established:

Proposition 4–2. *Under the assumption of absolute money wage rigidity, the emergence of a positive or negative gap in the product market will always induce adjustments in employment and output which tend to eliminate the gap.*

To complete our stability analysis, we have to take into consideration the Kahn–Keynes multiplier process, which will be triggered by the induced decline of total labor employment. To avoid repetition, however, we postpone its discussion until chapter 5, where we present a more detailed analysis of the dynamic workings of the economy with money wage inflexibility.

5. The Wicksellian Economy versus the Ultra-Keynesian Economy

Before us are two opposing systems of economy—the Wicksellian economy, which assumes perfectly flexible money wages, on the one side, and the ultra-Keynesian economy, which assumes absolutely rigid money wages, on the other.

In the Wicksellian economy, only the normal level of output and employment that balances the product and labor markets is compatible with Expectational equilibrium. Moreover, any deviation from that unique equilibrium sets off a cumulative inflation or deflation, which will drive the system further away. The Wicksellian economy thus has a knife-edge property.

By contrast, in the ultra-Keynesian economy, any scale of output and employment determined by an equilibrium balance between total demand and supply in the product market is compatible with Expectational equilibrium. Furthermore, any deviation from a given equilibrium position sets forces into operation that will tend to restore equilibrium. The ultra-Keynesian economy thus has a built-in stability in whichever equilibrium it has found itself.

The task of chapter 5 is to unite these two opposing systems on a higher plane.

CHAPTER 5

The Keynesian Theory of Slump and the Wicksellian Theory of Crisis: A Synthesis

1. On the Inflexibility of Money Wages

The labor market is not a "bourse" (see Dunlop 1944, chap. 2). Money wages are never quoted by symmetrical exchanges of biddings between large and approximately equal numbers of employers and workers circulating among each other. In a nonunionized labor market at least, it is in general the employer who takes the initiative and quotes a money wage on a take-it-or-leave-it basis. Thus, the most natural way to formalize the notion of money wage inflexibility in such monopsonistically competitive economy is to postulate that the employer incurs certain *adjustment costs* whenever the level of money wage is changed at the beginning of the period.

There exist several reasons why money wages are costly to adjust in the actual labor market. First, the act of changing the money wage itself may require a certain economic cost—administrative cost in particular. This cost is often regarded as minor by orthodox economists, but in complex decision processes of a firm it may not be negligible. Second, it should be recalled that the money wage which is unilaterally quoted by the employer on the take-it-or-leave-it basis can no longer be regarded as a mere exchange rate between workers' labor service and means of payment but as a public information signal that informs potential employees of the pecuniary working condition of a particular firm; the money wage therefore provides an incentive for them to reveal their true preferences in the form of labor supply offers. Then, as argued in section 4 of chapter 1, to serve this function the money wage must be fixed prior to the workers' labor supply decisions, and for it to serve this function effectively, it must be fixed for some length of time to secure its reliability. Since frequent changes of money wage is likely to depreciate its reliability as a signal, a change in money wage tends to reduce the supply of labor, thereby inflicting a certain cost upon the firm. How large this informational cost is is, however, ambiguous. Third, the recently developed theory of implicit labor contract emphasizes the function of fixed money wages as an efficient device for insuring workers, who are likely to be more risk averse than managers and shareholders,

128

against uncertainty in market conditions.[1] Fourth, it is important to note that if workers are heterogeneous, the employer's attempt to change money wage rates almost inevitably disrupts the existing "internal equity" within a heterogeneous work force and is likely to raise troublesome labor–management problem. The sociological cost associated with the disturbance of the internal equity structure is one of the major raisons d'être for the stickiness of money wages even in an unorganized labor market.

There is little reason to expect that four types of adjustment costs listed above are biased in either direction—upward or downward. However, once the problem of "external equity" between workers in different firms is introduced, a clear case for the downward rigidity of money wages emerges. As originally argued by Keynes, workers are very concerned with the relative position of their money wages vis-à-vis the money wages received by workers comparable as to skills, jobs, social backgrounds and the like. They tend to resist a cut in their money wages which they believe will jeopardize their relative wages (Keynes 1936, chap. 2; see also Ross 1948).[2] (On the other hand, they will not always resist a cut in their "real" wages brought about by an increase in the general price level, because it affects all workers equally and preserves the external equity structure of money wages virtually intact.) Since workers do not reject a proposed increase in their money wages (unless they are exceptionally self-sacrificing or skillfully aiming at a much higher increase), this sociological cost leads to the downward rigidity of money wages. This cause of downward rigidity would undoubtedly be reinforced by the existence of trade unions, but it is very important to note that it is far from negligible even if no unions exist. (A detailed discussion of the nature and implications of the downward money wage rigidity when the labor market is unionized is postponed until Chapter 8. Until then, we shall limit ourselves to the study of the behavior of the firm in a nonunionized labor market.)

More specific assumptions about wage adjustment costs are introduced in chapter 6. It suffices here to bear in mind that in the Keynesian economy the act of changing the money wage is no longer a free activity to the employer; it is a genuine economic activity which requires the input of certain economic resources for its own execution.

It should be emphasized, however, that for our purposes in this chapter, the precise rationalization of the inflexibility of money wages—though an undeniable empirical fact—is of little importance. For what we would like to establish is that, whether or not it is an outcome of workers' and/or employers' rational calculations, the inflexibility of money wages tends to stabilize an otherwise

---

1. For an exposition of this theory, see Baily (1974), Azariadas (1975), and Gordon (1975). Quite recently, however, certain theoretical difficulties of this approach have been pointed out. See, for instance, Akerlof and Miyazaki (1980).

2. Akerlof (1980) may be regarded as a modern formulation of their idea.

unstable monetary economy and restore, at least partially, a certain rationality to the dynamic workings of the system as a whole.

2. *A Simplifying Assumption*

To facilitate our subsequent exposition, it is convenient at this point to introduce a simplifying assumption. It is the assumption that all firms in our economy are symmetric with respect to the structure of product demand schedules, the structure of labor supply schedules, the technological relations, and the structure of their expectation-formation processes. Formally, this assumption of symmetry can be stated that all the elasticities, $\eta(i)$, $\varepsilon(i)$, $\gamma(i)$, $\lambda(i)$, and $\xi(i)$, all the probability distributions of surprises, $A_i(\cdot)$, $A_i^{(\tau)}(\cdot)$, and $B_i(\cdot)$, and all the other structural parameters, $\phi(i)$ and $\chi(i)$, are uniform across firms. It then follows that all the normal ratios, $g^*(i)$, $f^*(i)$, $u^*(i)$, and $v^*(i)$, also become uniform across firms and that all the aggregate normal ratios, G^* and F^*, become equal to the corresponding uniform normal ratios g^* and f^*. From now on, we are able to drop the burdensome firm-specific index i from these structural parameters.[3]

It should be emphasized, however, that this assumption by no means implies that firms behave identically from period to period. On the contrary, in the dynamic and uncertain world, firms' actual behaviors, which are made on the basis of their quite heterogeneous expectations, which are in turn formed on the basis of their quite heterogeneous market experiences, are quite diverse both cross-sectionally and intertemporally. (We have more to say on this in chapter 7.) It should be also stressed that this assumption of symmetry has been introduced here solely for convenience. The qualitative nature of all the propositions in what follows would remain valid even if asymmetry among firms were allowed into our model.

3. *The Class of Simple Wage Adjustment Rules*

The life of the firm in the Wicksellian labor market was rather uncomplicated. At the beginning of every period the firm processes new data acquired in markets in the previous period, forms the best expectations it can as to the tightness of labor supply and the briskness of product demand, and computes the level of money wage $w_t^*(i)$, which is expected to maximize the short-run gross profit on the basis of these newly revised expectations. It then announces $w_t^*(i)$ in the labor market. The level of $w_t^*(i)$ is an increasing function of the expectation of

---

3. As pointed out in appendixes 1–a and 1–b, both $\xi(i)$ and $\lambda(i)$ have to be equal to unity for all firms under the assumption of symmetry.

the briskness of product demand τ periods later, of the expectation of the tightness of labor supply in the current period, and of the index of labor productivity.

The life of the firm in the Keynesian economy is not as easy-going as that of its fellow firm in the Wicksellian economy. If the firm tried to set its money wage to the expected short-run profit-maximizing level $w_t^*(i)$ in every period, it would in the long run suffer an enormous amount of wage adjustment costs. If, on the other hand, the firm were slow in adjusting money wage, it could not cope with ever-changing market conditions and would in the long run suffer an enormous amount of opportunity costs. In the Keynesian economy there is therefore a trade-off between the cost of changing the money wage and the opportunity cost of failing to adapt it to novel situations; the firm has to devise a rule of wage adjustment which keeps a balance between these two conflicting costs. This is inherently a dynamic problem.

The strict neoclassical methodology would indicate that we assume that the firm chooses a wage adjustment rule which is expected to optimize a certain objective function (e.g., the discounted sum of the sequence of net profits) among all conceivable adjustment rules. In this book, however, we do not necessarily adhere to this assumption of the global rationality of the decision maker. Instead, we make an appeal to the bounded rationality of the firm (as well as to our own bounded rationality) in a complex and uncertain environment,[4] and suppose that the firm selects a wage adjustment rule only from a restricted class of simple rules whose forms are given a priori except for the values of a few decision parameters. Even if an infinite variety of adjustment rules are feasible from the purely formal standpoint, only the adjustment rules in this a priori restricted class are considered "feasible" to our firm. This would drastically reduce the complexity of the firm's decision problem (as well as of our own theoretical investigation).

Let $w_t(i)$ be the level of money wage actually quoted by the ith firm at the beginning of period t. With the existence of wage adjustment costs, the firm needs not and indeed does not set $w_t(i)$ equal to $w_t^*(i)$ (i.e., the optimal wage in the Wicksellian economy) in every period. For want of better terminology, we call the latter the "short-run optimal wage" in period t, although in the Keynesian economy it is no longer the optimal wage in the true sense of the world. This short-run optimal wage $w_t^*(i)$ will serve as an important benchmark for the specification of simple wage adjustment rules.

A simple wage adjustment rule that is considered to be feasible by our firm is assumed to be of the following form:

---

4. The notion of "bounded rationality" or "limited rationality" is due to H. A. Simon. See Simon (1955, 1959, 1972) and March and Simon (1958).

$$(5\text{-}1) \qquad \ln w_t(i) = \begin{cases} \ln w_{t-1}(i) \quad \text{(i.e., no wage adjustment)} \\ \quad \text{if } \theta_- \leqslant \ln w_t^*(i) - \ln w_{t-1}(i) \leqslant \theta_+, \\ \ln w_t^*(i) - \theta_0 \quad \text{(i.e., wage increase)} \\ \quad \text{if } \ln w_t^*(i) - \ln w_{t-}(i) > \theta_+, \\ \ln w_t^*(i) - \theta_0 \quad \text{(i.e., wage cut)} \\ \quad \text{if } \ln w_t^*(i) - \ln w_{t-1}(i) < \theta_-, \end{cases}$$

where "ln" stands for natural logarithm and θ_+, θ_-, and θ_0 are constant parameters satisfying the inequalities $\theta_- \leqslant \theta_0 \leqslant \theta_+$. θ_+ will be called the upper barrier, θ_- the lower barrier, and θ_0 the return point. The range $[\theta_-, \theta_+]$, bound from below by θ_- and above by θ_+, will be called the satisfactory range. Because of the symmetry assumption we introduced a short while ago, these parameters are uniform across firms.

In its present form, the structure of the simple wage adjustment rule (5–1) may not be easy to comprehend. For that reason, shortly we shall transform it into a slightly more transparent form. But to fill the interval, let us try to explain it in words.

At the beginning of every period, our firm computes the short-run optimal wage $w_t^*(i)$ for that period on the basis of newly revised expectations about market conditions. The firm then compares it with the level of money wage $w_{t-1}(i)$ quoted in the preceding period. If their proportionate difference, $\ln w_t^*(i) - \ln w_{t-1}(i)$, remains within the satisfactory range $[\theta_-, \theta_+]$, the firm is "satisfied" with the old wage level and defers adjustment in that period. If, on the other hand, $\ln w_t^*(i) - \ln w_{t-1}(i)$ strays away from this satisfactory range, the firm's "drives" overcome the rigidity of money wage. In particular, if $\ln w_t^*(i) - \ln w_{t-1}(i)$ surpasses the upper barrier θ_+, the money wage is raised, and if it drops below the lower barrier θ_-, the money wage is cut. In either case, the simple rule given above dictates the firm to set the logarithmic level of the new money wage, $\ln w_t(i)$, to be equal to the logarithmic level of the short-run optimal wage, $\ln w_t^*(i)$, minus the constant adjustment term θ_0 (which have been called the return point). Since in the Keynesian economy the short-run optimal wage $w_t^*(i)$ is not the optimal wage in the true sense, there is no necessity for the firm to adjust the money wage to that level; hence, the value of θ_0 may be positive or negative or zero.

If $\theta_+ = \theta_- = \theta_0$, then $w_t(i)$ is set always equal to $w_t^*(i)$, and the Wicksellian case of *perfect flexibility* of money wages obtains. If $\theta_- = -\infty$, the rule directs our firm to refuse any wage cut no matter how low $w_t^*(i)$ falls below $w_{t-1}(i)$. This is the case of the absolute downward rigidity of money wages. Similarly, if $\theta_+ = \infty$, the rule directs the firm to refuse any wage hike, regardless of the degree to which $w_t^*(i)$ exceeds $w_{t-1}(i)$. This is the case of absolute upward rigidity of money wages. As a combination, the case of $\theta_- = -\infty$ and $\theta_+ = \infty$ corresponds to the ultra-Keynesian assumption of absolute rigidity of money wages. Our simple wage adjustment rule therefore classifies both the Wicksellian and ultra-Keynesian as special cases.

The general case is that $-\infty < \theta_- < \theta_0 < \theta_+ < +\infty$. Then, money wages are inflexible but not absolutely rigid in either direction.

Let us denote by $z_t(i)$ the proportionate difference between the short-run and actual money wages of the ith firm in period t; that is, we put

$$(5\text{--}2) \qquad z_t(i) \equiv \ln w_t^*(i) - \ln w_t(i).$$

Since the short-run optimal wage $w_t^*(i)$ is by definition the level of money wage that would uniquely maximize the expected short-run gross profit in period t were it not for any wage adjustment costs, its deviation from the actual wage $w_t(i)$ can be used as an index which scales the extent of the firm's "frustration" over the currently quoted money wage. We shall therefore call $z_t(i)$ the firm's subjective labor market disequilibrium or simply the subjective disequilibrium in period t. Note that in the case of the flexible-wage Wicksellian economy, it would always and necessarily equal zero. Henceforth, this variable will play a central role in our theoretical investigation of the firm's wage adjustment activity.

If we note the obvious transformation

$\ln w_t^*(i) - \ln w_{t-1}(i)$
$\equiv \left[\ln w_{t-1}^*(i) - \ln w_{t-1}(i) \right] + \left[\ln w_t^*(i) - \ln w_{t-1}^*(i) \right]$
$\equiv z_{t-1}(i) + \Delta \ln w_{t-1}^*(i)$ where $\Delta \ln w_{t-1}^*(i) \equiv \ln w_t^*(i) - \ln w_{t-1}^*(i)$, the simple wage adjustment rule specified in (5–1) can be easily translated into the following rule for the adjustment of subjective disequilibrium:

$$(5\text{--}3) \qquad z_t(i) = \begin{cases} z_{t-1}(i) + \Delta \ln w_{t-1}^*(i) & \text{(i.e., no wage adjustment)} \\ \qquad \text{if } \theta_- \leqslant z_{t-1}(i) + \Delta \ln w_{t-1}^*(i) \leqslant \theta_+, \\ \theta_0 \qquad \text{(i.e., wage increase)} \\ \qquad \text{if } z_{t-1}(i) + \Delta \ln w_{t-1}^*(i) > \theta_+, \\ \theta_0 \qquad \text{(i.e., wage cut)} \\ \qquad \text{if } z_{t-1}(i) + \Delta \ln w_{t-1}^*(i) < \theta_-. \end{cases}$$

This transformation might make the nature of the simple wage adjustment rule easier to visualize. Figure 5–1 illustrates the dynamic motion of subjective disequilibrium $z_t(i)$. At the beginning of period t, the firm computes the rate of change in the short-run optimal wage $\Delta \ln w_{t-1}^*(i)$, and then adds it to the subjective disequilibrium $z_{t-1}(i)$ of the preceding period. Their sum, $z_{t-1}(i) + \Delta \ln w_{t-1}^*(i)$, is by definition equal to $\ln w_t^*(i) - \ln w_{t-1}(i)$. If this is found to be within the satisfactory range $[\theta_-, \theta_+]$, the firm defers the wage adjustment and sets $\ln w_t = \ln w_{t-1}$, which is equivalent to setting the new value of subjective disequilibrium $z_t(i)$ equal to $z_{t-1}(i) + \Delta \ln w_{t-1}^*(i)$. If, on the other hand, $z_{t-1}(i) + \Delta \ln w_{t-1}^*(i)$ hits the upper barrier θ_+, the new subjective disequilibrium would float above it unless the money wage were raised. In that case, the money wage is indeed raised in such a way that the new subjective disequilibrium $z_t(i)$ is pulled down to the return point θ_0. And, if $z_{t-1}(i) + \Delta \ln w_{t-1}^*(i)$ hits the lower

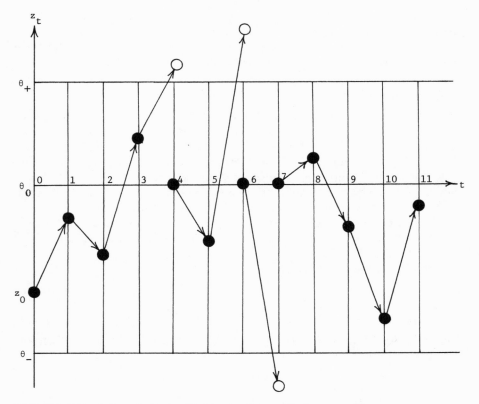

FIGURE 5–1. A Sample Path of Subjective Disequilibrium over Time

barrier, the money wage is cut so as to push up the new value of subjective disequilibrium $z_t(i)$ to the same return point θ_0. The reason θ_0 is called the return point should be evident by now.

We have thus formulated the notion of money wage inflexibility in a manner consistent with our view of the firm as a monopsonist in the labor market. Although there appear to be many alternative ways of formulating it, we have chosen this particular form primarily because it is "simple" and "good." (Why it is good is explained in appendix 6–a.)

It is, therefore, not surprising that for the object of the present chapter—a synthesis of Keynes and Wicksell—no further microeconomic analysis of the firm's wage adjustment activity is necessary. Accordingly, let us postpone a close analysis of the firm's money wage adjustment activity until part III, and suppose for now that the parameter values of θ_+, θ_-, and θ_0 are viewed by the firm as a legacy from the past. All that the firm is supposed to do here is to follow routinely a historically given rule of money wage adjustment. This is tantamount to saying that the firm here acts like a satisficer (H. A. Simon's term) in the short run.[5]

We are now able to proceed directly to the analysis of the short-run performance of the Keynesian economy as a whole.

4. The Generalized Fundamental Equation in the Labor Market

In the Keynesian economy, the fundamental equation of labor market, (3–17), becomes defunct. For it was deduced from the optimal wage equation (1–22), which is valid only under the assumption of the flexibility of money wages. It is then evident that in the Keynesian economy, proposition 3–2′ (which claims that all firms are capable of attaining their expectational equilibria concerning the tightness of the labor supply only if the labor market gap is equal to zero) breaks down *pari passu*. As a result, all the firms in the Keynesian labor market are, unlike their counterparts in the Wicksellian labor market, in principle capable of forming equilibrium expectations, even if the gap in the labor market is wide open. One of our main concerns in this chapter is to explore the implications of this breakdown of the fundamental equation of the labor market.

On the other hand, since we still keep the assumption that product prices are flexible at the beginning of every period, the fundamental equation of the product market (3–16) and consequently proposition 3–1′ remain effective even in the Keynesian economy. Thus, all firms are able to achieve their expectational equilibria concerning the briskness of product demand only if the product market gap happens to be equal to zero. Of course, this asymmetric treatment of wages and prices is certainly restrictive; for there are many products whose prices are as inflexible as money wages. The only justification for this is our belief that it is at least more realistic than an alternative assumption of equal inflexibility of prices and wages. For real wage rates appear to exhibit weak but by no means negligible variations in the normal course of business fluctuation.

The fundamental equation of the labor market (3–17) played a key role in our analysis of the process of disequilibrium in the Wicksellian labor market. It is now dead, so we have to search for a new equation that is as useful as the deceased one in analyzing the process of disequilibrium in the Keynesian labor market.

Now, the subjective disequilibrium $z_t(i)$ was defined as the proportional difference between the short-run optimal wage $w_t^*(i)$ and the actual money wage $w_t(i)$ [see (5–2)]. The short-run optimal wage, in turn, was defined as the level of money wage that is expected to equate the ratio of labor demand to supply with the constant subjective-normal ratio f^*. (Recall proposition

---

5. We say more on the analogy between our model of money wage adjustment and Simon's satisficing model in chapter 6.

1–3.) It then follows that if the firm sets its money wage at the level that is not expected to equate the ratio of labor demand to supply with the subjective-normal ratio, then the associated subjective disequilibrium has to deviate from zero. More formally, we have deduced the following relation in appendix 5–a:

$$(5-4) \qquad \ln \hat{E}\left[\frac{h_t(i)}{l_t(i)} : \delta_t(i)\right] - \ln f^* = \psi z_t(i),$$

where the multiplier ψ is a positive constant defined by

$$\psi \equiv \frac{\eta + \varepsilon\eta(1-\gamma) + \varepsilon\gamma}{\eta - \gamma(\eta-1)} > 0.$$

It is often convenient to approximate this relation as

$$(5-4') \qquad \psi z_t(i) \triangleq \left\{ \hat{E}\left[\frac{h_t(i)}{l_t(i)} : \delta_t(i)\right] - f^* \right\} \Big/ f^*.$$

We can interpret this as saying that the value of subjective disequilibrium $z_t(i)$ multiplied by ψ represents the proportional gap between the ratio of labor demand to supply and its subjective-normal ratio that the firm "expects" or "intends" to obtain in the current labor market.

Let Z_t be the market-wide average of the firm's subjective disequilibrium $z_t(i)$, defined by

$$(5-5) \qquad Z_t \equiv \sum_{i=1}^{I} \left[\frac{l_t(i)}{L_t}\right] z_t(i).$$

We shall call Z_t the aggregate subjective disequilibrium in period t. Multiply this by the constant ψ, and we obtain, in view of (5–4'), the following relation:

$$(5-6) \qquad \psi Z_t \triangleq \sum_{i=1}^{I} \left[\frac{l_t(i)}{L_t}\right] \left\{ \hat{E}\left[\frac{h_t(i)}{l_t(i)} : \delta_t(i)\right] - f^* \right\} \Big/ f^*.$$

We shall call this multiple of the aggregate subjective disequilibrium the "aggregate intended gap" in the labor market, for it is a market-wide aggregate of each firm's intended magnitude of the gap between the ratio of labor demand to supply and its normal value f^*.

No matter what their intentions are, however, the firms' money wage adjustment activities as a whole are necessarily constrained by macroeconomic conditions in the market. In fact, combining the adding-up equation (3–4) of the labor supply schedules and the definition (3–7) of total labor demand in chapter 3, we can easily deduce the following equation, which says that the proportional gaps between the actual ratio of labor demand to supply and its normal ratio across individual firms have to add up to the current value of labor market gap:[6]

$$(5\text{--}7) \qquad \sum_{i=1}^{I} \left[\frac{l_t(i)}{L_t} \right] \left[\frac{h_t(i)}{l_t(i)} - f^* \right] \bigg/ f^* = \left(\frac{H_t}{L_t} - f^* \right) \bigg/ f^*.$$

Thus, the existing size of the labor market gap determines the extent to which the *actual* ratios of labor demand to supply *as an aggregate* diverge from the corresponding normal ratios.

It then follows that if the aggregate intended gap ψZ_t is different in value from the size of the existing labor market gap $(H_t/L_t - f^*)/f^*$, the firms' intentions as an aggregate become incompatible with macroeconomic conditions in the labor market. Such incompatibility necessarily causes the expectations of at least one of the firms and often a majority of them to be upset by the actual market outcomes! We have thus established an endogenous explanation of the existence of surprises in the Keynesian labor market. Here, the cause for surprises on the part of firms is found not in the divergence of the labor market gap from zero as in the Wicksellian labor market, but in its divergence from the aggregate intended gap ψZ_t.

We are able to summarize this observation in the form of a single equation. To this end, let us rewrite the left-hand side of (5–4) as

$$\{\ln \hat{E}[h_t(i)/l_t(i) : \delta_t(i)] - \ln [h_t(i)/l_t(i)]\} + \{\ln [h_t(i)/l_t(i)] - \ln f^*\}$$
$$= \{\ln \hat{E}[b_t(i) : \delta_t(i)] - \ln b_t(i)\} + \{\ln [h_t(i)/l_t(i)] - \ln f^*\}.$$

Rearranging terms, we obtain

$$\ln b_t(i) - \ln \hat{E}[b_t(i) : \delta_t(i)] = \{\ln [h_t(i)/l_t(i)] - \ln f^*\} - \psi z_t(i).$$

Aggregating this across firms with weight equal to $l_t(i)/L_t$, *we get*

$$\sum_{i=1}^{I} \left[\frac{l_t(i)}{L_t} \right] \{\ln b_t(i) - \ln \hat{E}[b_t(i) : \delta_t(i)]\}$$
$$= \sum_{i=1}^{I} \left[\frac{l_t(i)}{L_t} \right] \{\ln [h_t(i)/l_t(i)] - \ln f^*\} - \psi Z_t.$$

If we approximate $\ln b_t(i) - \ln \hat{E}[b_t(i) : \delta_t(i)]$ by $b_t(i)/\hat{E}[b_t(i) : \delta_t(i)] - 1$, and $\ln [h_t(i)/l_t(i)] - \ln f^*$ by $(h_t(i)/l_t(i) - f^*)/f^*$, and then take note of the adding-up relation (5–7), we can finally come up with the "generalized fundamental equation of the labor market":

$$(5\text{--}8) \qquad \sum_{i=1}^{I} \left[\frac{l_t(i)}{L_t} \right] \left\{ \frac{b_t(i)}{\hat{E}[b_t(i) : \delta_t(i)]} - 1 \right\} \triangleq \left(\frac{H_t}{L_t} - f^* \right) \bigg/ f^* - \psi Z_t.$$

---

6. The derivation of this adding-up relation is analogous to that of the adding-up relation (3–13) of the product market gap. In fact, this relation was already employed in the deduction of the fundamental equation of the labor market (3–17), although it was not recorded explicitly there.

This new fundamental equation takes over the role played by the fundemantal equation of the labor market (3–17). Indeed, it now includes the latter as a special case in which the aggregate intended gap ψZ_t is always set equal to zero.

Our new fundamental equation states that the average surprise on the part of firms with respect to the state of labor supply, $\Sigma\,[l_t(i)/L_t]\,\{b_t(i)/\hat{E}\,[b_t(i):\delta_t(i)] - 1\}$, is completely determined by (and in fact equal in value to) the difference between the labor market gap $(H_t/L_t - f^*)/f^*$ and the aggregate intended gap ψZ_t. We can therefore establish the following:

> Proposition 5–1. *When the existing labor market gap exceeds the aggregate intended gap, firms as a whole are bound to underestimate the extent of the tightness of labor supply; and when the labor market gap falls short of the aggregate intended gap, at least one firm and usually a majority of them inevitably overestimate the extent of tightness of labor supply. It is when and only when the labor market gap equals the aggregate intended gap that the expectations of the firms become on average consistent with the realized market outcomes.*

If the number of the firms, I, is very large, we can strengthen proposition 5–1 in the following manner:

> Proposition 5–1′. *In the Keynesian economy, all firms are simultaneously capable of attaining expectational equilibrium with respect to the tightness of labor supply only if the actual labor market gap is (approximately) equal to the aggregate intended gap, that is, only if*

$$(5\text{–}9) \qquad\qquad \left(\frac{H_t}{L_t} - f^*\right)\!\bigg/ f^* \triangleq \psi Z_t.$$

5. *The Equilibrium Band in the Keynesian Labor Market*

We can drawn two implications from the new fundamental equation (5–8), one positive and the other negative.

In chapter 4 we resuscitated the Keynesian principle of effective demand under the assumption of absolute money wage rigidity. However, our rescue operation of the Keynesian principle has not been completed yet. For we have to see whether the principle still holds true even under the more general formulation of money wage inflexibility. It is the positive implication of the generalized fundamental equation that plays the key role in this part of our investigation. The negative implication then fixes the boundary of the applicability of the principle and at the same time provides the foundation for the reintroduction of the Wicksellian approach into our Keynesian disequilibrium dynamics.

The positive implication of the new fundamental equation consists of an observation that in the Keynesian labor market there is no longer one-to-one correspondence between the average surprise on the part of firms and the value of labor market gap. Even if the actual labor market gap is negative, as long as the aggregate intended gap is negative and equal in value, the Keynesian economy is capable of attaining Expectational equilibrium. By the same token, even if the labor market gap is positive, as long as the aggregate intended gap is positive and equal in value, the Keynesian economy is also capable of attaining Expectational equilibrium. In the Wicksellian economy, a zero labor market gap was necessary for the existence of Expectational equilibrium. By contrast, in the Keyensian economy, the inflexibility of money wages, even if it is not absolute, has enlarged the scope of Expectational equilibrium and allowed both negative and positive values of labor market gap to be consistent with it.

The foregoing observation should not be taken as an assertion that *any* value of labor market gap is compatible with Expectational equilibrium. On the contrary, unless money wages are absolutely rigid, there are in general a lower limit and an upper limit to the values of labor market gap that are compatible with the conditions of Expectational equilibrium. This is the negative implication of the new fundamental equation. As we saw in section 3, the position of subjective disequilibrium $z_t(i)$ for an individual firm fluctuates within the satisfactory range bound from below by the lower barrier θ_- and from above by the upper barrier θ_+. It follows trivially that the value of aggregate subjective disequilibrium Z_t, defined by (5–5), must be also bounded from below by θ_- and from above by θ_+, so that its multiple, ψZ_t, is able to fluctuate only within the range bound from below by $\psi\theta_-$ and from above by $\psi\theta_+$. Now, we know from proposition 5–1' that all the firms in our Keynesian economy are simultaneously capable of achieving their expectational equilibria only if the labor market gap $(H_t/L_t - f^*)/f^*$ is equal to the value of this ψZ_t. Hence, if a given value of the labor market gap is below the lower bound $\psi\theta_-$ or above the upper bound $\psi\theta_+$, then even in the Keynesian economy Expectational equilibrium is impossible to exist.

Let us call the lower bound $\psi\theta_-$ the barrier of crisis, and the upper bound $\psi\theta_+$ the barrier of inflationary hysteria. (The reason for such nomenclature will become clear as we proceed.) Let us also call the range of the values of the labor market gap that are bounded by these two barriers the band of labor market equilibrium or simply the equilibrium band. We can state then the following proposition:

Proposition 5–2. *The Keynesian economy is capable of achieving an Expectational equilibrium only if the existing labor market gap $(H_t/L_t - f^*)/f^*$ lies within the equilibrium band $[\psi\theta_-, \psi\theta_+]$. When the labor market gap strays from this band, the Keynesian economy is inevitably thrown out of its Expectational equilibrium.*

In the Wicksellian labor market the equilibrium band would degenerate into a unique point, the origin, whereas in the ultra-Keynesian labor market the equilibrium band would extend over the entire line. The knife-edge property of the former is now made blunt by the inflexibility of money wages, and the neutural character of the latter is bend by the reintroduction of certain flexibility of money wages.

Note in passing that since we shall prove in chapter 6 that the firm never sets the value of lower barrier θ_- to be positive and the value of upper barrier θ_+ to be negative, the barrier of crisis $\psi\theta_-$ is always nonpositive and the barrier of inflationary hysteria $\psi\theta_+$ always nonnegative.

6. *Equilibria and Disequilibria in the Keynesian Economy*

We have to distinguish three rather than two notions of equilibrium in the Keynesian economy.

The definition of Expectational equilibrium of the economy as a whole is the same as the one in the Wicksellian economy, although its nature is, as we shall soon see, markedly different from the latter. We then say that the Keynesian economy is in a state of Keynesian equilibrium if the product market gap $(X_t/Q_t - g^*)/g^*$ is zero *and* the labor market gap $(H_t/L_t - f^*)/f^*$ is equal to the aggregate intended gap ψZ_t. This generalizes the notion of Keynesian equilibrium introduced in chapter 4. The relaxation of the ultra-Keynesian assumption of absolute money wage rigidity has made it necessary to supplement the condition for mutual compatibility in the product market with another one in the labor market. Finally, we say that the Keynesian economy is in a state of Wicksellian equilibrium if the labor market gap $(H_t/L_t - f^*)/f^*$ stays within the equilibrium band $[\psi\theta_-, \psi\theta_+]$. Although not self-evident, this generalizes the Wicksellian equilibrium notion introduced in chapter 3.

It is evident from proposition 5–1′ that the conditions for Keynesian equilibrium are necessary preconditions for the existence of Expectational equilibrium. For if either the product market gap is nonzero or the labor market gap loses its multiple relation to the aggregate subjective disequilibrium, expectations of at least one of the firms (and usually a majority of them) will be inevitably upset by the very aggregate outcome of their own price or wage decisions. Needless to say, Keynesian equilibrium is not necessarily Expectational equilibrium. It is also plain that the condition for Wicksellian equilibrium is a necessary precondition for the existence of Keynesian equilibrium. For if the labor market gap deviates from the equilibrium band, it is impossible for the aggregate intended gap to become equal to the labor market gap. Again, needless to say. Wicksellian equilibrium is not necessarily Keynesian equilibrium.

The introduction of three concepts of equilibrium naturally leads us to distinguish *three* forms of disequilibrium in the Keynesian economy. The first is called Wicksellian disequilibrium. It refers to a set of situations in which the labor market gap is outside the equilibrium band. The second form is called Keynesian disequilibrium. It is a set of situations in which either the product market gap is nonzero or the labor market gap is out of line with ψZ_t but still within the equilibrium band. The third form of disequilibrium is called "secondary disequilibrium." It refers to a set of situations in which even if the economy is in a state of Keynesian equilibrium, some of firms fail to achieve their expectational equilibria.

Since the fulfillment of the conditions of Keynesian equilibrium renders the simultaneous attainment of expectational equilibria by firms a logical possibility, errors of expectations in secondary disequilibrium should be regarded as the very cause of disequilibrium. The cause of secondary disequilibrium is, in other words, purely microscopic. In contrast, in Keynesian or Wicksellian disequilibrium, expectations of at least one firm (and usually a majority of them) are necessarily upset by the very aggregate outcome of their separate and yet mutually interacting price and/or wage decisions. In Keynesian or Wicksellian disequilibrium, therefore, surprises in the individual firm's expectation-formation process are merely an inevitable *result* of an imbalance in macroeconomic conditions, which are beyond the control of the individual firm. The cause of these two forms of disequilibrium can be thus regarded as macroeconomic.

However, even though both Keynesian and Wicksellian disequilibrium are caused by a macroeconomic imbalance, their reactions to it are qualitatively different. It will be shown later that Keynesian disequilibrium has a tendency to correct itself mainly through adjustments of quantity variables, but that Wicksellian disequilibrium has the tendency to drive itself away from the original position of Wicksellian equilibrium.

Figure 5–2 illustrates, albeit too schematically, the hierarchic relationship among three forms of equilibrium and three forms of disequilibrium in our Keynesian economy. The reader is warned, however, that this is, like figure 3–1, an extremely distorted diagram. The set of Expectational equilibria in effect occupies only a negligible subset of the whole set of Keynesian equilibria, which in turn occupies only a negligible subset of the whole set of Wicksellian equilibria, which in turn occupies only a very tiny subset in the whole collection of possible states of the economy.

It is convenient here to classify various phases of Keynesian and Wicksellian disequilibrium according to the sign of the labor market gap. We shall say that Keynesian disequilibrium is in a slump when the labor market gap is negative, and is enjoying a boom when the labor market gap is positive. (To be more taxonomic, we may call a slump with a nonpositive product market gap a pure slump, a slump with a positive product market gap stagflation, a boom with a nonnegative product market gap a pure boom, and a boom with a negative product market gap a deflationary boom.) We shall also say that Wicksellian disequilibrium is in a crisis phase when the labor market gap sinks below the barrier of crisis, and in an inflationary hysteria phase when

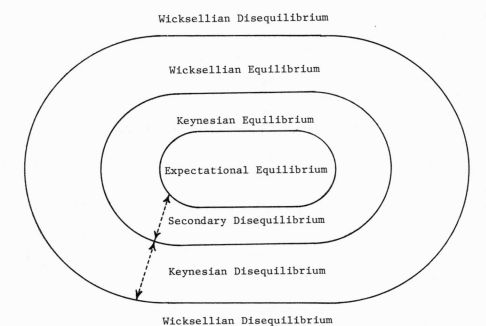

FIGURE 5–2. Hierarchical Relations among Equilibria and Disequilibria in the
Keynesian Economy

the labor market gap floats above the barrier of inflationary hysteria.

The relationship among various phases of Keynesian and Wicksellian
disequilibrium is (again schematically) summarized in figure 5–3.

7. The Keynesian Principle of Effective Demand, Once Again

In chapter 4 we introduced the notions of total demand schedule $X_t = X(N_t, N_{t-1}, \ldots)$ and total supply schedule $Q_t = Q(N_{t-\tau})$, and argued that for the economy to be in Expectational equilibrium, the level of total labor employment $N_{t-\tau}$ or its time path has to be a solution to the following market-clearing condition for output as a whole:

$$(5\text{–}10) \qquad \left(\frac{X_t}{Q_t} - g^*\right)\bigg/ g^* = 0.$$

Otherwise, firms' simultaneous attempts at relative price adjustment would become mutually incompatible and surprises on their part would inevitably be created in the product market. This is the essence of the Keynesian principle of effective demand.

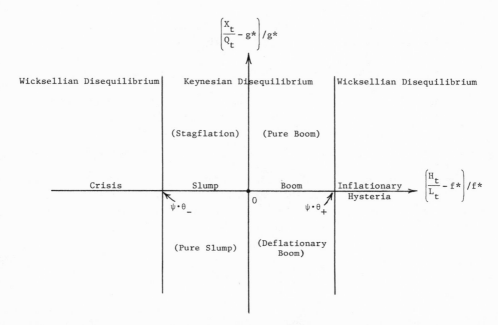

FIGURE 5-3. Various Phases of Keynesian and Wicksellian Disequilibria

Under the assumption of absolute rigidity of money wages, *any* equilibrium level of employment thus "solved" would be consistent with Expectational equilibrium of the economy as a whole. Since firms are by assumption unable to change their money wages, the problem of mutual incompatibility of their simultaneous relative wage adjustment would not arise in the labor market.

Once we drop the ultra-Keynesian assumption and allow certain flexibility in firms' money-wage-adjustment activities, we can no longer ignore the problem of mutual compatibility, even in the labor market, for firms start attempting to adjust their relative wages, albeit sluggishly, to control the position of their subjective disequilibrium. This now compels us to examine whether the level of total labor employment fixed by the Keynesian principle of effective demand is indeed consistent with the condition for mutual compatibility of intentions in the labor market. We thus have to leave Keynes behind and look more closely at the complex structure of the labor market. In particular, we must study how the level of total labor employment is actually determined in the market for it, and then compare that level with the one solved by the principle of effective demand. Since there is a one-to-one correspondence between the level of total labor employment N_t and the aggregate rate of involuntary unemployment $U_t \equiv (L_t - N_t)/N_t$, once the level of total labor supply L_t is given, this will lead us to study the determination of the aggregate rate of involuntary unemployment in the Keynesian labor market.

8. *The Aggregate Unemployment Schedule*

In the Keynesian labor market, some firms have excess labor supplies and leave part of the willing workers involuntarily unemployed; the others have excess labor demands and are unable to fill all their job vacancies. For those firms that have excess labor supplies, the rates of involuntary unemployment are by definition positive, whereas for those that have excess labor demands, they are simply zero. (On the other hand, for the former the rates of unfilled vacancies are zero, whereas for the latter they are positive.) The aggregate rate of involuntary unemployment $U_t \equiv (L_t - N_t)/L_t$ is of course a market-wide aggregate of those individual rates of involuntary unemployment, which is by (3–9) defined as

$$(5\text{--}11) \qquad U_t = \sum_{i=1}^{I} \left[\frac{l_t(i)}{L_t} \right] u_t(i).$$

Now, the individual rate of involuntary unemployment $u_t(i)$ actually realized may overshoot or fall short of its (objective) expected value $E[u_t(i):\delta_t(i)]$ in an uncertain labor market. Viewed macroscopically, however, these individual deviations tend to cancel, and by the strong law of large numbers their aggregate can be approximated by the market-wide average of the *expected* rates of involuntary unemployment as follows:[7]

$$(5\text{--}12) \qquad U_t \triangleq \sum_{i=1}^{I} \left[\frac{l_t(i)}{L_t} \right] E[u_t(i):\delta_t(i)].$$

Hence, the forces determining the aggregate rate of involuntary unemployment can be revealed first by analyzing the forces determining the expected value of each firm's rate of involuntary unemployment, and then by aggregating them across firms.

Such an analysis, whose detail will be given in appendix 5–b, has enabled us to deduce the following approximate equation, which pins down the forces determining the aggregate rate of involuntary unemployment in the Keynesian economy:

$$(5\text{--}13) \qquad U_t \triangleq u^* + u^{***}D_t - \left[u^{**}\left(\frac{H_t}{L_t} - f^* \right) \middle/ f^* - u^{***}\left(\frac{H_t}{L_t} - f^* \right)^2 \middle/ f^{*2} \right],$$

---

7. According to the strong law of large numbers of appendix 3–a, $\Sigma_{i=1}^{I}(l_t(i)/L_t)[u_t(i) - E(u_t(i):\delta_t(i))]$ approaches zero as I goes to infinity, if the variances of $u_t(i) - E(u_t(i):\delta_t(i))$ are uniformly bounded and the average of their covariance terms dwindles at a sufficient speed as I increases.

where u^*, u^{**}, and u^{***} are all positive constants whose values are fixed by the basic structural parameters of the economy; in particular, the first term, u^*, is the normal rate of involuntary unemployment defined by (2–25). The new variable, D_t, in the second term is defined by the following formula:

$$(5\text{–}14) \qquad D_t \equiv \sum_{i=1}^{I} \left[\frac{l_t(i)}{L_t} \right] \left\{ E\left[\frac{h_t(i)}{l_t(i)} : \delta_t(i) \right] - \frac{H_t}{L_t} \right\}^2 \Big/ f^{*2}.$$

We shall call this the cross-section dispersion index in period t, for it measures how dispersively the expected ratios of labor demand to supply are distributed across firms.

Equation (5–13) will be called the aggregate unemployment schedule. It has decomposed the aggregate rate of involuntary unemployment into three more-or-less independent terms.

1. The first term, u^*, is the normal rate of involuntary unemployment, which is positive and constant over time.

2. The second term is proportional to the cross-section dispersion index D_t. It says that, other things being equal, the more dispersively the expected ratios of labor demand to supply are scattered across firms, the higher is the aggregate rate of involuntary unemployment. This relation is illustrated by figure 5–4.

3. The third term is related to the labor market gap $(H_t/L_t - f^*)/f^*$, which represents the overall tightness of the current labor market. Since u^{**} is positive, it says that, other things being equal, an increase in the labor market gap reduces the aggregate rate of involuntary unemployment. Moreover, since u^{***} is also positive, the marginal contribution of the increase in the value of labor market gap to the decline of the aggregate rate of involuntary unemployment becomes less and less as the former increases more and more. [According to (5–13), the effect of the former upon the latter will be reversed when the latter becomes exceedingly large. But this perversity is due solely to our neglect of the third- and higher-order effects in our approximation.] This relation is illustrated in figure 5–5.

Let us explain the economic logic behind the aggregate unemployment schedule. In the Wicksellian economy, in which no costs are involved in wage adjustment, each firm always adjusts money wage to the level that is expected to equate the ratio of labor demand to supply with the subjective-normal ratio f^*. The value of f^* depends upon the asymmetry of costs/benefits between excess demand and excess supply situations, and may be greater or less than unity. But even if f^* is greater than unity, so that the firm does not expect to have an unemployment ex ante, it might end up leaving some willing workers unemployed ex post. For expectations are always liable to disappointment; and the realized supply of labor might exceed the firm's effective demand when the firm has grossly underestimated the number of workers willing to work for it. Therefore, as long as the firm is not free of expectation errors, the chance

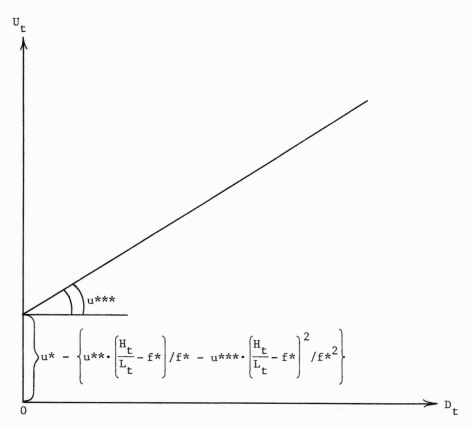

FIGURE 5-4. The Relation between the Aggregate Rate of Involuntary Unemployment and the Cross-Section Dispersion Index

that some workers are involuntarily unemployed always exists, even in the
Wicksellian economy, so that on average the rate of involuntary unemployment can never be reduced to zero. It is this rate that the normal rate of involuntary unemployment u^* represents. Its value thus reflects the "inherent
uncertainty" which the firm quoting a money wage on a take-it-or-leave-it
basis has to swallow in the labor market. (Note, however, that the *actual* rate
of involuntary unemployment often declines below u^*, which represents only
the *average* rate in Expectational equilibrium.)

Even in the Keynesian economy, a part of the rate of involuntary unemployment reflects such inherent uncertainty, and it is this rate which constitutes the first term u^* in the aggregate unemployment schedule (5–13). The
value of this normal rate of involuntary unemployment is fixed solely by the
structural parameters of the economy and is totally invariant to any short-
run changes in market conditions.

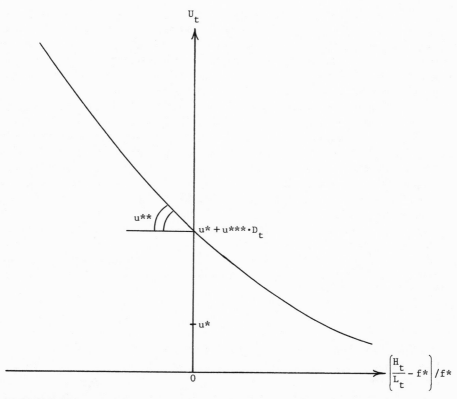

FIGURE 5–5. The Relation between the Aggregate Rate of Involuntary Unemployment and the Value of the Labor Market Gap

In the Keynesian economy, however, owing to the existence of money-wage-adjustment costs, the firm no longer attempts to adapt its money wage to every anticipated change in market conditions. In consequence, the firm does not necessarily cut the money wage and attempt to restore subjective-normal ratio f^*, even if the ratio of labor demand to supply is expected to be lower than f^*, and the firm does not necessarily raise the money wage even if this ratio is expected to be higher than f^*. In the Keynesian economy, therefore, part of involuntary unemployment is not the incidental consequence of the inherent uncertainty that the firm cannot avoid, but is an intended outcome of the firm's conscious (nonetheless frustrating) money-wage-adjustment activity under the inflexibility of money wage.

Now there are many firms in the Keynesian labor market, each independently adjusting its money wage from period to period. Consequently, in every period there are some firms that are expected to have subnormal ratios of labor demand to supply and some firms that are expected to have supernormal ratios of labor demand to supply. It is clear that the overall balance between supernormal and subnormal ratios of labor demand to supply is determined by the existing size of the labor market gap $(H_t/L_t - f^*)/f^*$. Other things being equal, the larger the value of the labor market gap, the fewer firms expected to have subnormal ratios of labor demand to supply, and hence the lower the aggregate rate of involuntary unemployment. The third term in the aggregate unemployment schedule (5–13) captures this overall tightness effect.

This does not, however, exhaust the determining forces of the aggregate involuntary unemployment rate. We still have to explain the second term of (5–13). To see the import of this term, it is useful to recall the definition (3–10) of aggregate rate of unfilled vacancies V_t. Since we know from (1–27) that the difference between the rate of unfilled vacancies and the rate of involuntary unemployment of an individual firm is identically equal to the ratio of labor demand to supply minus 1 [that is, $v_t(i) - u_t(i) \equiv h_t(i)/l_t(i) - 1$], the difference between the aggregate rate of unfilled vacancies and the aggregate rate of involuntary unemployment must also be identically equal to the aggregate ratio of labor demand to supply *minus* 1; that is, $V_t - U_t \equiv (H_t/L_t - 1)$. If we note another (obvious) identity, $v^* - u^* \equiv f^* - 1$, given by (1–30), we can rewrite the foregoing identity in the following slightly more illuminating manner:

$$(5\text{–}15) \qquad (V_t - v^*) - (U_t - u^*) \equiv \frac{H_t}{L_t} - f^*.$$

This identity amounts to saying that the labor market gap $(H_t/L_t - f^*)/f^*$ represents merely the relative balance between the aggregate rate of involuntary unemployment in excess of its normal rate $U_t - u^*$ and the aggregate rate of unfilled vacancies in excess of its normal rate $V_t - v^*$. A given value of labor market gap is consistent with a wide range of the values of U_t and V_t as long as they maintain identity (5–15). To determine both of them simultaneously, we therefore have to look not only at the overall balance but also at the "dispersion" of disequilibria across firms. For if each excess supply firm has a larger excess supply and at the same time each excess demand firm has an equally larger excess demand, both aggregate involuntary unemployment and aggregate unfilled vacancies tend to increase, even though the overall balance of disequilibria remains the same. Thus, given the overall balance represented by the labor market gap, the more dispersively the demand/supply ratios are distributed across firms, the larger the values of both U_t and V_t. D_t in the second term of the aggregate involuntary unemployment schedule (5–13) represents nothing but this dispersion effect.

Then, what determines D_t? We shall be concerned in part III with identifying the factors that in the long run govern the magnitude of the cross-section dispersion index D_t. It will be demonstrated there that it is determined not only by those real market characteristics by which the normal rate of involuntary unemployment is determined, but also by such factors as the costs of money wage adjustment, the measure of the volatility of the labor market, and most important, the long-run rate of change in the general money wage level. It is reasonable to expect that the cross-section dispersion D_t moves rather slowly and that its value is determined more or less by the same sort of factors even in the short run. The sum of the first and second terms in relation (5–15) thus corresponds to the long-run determinants of the aggregate rate of involuntary unemployment.

The short-run determinant is therefore represented exclusively by the third term, which is negatively related to the labor market gap $(H_t/L_t - f^*)/f^*$. When the labor market is slack in the sense that the gap in it is negative, the aggregate rate of involuntary unemployment tends to exceed the long-run level (i.e., the sum of the first and third terms), and when the labor market is tight in the sense that the gap in it is positive, the aggregate rate of involuntary unemployment tends to fall short of the long-run level. It is only when the labor market gap happens to be zero that the aggregate rate of involuntary unemployment is pegged by its long-run determinants.

Before leaving this section, let us note that our discussion of the determination of the aggregate rate of unemployment can be recast in terms of the well-known unemployment-vacancies map of Dow and Dicks-Mireaux (1959), adopted in figure 5–6. In this figure, the aggregate rate of involuntary unemployment U is measured on the horizontal axis and the aggregate rate of unfilled vacancies V on the vertical axis. Each of the 45° lines represents the positive relation between U and V for a given value of labor market gap $(H/L - f^*)/f^*$. It depicts the identity (5–15): $(V - v^*) - (U - u^*) \equiv H/L - f^*$. The line passing through the point (u^*, v^*) and cutting the V axis at $v^* \equiv u^* + f^* - 1$ therefore corresponds to the situation of zero labor market gap. An increase (decrease) in the value of labor market gap then shifts this positive relation between U and V to the northwest (to the southeast). On the other hand, each of the concave curves represents the inverse relation between U and V, for a given value of the cross-section dispersion index D. It depicts the equation $U - u^* + (u^{**}/f^*)[(V - v^*) - (U - u^*)] - (u^{***}/f^{*2})[(V - v^*) - (U - u^*)]^2 \triangle u^{***}D$, which can be obtained by substituting (5–15) into (5–13) and eliminating $(H/L - f^*)/f^*$. The curve passing through the point (u^*, v^*) therefore corresponds to the situation in which there is *no* dispersion of expected ratios of labor demand to supply across firms. It, in other words, represents the relation between U and V in the Wicksellian economy. Then, an increase in the cross-section dispersion shifts this inverse relation in the northeast direction, which worsens the trade-off between U and V. In sum, figure 5–6 says that when the value of the cross-section dispersion is given, an increase in the value of labor market gap moves V upward and U downward *along* the corresponding concave curve. When the value of labor market gap is fixed, an increase in the cross-section dispersion raises both U and V by the same magnitude along the corresponding 45° line.

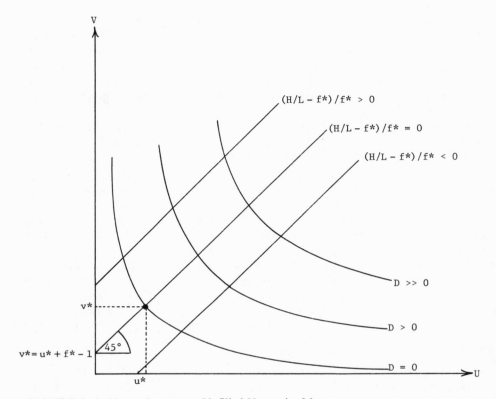

FIGURE 5–6. Unemployment—Unfilled Vacancies Map

9. *The Modified Keynesian Principle of Effective Demand*

We have thus seen that the aggregate rate of involuntary unemployment U_t is determined in the short run by the value of the labor market gap $(H_t/L_t - f^*)/f^*$. Now, proposition 5–2 asserts that for all firms to be in expectational equilibrium, it is necessary that the labor market gap be within the equilibrium band $[\psi\theta_-,$ $\psi\theta_+]$. Consequently, there must also exist both an upper and a lower bound to the aggregate rate of involuntary unemployment which is consistent with Expectational equilibrium. In view of the aggregate unemployment schedule (5–13), this equilibrium band of the aggregate rate of involuntary unemployment is given by the following inequality:

$$(5–16) \qquad u^* + u^{***}D_t - (u^{**}\psi\theta_- - u^{***}\psi^2\theta_-^2)$$

V/

$$U_t \equiv \frac{L_t - N_t}{L_t}$$

$$\vee\!/$$

$$u^* + u^{***}D_t - (u^{**}\psi\theta_+ - u^{***}\psi^2\theta_+^2)$$

When for some reason unemployment rate strays away from the foregoing equilibrium band, the economy is inevitably thrown out of Expectational equilibrium.

We can now state a qualified version of the principle of effective demand in our Keynesian economy:

Proposition 5–3. *In a state of Expectational equilibrium, the total labor employment N_t is fixed at whatever level is required to solve the following equilibrium condition between total demand and supply schedule:*

$$\left(\frac{X_{t+\tau}}{Q_{t+\tau}} - g^*\right)\Big/g^* = 0$$

as long as the associated value of aggregate rate of involuntary unemployment $U_t \equiv (L_t - N_t)/N_t$ remains within the equilibrium band given by (5–16). If, however, the associated aggregate rate of involuntary unemployment deviates from this equilibrium band, the economy will be immediately displaced from Expectational equilibrium.

Although somewhat qualified, our new Keynesian principle of effective demand is still an equilibrium-theoretic principle. As such, we can apply the method of comparative statics and compare different equilibrium levels of total employment and output, corresponding to different sets of exogenous factors, such as the schedule of the marginal efficiency of investment, the propensity to consume, the liquidity preference schedule, the central bank's monetary policy, and the government's tax and expenditure policies. All these are in any standard textbook of macroeconomics.

Like all equilibrium analyses in economics, however, the Keynesian principle of effective demand would remain a mere exercise in mental gymnastics unless its use is justified by a stability analysis which shows the existence of a tendency toward it. Like all equilibrium theories in economics, the principle of effective demand in itself is incapable of describing the causal process through which the Keynesian economy will gradually approach or diverge from an equilibrium position. The method of comparative statics, which compares two equilibria with two different sets of exogenous variables, cannot serve a substitute for the dynamic analysis of a transition process from one position to another.

We now embark upon such a causal analysis.

10. *Secondary Disequilibrium*

To begin, let us briefly study secondary disequilibrium. It is a Keynesian equilibrium state in which, although there remains no endogenous force that upsets firms' expectation-formation processes, some firms are, nonetheless, out of expectational equilibrium.

Now, in a state of secondary disequilibrium, there is no necessity for the development of cumulative price inflation or deflation in the product market, and all the necessary adjustments therein are effected through changes in the system of relative prices of products. As we saw in section 12 of chapter 3, as long as most products are gross substitutes in the eyes of spenders, firms' simultaneous error-learning processes and the induced adjustments of their relative prices reinforce each other and smoothly move the product market toward Expectational equilibrium. The restoration of a new order is, unless disrupted by new exogenous disturbances, merely a question of time.

In the Keynesian labor market, however, the rigidity of money wages emasculates the power of the Invisible Hand in guiding and strengthening individual firms' error-learning activities. The restoration of Expectational equilibrium in the labor market therefore has to rely primarily upon trial-and-error calculations of individual firms. It is an act of faith to believe that individual firms' error-learning processes will, without any help from outside, instantaneously move the labor market toward equilibrium. But as long as the conditions for Keynesian equilibrium are retained, there is also little reason to expect individual firms' expectation-formation activities to be grossly biased one way or the other over a long period. In secondary disequilibrium, there is no endogenous force that inevitably misguides their expectation-formation processes. Thus, if the market environment remains transquil, we may expect each individual firm to approach its expectational equilibrium by intermittently accommodating its subjective model of the economy to the demand of reality over a long period of time.

On balance, it is likely that even in a sticky-wage Keynesian economy, the secondary disequilibrium has a tendency to correct itself in the long run. But its self-correcting tendency is expected to be weaker than that of a Wicksellian economy.

Next, discuss a more serious part of our Keynesian dynamics.

11. *Keynesian Disequilibrium*

Imagine a Keynesian economy that has been in a state of Keynesian equilibrium for a long time. The product market gap has been continuously filled up, and the labor market gap has continuously sustained its equality with the aggregate intended gap.

Suppose now that in period zero, the volume of total product demand suddenly declines, and then resumes the past trend growth rate (but not the past trend level) from the next period on. Whatever the cause of this decline, it will certainly create a negative gap in the product market, at least for a couple of periods afterward:

$$(5-17) \qquad \left(\frac{X_t}{Q_t} - g^*\right)\bigg/ g^* < 0.$$

The economy has now found itself in a state of Keynesian disequilibrium.

In section 3 of chapter 4, we elucidated a mechanism that explains the way in which, under the assumption of absolute rigidity of money wages, a negative product market gap eliminates itself primarily through the adjustment of quantity variables. For convenience in the following discussion, let us first recapitulate the argument given there.

When there emerges a negative gap in the product market, a majority of firms inevitably experience subnormal demands for their products. Sooner or later, they will revise downward their expectations of the state of product demand and lower their prices accordingly. This will set off a cumulative price deflation in the product market. If, furthermore, the firms expect the sluggish condition in the product market to continue in the future, they will curtail their effective demands for labor so as to contract the output supply in the future. This will tend to decrease employment in the labor market and after τ periods decrease total supply in the product market as well. As a result, it will tend to eliminate the negative product market gap. Moreover, even if the induced decline in total product supply had failed to close the negative product market gap completely, the cumulative price deflation caused by the remaining negative gap would back up its stabilizing tendency. For the ongoing decline of price will probably make firms more pessimistic about the state of product demand in the future and further discourage their effective demands for labor. Such an adjustment process will continue until the gap in the product market is completely closed.

In our entire discussion of the stability of Keynesian equilibrium in chapter 4, we did not have to look more closely at the development of disequilibrium in the labor market. The labor market gap or the aggregate rate of involuntary unemployment expands or contracts as firms revise their expectation of the state of product demand in the future and adjust their effective demand for labor accordingly. But those fluctuations are only a result of the development of disequilibria in the product market. Disequilibrium conditions in the labor market do not themselves have direct causal effects, except for the possible roundabout repercussions that pass through the product market. But once we have abandoned the assumption of absolute rigidity and have allowed a certain degree of flexibility in money wages, we can no longer assign a passive role to disequilibria in the labor market. Indeed, we now have to study in detail how disequilibria in the labor market react to themselves.

In our Keynesian economy, the extent of macroscopic imbalance in the labor market is represented by the divergence between the existing labor market gap $(H_t/L_t - f^*)/f^*$ and the aggregate intended gap ψZ_t. We already noted that the initial decline of total product demand will sooner or later induce firms to revise downward their expectations of the future state of product demand and then discourage their effective demands for labor. This will, of course, work to decrease the value of labor market gap. But it is not hard to see that such a pessimistic revision of firms' expectations will, at the same time, work to decrease the value of the aggregate intended gap. It is therefore necessary to gauge the relative decline of these two aggregate variables in order to ascertain the impact of the decline of total product demand on the state of disequilibrium in the labor market.

Suppose, for the sake of argument, that money wages are absolutely rigid downward. Then it is not difficult to see that firms' pessimistic revisions of their expectations of the future product demand reduce both the labor market gap and the aggregate intended gap equally. In fact, other things being equal, a one percentage point decline in $\hat{E}[a_{t+\tau}(i):\delta_t(i)]$ reduces both of them by $100/[\eta - \gamma(\eta - 1)]$ percentage point.[8] In this case, the overall balance in the labor market remains unperturbed in spite of the decline of total product demand. In general, however, money wages have some flexibility even downward. A decline in expectations of the future product demand is thus likely to force a certain fraction of firms to cut, willy-nilly, their money wages. Such reductions of actual money wages then tend to offset, to a certain extent, the original decline of the labor market gap and the aggregate intended gap. Indeed, they affect differently the two aggregate variables. Other things being equal, whereas a one percentage point decline of the actual money wage stimulates the labor market gap by $100\eta/[\eta - \gamma(\eta - 1)]$ percent, it raises the aggregate intended gap by the larger $100\psi \equiv 100\{\varepsilon + \eta/[\eta - \gamma(\eta - 1)]\}$ percent. (Again see footnote 8.) Thus, if we take account of these compensating effects, we can maintain that as long as money wages are not absolutely rigid downward, the pessimistic revision of the expectations of the future product demand tends to reduce the labor market gap more than the aggregate intended gap, thereby giving rise to an inequality

---

8. Recall the definition of $h_t(i)$ given by (1–16):

$$h_t(i) = \left[\frac{\gamma(\eta - 1)\phi\chi}{\eta} j_t(i)^{(\eta - 1)} w_t(i)^{-\eta} \frac{\hat{E}(a_{t+\tau}(i):\delta_t(i))}{g^*}\right]^{1/[\eta - \gamma(\eta - 1)]}$$

and the definition of $w_t^*(i)$ given by (1–23):

$$w_t^*(i) = \left\{\frac{\gamma(\eta - 1)\phi\chi}{\eta} j_t(i)^{(\eta - 1)} \left[\frac{\hat{E}(a_{t+\tau}(i):\delta_t(i))}{g^*}\right]\right.$$
$$\left. \times \left[\frac{\hat{E}(b_t(i):\delta_t(i))}{f^*}\right]^{\eta - \gamma(\eta - 1)}\right\}^{1/[\eta + \varepsilon\eta(1 - \gamma) + \varepsilon\gamma]} .$$

(5–18) $$\left(\frac{H_t}{L_t} - f^*\right)\bigg/f^* < \psi Z_t.$$

As long as the declined labor market gap remains above the barrier of crisis $\psi\theta_-$, our Keynesian economy now finds itself in the (pure) slump phase of Keynesian disequilibrium.

12. The Stability of Keynesian Equilibrium

Let us examine more closely the adjustment process in the labor market. Here, there is a negative difference between the labor market gap and the aggregate intended gap, as represented by (5–18). Such a negative difference tends to be widened if a cumulative price deflation is being developed in the product market. For when the general price level is declining or slowing down unexpectedly, firms revise downward their expectations of the general price level and hence those of the state of product demand in the future. Then, for the same reason as we deduced with regard to inequality (5–18), we can say that this will reduce the labor market gap more than the aggregate intended gap. Now, our generalized fundamental equation of the labor market (5–8) (or proposition 5–1) maintains that, when the labor market gap falls short of the aggregate intended gap, at least one firm, and usually a majority of them, will inevitably overestimate the tightness of labor supply. Having discerned this, they will start revising their expectations downward. Since the short-run optimal wage $w_t^*(i)$ is (by the formula in footnote 8) an increasing function of the expectation of the tightness of labor supply, they will then reduce their short-run optimal wages.

Suppose, again for the sake of argument, that money wages are absolutely rigid downward. Then a decline of $w_t^*(i)$ will not reduce the actual money wage $w_t(i)$; it will, instead, reduce the subjective disequilibrium $z_t(i) \equiv \ln w_t^*(i) - \ln w_t(i)$, by the same proportion. As a result, the aggregate subjective disequilibrium Z_t and thereby its multiple ψZ_t will decline as well. On the other hand, as long as $w_t(i)$ has refused to decline, the decline of the expectation of the tightness of labor supply will itself have no impact on the firm's effective labor demand and hence upon the value of labor market $(H_t/L_t - f^*)/f^*$. Therefore, under the supposition of absolute downward rigidity of money wages, any existing Keynesian disequilibrium, represented by the inequality (5–18), will disappear quickly.

Even in the Keynesian economy, however, there may exist some firms that take trouble to cut money wages. They will raise their subjective disequilibrium $z_t(i)$ to the level of return point θ_0. Consequently, the decline of ψZ_t will be checked in proportion to the number of wage-cutting firms. The self-correcting tendency of Keynesian disequilibrium in the labor makret, noted above, will then be mitigated. Of course, a reduction of actual money wages

will relieve firms of the burden of wage cost and stimulate their effective demands for labor. It will certainly raise the value of the labor makret gap or at
least slow its declining tendency effected by the ongoing cumulative price
deflation. But this compensatory effect turns out to be a less effective way of
eliminating Keynesian disequilibrium in the labor market than the effect on
it of the nonreduction of money wages. For whereas the decline of money wage
by 1 percent tends to raise the effective labor demand and thereby the value
of labor market gap by $100\eta/[\eta - \gamma(\eta - 1)]$ percent, resistance to it directly
lowers the aggregate intended gap by 100ψ percent (see footnote 8). Of course,
$\psi \equiv \varepsilon + \eta/[\eta - \gamma(\eta - 1)]$ is greater than $\eta/[\eta - \gamma(\eta - 1)]$.

Furthermore, the stimulating effect of the decline of actual money wages
upon effective labor demands will counterbalance the depressing effect of the
cumulative price inflation and will work to weaken the self-correcting tendency
of Keynesian disequilibrium in the product market. Thus, the weaker the
downward rigidity of money wages, the weaker the self-correcting tendency of
Keynesian disequilibrium in *both* labor and product markets. Hence, we have:

> Proposition 5–4. *Keynesian disequilibrium in both product and labor
> markets has an automatic tendency to eliminate itself and restore the posi-
> tion of Keynesian equilibrium. This self-correcting tendency of Keynesian
> disequilibrium is, however, weakened as money wages become less rigid.*

It should be borne in mind that the stability of the position of Keynesian
equilibrium, established above, is totally independent of the existence of the
Keynes and/or Pigou effects, upon which the stability of Wicksellian equilibrium had to rely in the Wicksellian economy. This essential characteristic of
the Keynesian economy results directly from the very inflexibility of money
wages.

It is now possible to maintain that in the Keynesian economy, Expectational equilibrium has a gravitational force that can reach as far as the boundary
of the domain of Wicksellian equilibrium, which encompasses not only Keynesian equilibria (hence secondary disequilibria) but also Keynesian disequilibria. As long as this gravitational force is at work, the Keynesian principle
of effective demand has a secure ground for workability.

13. *The Downward Multiplier Process during a Slump*

So far, our discussion of the slump phase of Keynesian disequilibrium has
supposed implicitly that the volume of total product demand is given exogenously. This supposition is of course untenable, because as argued in sections
11 and 12, the initial decline of the volume of total product demand and the
induced cumulative price deflation will reduce the level of total labor employment through their adversary effect on effective demands for labor. This will
reduce the volume of total earned income in the hands of spenders. We all

know from standard macroeconomics textbook that such a reduction of total income will then reduce—primarily through the aggregate consumption schedule of consumers and partly through the aggregate investment schedule of producers—the scale of total product demand in the subsequent periods. A new negative product market gap and hence a new Keynesian disequilibrium will then emerge in the economy. This will induce another decrease in total labor employment, in the same manner as its initial induced decrease, and will prepare the ground for a further induced decline of total labor employment. A Kahn–Keynes multiplier process will thus be triggered, and the decline in total product demand and the decline in total labor employment will reinforce each other and aggravate the downturn of business activity. This downward multiplier process represents the major feature of the slump phase of Keynesian disequilibrium.

To be complete, we must point out various repercussions that occur during the slump. The following are likely to be the most important.

1. The decline in total income tends to reduce the transactions demand for cash balance and release part of money stock previously tied up for that purpose for the use of the precautionary and speculative motives. Other things being equal, this will lower the rates of interest in financial markets and may stimulate the demand for investment goods. This effect tends to weaken the downward multiplier process.

2. If the income tax schedule is progressive, the decline in total income tends to reduce the average rate of income tax. This may also weaken the downward multiplier process.

3. As we saw in previous sections, the general price level tends to diminish more than the general money wage level during the course of the slump. This has an effect of redistributing real income from non-wage earners to wage earners. Since the marginal propensity to consume out of wage incomes seems to be higher than the marginal propensity to consume out of nonwage incomes, this effect is likely to weaken the downward multiplier process.

As long as the magnitude of the induced decline of total product demand is smaller than the magnitude of the originating decline, that is, as long as the marginal propensity to spend is less than unity, the downward multiplier process will gradually slow down and eventually disappear. As long as the associated labor market gap remains within the equilibrium band, the position of Keynesian disequilibrium thus reached will be likely to restore the conditions for Keynesian equilibrium in the course of time, but with a much larger negative labor market gap than in the old equilibrium.

14. *Crisis!*

Suppose now that the initial decline of total product demand was so massive, or that the later stage decline in total product demand during the downward

multiplier process was so large, that the induced decline in total labor demand
has sunk the value of labor market gap well below the barrier of crisis,

$$(5-19) \qquad\qquad \left(\frac{H_t}{L_t} - f^*\right)\Big/f^* < \psi\theta_-.$$

Our Keynesian economy has now entered the crisis phase of Wicksellian disequilibrium.

As long as the labor market gap is below the barrier of crisis, Proposition
5–2 tells us that at least one firm, and usually most, now becomes incapable
of achieving their expectational equilibrium with respect to the tightness of
labor supply, no matter what value the aggregate intended gap takes. In consequence, at the end of the period, most firms learn, to their disappointment,
that they have overestimated the tightness of labor supply. Sooner or later,
they will revise their expectations downward and then adjust the values of
their short-run optimal wages downward as well. It is then likely that some of
the firms will find the money wage they quoted in the preceding period too
low [in the sense that $\ln w_t^*(i) - \ln w_{t-1}(i) = z_{t-1}(i) + \Delta \ln w_{t-1}^*(i) < \theta_-$].
Those firms will, of course, cut their money wage so as to return the position
of their subjective disequilibrium to θ_0. This will probably increase the aggregate subjective disequilibrium Z_t in the next period.

But no matter what happens to the value of aggregate subjective disequilibrium, such simultaneous cuts in money wages cannot themselves correct
their own overestimation of the tightness of labor supply. For proposition
5–2 keeps telling us that as long as the labor market gap remains below the
barrier of crisis, firms will again learn their overestimation of the tightness
of labor supply in the next period. They will then revise their expectations
downward and once again reduce their short-run optimal wages. This will, of
course, lead to another round of simultaneous money wage cuts. But, as before,
as long as the value of the labor market gap is below the barrier of crisis, most
firms will inevitably discover that they have once again overestimated the
tightness of labor supply. Further downward revisions of the expectation of
the state of labor supply and another wave of wage cuts will follow. Our Keynesian economy will plunge deeply into a crisis.

Summarizing, we have:

Proposition 5–5. *As long as the gap in the labor market stays below the
barrier of crisis, the crisis of the Keynesian economy, in which the level of
general money wage declines massively and cumulatively, will continue
indefinitely.*

Let us now drop the tentative supposition that the value of the labor
market gap is kept below the barrier of crisis. We then have to examine the
influence of the cumulative wage deflation on the level of total labor demand
and hence on the value of labor market gap. Evidently, other things being

equal, a decline of money wages will lighten the burden of wage cost and encourage firms to expand their effective demands for labor. This will tend to raise total labor demand and hence the value of labor market gap. If this stimulating effect is sufficiently strong, the labor market gap may even float above the barrier of crisis, and brake the development of cumulative wage deflation process. This, however, is likely to be a temporary pause in the development of the crisis. For an increase in total labor demand will push up the scale of labor employment and after one production period has elasped, will raise the total supply in the product market. (Or, if the declining tendency of total product supply is strong, its pace will be somewhat retarded.) The gap in the product market will turn negative and a cumulative price deflation will be set off. Or, if the product market gap is already negative, it will widen further, and the ongoing cumulative price deflation will be accentuated. A decline of the general price level is, if it is expected to continue in the future, detrimental to firms' effective demand for labor. At the same time, a slow-down in the cumulative wage deflation, affected by the shrinkage of the negative labor market gap, also works to discourage the effective demand for labor. As a result, the labor market gap will again start to decline and will soon find itself returning to a position below the barrier of crisis. The cumulative wage deflation will resume its pace from then on. Thus, once the labor market gap has been trapped in a position below the barrier of crisis, its upward motion will be constantly checked by the adjustment of the rate of price deflation relative to that of wage deflation. Thus, removal of the tentative supposition that labor market gap remains below the barrier of crisis will not change our story in any essential manner.

It should be noted that the barrier of crisis does not necessarily form a sharp line between crisis and slump. When the gap in the labor market is negative but small, the probability that a slump will turn into a crisis is also small. But as the labor market gap declines and approaches the barrier, this probability will gradually increase; and when the labor market gap sinks below the barrier of crisis, this probability approaches unity.

15. *The Money Wage Problem, Again*

Although movement in a crisis situation is the reverse of that in the process of cumulative inflation, the two are qualitatively analogous. Thus, the question of whether the Keynesian economy is capable of rebounding from the crisis phase of Wicksellian disequilibrium without outside helps can be analyzed in the same way as was the stability problem in the Wicksellian economy. We can therefore argue that the stability of the Keynesian economy in the crisis phase is in the end determined by whether massive and cumulative money wage reductions and accompanying cumulative price reductions are capable of engineering enough stimulus to the scale of total product demand, raising the level of total labor demand and then pushing up the labor market gap above the barrier of crisis. This is again the money wage problem discussed in section 20 of chapter 3. In the first place, a fall in wages and prices will increase the real value of cash balances and may directly stimulate expenditures by consumers who feel richer because of this. This was called the Pigou effect. Second, in order for asset holders to be induced to hold the same level of cash balances, which now have, however, a higher *real* value, the rate of interest—the opportunity cost of shifting one's wealth from nonliquid to liquid form—must decline, unless the economy has already fallen to the liquidity trap. This will have a tendency to encourage firms to finance more of their investment in financial markets and stimulate their demands for investment goods. This mechanism was called the Keynes effect. Obviously, both the Pigou effect and the Keynes effect will work to raise the total product demand and help the economy from rebounding from the crisis situation. If, however, the supply of bank credit (inside money) responds, through the credit multiplier process, in positive comformity to the demands of business activity, these two effects will be, at least partly, paralyzed. Indeed, in the extreme case of a pure credit economy that does not use cash in transactions, their stabilizing power will become completely ineffectual. We also have to note the impact of a fall in wages and prices on the real value of private debt, which works favorably to the creditors but unfavorably to the debtors. Since in a modern capitalist economy, creditors consist largely of banks and financial institutions which appear to have a small propensity to spend, whereas the largest fraction of debtors consists of business firms whose propensity to spend is nearly unity, the net effect will probably be detrimental to the level of total demand. This negative spending effect of the redistribution of the real value of private debts will thus have a tendency to counteract the stabilizing Pigou effect. Furthermore, if the fall of wages and prices goes far and increases the real burden of the debtors to the point of insolvency, quite a large amount of liquidity will be wiped out in the financial markets. This negative impact upon liquidity will probably not be offset by a possible increase in demands for nonliquid assets by creditors, whose real wealth has increased at the expense of debtors. This mechanism, called the debt-deflation process by Irving Fisher, will work to counterbalance the stabilizing Keynes effect. Finally, once it is widely believed that the ongoing fall in wages and prices will continue in the future, people will start postponing their current spending plans. Business firms will reduce their purchases of investment goods and households will curtail their current spending on consumption goods. This price-expectation effect will, of course, decrease the level of current total product demand and work as a destabilizer of the monetary economy.

All the effects cited above are not peculiar to the Keynesian economy; they are expected to work in both the Wicksellian and Keynesian economies. The possible effect of wage and price reductions on the cost of a wage cut is, however, peculiar to the Keynesian economy. If workers believe that the ongoing crisis will be short-lived, it is likely that they strengthen their resistance to employers' attempts to cut wages and hence raise the cost of wage cuts to employers. This has the effect of checking further reductions in money wages and works favorably toward stabilizing the system. If, on the other hand, workers begin to believe that the crisis will persist, then the consequent decline in their morale may weaken their resistance and invite further wage reductions. This is, of course, disadvantageous to stability.

Orthodox economists would recommend a reduction in money wages as a way to overcome the crisis on the ground that it would reduce real wages and thus stimulate firms' effective demands for labor. However, by the same reason as that used at the end of section 14, the reduction of money wages in itself has no lasting tendency to stimulate the effective demand for labor, except for its direct influence on the scale of total product demand. Suppose, for the sake of argument, that a massive reduction of money wages has at least temporarily been accompanied by lower real wages and has thus succeeded in increasing the total demand for labor. Then, total labor employment is likely to increase, which will result in an increase in the total product supply τ periods later. If there has already been a negative gap in the product market, it will be widened further and the ongoing cumulative price deflation process will be intensified. If there has been no negative gap before, a negative product market gap will be created and a cumulative price deflation process will be triggered. Real wages will then begin to bounce back, and the initial gain in the amount of total effective demand for labor will soon be lost. In the entire course of events during the crisis, real wages may fluctuate up and down, but the net effect is only to redistribute the fundamental disequilibrium between two markets; it has little direct impact upon the fundamental disequilibrium itself.

The foregoing discussion by no means exhausts all the possible repercussions of wage reductions, but it seems to cover the most important ones. Its clear implication is that there exists no a priori reason to believe in the existence of an automatic self-adjusting mechanism capable of pulling the Keynesian economy out of its crisis phase without outside help. Although there are forces working favorably toward stabilizing the system, there are other forces working adversely. We simply do not know a priori which forces are relatively stronger. In order to determine which forces are actually stronger, we have to analyze the causal process in the crisis phase step by step, without prejudgment of its final outcome.

16. *The Inflexibility of Money Wages and the Stability of a Monetary Economy*

Neoclassical economics is founded on the belief that a market economy has under the perfect flexibility of wages and prices a built-in self-correcting mechanism in which a deviation from equilibrium brings about forces that tend to eliminate it. Hence, when there is a maladjustment, the inflexibility of wages and prices and its supposed causes—trade unions, the minimum wage law, unemployment insurance, price support schemes—are held responsible.

However, our Wicksellian theory of economic disequilibrium developed in part I demonstrated the untenability of such belief. In an economy where prices and wages are completely flexible at the beginning of each period, most firms' expectations are inevitably upset by the aggregate consequences of their own price and wage decisions unless gaps in both product and labor markets happen to be zero. It was then shown that the position of (Wicksellian) equilibrium possesses a character completely different from that of neoclassical equilibrium: a deviation from equilibrium starts a cumulative inflation or deflation that would continue indefinitely as long as the cause that gave rise to it continued to exist. And the stability depends upon special circumstances which determine the relative balance between stabilizing and destabilizing forces, which continuously breed themselves and incessantly counteract with each other during the whole course of the cumulative process. The equilibrium may be unstable, or even if it is stable, its stable tendency may be too weak to rely upon.

On the other hand, our synthesis of Wicksellian approach and Keynesian theory in this chapter has shown that the inflexibility of money wages widens the range of values of the labor market gap that are consistent with the conditions for Expectational equilibrium; from the knife-edge "zero" position, it now encompasses a wide band. As long as the labor market gap remains within this equilibrium band, the Keynesian economy is capable of attaining Expectational equilibrium; it is only when the labor market gap sinks below the barrier of crisis or jumps over the barrier of inflationary hysteria that a cumulative wage deflation or inflation process will start its motion. Moreover, if money wages are relatively rigid downward, a cumulative wage deflation process or crisis is a possibility, but its occurrence is very unlikely.

Therefore, contrary to the position of neoclassical economics, we can claim that it is the inflexibility of money wages rather than their flexibility that is stabilizing the monetary economy. An attempt to fluidize money wages would inject great instability into the monetary economy. The more flexible money wages are, the greater the danger that the economy will be thrown into a crisis or into inflationary hysteria by a sudden change in the economic and noneconomic environment.

In *The General Theory*, Keynes wrote:

> If...money wages were to fall without limit wherever there was a tendency for less than full employment...., there would be no resting place below full employment until either the rate of interest was incapable of falling further or wages were zero. In fact, we must have *some* factor, the value of which in terms of money is, if not fixed, at least sticky, to give us any stability of values in a monetary system. [1936, pp. 303, 304]

Although form a different perspective, we have reached exactly the same conclusion.

17. Movements of Prices and Wages during the Great Depression

Let us trace the movements of prices and wages during the entire course of a business downturn.

1. The economy has been in a state of Expectational equilibrium until it is suddenly disturbed by a decline of total product demand.
2. A negative product market gap is opened up.
3. Prices will fall cumulatively.
4. Concurrently with the price deflation, pessimistic revisions of the expected sales revenue in the future will curtail total labor demand.
5. The labor market gap will turn negative.
6. But as long as the value of this gap remains within the equilibrium band, money wages are unlikely to decline as much as product prices.
7. The resulting increase in aggregate real wages will further reduce total labor demand.
8. Total labor employment will decline *pari passu*.
9. This will reduce the scale of total product supply in the product market.
10. The negative product market gap will shrink.
11. Cumulative price deflation will slow down.
12. Concurrently, the decline of total labor employment and total product supply, noted in stages 8 and 9, will reduce spenders' disposable incomes and discourage their demands for products.
13. Stages 1 to 9 will be repeated by this induced decline in total product demand.
14. A downward multiplier process will be set forth.
15. At some point in the course of this business downturn, the gradual decline of total labor demand will depress the value of the labor market gap below the barrier of crisis—the beginning of a crisis!
16. Money wages will start declining massively and cumulatively.
17. The aggregate real wage rate will start slipping.
18. The declining tendency of total labor demand will be checked.
19. The declining tendency of total labor employment and total product supply will also be checked.
20. The negative product market gap will again widen.
21. Cumulative price deflation will be rekindled.
22. The decline in the aggregate real wage rate will be halted.
23. *Both* prices and money wages will fall massively and cumulatively, keeping the aggregate real wage wage rate more-or-less stable.

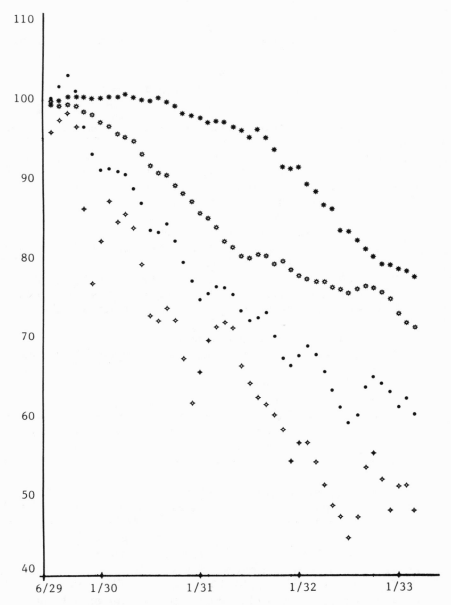

FIGURE 5–7. Wages, Prices, Output, and Employment in the United States, June 1929–March 1933. June 1929 = 100.

* = average hourly earnings of all wage earners. o = wholesale price index of all products except farm products and foods. # = industrial production of all manufactures. ● = factory employment.

Source: Department of Commerce, *Survey of Current Business*, October 1936, 1932 and 1936 Supplements.

The role of economic theory is to provide a framework of thinking which helps us to arrange various empirical facts in a meaningful way. This book is no exception; it does not intend to present in miniature the workings of an actual monetary economy. It is thus a little surprising that the "theoretical" account of a business downturn given above appears to fit so well the actual course of events during the Great Depression. Figure 5–7 charts the movements of average hourly earnings of all wage earners, the wholesale price index of all products (except farm products and foods), the industrial production of all manufactures, and factory employment in the United States from June 1929 (the peak before the Great Depression) to March 1933 (the trough of the Great Depression).[9]

18. *Boom and Inflationary Hysteria*

It is possible to examine in an analogous manner the slump and crisis of our Keynesian economy caused by an increase in the level of total labor supply. It is also possible, and very interesting, to examine the stagflation phase in our Keynesian economy, which is caused by a uniform decline in labor produc-

---

9. This observation may resolve the well-known Keynes versus Dunlop and Tarshis controversy on the cyclical movements of real wage rates. In *The General Theory*, Keynes, relying upon the assumption of perfect competition and the marginal productivity principle of neoclassical theory, argued that because of the law of diminishing marginal productivity the real wage in the short period tends to move in the opposite direction to the level of output. His view was soon challenged by empirical inquiries by Dunlop (1938) and Tarshis (1939), both claiming that real wage rates are more likely to move in the same direction as the level of output. [See Bodkin (1969) for the postwar analysis.] This led Keynes to say: "I now recognize that the conclusion is too simple, and does not allow sufficiently for the complexity of the facts. But I still hold to the main structure of the argument and believe that it needs to be amended rather than discarded" (1939, p. 40). Indeed, he quoted the statistical study of the Great Depression done by J. E. Meade as a partial support for his original conclusion. [In fact, a recent study by Otani (1978) has demonstrated a negative relationship, often statistically significant, between real wages and output for most OECD countries. Moreover, a positive relationship found in the United States, Germany, and Netherlands turns out to be statistically insignificant.]

The theoretical chronology of the movement of real wage rates given above has demonstrated that real wage rates tend to rise during the earlier phase of a business downturn but start to decline once the economy plunges into the phase of crisis. Indeed, after the economy has sunken deep into crisis, both prices and money wages decline in a parallel manner, thereby keeping the movement of real wage rates more or less stable. By the same token, we can also argue that real wage rates tend to decline during the earlier phase of a business upturn but start to catch up with their past rates as soon as the economy enters into the phase of inflationary hysteria. We can thus conclude that the view of Keynes prevails insofar as mild business fluctuations (which we called booms and slumps) are concerned, but that it has to succumb to that of Dunlop and Tarshis when the economy is trapped into crisis or inflationary hysteria. A blanket assertion as to counter- or pro-cyclical movements of real wage rates is unwarranted.

tivities across firms. However, we leave these investigations to the interested reader.

The process of boom is the reverse of that of slump. It is the phase of Keynesian disequilibrium in which the product market gap is positive, whereas the labor market gap is still within the band of equilibrium. Its main feature is thus the development of the upward multiplier process. The phase of inflationary hysteria in Wicksellian disequilibrium is the reverse of that of crisis. In the capitalist economy, money wages are expected to be much more rigid downward than upward. It is therefore more likely that the height of the barrier of inflationary hysteria, $|\psi\theta_+|$, is much lower than the absolute height of the barrier of crisis, $|\psi\theta_-|$. Thus, under the downward rigidity of money wages, the probability of a boom turning into an inflationary hysteria is much higher than the probability of a slump turning into a crisis. The prosperous side of the Keynesian economy therefore looks very much like that of the Wicksellian economy, and our theoretical account of the cumulative inflation process in the latter, given in chapter 3, can be applied, with little modification, to the process of inflationary hysteria in the former.

19. *Summary*

The inflexibility of money wages is one of the most characteristic features of our modern capitalist economy. In this chapter we have proposed a novel formalization of the notion of money wage inflexibility, which is compatible with our view that in most of nonunionized labor markets, money wages are quoted by employers on a take-it-or-leave-it basis. More specifically, it has been assumed that the firm in the short run adjusts its money wage only when its subjective disequilibrium (defined as the proportionate gap between the level of money wage that would maximize the expected profit were it not for money wage inflexibility and the actual level of money wage) deviates from a given satisfactory range bound by two barriers. The firm in this Keynesian economy is, in other words, supposed to behave like a "satisficer" in the short run.

Such formalization of the notion of money wage inflexibility includes, as two polar cases, both the Wicksellian assumption of perfect flexibility and the ultra-Keynesian assumption of absolute rigidity. It thus provides us with the basis for forming a synthesis of the Wicksellian theory of cumulative process, reconstructed in chapter 3 under the Wicksellian assumption, and the Keynesian principle of effective demand, reestablished in chapter 4 under the ultra-Keynesian assumption.

Since the fundamental equation of the labor market, which played a crucial role in our study of the Wicksellian cumulative process, has become defunct under the assumption of money wage inflexibility, it is necessary for us to replace it by a new formula, called the generalized fundamental equation of the labor market. This new fundamental equation states that the market-wide average of firms' surprises with respect to their expectations of the tightness of labor supply is equal in value to the deviation of the existing labor market gap, not from zero as in the old fundamental equation, but from what we call the aggregate intended gap, which is defined as a given constant multiple of the market-wide average of the firm's subjective disequilibrium. Since in this Keynesian economy an individual firm's subjective disequilibrium fluctuates within a given satisfactory range, the value of the aggregate intended gap thus defined can take any value, as long as it remains within a range, called the equilibrium band, which is no more than a multiple enlargement of each firm's satisfactory range. (The upper bound of this equilibrium band is called the barrier of inflationary hysteria, and the lower bound, the barrier of crisis.) From this simple observation we can obtain two important implications, one positive and the other negative. The positive implication is that, as long as the value of the labor market gap remains within the equilibrium band, all frims are simultaneously capable of attaining their expectational equilibrium. For in this case the aggregate intended gap can adjust itself and maintain an equality with the existing labor market gap. Expectational equilibrium of the Keynesian economy as a whole is therefore compatible with a wide range of the values of the labor market gap. This positive implication constitutes the foundation of our reconstruction of the Keynesian principle of effective demand. The negative implication of the new fundamental equation, on the other hand, is that if the labor market gap sinks below the barrier of crisis or floats above the barrier of inflationary hysteria, firms in the Keynesian labor market are incapable of achieving their expectational equilibrium simultaneously, no matter what value the aggregate intended gap takes. Just as in the Wicksellian economy, surprises are produced inevitably within the system in this case. This negative implication constitutes the foundation of our Wicksellian theory of crisis and inflationary hysteria.

In the Keynesian economy, we have to introduce, in addition to the concept of Expectational equilibrium of the economy as a whole, two other concepts of equilibrium, those of Keynesian equilibrium and Wicksellian equilibrium. The former is defined as a state in which the product market gap is zero and the labor market gap is equal to the aggregate intended gap; and the latter is defined as a state in which the labor market gap remains within the equilibrium band. The condition for Wicksellian equilibrium is a necessary condition for Keynesian equilibrium, and the conditions for Keynesian equilibrium are necessary conditions for Expectational equilibrium.

These three equilibrium concepts allow us to distinguish three forms of disequilibrium. We say that the Keynesian economy is in a state of Wicksellian disequilibrium if the labor market gap strays away from the band of equilibrium; is in a state of Keynesian disequilibrium if the product market gap is nonzero, or if the labor market gap fails to maintain an equality with the aggregate intended gap but still remains within the equilibrium band; and is in a state of secondary disequilibrium if, even though the product market gap is zero and the labor market gap equals the aggregate intended gap, at least one firm fails to attain its expectational equilibrium. Thus, in the case of secondary disequilibrium, the disequilibrium *is* the disappointment of expectations (just as in the Wicksellian economy), whereas in the case of both Keynesian and Wicksellian disequilibrium, the disequilibrium *causes* the disappointment of expectations.

We can further classify both Keynesian and Wicksellian disequilibria into two phases. We say that Keynesian disequilibrium is in the slump phase if the labor market gap is negative, and in the boom phase if it is positive. We also say that Wicksellian disequilibrium enters the crisis phase if the labor market gap sinks below the barrier of crisis, and the inflationary hysteria phase if it floats above the barrier of inflationary hysteria. Such a taxonomy makes it easier to grasp the nature of various equilibria and disequilibria of the Keynesian economy.

In the Keynesian economy it is an easy matter to reestablish the Keynesian principle of effective demand in a state of Expectational equilibrium. Since in order for the Keynesian economy to be in Expectational equilibrium, the product market gap has to be zero, all we need to do is to equilibriate the schedule of total product demand, which relates the level of total product demand to the level of labor employment, with that of total product supply, which relates the level of total product supply to the level of labor employment in the past, and then to find the level of labor employment that is consistent with this equilibrium condition. The only proviso for the validity of this principle is that the value of the labor market gap, which is associated with the equilibrium level of labor employment, should remain within the equilibrium band. This can be checked easily by the use of the aggregate involuntary unemployment schedule, which stipulates the relationship between the aggregate rate of involuntary unemployment (and, by implication, the level of total employment) and the value of the labor market gap.

But the Keynesian principle of effective demand thus reestablished is purely an equilibrium-theoretic principle, which is incapable of describing the causal process by which the economy is moved from one position to another. In order to analyze such a process, we have to divert our attention from Expectational equilibrium.

In the first place, it can be shown that the secondary disequilibrium of the Keynesian economy has a self-correcting tendency, although the inflexibility of money wages tends to weaken the power of the Invisible Hand in strengthening the individual firms' error-learning activities in the labor market. But the secondary disequilibrium is merely a secondary form of disequilibrium; the fundamental forms of disequilibrium in the Keynesian economy are, of course, what we have called Keynesian disequilibrium and Wicksellian disequilibrium. These two forms of disequilibrium, however, are likely to exhibit patterns of dynamic behaviors that are markedly different from each other.

Consider a Keynesian economy that has been thrown away from a Keynesian equilibrium state by a sudden drop in the volume of total product demand. A negative gap appears in the product market and a negative difference between the labor market gap and the aggregate intended gap is likely to emerge in the labor market. If the decreased labor market gap still remains above the barrier of crisis, the economy finds itself in the slump phase of Keynesian disequilibrium. The negative product market gap will sooner or later set out a cumulative price deflation. But as long as the labor market gap stays above the barrier of crisis, the downward inflexibility of meney wages tends to arrest the full deployment of the cumulative wage deflation. The sluggishness of the decline of money wages, which results in a rise in the real wage rate, discourages the effective labor demands and reduces the scale of total product supply relative to that of total product demand, thereby empowering the Keynesian disequilibrium in the product market with a self-correcting tendency. Furthermore, the resistence of money wages to decline tends to reduce the aggregate intended gap faster than the labor market gap, and also enables Keynesian disequilibrium to eliminate itself in the labor market. In the slump phase of Keynesian disequilibrium, the downward inflexibility of money wages thus prevents the destabilizing nature of price mechanism from exerting itself and invites the adjustment of quantity variables to anchor the economy to one of Keynesian equilibrium states.

During the slump phase of Keynesian disequilibrium, the decline in total product demand and the decline in total labor employment reinforce each other and aggravate the downturn of business conditions.

If such a downward multiplier process depresses the labor market gap below the barrier of crisis (or if the initial decline of the volume of total product demand is very massive), the economy slips into the crisis phase of Wicksellian disequilibrium. Then a majority of firms are bound to underestimate the tightness of the labor supply and start cutting their money wage simultaneously in order to eliminate an abnormally large excess labor supply. But, as long as the labor market gap remains below the barrier of crisis, these simultaneous cuts of money wage merely result in disappointing firms' intentions, which are, after all, mutually incompatible from the beginning. Then, as in the cumulative deflation process of the Wicksellian economy, the expectations of the general money wage level and the realized level of general money wage start to chase each other downward. A massive and cumulative deflation of money wages forms the major feature of the crisis of the Keynesian economy.

During the crisis phase of Wicksellian disequilibrium, the massive decline of money wages may reduce the real wage rate and act as a stimulus to the economy. But this favorable effect will soon be wiped out by an equally massive decline of product prices, which is bound to take place as the very effect of the fall in the real wage and the consequent recovery of total product supply in relation to total product demand.

Since the cumulative deflation of money wages and prices continues indefinitely unless the labor market gap rises above the barrier of crisis, the stability of the Keynesian economy in its crisis phase, that is, whether it is capable of rebounding from the crisis without outside help, hinges critically upon whether a massive wave of wage and price reduction acts as a stimulus upon the volume of total product demand and thus upon the level of total effective labor demand. This is exactly the money wage problem of Keynes. The Keynes and Pigou effects are stabilizers, whereas the spending effect of the redistribution of private real wealth from debtors to creditors, the debt-deflation process of Irving Fisher, and the price expectation effect make it more difficult for the Keynesian economy to recover from the crisis. Furthermore, if the cost of wage cuts decrease as the wage deflation deepens, the stability of the Keynesian economy is weakened further. The general conclusion is that there is no a priori reason to believe in the existence of any self-correcting tendency in the crisis phase of Wicksellian disequilibrium.

The boom and the inflationary hysteria are qualitatively the mirror images of the slump and the crisis. But under the assumption of the downward inflexibility of money wages, the barrier of inflationary hysteria is much closer to zero than is the barrier of crisis, and the likelihood of a boom turning into inflationary hysteria is much larger than is the likelihood that a slump will turn into a crisis.

20. Is the Keynesian Principle a Special Case of the Neoclassical Theory?

The reader may find it anticlimactic to be told that the Keynesian principle of effective demand is, after all, an equilibrium theory of a monetary economy with the downward rigidity of money wages.[10] This has been a standard interpretation of the economics of Keynes for the last forty years.[11] It should be noted, however, that the standard interpretation maintains at the same time that the economics of Keynes is merely a special case—the "Keynesian special case"—of neoclassical equilibrium theory and is valid only under the ad hoc but "realistic" assumption of inflexible money wages.[12] Implicit in this view

---

10. This conclusion is in contradistinction to the recent and influential interpretation of *The General Theory* by Leijonhufvud (1968, 1969). See Jackman (1974) for a forceful criticism of Leijonhufvudian Keynesianism.

11. For such an interpretation, see Hicks (1937), Modigliani (1944, 1963), Hansen (1953), Samuelson (1964), Johnson (1958), or any mainstream textbooks on macroeconomics.

12. According to Harry Johnson:

Keynes presented his theory . . . as a general theory of which the classical theory was a special case. It turns out that Keynes' theory is a special case of the classical—

is a belief that if money wages were flexible, all the peculiarities of the Keynesian system would disappear and the harmonious world of neoclassical equilibrium theory would return. Quite an opposite conclusion was arrived at in this chapter. Indeed, it was argued that the "fluidification" of money wages would never resurrect the harmonious world of neoclassical economics. It would only replace the stable Keynesian economy by the Wicksellian economy, which is always in danger of being propelled into a crisis or inflationary hysteria by a sudden change in macroeconomic conditions. Contrary to the orthodox belief, there is *no* Invisible Hand to rely upon without Say's laws. Indeed, the laissez-faire price mechanism is itself the source of instability in the monetary economy. If there is any stability in the monetary economy, it is likely to be due to the inflexibility of money wages, which limits the free play of the price mechanism. "To suppose a flexible wage policy is a right and proper adjunct of a system which on the whole is one of laissez-faire, is the opposite of the truth. It is only in a highly authoritarian society, where sudden, substantial, all-round changes could be decreed that a flexible wage-policy could function with success" (Keynes 1936, p. 269). One can imagine it in operation only in the paradigm of neoclassical equilibrium theory, in which all prices and wages are controlled by highly authoritarian "market auctioneers."

However, the position to which the inflexibility of money wages anchors the economy is *not* that of neoclassical equilibrium but one of Keynesian equilibria. It is only by coincidence that the economy attains the normal level of labor employment; and for that reason, government's or the central bank's conscious economic policy becomes necessary to maintain the normal or any other desirable level of employment. Thus, the enhancement of the stability of the monetary economy is obtained at a price. One of the tasks of part III is to explore further the nature of this price.

---

or rather of the neoclassical theory, since a satisfactory "classical" theory was not worked out until after the Keynesian revolution. But this sort of argument about a theory is not particularly interesting; what is more important is that Keynes' theory started from an empirically relevant special assumption, derived some important meaningful results from it, and provided an approach which has since proved its usefulness for a wide range of problems. [1958]

Keynesian Disequilibrium Dynamics in the Long Run

CHAPTER 6

A Keynesian Model of Wage Adjustment

1. *Introduction: Keynes on the Long Run*

The primary purpose of part III is to demonstrate that an economy with wage inflexibility will *never* lose its Keynesian features, no matter how long it is run. Rather paradoxically, however, Keynes himself seems to have entertained an opposite view in *The General Theory*:

> Our criticism of the accepted [neo-]classical theory of economics has consisted not so much in finding logical flaws in its analysis as in pointing out that its tacit assumptions are seldom or never satisfied, with the result that it cannot solve the economic problems of the actual world. But if our central controls succeed in establishing an aggregate volume of output corresponding to full employment as nearly as is practicable, the [neo-]classical theory comes into its own again from this point onwards. [1936, p. 378]

This remark of Keynes has since become the foundation of the "neoclassical synthesis," and we need little textual evidence to assert that most contemporary economists more or less share the same view.[1]

By the [neo-]classical theory, Keynes of course meant a set of doctrines according to which all the real variables, such as employment of resources, production and consumption of commodities, and their relative prices, are determined by the equilibrium relations between demand and supply in competitive markets; whereas all the monetary variables, such as nominal prices and money wages, are left to be pegged by the equilibrium relation between the demand and supply of the money stock. The neoclassical description of the economy can thus be characterized by the following two interdependent

---

Section 10, "The Nature of the Best Wage Adjustment Rule (II)," may be regarded as optional reading.

1. See, for example, Samuelson (1976) for the most authoritative textbook of the neoclassical synthesis.

propositions: (a) that there is no such thing as involuntary unemployment of resources and (b) that money is neutral in the sense that all the real variables are determined independently of the nominal quantity of money stock.[2]

Clearly, the normal rate theory of unemployment, a version of which we presented in chapter 2, can be regarded as a sophisticated restatement of these two neoclassical propositions. The normal rate theory claims, in place of the first neoclassical theorem (that there is no such thing as involuntary unemployment), that since rational people's anticipations about the rate of inflation should on the average coincide with the actual rate of inflation, the rate of unemployment is on the average equal to the normal rate of unemployment, whose magnitude reflects various market frictions and is generally greater than zero. And the second neoclassical proposition (that money is neutral) is modified in such a way that this normal rate of unemployment should be independent of the time pattern of any monetary variables, in particular of the rate of inflation. In short, the normal rate theory of unemployment maintains that the long-run Phillips curve is vertical at a given positive normal rate of unemployment. Indeed, Milton Friedman has characterized the normal rate of unemployment as the rate "that would be ground out by the Walrasian system of general equilibrium equations, provided there is imbedded in them the actual structural characteristics of the labor and commodity markets, including market imperfections, stochastic variability in demands and supplies, the cost of gathering information about job vacancies and labor availabilities, the cost of mobility, and so on" (1968, p. 8).

In part I, however, we demonstrated that it is logically untenable to postulate the rationality of expectations as a behavioral hypothesis in the economy without Say's laws. We then showed in part II that once the inflexibility of money wages is brought into our picture of the economy, the aggregate rate of involuntary unemployment becomes determined, in the short run, by the volume of total product demand (or by the effective demand) and not by the normal rate of unemployment, even if firms' expectations are consistent with actual market outcomes. The analysis of the determination of the aggregate rate of involuntary unemployment in the long run, however, remains to be given; the following two chapters address this long-run problem. It will indeed complete our critique of the neoclassical equilibrium theory and of its derivative, the normal rate theory of unemployment. For we establish in this final part that in an economy with inflexibile money wages, not only does the involuntary unemployment persist in the long run but its aggregate rate stays permanently above the normal rate of unemployment. We demonstrate further that in an economy with a downward inflexibility of money wages, the long-

---

2. Here we have ignored the possibility of the nonneutral influences of the monetary growth rate on the rate of real savings in neoclassical growth models. See, for example, Tobin (1965) for this point.

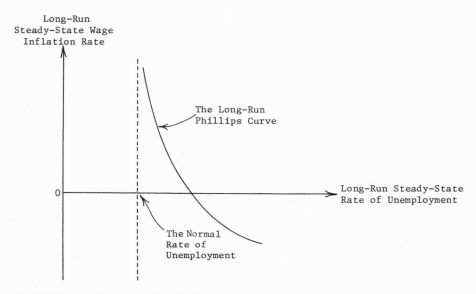

FIGURE 6–1. The Long-Run Phillips Curve

run equilibrium rate of involuntary unemployment will be inversely related to the equilibrium rate of wage inflation. Or, to put these propositions differently, we prove that, as is illustrated in figure 6–1, the long-run Phillips curve will be located to the right of the normal rate of unemployment and will never turn vertical. The economy we happen to live in thus can never approach the beautiful and optimum neoclassical world even in the economists' never-never land of the long run.

Our task is by no means straightforward. For what we have to prove is *not* that the inflexibility of money wages has certain transient effects on the determining process of the real variables in the economy (the rate of involuntary unemployment, in particular), with which no one disagrees, but that they exert *permanent* influences on them. In fact, it is easy to see that the conventional Keynesian analysis of the phenomenon of involuntary unemployment (as well as our ultra-Keynesian model of chapter 4) is incapable of undertaking such a task. This is easily seen in figure 6–2, a form of diagram that can be found in almost any macroeconomics textbook. In this diagram the horizontal axis measures the level of employment and the vertical axis the rate of aggregate money wage; the demand curve for labor is drawn as downward-sloping and the supply curve of labor as upward-sloping; their intersection representing full-employment equilibrium with the equilibrium money wage rate W^*. If, by a minimum wage law, trade union pressure, a convention, or by mere inertia the rate of money wage becomes rigid downward at the level W (which is higher that W^*), the number of workers willing to work at this rigidly fixed money

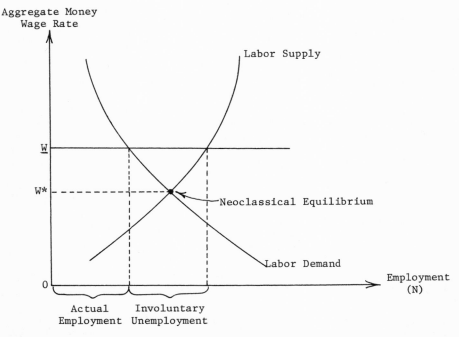

FIGURE 6–2. The Textbook Keynesian Analysis of Involuntary Unemployment

wage exceeds the demand, thereby creating involuntary unemployment, the extent of which is represented by the difference between the supply and demand at W. It is, however, plain that this textbook account of the phenomenon of involuntary unemployment is valid only in the short run. Other things that were assumed to be constant when we drew the demand and supply curve will not remain constant in the long run, or are at least subject to the control of the fiscal authority and the central bank. In general, as long as workers and employers are free of money illusions, both the demand for and the supply of labor are functions not of the money wage rate but of the real wage rate. Moreover, standard Keynesian macroeconomics has taught us that, at least when it is out of the neoclassical equilibrium position, the demand for labor is also a function of the level of product demand (or, more precisely, employers' expectations of the state of product demand). Therefore, if the fiscal authority or central bank decided to adopt an expansionary policy and began to stimulating the economy, the resulting increase in prices would reduce the rate of the real wage corresponding to the rigid money wage W and shift upward both the demand and supply curves of labor. More important, even if the general price level did not increase and the rate of real wage did not decrease, the increase in total demand for products brought about by an expansionary government policy would be expected to push upward the demand curve for labor. In either case, involuntary unemployment will gradually diminish and, when the demand and supply curves have been pulled up sufficiently, will disappear completely from the labor market.

Thus, to explain the persistence of involuntary unemployment in the long run—our main objective in part III—we cannot adopt the conventional Keynesian fixed-wage method.[3] A novel formulation of the notion of wage inflexibility is needed.

Fortunately, we laid the basic framework for such a reformulation in chapter 5, and here in chapter 6 we only have to follow up what was left unfinished. In chapter 7 we explore the implications of the inflexibility of money wages for the long-run performance of the Keynesian economy as a whole. Finally, in chapter 8, an attempt will be made to extend our theory to the situation in which labor markets are fully organized by trade unions.

2. The Simple Rule of Money Wage Adjustment

To refresh our memories, let's recapitulate the model of a firm's wage adjustment activity introduced in chapter 5. Since the present chapter is concerned exclusively with the wage adjustment activity of a single firm, in the following exposition we drop the firm-specific index i.

In the Wicksellian economy, where the firm is able to adjust its money wage without incurring any cost, at the beginning of each period a firm quotes the level of money wage that is expected to maximize its gross profit in that period. We have denoted this wage level by w_t^* and called it the short-run optimal wage in period t. In the Keynesian economy, in which the cost of money wage adjustment is not negligible, it does not pay for the firm to attempt to maximize its short-run expected gross profit in each period. Here the firm would tolerate, within certain bounds, the existence of subjective disequilibrium in order to save the cost of wage adjustment. At the same time, however, the firm has to adjust its money wage occasionally in order to adapt itself to changing market conditions. There emerges, therefore, a trade-off between the cost of adjusting the money wage and the opportunity cost of failing to accommodate it to the never-steady market environment. The firm in the Keynesian economy has to devise a rule for money wage adjustment which takes due account of such a trade-off.

In chapter 5 we measured the firm's subjective disequilibrium in the labor

---

3. It should be noted that recent attempts at incorporating the assumption of fixed prices and wages into the framework of the Walrasian general equilibrium model share the same features as textbook Keynesian analysis and hence are incapable of explaining the persistence of involuntary unemployment in the long run or the existence of the permanent trade-off between inflation and unemployment. Examples are Barro and Grossman (1971), Bennasy (1975), Drèze (1975), Grandmont and Laroque (1976), and Malinvaud (1977).

market by the proportionate difference between the short-run optimal wage w_t^* and the level of money wage w_t actually quoted, and denoted it by z_t. We then supposed that the firm adjusts (or does not adjust) its money wage w_t and hence its subjective disequilibrium z_t, according to the following simple rule:

$$(6\text{-}1) \quad z_t = \begin{cases} z_{t-1} + \Delta \ln w_{t-1}^* & (\text{or } \ln w_t = \ln w_{t-1}) \\ \quad \text{if } \theta_- \leqslant z_{t-1} + \Delta \ln w_{t-1}^* \leqslant \theta_+ \\ \quad (\text{or } \theta_- \leqslant \ln w_t^* - \ln w_{t-1} \leqslant \theta_+), \\ \theta_0 \quad (\text{or } \ln w_t = \ln w_t^* - \theta_0) \\ \quad \text{if } z_{t-1} + \Delta \ln w_{t-1}^* > \theta_+ \quad (\text{or } \ln w_t^* - \ln w_{t-1} > \theta_+), \\ \theta_0 \quad (\text{or } \ln w_t = \ln w_t^* - \theta_0) \\ \quad \text{if } z_{t-1} + \Delta \ln w_{t-1}^* < \theta_- \quad (\text{or } \ln w_t^* - \ln w_{t-1} < \theta_-), \end{cases}$$

where $\theta_- \leqslant \theta_0 \leqslant \theta_+$. In words, the firm defers wage adjustment, thereby automatically setting the value of subjective disequilibrium $z_t \equiv \ln w_t^* - \ln w_t$ equal to $z_{t-1} + \Delta \ln w_{t-1}^*$ ($\equiv \ln w_t^* - \ln w_{t-1}$), as long as the latter stays within a satisfactory range bound from below by the lower barrier θ_- and from above by the upper barrier θ_+. It raises its money wage and sets the value of subjective disequilibrium z_t equal to the return point θ_0 only when $z_{t-1} + \Delta \ln w_{t-1}^*$ floats above θ_+; and it lowers its money wage and sets z_t equal to the same θ_0 only when $z_{t-1} + \Delta \ln w_{t-1}^*$ sinks below θ_-. The nature of this rule was already illustrated by figure 5–1.

Money wage adjustment rule (6–1) is indeed very "simple," for it is characterized completely by three parameters: θ_+, θ_-, and θ_0. Hence a firm's search for a better adjustment rule in the long run can be reduced to the simpler activity of searching for the better values of these three parameters. This is, of course, still a dynamic problem; but it is at least a tractable one, even within the boundaries of the firm's (and our own) rationality.

Furthermore, our simple wage adjustment rule is not only simple but also "good." In fact, it is argued in appendix 6–a that the form of this simple rule may turn out to be the optimal one under certain reasonable conditions. If this is indeed the case, the selection of the best rule out of the restricted class of simple rules would incidentally ensure the selection of the globally optimal wage adjustment rule and could blur the distinction between the neoclassical global-rationalistic view and our bounded-rationalistic view, at least from a long-run perspective.

3. The Firm as a Satisficer in the Short Run

As in our theory of expectation formation presented in chapter 2, it is useful to comprehend the firm's wage adjustment activity as an outcome of the continual interaction between its short-run and long-run activities.

In the short run, the wage adjustment rule is a legacy from the past. The value of the upper barrier θ_+, the lower barrier θ_-, and the return point θ_0 are all regarded by the firm as historically given data into which its long-term expectations formed in the past have been congealed. Thus, the firm's wage adjustment rule in the short run is only to follow the given rule routinely: (a) be content with the old wage if the proportionate difference between the current short-run optimal wage and the level of money wage quoted in the last period remains within a historically given satisfactory range; (b) raise the money wage so as to pull down the subjective disequilibrium to a given return point if the difference overshoots a given upper barrier; and (c) cut the money wage so as to push up the subjective disequilibrium to the return point if the difference falls short of a given lower barrier. In other words, our firm behaves in the short run like a firm postulated in the behavioral theory of the firm, which "satisfices" rather than optimizes.[4] Indeed, the upper barrier θ_+ and the lower barrier θ_- in our wage adjustment rule play a role that is quite analogous to the role played by the aspiration level in the behavioral approach.

In the long run, however, our firm adjusts the rule of wage adjustment itself. If the firm has been persistently disappointed at the performance of its long-term expectations frozen in the existing wage adjustment rule, it will inspect its own subjective model of the environment, revise its long-term expectations, and finally switch to a new wage adjustment rule which it thinks is better adapted to the present market situation. Here, the process of the firm's search for a better rule is ignored, and it is simply assumed that in the long run the firm chooses one of the simple rules that optimizes a certain long-term criterion (to be specified later) evaluated by the newly revised long-term expectations. The rationale for our adoption of such an optimization hypothesis for the description of the firms' long-run wage adjustment activity is, however, primarily strategic. For one of the main purposes of part III is to show that, in an economy with inflexible money wages, even if firms were optimizers, the economy would never approach the state described by neoclassical equilibrium theory. If firms did not even bother to optimize in the long run, our theme would, of course, be greatly strengthened.

For the time being, however, let us concentrate on an analysis of the behavior of the firm as a satisficer, postponing until section 6 an analysis of how the firm chooses the wage adjustment rule itself in the long run. Let us suppose until then that the values of the upper barrier θ_+, the lower barrier θ_-, and the return point θ_0 are all arbitrarily given constants.

Now, as is easily seen in figure 5–1, the dynamic motion of the subjective disequilibrium z_t is completely governed by the dynamic motion of the rate of change in the short-run optimal wage $\Delta \ln w_{t-1}^*$ once the parameter values θ_0, θ_+, and θ_- and the initial subjective disequilibrium z_0 are fixed. It is clear from equation (1–23), which determines the short-run optimal wage, that the

---

4. The term "satisficing" was recoined by H. A. Simon from the Old Scottish in order to designate the behavior of a decision maker who does not care to optimize but simply wants to obtain a satisfactory utility or return. See Simon (1955, 1959, 1972) and March and Simon (1958). The more recent contributions of the behavioral school are from Cyert and March (1963), and Nelson and Winter (1974, 1975).

dynamic motion of $\Delta \ln w_t^*$ is, in turn, governed by the rates of change in the firm's subjective expectation of the future briskness of product demand, by its subjective expectation of the tightness of the current labor supply, and by the rate of change in labor productivity. Therefore, how $\ln w_{t-1}^*$ changes from period to period is guided primarily by how the firm revises its subjective expectations from period to period in response to changing market conditions. But how the firm will revise these subjective expectations in the future is in general unknown in the present period, for its future subjective expectations will have to be formed, at least partially, on the basis of a set of yet-unknown market data in the future. Hence, we have no choice but to regard future $\Delta \ln w_t^*$'s as random variables and assign them an objective probability distribution.

Let us assume that the sequence of the rates of change in the short-run optimal wage, $\Delta \ln w_0^*$, $\Delta \ln w_1^*$, ..., $\Delta \ln w_{t-1}^*$, ..., are mutually independent random variables drawn from the same objective probability distribution:

$$(6–2) \qquad \Omega(x) \equiv \Pr\{\Delta \ln w_t^* \leqslant x\} \qquad \text{for } t = 1, 2, \ldots .$$

Let us denote the objective expectation of $\Delta \ln w_t^*$ by

$$(6–3) \qquad \omega \equiv \int_{-\infty}^{\infty} x \, d\Omega(x).$$

In short, we assume that the short-run optimal wage w_t^* in the future will undergo a multiplicative random walk with a drift equal to ω. This is hardly an innocuous assumption, but we believe it to be a useful first-order approximation. Note that the probability distribution $\Omega(\cdot)$ summarizes not only the stochastic properties of the relevant random variables (i.e., the briskness of product demand, the tightness of labor supply, and the index of labor productivity) that influence the firm's market and technological environment, but also the statistical properties of the firm's measurement errors pertaining to random variables.

Then the dynamic motion of the subjective disequilibrium z_t constitutes a random-walk process with two return barriers at θ_+ and θ_- and a given return point θ_0. We shall relegate detailed mathematical study of the nature of this particular class of stochastic processes to the mathematical supplement to chapter 6. Here, we simply summarize the results obtained in the supplement and interpret them economically.

4. The Stochastic Steady State

Let the transition probability distribution $\Pi_t(z : z_0)$ summarize our prediction of the position of subjective disequilibrium in period t, formed on the basis of information about its position in period zero given by z_0; that is, we put for $t = 1, 2, 3, \ldots,$

(6–4) $\Pi_t(z : z_0) \equiv \Pr\{z_t \leqslant z : z_0\}$ for $\theta_- \leqslant z \leqslant \theta_+$.

By convention we set $\Pi_t(z : z_0) = 0$ for $z < \theta_-$ and $\Pi_t(z : z_0) = 1$ for $z \geqslant \theta_+$. In words, $\Pi_t(z : z_0)$ represents the probability that the subjective disequilibrium in period t is at most as large as a given constant z, on the condition that it start from z_0 in period zero. [See appendix 6–b for the recurrence relation that determines the whole sequence of $\Pi_t(z : z_0)$ for $t = 0, 1, 2, \ldots$.]

As time goes on, the level of money wage and hence the value of subjective disequilibrium will be adjusted again and again. It is then reasonable to predict that the influence of the initial position z_0 will gradually fade away, and after a sufficiently long period of time, the stochastic motion of subjective disequilibrium will produce a regularity of its own, breaking the spell of the initial condition. It will, in other words, settle down to a "stochastic steady state" (see figure 6–3). In the mathematical supplement to chapter 6, we are indeed able to prove the following proposition (theorem S–1 of the supplement), which provides a rigorous justification of this intuitive prediction:

> Proposition 6–1 (The Steady-State Theorem). *If* (a) *both* θ_+ *and* θ_- *are finite;* (b) θ_+ *is infinite,* $\theta_- = -\infty$ *and* $0 < \omega < \infty$; *or* (c) θ_- *is finite,* $\theta_+ = +\infty$ *and* $-\infty < \omega < 0$, *then as* $t \to \infty$ *the transition probability distribution* $\Pi_t(z : z_0)$ *converges to a limit distribution* $\Pi^\infty(z)$, *independently of the initial condition* z_0; *that is, we have*
>
> (6–5) $\displaystyle\lim_{t \to \infty} \Pi_t(z : z_0) = \Pi^\infty(z)$ *for any* z_0.

In words, if (a) the money wage is not absolutely rigid either upward or downward, or if (b) the money wage is absolutely rigid downward but the short-run optimal wage is on the average growing at a positive rate, or if (c) the money wage is absolutely rigid upward but the short-run optimal wage is on the average declining at a positive rate, the position of subjective disequilibrium will in the long run approach a stochastic steady state, hence enabling us to predict its motion in the distant future by the limit distribution $\Pi^\infty(z)$, independent of its initial condition.

The shape of the limit distribution $\Pi^\infty(z)$ is determined by the three parameters θ_+, θ_-, and θ_0 and the probability distribution $\Omega(\cdot)$. Its detailed characterization is, however, relegated to the mathematical supplement.

This limit distribution is called the steady-state distribution, because it is that probability distribution which is capable of reproducing itself from period to period once it is achieved. It is, in other words, the (unique) self-perpetuating probability distribution of the position of subjective disequilibrium.[5] Alterna-

---

5. Namely, the steady-state distribution $\Pi^\infty(z)$ uniquely satisfies the following "steady-state" or "invariant" or "self-perpetuating" relation for any t' and t (> 0):

$$\Pi^\infty(z_{t'+t}) = \int_{\theta_-}^{\theta_+} \Pi_t(z_{t'+t} : z_{t'}) \, d\Pi^\infty(z_{t'}).$$

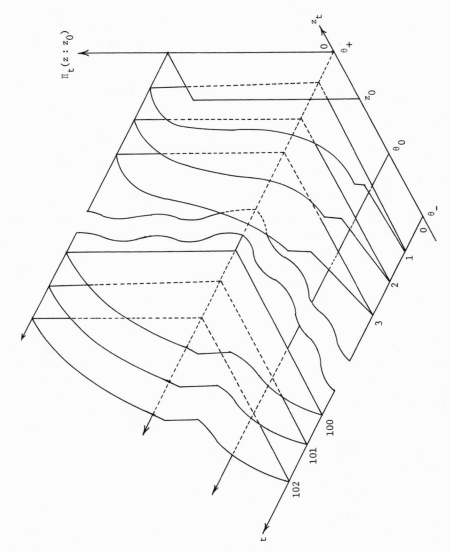

FIGURE 6–3. Evolution of the Transition Probability Distribution over Time

tively, the same limit distribution can be interpreted as the long-run average description of the intertemporal movement of the subjective disequilibrium. For according to the strong law of large numbers for Markov processes explained in appendix 6–c, the steady-state probability distribution also represents the average proportion of periods z_t is expected to spend in a half-interval $(-\infty, z]$ in the long, long run. We therefore call $\Pi^\infty(\cdot)$ either the steady-state distribution or the long-run average distribution.

Our interest in the steady-state or long-run average behavior of the subjective disequilibrium z_t is twofold. In the first place, since our steady-state theorem characterizes the long-run average performance of our firm's wage adjustment activity, a study of its properties will be useful for the determination of the best wage adjustment rule that can be expected to optimize a certain long-run objective function. In this chapter, our attention will be focused on this microeconomic application of the steady-state theorem. However, the second (and no less important) reason arises from the fact that if we start analyzing the dynamic behavior of the Keynesian economy as a whole, in which numerous firms are making wage decisions independently, this long-run average distribution could be given an entirely different interpretation as the *cross-sectional description* of the economy's macroscopic steady state—a steady state of the entire labor market, which is maintained by offsetting motions of a large number of firms perpetually thrown out of equilibrium by incessant disturbances of product demand, labor supply, capital accumulation, and technology across firms. The concept of macroscopic steady state is studied closely in chapter 7.

5. The Rate of Wage Change in the Short and Long Runs

The motion of the rate of change in money wage, $\Delta \ln w_t$, is essentially discrete. There is an upward jump when $z_t + \Delta \ln w_t^* > \theta_+$ and a downward jump when $z_t + \Delta \ln w_t^* < \theta_-$; otherwise, there is no adjustment at all. But it is still possible to obtain some useful insight into the nature of the wage adjustment process by examining its short- and long-run average behaviors.

We represent by $E(\Delta \ln w_{t-1} : z_0)$ the expected rate of wage change in period t, predicted on the basis of the data in period zero. In particular, the expected rate of wage change in the first period can be given the following more illuminating expression:

$$(6\text{--}6) \qquad E(\Delta \ln w_0 : z_0) = \omega - E(z_1 - z_0 : z_0)$$

$$= \omega - \left[\int_{\theta_-}^{\theta_+} (z - \theta_0) d\Omega(z - z_0) + \theta_0 - z_0 \right].$$

[Here, we have employed the adjustment rule (6–1) or the recurrence relation (A6–2) in appendix 6–2 to deduce the last line.] Although it cannot be shown in general that $E(\Delta \ln w_0 : z_0)$ is a nondecreasing function of z_0, it is, as shown in appendix 6–d, indeed the case in many reasonable special cases. Thus, at least in these special cases we can regard (6–6) as an ex ante law of demand and supply in the labor market, for it states that the expected rate of wage change from period zero to period one is nonnegatively correlated with a given initial subjective disequilibrium z_0 in the labor market. This ex ante law of demand and supply in the Keynesian labor market should not be confused with the ex post law of demand and supply in the Wicksellian labor market deduced in section 5 of chapter 2. The latter is a law relating the *actual* rate of change in money wage to the gap between the subjective-normal and observed ratios of labor demand to supply, and has nothing to do with their ex ante correlation. Indeed, in the Wicksellian economy the firm's optimal wage policy is to set $z_t \equiv \ln w_t^* - \ln w_t$ equal to zero at the beginning of every period, thereby leaving no room for the working of the ex ante law of demand and supply. In the Keynesian economy, on the other hand, the existence of a wage adjustment cost prevents the ex post law of demand and supply from working smoothly in the labor market.

In the long run, however, this ex ante law of demand and supply in the labor market disappears! Let $E^\infty(\Delta \ln w)$ represent the expected rate of money wage change in a stochastic steady state. It also represents the long-run average rate of money wage change according to the law of large numbers of appendix 6–c. Then we can indeed establish:

Proposition 6–2. *As $t \to \infty$, $E(\Delta \ln w_t : z_0)$ converges to ω, a given constant value of the expected rate of change in the short-run optimal money wage, independently of the initial condition z_0; that is, we have*

(6–7) $$E^\infty(\Delta \ln w) = \omega.$$

That is, as time goes on, the influence of the initial subjective disequilibrium z_0 will gradually melt away, and after a sufficiently long passage of time the expected rate of wage change will converge to the constant expected rate of change in the short-run optimal wage ω, whose value is totally independent of the initial condition. The proof of this proposition is trivial and is given below.

Proof. As $t \to \infty$, both $\Pi_t(z : z_0)$ and $\Pi_{t+1}(z : z_0)$ approach the same steady-state distribution $\Pi^\infty(z)$. Hence, by (6–6),

$$(6\text{–}8) \qquad E(\Delta \ln w_t : z_0) = \omega - E(z_{t+1} - z_t : z_0)$$

$$= \omega - \left[\int_{\theta-}^{\theta+} z \, d\Pi_{t+1}(z) - \int_{\theta-}^{\theta+} z \, d\Pi_t(z) \right]$$

$$\to \omega - \left[\int_{\theta-}^{\theta+} z \, d\Pi^\infty(z) - \int_{\theta-}^{\theta+} z \, d\Pi^\infty(z) \right] \qquad \text{as } t \to \infty$$

$$= \omega \qquad\qquad\qquad\qquad\qquad \text{(Q.E.D.)}$$

Note that this proposition depends on neither the parameter values θ_0, θ_+, and θ_0, nor on specification of the subjective probability distribution $\Omega(\cdot)$; it requires only that one of the conditions for the existence of a steady-state distribution stated in proposition 6–1 be fulfilled.[6]

6. *The Firm as an Optimizer in the Long Run*

Let us now go to the longer-run side of our model and study the behavior of the firm as an optimizer. For this purpose we must first specify the firm's inner perception about the dynamic structure of the market environment relevant to its wage adjustment activity.

Assume that the firm believes that the sequence of the rates of change of its short-run optimal wage are mutually independent random variables drawn from the time-invariant subjective probability distribution:

(6–9) $$\hat{\Omega}(x) \equiv \hat{\text{Pr}}\{\Delta \ln w_t^* \leqslant x\} \qquad \text{for } t = 1, 2, \ldots,$$

where, as before, the caret indicates a subjectively formed parameter. The subjective expected value of the rate of change in the short-run optimal wage is then denoted by

(6–10) $$\hat{\omega} \equiv \int_{-\infty}^{\infty} x \cdot d\hat{\Omega}(x).$$

Note that the subjective probability distribution $\hat{\Omega}(\cdot)$ summarizes not only the firm's view of the statistical properties of the random variables which represent its own market and technological environment but also the firm's evaluation of the statistical properties of its own measurement errors pertaining to these random variables.

Under this assumption the firm is able to view the motion of the position

---

6. Compare our result with that of the model of price adjustment of Barro (1972). Barro's model can be made mathematically equivalent to ours by substituting his price variable for the logarithmic level of money wage and setting the drift ω equal to zero. In that paper he calculated the ratio of the expected rate of price change to the expected duration of time up to the first price change and showed that it is an increasing function of the size of the initial disequilibrium. Unfortunately, it is hard to give any meaningful economic interpretation to this ratio. In particular, if it had been calculated as the approximation of the long-run average rate of price change, the result would have been mistaken. For our proposition 6–2 demonstrated that it is zero (i.e., equal to ω) independently of the size of the initial subjective disequilibrium! That is, the law of demand and supply he tried to deduce will evaporate if it is averaged out over long period of time. If, on the other hand, he had tried to approximate the short-run expected rate of price change, the ratio he calculated would have been superfluous. It would have been enough to examine the expected rate of price change in the first period, whose calculation requires only elementary arithmetic, as shown in appendix A6–d.

of its own subjective disequilibrium z_t in the future as constituting a random walk with two barriers at θ_+ and θ_- and a return point θ_0 that is generated by the subjective probability distribution $\hat{\Omega}(\cdot)$. The firm can thus analyze its nature by the same method as that developed in sections 4 and 5. Accordingly, let $\hat{\Pi}_t(z : z_0)$ be the subjective transition probability distribution, representing the firm's probabilistic prediction of the position of subjective disequilibrium in period t, formed on the basis of the firm's knowledge of the initial condition z_0; that is,

$$(6\text{–}11) \qquad \hat{\Pi}_t(z : z_0) \equiv \hat{\Pr}\{z_t \leqslant z_0 : z_0\} \qquad \text{for } t = 1, 2, \ldots$$

Proposition 6–1 then assures the firm that as $t \to \infty$,

$$(6\text{–}12) \qquad \hat{\Pi}_t(z : z_0) \to \hat{\Pi}^\infty(z),$$

independent of the initial condition z_0. The firm is then able to predict the position of its own subjective disequilibrium in the distant future without being bothered by where it starts. We shall call this limit distribution either the subjective steady-state distribution or the subjective long-run average distribution. Its shape is dependent upon the three parameters θ_+, θ_-, and θ_0 and the shape of the subjective probability distribution $\hat{\Omega}(\cdot)$.

This subjective steady-state or long-run average distribution, $\hat{\Pi}^\infty(z)$, will play a key role in formulating the firm's long-run optimization problem. But before we investigate that point, we must look more closely at the firm's cost structure so that we can set up the long-run objective function that the firm seeks to optimize.

7. Specification of the Cost Structure

In appendix 6–e it is shown that the subjective expectation of short-run gross profit (exclusive of any costs associated with the wage adjustment) evaluated at the beginning of period t can be represented by the following functional form:

$$(6\text{–}13) \qquad \hat{E}(r_{t+\tau} : \delta_t \text{ and } w_t) = v_t \rho(z_t).$$

Since the definitions of the variable v_t and the function $\rho(\cdot)$ are fairly messy, we have relegated them to appendix 6–e. But it is easy to interpret them here. The variable v_t, defined by (A6–8), can be interpreted as the trend factor of the firm's short-run expected gross profit, the motion of which is beyond the control of the firm's short-run wage adjustment policy, although its long-run motion may be influenced by the firm's long-term policies concerning fixed capital investment, investment in research and development, marketing strategies, and other factors. However, the function $\rho(\cdot)$, defined by (A6–7), is a function only of the subjective disequilibrium z_t. Its functional form is determined by the subjective parameters that summarize the firm's subjective model of the market environment. This function, which we call the detrended short-run expected profit function, represents the fraction of short-run gross profit that is sensitive to the firm's wage adjustment activity. It then follows from the very characterization of the short-run optimal wage w_t^* (i.e., that it would uniquely maximize the expected gross profit if the costs of wage change were zero) that the detrended short-run expected profit function $\rho(z)$ should attain a unique maximum at the point where the subjective disequilibrium vanishes, (where $w_t = w_t^*$ or, equivalently, $z_t = 0$); that is, $\rho(0) > \rho(z)$ for any $z \neq 0$. This, of course, implies the following first- and second-order conditions for the maximum:

(6–14a) $$\rho'(0) = 0$$

and

(6–14b) $$\rho''(0) < 0.$$

[We should point out that the first-order condition (6–14a) is equivalent to equation (1–17), which defined the subjective-normal ratio of labor demand to supply $\hat{f}^*$.] In general, the further the actual money wage w_t deviates from the short-run optimal wage w_t^*, and hence the larger the absolute value of the subjective disequilibrium z_t, the smaller the short-run gross profit the firm expects to earn. Clearly, the difference between the maximum attainable short-run expected gross profit $v_t\rho(0)$ and the current short-run expected gross profit $v_t\rho(z_t)$ measures the opportunity cost associated with the firm's failure to set w_t equal to w_t^* or z_t equal to zero. For ease of discussion we call this the disequilibrium cost (see figure 6–4).

If we approximate this disequilibrium cost up to the second-order term, we obtain

(6–15) $$v_t\rho(0) - v_t\rho(z_t) \triangleq v_t\left[-\frac{\rho''(0)}{2} \right]z_t^2,$$

where use has been made of the first-order condition (6–14a). The disequilibrium cost is thus seen to be approximately proportional to z_t^2, the square of the value of the subjective disequilibrium, with constant coefficient $-\rho''(0)/2$ which is positive by the second-order condition (6–14b). In what follows, we employ only this quadratic approximation of the disequilibrium cost.

Against the disequilibrium cost, the cost of adjusting money wage has to be weighted. Since we discussed the general nature of wage adjustment costs in section 1 of chapter 5, in the present section we have only to specify their formal structure. We assume that if the money wage is raised at the beginning of period t, the firm will incur a cost equal to $v_t c_+$ in dollar value in that period, and that if the money wage is cut at the beginning of period t, it will cost the firm $v_t c_-$ in dollar value (v_t stands for the trend factor of the expected short-run gross profit). It is further assumed that these upward and downward

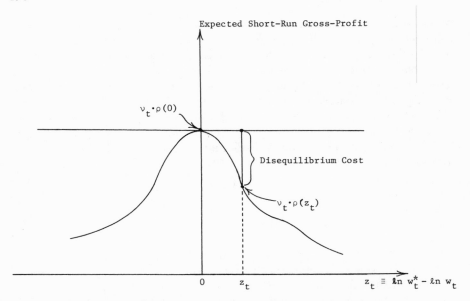

FIGURE 6–4. A Graphic Representation of Disequilibrium Cost

adjustment costs are of lump-sum type, so that the detrended adjustment costs, c_+ and c_-, are constants whose values are insensitive to the rate of wage change.

Whether the wage adjustment cost can be adequately represented by a lump-sum cost is a question whose definite answer requires careful empirical analysis. But our casual empiricism strongly suggests that, unlike the production cost with which conventional economic theory has been almost exclusively concerned, the administrative, informational, and sociological costs (and of course the cost of strikes in the case of the unionized labor market) listed as the chief constituents of wage adjustment cost in chapter 5 contain a good deal of lumpiness. (In fact, this seems to be the very reason why conventional economic theory has not been successful in incorporating these nonproduction costs into its framework.) Although it is not altogether impossible to incorporate adjustment cost that is dependent upon the size of wage change, we shall not, for the reason of expositional simplicity, seek such a generalization in this book. The main themes of part III are not likely to be affected by the introduction of such size-dependent costs of wage adjustment.

Now, if $c_+ = c_- = 0$, we are back to the old Wicksellian economy. The model of wage determination in the Wicksellian economy is therefore a very special case of the model of wage determination in the Keynesian economy. If $c_- > 0$, the money wage is inflexible downward, and if $c_+ > 0$, it is inflexible upward. If c_- is infinite, we say that the money wage is absolutely rigid downward, and if c_+ is infinite, we say that it is absolutely rigid upward. Finally, if c_- is greater than c_+, we say that the money wage is relatively inflexible downward. This is our precise formalization of the notion of downward wage inflexibility in the Keynesian economy. Later, we examine how the structure of wage adjustment cost thus formulated is transformed, via the firm's long-run optimizing efforts, into the structure of the chosen wage adjustment rule, represented by the three parameters θ_+, θ_-, and θ_0.

8. *The Determination of Long-Run Average Total Cost*

The total cost in period t is the sum of disequilibrium cost and adjustment cost. The disequilibrium cost is (approximately) equal to $v_t[-\rho''(0)/2]z_t^2$, whereas the wage adjustment cost is zero if the wage is kept constant, $v_t c_+$ if the wage is raised, and $v_t c_-$ if the wage is cut. The detrended total cost in period t, denoted Λ_t, is thus given by

$$\Lambda_t \equiv [-\rho''(0)/2]z_t^2 \begin{cases} + c_+ & \text{if } z_{t-1} + \Delta \ln w^*_{t-1} > \theta_+ \\ + c_- & \text{if } z_{t-1} + \Delta \ln w^*_{t-1} < \theta_-. \end{cases}$$

Let us assume that the firm as a long-run optimizer is concerned only with the detrended costs and has a very long planning horizon. (This is roughly tantamount to saying that the firm's time-discount rate is equal to the expected growth rate of the trend factor v_t.) To put this in more formally, let's assume that the firm chooses the wage adjustment rule that minimizes the long-run average detrended total cost, given by $\lim_{T \to \infty} \Sigma_{t=1}^{T} \Lambda_t/T$. This is by no means the most general form of the objective function, but if we take account of the bounded rationality of our firm, this does not seem an unreasonable assumption to make. In any case, it would not be so difficult to work out the model with the more complicated objective function, such as the discounted sum of un-detrended total costs.[7] Now, according to the strong law of large numbers, the long-run average is equal to its steady-state expectation. Hence, our firm's determination of the best wage adjustment rule can be reduced to a simple minimization of the steady-state expectation of the detrended total cost, denoted $\hat{E}^\infty(\Lambda)$, evaluated by its subjective steady-state distribution $\Pi^\infty(z)$.[8] Let us compute this.

---

7. In the case of the minimization of the discounted sum of total costs, the firm has to determine the best wage adjustment rule by applying the successive approximation method of the dynamic programming.

8. See appendix 6–c. Since Λ_t is a function of the Markovian random variable z_t, we can directly apply the strong law of large numbers for Markov process and assert that as T goes to infinity,

$$\sum_{t=1}^{T} \Lambda(z_t)/T \to \hat{E}^\infty(\Lambda) \equiv \int \Lambda(z)\, d\hat{\Pi}^\infty(z)$$

with probability 1.

First, let $\hat{V}ar^\infty(z)$ represent the steady-state or long-run average variance of z_t, defined by

$$(6\text{--}16) \qquad \hat{V}ar^\infty(z) \equiv \int_{\theta_-}^{\theta_+} [z - \hat{E}^\infty(z)]^2 d\hat{\Pi}^\infty(z).$$

This is the firm's subjective measure of the volatility of the position of subjective disequilibrium over a long period (this will become an important statistic later). Second, let $\hat{\pi}_+^\infty$ and $\hat{\pi}_-^\infty$ be the probability of wage increase and the probability of wage decrease in a stochastic steady state, respectively. They can be easily calculated as

$$(6\text{--}17) \qquad \hat{\pi}_+^\infty = \int_{\theta_-}^{\theta_+} [1 - \hat{\Omega}(\theta_+ - z)] d\hat{\Pi}^\infty(z)$$

$$\hat{\pi}_-^\infty = \int_{\theta_-}^{\theta_+} \hat{\Omega}(\theta_- - z) d\hat{\Pi}^\infty(z).$$

Then the expected detrended costs of wage hike and of wage cut in a stochastic steady state can be given by $c_+ \hat{\pi}_+^\infty$ and $c_- \hat{\pi}_-^\infty$, respectively.

Putting these calculations together, we can express the steady-state expectation or long-run average of the detrended total cost as follows:

$$(6\text{--}18) \qquad \hat{E}^\infty(\Lambda) = \left[\frac{-\rho''(0)}{2} \right] [\hat{V}ar^\infty(z) + \hat{E}^\infty(z)^2] + c_+ \hat{\pi}_+^\infty + c_- \hat{\pi}_-^\infty.$$

This is evidently a function only of the decision parameters θ_0, θ_+, and θ_-. Thus, the firm's long-run problem of selecting the best wage adjustment rule has been now reduced to the choice of those values of the three parameters that minimize the value of the function. This is a static minimization problem that is clearly within the capacity of the firm's bounded rationality. Let us show how the firm solves this minimization problem.

9. *The Nature of the Best Wage Adjustment Rule* (I)

In the first place, it is easy to establish one of the necessary conditions for the best wage adjustment rule:

Proposition 6–3. *One of the conditions for the best wage adjustment rule is that the value of the return point θ_0^* be chosen in such a way that the long-run average of subjective disequilibrium is equal to zero; that is,*

$$(6\text{--}19) \qquad \hat{E}^\infty(z) \equiv \int_{\theta_-}^{\theta_+} z \, d\hat{\Pi}^\infty(z) = 0.$$

Although the formal proof is relegated to appendix A6–f, its idea is rather trivial. When there is a positive subjective disequilibrium, the firm incurs a disequilibrium cost proportional to its square value, and when there is a negative subjective disequilibrium with the equal absolute magnitude, the firm has to incur the same amount of disequilibrium cost. It is thus easy to see that because of the quadratic nature of the disequilibrium cost, if the firm chooses the return point θ_0^* in such a way that positive and negative subjective disequilibria balance each other in the long run, the disequilibrium cost will, on average, be reduced to the minimum.

A trivial consequence of this proposition is:

Corollary to Proposition 6–3. *The upper barrier θ_+ is always positive and the lower barrier θ_- always negative unless the steady-state distribution is degenerated into a single atom. The optimal return point θ_0^*, on the other hand, can be positive or zero or negative, depending upon the particular values of the basic subjective parameters.*

Proof. If this were not so, the mean of the nondegenerated probability distribution $\hat{\Pi}^\infty(z)$ defined over the interval $[\theta_-, \theta_+]$ could never be zero! (Q.E.D)

This corollary implies that the firm never cuts its money wage when it has a positive subjective disequilibrium and never raises its money wage when it has a negative disequilibrium. This is a self-evident implication of the fact that a positive subjective disequilibrium represents the extent of the firm's frustration over its failure to raise the money wage and that a negative subjective disequilibrium represents the extent of its frustration over its failure to cut the money wage.

By virtue of proposition 6–3, we are now able to rewrite the long-run average of the detrended total cost (6–18) as follows:

$$(6\text{–}20) \qquad \hat{E}^\infty(\Lambda)|_{\theta_0=\theta_0^*} = \left[-\frac{\rho''(0)}{0} \right] \hat{V}\mathrm{ar}^\infty(z) + c_+ \hat{\pi}_+ + c_- \hat{\pi}_- .$$

The firm is now faced with a sharp trade-off in its determination of the best values for the upper and lower barriers. If these barriers are set too far apart, the cost of wage adjustment is expected to diminish, while the variance of subjective disequilibrium and hence the disequilibrium cost rise. If, on the other hand, the barriers are set too close, the disequilibrium cost can be reduced tremendously but only at the expense of the higher expected cost of adjustment. The firm has to find the best balance between these conflicting costs.

10. *The Nature of the Best Wage Adjustment Rule (II)*

To obtain more quantitative information about the nature of the best wage adjustment rule, it is necessary to specify the functional form of the subjective probability distribution $\hat{\Omega}(\cdot)$. For our purposes we suppose that the firm believes that the short-run optimal wage w_t^* is generated by a multiplicative Bernoulli-trial random-walk model. It is well known that the Bernoulli-trial random walk is a discrete-time, discrete-state analog of the celebrated Wiener–Gauss random process.[9]

In the case of the Bernoulli-trial random-walk model, there are only two alternative states in each period: either w_t^* increases by the rate equal to $\hat{s}$ (>0) with probability $\hat{\pi}$ ($0 < \hat{\pi} < 1$) or w_t^* decreases by the same absolute rate with probability $1 - \hat{\pi}$. Thus, the subjective probability distribution $\hat{\Omega}(\cdot)$ can be specified as

$$d\hat{\Omega}(\hat{s}) \equiv \Pr\{\Delta \ln w_t^* = \hat{s}\} = \hat{\pi}, \qquad d\hat{\Omega}(-\hat{s}) \equiv \Pr\{\Delta \ln w_t^* = -\hat{s}\} = 1 - \hat{\pi}.$$

Then the subjective expectation of $\Delta \ln w_t^*$ can be calculated as

$$\hat{\omega} \equiv \hat{E}(\Delta \ln w_t^*) = (2\hat{\pi} - 1)\hat{s};$$

and the subjective second-moment of $\Delta \ln w_t^*$ is given by

$$\hat{E}(\Delta \ln w_t^{*2}) = \hat{s}^2.$$

(The subjective variance of $\Delta \ln w_t^*$ is therefore equal to $\hat{s}^2 - \hat{\omega}^2$). While $\hat{\omega}$ represents the firm's anticipation of the trend growth rate of the short-run optimal wage, $\hat{s}$ represents the firm's view of its changeability.[10,11]

In this special example (see appendix 6–g) it is possible to write down explicitly the subjective steady-state expectation of detrended total cost $\hat{E}^\infty(\Lambda)|_{\theta_0 = \theta_0^*}$ as a function of the two decision parameters θ_+ and θ_- and of the given subjective parameters of the model. Maximizing it with respect to θ_+ ($\geqslant \theta_0^*$) and θ_- ($\leqslant \theta_0^*$), the firm can obtain the optimal parameter values θ_+^* and θ_-^*, and from them the value of θ_0^*, as functions of the given subjective parameters of the model. Unfortunately, even in this special Bernoulli-trial example it is in general impossible to obtain the closed-form solutions of the optimal parameters using pencil and paper. This time-honored computational technique has therefore yielded to the power of the modern electronic computer.

---

9. See, for instance, Cox and Miller (1965) for the relation between Bernoulli-trial random walk and the Wiener process. See footnote 10.

10. Our choice of $\hat{s}$ rather than ($\hat{s}^2 - \hat{\omega}^2$), as the representation of the measure of volatility is motivated by the fact that while the former is invariant to the choice of the length of a unit period, the latter is not. In fact, if we denote by τ the length of a unit period, then for small τ our Bernoulli random walk can be approximated by a Wiener process with drift $\hat{\omega}/\tau$ and variance $\hat{s}^2/\tau$. See, for instance, Cox and Miller (1965).

11. Quite a similar story can be told about the optimal wage adjustment rule even if we replace the Bernoulli-trial random-walk model by another random-walk model which specifies $\hat{\Omega}(\cdot)$ as a mixture of positive and negative exponential probability distributions: $d\hat{\Omega}(x) = e^{-x/\alpha}/(\alpha + \beta)$ for $x > 0$, and $= e^{x/\beta}/(\alpha + \beta)$ for $x < 0$, where $\alpha > 0$ and $\beta > 0$. This random-walk model is known to be a discrete-time analog of another celebrated stochastic process called the birth-and-death process. Since virtually no *new* information could be gained from this case, it will not be explicitly considered in the following discussion.

(There is, however, one special case in which the pencil-and-paper method is still effective. It is the case where the money wage is absolutely rigid downward in the sense that the downward adjustment cost c_- is infinite. Appendix A6–h is devoted to an examination of this special case.)

Let us now summarize very briefly the results obtained by computer analysis. Figure 6–5 illustrates how the optimal parameter values θ^*_-, θ^*_0, and θ^*_+ vary as the value of the expected rate of change in the short-run optimal wage $\hat{\omega}$ varies, in a case where money wage is perfectly flexible upward ($c_+ = 0$) but imperfectly flexible downward ($c_- > 0$). Here the parameter values of $\hat{s}$ and $-\rho''(0)/2$ are fixed throughout at 0.1 and 1.0, respectively, but the downward adjustment cost c_- is specified at 0.1, 1.0, 10, and 100, respectively [figure 6–5(a), (b), (c), and (d)]. The first observation we can make is that the optimal upper barrier θ^*_+ coincides with the optimal return point θ^*_0, implying that the firm is ready to raise the money wage even just after its return to return point θ^*_0, if there is an upward jump in the short-run optimal wage in the next period. Second, we can observe that the upper barrier θ^*_+ as well as the return point θ^*_0 are monotonically decreasing in $\hat{\omega}$ but never become nonpositive. Third, the lower barrier θ^*_- is monotonically increasing in $\hat{\omega}$ for all negative values and some relatively small positive values of $\hat{\omega}$, but starts decreasing as $\hat{\omega}$ exceeds a critical positive value. This lower barrier θ^*_- is always negative. Finally, by comparing figure 6–5(a), (b), (c), and (d), we can easily conclude that the satisfactory range $[\theta^*_-, \theta^*_+]$ widens as the downward adjustment cost c_- increases. That is, the more inflexible the money wage, the more "tolerant" the firm becomes toward its own subjective disequilibrium.

Figure 6–6 illustrates the responses of the optimal parameter values θ^*_-, θ^*_0, and θ^*_+ to the variation of $\hat{\omega}$ in the general case in which money wage is inflexible both downward and upward. Here again the parameter values $\hat{s}$ and $-\rho''(0)/2$ are fixed at 0.1 and 1.0, respectively, and the downward adjustment cost c_- is specified at 0.1, 1.0, 10, and 100, respectively, in figure 6–6(a), (b), (c), and (d); but the value of the upward adjustment cost c_+ is now pegged at a positive level 1.0. In the first place, we can observe that, unlike the special case of zero upward adjustment cost, the optimal upper barrier θ^*_+ no longer coincides with the optimal return point θ^*_0. Second, whereas the optimal return point θ^*_0 is monotonically decreasing in $\hat{\omega}$ for all values of c_-, both the optimal upper and lower barriers, θ^*_+ and θ^*_-, lose monotonic relations to $\hat{\omega}$. Third, it is important for our subsequent analysis to note that in figure 6–6(c) and (d), where the money wage is relatively inflexible downward (i.e., $c_- > c_+$), the satisfactory range $[\theta^*_-, \theta^*_+]$ narrows monotonically as the value of $\hat{\omega}$ gradually increases, for all negative values and for relevant positive values of $\hat{\omega}$, and starts widening out only after a certain positive value of $\hat{\omega}$ is exceeded. [We can observe the opposite in figure 6–6(a), in which the money wage is relatively inflexible upward.] Finally, if we compare figure 6–6(a), (b), (c), and (d), it is easy to see again that the satisfactory range widens as the cost of downward

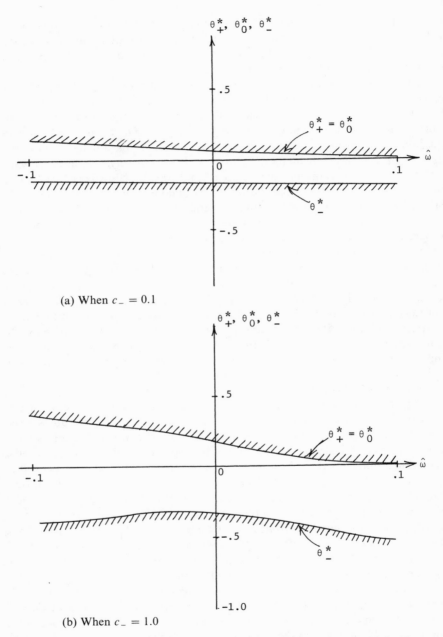

(a) When $c_- = 0.1$

(b) When $c_- = 1.0$

FIGURE 6–5. Relations between the Optimal Decision Parameters and the Expected
Rate of Change in the Short-Run Optimal Wage in the Case of the
Complete Upward Flexibility of Money Wage (i.e., $c_+ = 0$)

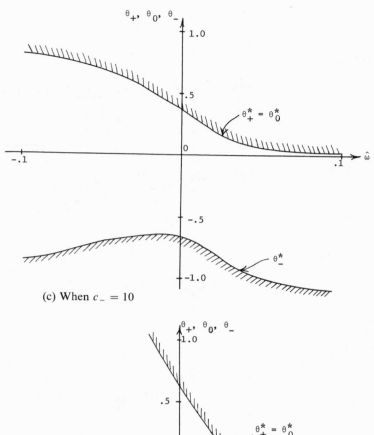

(c) When $c_- = 10$

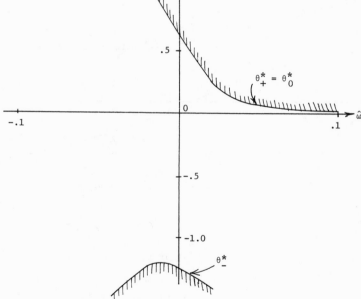

(d) When $c_- = 100$

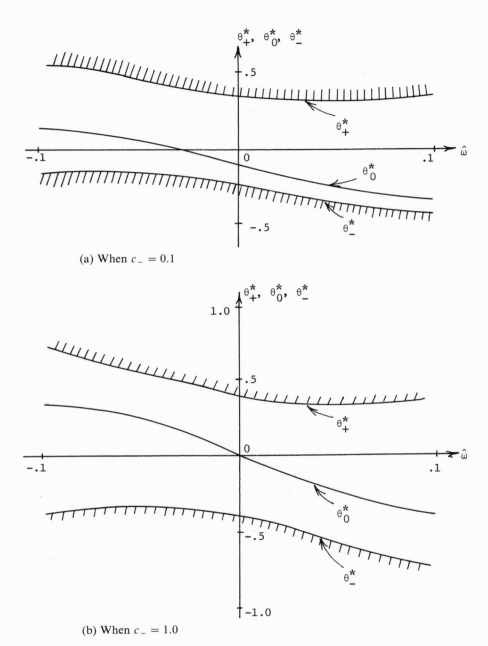

(a) When $c_- = 0.1$

(b) When $c_- = 1.0$

FIGURE 6–6. Relations between the Optimal Decision Parameters and the Expected Rate of Change in the Short-Run Optimal Wage in the Case of the Incomplete Upward Flexibility of the Money Wage (i.e., $c_+ = 1.0$)

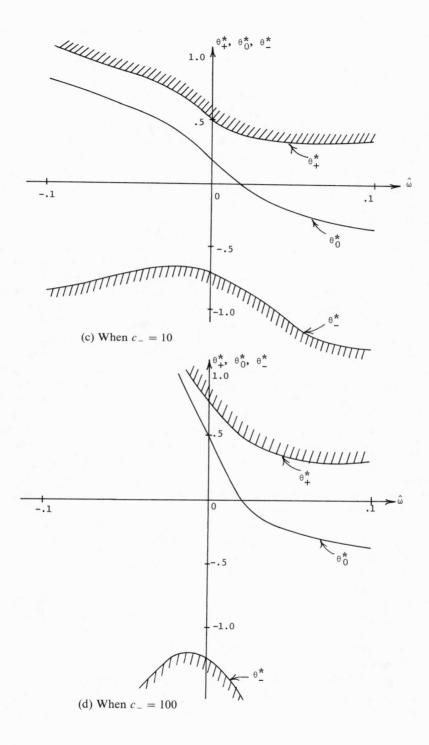

(c) When $c_- = 10$

(d) When $c_- = 100$

wage adjustment c_- increases (while keeping the value of upward adjustment cost c_+ constant).

As for the relations between the optimal parameter values and $\hat{s}$, the measure of volatility of the rate of change in the short-run optimal wage, we are unable to discern any systematic pattern worth reporting here.

If we blow up the satisfactory range determined above by the factor ψ, we obtain the equilibrium band of the Keynesian labor market $[\psi\theta_-^*, \psi\theta_+]$, which played the key role in our analysis of the short-run behavior of the Keynesian economy in chapter 5.

11. How Volatile Is the Stochastic Steady State?

Proposition 6–3 showed that if a firm keeps adopting the best wage adjustment rule, other things being equal, the deviation from zero of its subjective disequilibrium position has a tendency to average out in the long run. To put this slightly differently, the short-run optimal wage w_t^*, which itself has no genuine optimality property in the Keynesian economy, has now reestablished itself as the optimal wage *from the long-run average standpoint*.

Does this really mean that even in this sticky-wage Keynesian economy, no trace of subjective disequilibrium will be left in the long run? The answer seems definitely to be no, but to support this view we have to study in some detail the long-run implications of the adoption of the best wage adjustment rule.

The stochastic steady state the firm's subjective disequilibrium is expected to approach in the long run is not a tranquil environment. In fact, it is just the opposite. In a stochastic steady state, the position of subjection disequilibrium is constantly fluctuating between the upper and lower barriers; its period-to-period behavior exhibits no tendency toward any sort of steadiness or regularity. Regularity would emerge only if the subjective disequilibrium motion is observed for a sufficiently long period of time and then only if it is analyzed using statistical methods.

How volatilely the subjective disequilibrium fluctuates over time can best be measured by its long-run average or steady-state variance $\hat{\text{Var}}^\infty(z)$.

If we substitute the optimal decision parameters θ_0^*, θ_+^*, and θ_-^* obtained in section 10, the steady-state variance of the subjective disequilibrium can be expressed as a function of the basic subjective parameters $\hat{\omega}$, $\hat{s}$ (a measure of the volatility of $\Delta \ln w_t^*$), c_+, c_-, and $-\rho''(0)/2$. Although it is generally impossible to obtain a closed-form expression (except for the special case of absolute downward wage rigidity, as shown in appendix A6–8), it is not so difficult to examine its various properties by the method of numerical analysis. Let us look at the results obtained by such a method.

Figure 6–7 illustrates the relation between $\hat{\text{Var}}^\infty(z)$ and the expected rate of change in the short-run optimal wage $\hat{\omega}$ for selected values of the cost of wage cut c_- in the case of complete upward wage flexibility (i.e., $c_+ = 0$). The

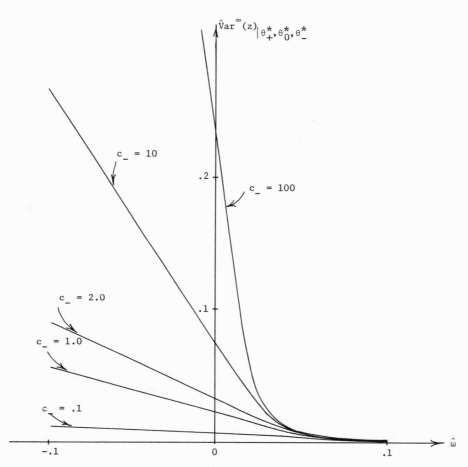

FIGURE 6–7. The Relation between the Steady-State Variance of Subjective
Disequilibrium and the Expected Rate of Change in the Short-Run
Optimal Wage in the Case of Complete Upward Flexibility of the
Money Wage (i.e., $c_+ = 0$)

first obvious observation is that $\hat{\text{Var}}^\infty(z)$ is, other things being equal, a monotonically decreasing function of $\hat{\omega}$ for any value of c_-. The next observation
is that the higher the value of c_-, the more marked does this inverse relationship
become. Figure 6–8, on the other hand, illustrates the relationship between
$\hat{\text{Var}}^\infty(z)$ and $\hat{\omega}$ for selected values of c_- in the general case where the money
wage is somewhat rigid upward as well. As is easily seen from the figure, once
the money wage ceases to be perfectly flexible upward, the monotone relation
between $\hat{\text{Var}}^\infty(z)$ and $\hat{\omega}$ breaks down and the former becomes an increasing
function of the latter for the relatively higher values of the latter. The crucial

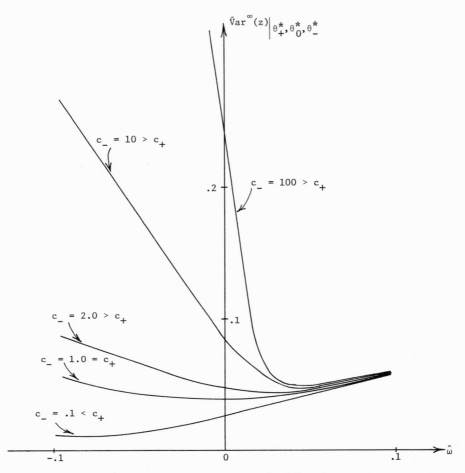

FIGURE 6–8. The Relation between the Steady-State Variance of Subjective
Disequilibrium and the Expected Rate of Change in the Short-Run
Optimal Wage in the Case of Incomplete Upward Flexibility of the
Money Wage (i.e., $c_+ = 1.0$)

point, however, is that, as long as the money wage is relatively inflexible down-
ward in the sense of $c_+ < c_-$, $\hat{V}ar^\infty(z)$ remains a decreasing function of $\hat{\omega}$ for
all the negative values and for the relatively lower positive values of $\hat{\omega}$. As
before, this inverse relation between $\hat{V}ar^\infty(z)$ and $\hat{\omega}$ for the relevant range of
the values of the latter becomes more acute as the value of c_- increases relative
to the value of c_+.

Finally, figure 6–9 illustrates the *typical* relation between $\hat{V}ar^\infty(z)$ and $\hat{s}$—
the measure of the volatility of the rate of change in the short-run optimal
wage. It says that in general the volatility of the subjective disequilibrium is

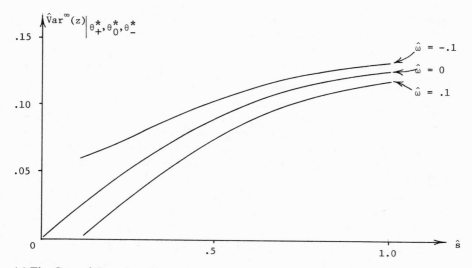

(a) The Case of Complete Upward Wage Rigidity (i.e., $c_+ = 0$ and $c_- = 1.0$)

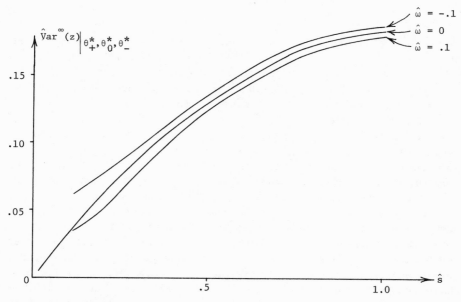

(b) The Case of Relative Downward Wage Rigidity (i.e., $c_+ = 0.5 < c_- = 1.0$)

FIGURE 6–9. The Relation between the Steady-State Variance of Subjective Disequilibrium and the Measure of the Volatility of the Rate of Change in the Short-Run Optimal Wage

positively correlated with the volatility of the rate of change in the short-run optimal wage—its own motive force. We would be surprised at any other result.

It is convenient to summarize the results obtained in the present section:

Proposition 6–4. *The long-run average variance of subjective disequilibrium* $\hat{\text{Var}}(z)$, *associated with the best wage adjustment rule, (a) decreases monotonically as the expected rate of change in the short-run optimal wage $\hat{\omega}$ increases, if the money wage is perfectly flexible upward but imperfectly flexible downward; (b) decreases monotonically as $\hat{\omega}$ increases until a certain positive value of $\hat{\omega}$ is reached but starts increasing as $\hat{\omega}$ is further increased beyond that point, if the money wage is relatively inflexible downward; (c) increases as the measure of the volatility of the rate of change in the short-run optimal wage $\hat{s}$ increases; and (d) increases as either the cost of wage hike c_+ or the cost of wage cut c_- increases.*

In chapter 7 these microeconomic relations are translated into macroeconomic relations and then employed to characterize the long-run Phillips curve.

12. *Summary*

In the present chapter I have developed a model of money wage adjustment that incorporates the cost of money wage change, a formalization of the notion of wage inflexibility in a monopsonistically competitive economy.

In the Wicksellian economy in which the act of wage change is costless at the beginning of every period, the firm determines its money wage so as to maximize the expected gross profit in every period. If, however, the cost of wage adjustment is not negligible, the firm no longer maximizes the expected gross profit in every period, but satisfices in the short run. In the first place, we measured the firm's subjective disequilibrium in the labor market by the proportionate difference between the level of money wage that would maximize the short-run expected gross profit (exclusive of the cost of wage change) and the level of money wage currently quoted. We then supposed that the firm deters wage change as long as its subjective disequilibrium stays within the satisfactory range bound from above by a positive number called the upper barrier and from below by a negative number called the lower barrier, and that it is only when its subjective disequilibrium strays away from this satisfactory range that the firm raises or cuts money wage and adjusts its subjective disequilibrium to another constant called the return point. The upper and the lower barriers of the firm's wage adjustment rule therefore play a role analogous to that of the aspiration level in the satisficing model of H. A. Simon. Like the aspiration level, the position of these barriers, as well as that of the return point, are viewed by the firm as a legacy from the past in the short run.

In the long run, however, the firm's wage adjustment rule itself is subject to change. It will be intermittently adjusted to the demand of reality as the firm accumulates experiences and revises its long-term expectations about market environment. In this book I have not described the process of search but simply supposed that in the long run the firm chooses the values of the upper and the lower barriers and the return point so as to minimize the long-run average total (detrended) cost. Such an adaptation of the wage adjustment rule in the long run will not, however, drive our firm to act like a producer in neoclassical equilibrium theory. In fact, we have succeeded in demonstrating that the motion of the subjective disequilibrium will only approach a stochastic steady state in which the firm's period-to-period wage adjustment activity shows no tendency to assimilate that of the short-run-expected-profit-maximizing firm.

We have seen in this chapter that a firm chooses a value for the return point in such a way that the long-run average of its subjective disequilibrium becomes equal to zero. But we have also seen that, as long as the cost of wage adjustment is not negligible, the variance of subjective disequilibrium, a measure of its long-run volatility, never shrinks to zero. The stochastic steady state is therefore by no means static. Steadiness would emerge only if the motion of subjective disequilibrium is observed for a long period and then analyzed by a statistical method. Furthermore, if the money wage is relatively rigid downward —a reasonable assumption in an advanced capitalist economy—the long-run average variance of subjective disequilibrium can be shown to be inversely related to the long-run average rate of money wage change, at least for the relevant range of the values of the latter.

We have no intention of denying the fact that while Simon's satisficing model was proposed as an alternative to the concept of "economic man as an optimizing animal," our model of money wage adjustment has been developed on the hypothesis that the firm optimizes in the long run. However, if we interpret the cost of wage adjustment in our model as the cost associated with the process of decision making in an organization consisting of heterogeneous groups of people with different motivations, constraints, behavioral traits, knowledge, and so on, it becomes difficult to draw a clear-cut dividing line between our long-run optimizing model and Simon's satisficing model. In fact, the satisficing model does not claim that people are irrational; all it claims is that it is more rational for a complex organization under numerous constraints and considerable risks to satisfice rather than to optimize. In particular, the model of union strike activity developed in chapter 8 as a straightforward extension of the model constructed here, can be regarded as an attempt to analyze an organizational decision process that involves at least three very heterogeneous groups: management, the union leadership, and the union rank and file. The cost of a strike can then be interpreted as the cost associated with the complex decision process during a wage negotiation.

In any case, both the satisficing model and our model of wage adjustment have much richer implications for monetary theory and economic dynamics than does the conventional neoclassical model of the firm, for both models are devised primarily for the analysis of disequilibrium, which is what monetary theory and economic dynamics are all about.

CHAPTER 7

Macroscopic Steady State and the Long-Run Phillips Curve

1. Three Strategic Assumptions

"The myth of macroeconomics," says James Tobin, "is that relations among aggregates are enlarged analogues of relations among corresponding variables for individual households, firms, industries, and markets. The myth is a harmless and useful simplification in many contexts, but sometimes it misses the essence of the phenomena" (1972, p. 9). My aim in this chapter is to show that this myth has indeed been the very root of the persistent failure of conventional economics to explain the persistence of involuntary unemployment as well as the persistence of a trade-off between inflation and unemployment in our modern capitalistic economy.

There are a large number of firms in our Keynesian labor market, each independently quoting wages, hiring workers, and engaging in production. The macroscopic behavior of the labor market is the aggregate outcome of the numerous decentralized decisions of individual firms in it. The aim of this chapter is to show that this macroscopic behavior has its own laws that are fundamentally different from those governing the behavior of individual firms.

We have to introduce two assumptions at the outset. In the first place, we assume throughout the chapter that the Keynesian economy we are going to analyze happens to be in a state of Expectational equilibrium. This is, of course, a stringent assumption to make. But its stringency is by design, for the whole purpose here is to demonstrate that even in a state of Expectational equilibrium—the home ground of neoclassical equilibrium theory—the Keynesian features would never disappear from our Keynesian economy. It is, in other words, a strategic assumption.

Next, we assume that all the firms in our Keynesian economy have already accommodated their wage adjustment rule to their (now correct) expectations in the sense that the rules they have chosen are the best in the class of simple rules. This is again a strategic assumption. For what we would like to show here is that even if all firms act as optimizers in the long run, the Keynesian features cannot be wiped out from our Keynesian economy.

Finally, it is convenient here to recall the assumption, made at the outset of chapter 5, that all firms in our economy are symmetric with respect to the structure of their demand schedules, the structure of their labor supply schedules, their technological relations, the structure of their expectation-formation processes, and so on. It must again be stressed that this assumption *on no account* implies that all firms in our Keynesian economy behave identically. On the contrary, in our dynamic and hence uncertain world, their actual behaviors are quite heterogeneous, both cross-sectionally and intertemporally. Indeed, this is the whole point of the chapter! Workers' relative preferences for a particular firm's working conditions shift gradually over time; spenders' relative preferences for a particular product fluctuate from period to period; the introduction of new production processes, new marketing techniques, and new recruiting methods is never uniform across firms; and accumulation of both tangible and nontangible capital, which is made on the basis of different long-term expectations, follows a different pattern from firm to firm. In consequence, firms gather quite different experiences from their activities in the past and form quite heterogeneous expectations about the conditions of the labor and product markets both at present and in the future. Since the short-run optimal wage $w_t^*(i)$ is constructed on the basis of each firm's own subjective expectations about these market conditions, the motion of the actual wage $w_t(i)$, which is adjusted intermittently in order to keep up with the long-run motion of $w_t^*(i)$, will follow a stochastic path which is quite heterogeneous from firm to firm. In this sense, our assumption of symmetry is once more a strategic one, for what we endeavor to exhibit here is that, even if all firms are symmetric, the behavior of the Keynesian labor market as an aggregate has nothing in common with the behavior of a single firm in it.

Let $\Pi_t(z:z_0)$ be, as before, the objective probability of the position of subjective disequilibrium of a firm, which happens to start at a given subjective disequilibrium z_0 in the initial period. In virtue of the assumption of symmetry, this objective transition distribution is uniform across firms and does not explicitly contain the firm-specific label i.

2. Macroscopic Steady State

For the time, suppose that *all* firms in the economy happen to start at position z_0 in period zero. [This assumption is employed solely for expositional brevity. The following argument requires little change even if subjective disequilibria in period zero are distributed according to an initial distribution $\Pi_0(z)$.] From period zero on, each firm adjusts its money wage according to the identical adjustment rule but on the basis of different market experiences unfolding over time. Since the probability that the subjective disequilibrium will transit to a position not higher than z is represented by the same $\Pi_t(z:z_0)$ for every firm, the expected number of firms whose subjective disequilibrium is not higher than z in period t must equal $I\,\Pi_t(z:z_0)$, where I is the number of firms in the economy. Furthermore, if I is sufficiently large (and, in fact, we so assumed it to be), by the strong law of large numbers of appendix 3–a, we can regard $I\,\Pi_t(z:z_0)/I = \Pi_t(z:z_0)$ as approximating the *actual proportion of firms* whose subjective disequilibrium is not higher than z in period t; that is, we have

(7–1) $\Pi_t(z:z_0)\,\underline{\Delta}$ the actual proportion of firms in period t whose
               subjective disequilibrium $z_t(i)$ is not higher than z
               provided that they all started from the same initial
               position z_0 in period zero.

Accordingly, $\Pi_t(z:z_0)$ can be interpreted as the cross-section distribution of subjective disequilibria in period t. The transition probability distribution, introduced in chapter 6 as a summary representation of the intertemporal motion of the subjective disequilibrium of an individual firm, has now reappeared as the cross-sectional picture of the labor market as a whole, describing how subjective disequilibria are distributed across firms within each period. This equivalence between the intertemporal picture of a single firm and the atemporal snapshot of numerous firms in the market constitutes the foundation of our synthetic treatment of micro and macro structures of the Keynesian economy. In fact, it will allow us to apply, with little modification, all the propositions of chapter 6 to the analysis of the atemporal structure of the labor market as a whole.

Let us first make use of proposition 6–1 (the steady-state theorem). It says that after a sufficiently long passage of time, the transition distribution $\Pi_t(z:z_0)$, which now represents the cross-section distribution of subjective disequilibria, converges to the steady-state distribution $\Pi^\infty(z)$:

(7–2) $\Pi_t(z:z_0) \to \Pi^\infty(z)$,

independently of the initial position z_0. (Thus, the assumption that all firms happened to start at the same initial disequilibrium is made immaterial!)

In chapter 6 this steady-state distribution was interpreted as the probabilistic prediction of the position of subjective disequilibrium of a single firm in a stochastic steady-state. It was also pointed out that the same steady-state distribution is the long-run average summary of the randomly fluctuating subjective disequilibrium of a single firm.

In this chapter, which is concerned with the macroscopic structure of the labor market, this steady-state distribution can be interpreted as the cross-sectional picture of the positions of subjective disequilibrium of all the firms in a "macroscopic steady state"—the steady state of the labor market as a whole, which is maintained by offsetting motions of a large number of firms perpetually thrown out of subjective equilibrium by incessant stochastic disturbances of labor supplies, product demands, capital stocks, technical knowledge, and other factors.[1] It is a state of the labor market in which the cross-section picture of subjective disequilibria in it can be described by the same steady-state distribution $\Pi^\infty(z)$ from period to period. However, it is by no means a static situation. To the contrary, it is a state of continual flux; the subjective disequilibrium of *each* firm fluctuates stochastically from positive to negative and from negative to positive and never exhibits any tendency toward tranquility. [As a matter of fact, the prediction of the position of the subjective disequilibrium $z_{t+t'}$ in period $(t + t')$ of the individual firm whose subjective disequilibrium in period t is z_t is still given by the transition probability $\Pi_{t'}(z : z_t)$, even in this macroscopic steady state; and the steady-state distribution $\Pi^\infty(z)$ has nothing to do with the short-run movement of an individual firm's subjective disequilibrium.] That the labor market as a whole is in a macroscopic steady state means only that a large number of transitions of subjective disequilibria in opposite directions balance each other and keep reproducing the same cross-section distribution from period to period.

A macroscopic steady state is an *equilibrium of microscopic disequilibria*. Its characteristic feature lies in the marked contrast between the tranquil and homogeneous aggregative behavior and the volatile and heterogeneous individual behaviors. To use a biological analogy (which is certainly a bad habit of economists), it would be likened to a swarm of mosquitoes which, observed from a distance, appears merely as a white cloud more or less stable in its figuration. But on closer examination (which we do taking some care not to be stung), it would be found to be a cluster of thousands of mosquitoes, each dancing wildly to and fro and up and down. Similarly, if we are content to examine only the aggregate behavior of the labor market, we will never understand the actual dynamic behavior of individual firms in it. If, on the other hand, we focus our attention only on the short-run behavior of an individual firm, we easily lose the sight of the structure of the labor market as a whole. Only if we succeeded in synthesizing the micro- and macroscopic analyses would a complete picture of the dynamic and complex labor market emerge before our eyes.

3. *How to Aggregate?*

We are now in a position to analyze more closely the aggregate structure of the Keynesian labor market when it has settled into a macroscopic steady state. The key to this macroscopic analysis is the observation, already put

---

1. A notion similar to the macroscopic steady state was first introduced into macroeconomics by Tobin (1972). Analogous notions have also appeared in other branches of economics: for example, the description of the long-run equilibrium size distribution of incomes in Champernowne (1953) and the description of the long-run equilibrium size distribution of business firms in Simon and Bonini (1958), to name a few.

forth, that $\Pi^{\infty}(z)$ can be interpreted from the microscopic viewpoint as the steady-state probability distribution of the position of an individual firm's subjective disequilibrium, and from the macroscopic viewpoint as the cross-section distribution of subjective disequilibria in a macroscopic steady state. For this suggests to us that we can translate all the propositions established in chapter 6 pertaining to the *long-run average* motions of an individual firm's subjective disequilibrium and other random variables, into macroscopic laws characterizing the relations among their economy-wide averages in a macroscopic steady state.

To illustrate this method of translation, let $k_t(1), k_t(2), \ldots, k_t(I)$ be a set of variables distributed across firms, and let K_t represent their economy-wide weighted average $\Sigma_{i=1}^{I} \gamma_t(i) k_t(i)$, with weights $\gamma_t(1), \gamma_t(2), \ldots, \gamma_t(I)$ adding to unity. If the variable $k_t(i)$ and the corresponding weighted $\gamma_t(i)$ are not strongly correlated with each other, this weighted average can be approximated by the arithmetic average $(1/I)\Sigma_{i=1}^{I} k_t(i)$.[2] Furthermore, if each of the variables $k_t(i)$ is a function only of the value of subjective disequilibrium $z_t(i)$ and is representable as $k_t(i) = k[z_t(i)]$, then the value of this arithmetic average in a macroscopic steady state can be calculated, by means of the cross-section distribution $\Pi^{\infty}(z)$, as $\int k(z)d\Pi^{\infty}(z)$. But this expression is simply $E^{\infty}[k(z)]$, the steady-state expectation or the long-run average of the random variable $k_t(i)$ for an arbitrarily chosen firm in the economy. Hence, we have established a formal equivalence between the economy-wide aggregate of the micro variables distributed across firms in a macroscopic steady state and the long-run average of each of these micro variables; that is,

$$K_t \triangleq E^{\infty}[k(z)].$$

We are thus able to proceed, without any further preparation, to an analysis of the laws that govern the relations among aggregate variables in a macroscopic steady state. Indeed, all we have to do is to apply this method of translation almost mechanically to the results we obtained in chapter 6.

Before we proceed, however, let me emphasize at this point, to avoid any confusion, that our discussion here of the formal equivalence between the economy-wide average in a macroscopic steady state and the long-run average for an individual firm by no means implies a vindication of the "myth of macroeconomics." On the contrary, the point made earlier must be repeated—the

---

2. K_t can be rewritten

$$K_t \equiv \sum_{i=1}^{I} \gamma_t(i)k_t(i)$$

$$= \frac{1}{I}\sum_{i=1}^{I} k_t(i) + \sum_{i=1}^{I}\left[\gamma_t(i) - \frac{1}{I}\right]k_t(i).$$

Hence, if $\gamma_t(i)$ and $k_t(i)$ are not correlated, the second term approaches zero as I gets larger.

behavior of an individual firm *at each moment in time* is almost totally dissimilar to the behavior of the aggregate and should never be regarded as being representative of the aggregate. Our equivalence principle merely insists on the formal equivalence between the average over time and the average over the population of firms, that is, between two averages, *not* between an individual and the average.

4. *The Rate of Change in the General Money Wage Level in a Macroscopic Steady State*

To begin with, let us apply our method of translation to the determination of the rate of change in the general money wage level. First, as shown in appendix 7–a, the proportionate change in the general wage level $\Delta \ln W_t$ can be expressed as the following weighted average of individual rates of money wage changes:

$$(7-3) \qquad \Delta \ln W_t = \sum_{i=1}^{I} \sigma_t(i) \Delta \ln w_t(i),$$

where the weight $\sigma_t(i)$ is defined by (A7–4). Now the rate of change in the money wage of an individual firm, $\Delta \ln w_t(i)$, almost always deviates from its expected value $E[\Delta \ln w_t(i) : z_t(i)]$. But for the labor market as a whole, these individual deviations tend to cancel each other out. In fact, by the strong law of large numbers, we can approximate, under certain reasonable conditions, the average of realized rates of money wage change by the average of expected rates of money wage change and obtain

$$(7-4) \qquad \Delta \ln W_t \underset{\Delta}{} \sum_{i}^{I} \sigma_t(i) E[\Delta \ln w_t(i) : z_t(i)].$$

Since we know from (6–7) that $E[\Delta \ln w_t(i) : z_t(i)]$ is a function only of $z_t(i)$, we are now able to apply our method of translation to the right-hand side of the approximate equation (7–4) and obtain

$$(7-5) \qquad \Delta \ln W^{\infty} \underset{\Delta}{} E^{\infty}(\Delta \ln w),$$

where ∞ on the right shoulder of an aggregate variable indicates the macroscopic steady state. That is, the rate of change in the general money wage in a macroscopic steady state is shown to be approximately equal to $E^{\infty}(\Delta \ln w)$, the long-run average rate of money wage change for any firm in the economy. But we know from proposition 6–2 that this long-run average of the rate of change in the money wage is, in turn, equal to the expected rate of change in the short-run optimal wage, $\omega \equiv E(\Delta \ln w_t^*)$. We have thus established:

> Proposition 7–1. *In a macroscopic steady state the rate of change in the general money wage level is approximately equal to the constant expected rate of change in the short-run optimal wage ω:*

(7–6) $\qquad\qquad\qquad \Delta \ln W^\infty \underset{\Delta}{=} \omega.$

In appendix 7–b it is shown that in a macroscopic steady state, the rate of change in the general wage level $\omega \underset{\Delta}{=} \Delta \ln W^\infty$ is determined roughly by the growth rate of the nominal total product demand per worker, which may be represented by $\Delta \ln (PX/L)^\infty$. However, unless the total product demand schedule, total labor supply schedule, and the way the government and the central bank conduct their policies are specified in detail, we cannot say anything definite about the factors that ultimately govern the long-run motion of the per capita nominal total product demand.

In any case, insofar as the macroscopic steady state is concerned, a change in ω or, more generally, a shift in the probability distribution of the rate of change in the short-run optimal wage $\Omega(\cdot)$ is the only route through which changes in macroeconomic conditions, both real and monetary, are capable of being transmitted to the Keynesian labor market. Needless to say, however, once the economy is thrown out of the macroscopic steady state, changes in macroeconomic conditions find many other routes for the exertion of influence on the aggregative performance of the Keynesian labor maket, as we have seen in chapter 5.

5. The Labor Market Gap in a Macroscopic Steady State

The second application of our method of translation is concerned with a determination of the value of the labor market gap in a macroscopic steady state. For this purpose, let us first recall proposition 5–1, which maintains that for the economy to be in Expectational equilibrium, the labor market gap has to be approximately equal to the aggregate intended gap, a constant multiple of the aggregate subjective disequilibrium:

(7–7) $\qquad\qquad\qquad \left(\dfrac{H_t}{L_t} - f^* \right) \Big/ f^* \underset{\Delta}{=} \psi Z_t.$

Now, the aggregate subjective disequilibrium Z_t is by definition (5–5) the weighted average of the subjective disequilibria for all the firms in the economy: $Z_t \equiv \Sigma_{i=1}^I [l_t(i)/L_t] z_t(i)$. To this we can directly apply our method of translation and assert that in a macroscopic steady state the aggregate subjective disequilibrium is approximately equal to the long-run average value of any firm's subjective disequilibrium:

(7–8) $\qquad\qquad\qquad Z^\infty \underset{\Delta}{=} E^\infty(z).$

But by proposition 6–3, $E^\infty(z)$ is equal to zero! Hence, in view of (7–7), we have obtained:

Proposition 7–2. *In a macroscopic steady state, the labor market gap is approximately equal to zero:*

(7–9) $$\left(\frac{H^\infty}{L^\infty} - f^*\right)\bigg/ f^* \underline{\triangle}\, 0.$$

It is thus demonstrated that, even in the sticky-wage Keynesian economy, once a macroscopic steady state is reached, the demand for and the supply of workers as a whole restore their normal balance. It is now tempting to draw the conclusion that in spite of the supposed inflexibility of money wages, the beautiful neoclassical picture of the economy would reassert itself in a macroscopic steady state. Such a conclusion would, however, be mistaken. The restoration of a normal balance between total labor demand and total labor supply is by no means the same as the evaporation of disequilibria from the labor market. On the contrary, stochastic disturbances to the market environment, coupled with the inflexibility of money wages, constantly force firms away from their subjective equilibrium. The macroscopic steady state is merely a state in which the macroscopic composition of their subjective disequilibria happens to be steady over time. This disequilibrium nature of the macroscopic steady state should have significant implications for the determination of the aggregate rate of involuntary unemployment therein, as we see shortly.

6. *The Aggregate Rate of Involuntary Unemployment in a Macroscopic Steady State*

In a macroscopic steady state of the Keynesian economy, the absence of a labor market gap simply indicates the existence of a normal balance between the aggregate rate of involuntary unemployment and the aggregate rate of unfilled job vacancies; on no account should it be thought to imply that the aggregate rate of involuntary unemployment itself equals its normal rate. Economic forces determining the value of labor market gap therein are of a different type from those that are working for the determination of the aggregate rate of involuntary unemployment.

What, then, determines the aggregate rate of involuntary unemployment? In section 8 of chapter 5 we were able to deduce a schedule that decomposes the aggregate rate of involuntary unemployment into three more or less independent components. For convenience, let us reproduce this aggregate unemployment schedule (5–13) here:

(7–10) $$U_t \underline{\triangle}\, u^* + u^{***}D_t - \left[u^{**}\left(\frac{H_t}{L_t} - f^*\right)\bigg/ f^* - u^{***}\left(\frac{H_t}{L_t} - f^*\right)^2 \bigg/ f^{*2}\right],$$

where $u^* > 0$ is the constant normal rate of involuntary unemployment, and $u^{**} > 0$ and $u^{***} > 0$ are positive constants whose values are determined by the same structural parameters as those determining u^*; D_t in the second term is the cross-section dispersion index, which measures how dispersively the expected ratios of labor demand to supply are scattered across firms; and the third term is related inversely to the value of labor market gap, which represents the overall tightness of the labor market.

If we confine our attention to a macroscopic steady state, proposition 7–2 tells us that the labor market gap approaches zero, so that the third term in schedule (7–10) vanishes. In consequence, the aggregate rate of involuntary unemployment in a macroscopic steady state is pegged by the normal rate of involuntary unemployment u^* and the dispersion index D_t. Since u^* is a constant, a determination of the aggregate rate of involuntary unemployment in the long run boils down to a determination of the value of D_t, that is, to a determination of the dispersion of the expected labor demand/supply ratios across firms in a macroscopic steady state. What, then, determines D_t in a macroscopic steady state?

To answer this question, let us rewrite the definition (5–14) in a slightly different manner:

$$(7\text{--}11) \qquad D_t = \sum_{i=1}^{I} \left[\frac{l_t(i)}{L_t}\right] \left\{ \frac{E[h_t(i)/l_t(i):\delta_t(i)] - f^*}{f^*} - \frac{H_t/L_t - f^*}{f^*} \right\}^2.$$

Now, insofar as a state of Expectational equilibrium is concerned, the proportionate gap between the expected ratio of labor demand to supply and its normal ratio, $\{E[h_t(i)/l_t(i):\delta_t(i)] - f^*\}/f^*$, is by (5–4) equal to the constant multiple of the subjective disequilibrium $\psi z_t(i)$, and the labor market gap $(H_t/L_t - f^*)/f^*$ is by (7–7) approximately equal to the same constant multiple of the aggregate subjective disequilibrium ψZ_t. D_t is therefore approximately proportional to the weighted variance of subjective disequilibria distributed across firms in the labor market:

$$(7\text{--}12) \qquad D_t \triangleq \psi^2 \sum_{i=1}^{I} \left[\frac{l_t(i)}{L_t}\right] [z_t(i) - Z_t]^2.$$

Once again we can apply our method of translation to relation (7–12) and conclude that in a macroscopic steady state the cross-section dispersion index becomes approximately proportional to the steady-state variance of the motion of an individual firm's subjective disequilibrium:

$$(7\text{--}13) \qquad\qquad\qquad D^\infty \triangleq \psi^2 \operatorname{Var}^\infty(z),$$

If we substitute this result (as well as proposition 7–2) into the aggregate unemployment schedule (7–10), we obtain:

Proposition 7–3. *In a macroscopic steady state, the aggregate rate of involuntary unemployment is approximately equal to the sum of the constant normal rate of involuntary unemployment u^* and the term proportional to the steady-state variance of the subjective disequilibrium $\operatorname{Var}^\infty(z)$ of any firm in the economy:*

$$(7\text{--}14) \qquad\qquad\qquad U^\infty \triangleq u^* + u^{***} \psi^2 \operatorname{Var}^\infty(z).$$

We have thus reduced the question "what determines the aggregate rate of involuntary unemployment in a macroscopic steady state?" to the very specific question "what determines the steady-state variance of subjective disequilibrium of an individual firm?" We already have an answer to this question, for it was shown in chapter 6 that the steady-state variance of subjective disequilibrium (under the assumption of Expectational equilibrium) is determined by the objective elasticities of product demand and labor supply (η and ε), the degree of return to labor input (γ), the objective probability distributions of the firm's expectation errors $[A(\cdot), B(\cdot), \text{and } A^{(\tau)}(\cdot)]$, the costs of money wage change (c_+ and c_-), and the objective probability distribution of the rate of change in the short-run optimal wage $[\Omega(\cdot)]$. The fact that it is dependent upon $\Omega(\cdot)$ and, in particular, upon the expected rate of change in the short-run optimal wage ω is the most crucial. For proposition 7–1, which demonstrated that in the macroscopic steady state the rate of change in the general money wage level $\Delta \ln W^\infty$ is brought into equality with this constant number ω, immediately implies:

Proposition 7–4. *Even in a macroscopic steady state the aggregate rate of involuntary unemployment is correlated with the rate of change in the general money wage level $\Delta \ln W^\infty$, which registers expected long-run changes in the economy's macroeconomic conditions, both real and monetary.*

Thus, even if we supposed that all the firms happen to be in their expectational equilibrium and even though we confined our attention to a macroscopic steady state, the *nonneutrality of money* ceases to disappear from our Keynesian economy! The aggregate rate of involuntary unemployment, one of the most important "real" variables, is found to be correlated, even in the long run, with the time pattern of the general money wage level, which is one of the most important nominal variables. It is true that this long-run nonneutrality of money in our Keynesian economy is due to the assumed stickiness of money wages. If this stickiness of money wages were regarded as a manifestation of a certain money illusion involved in firms' wage adjustment activity, it would be this money illusion that is the raison d'être of the monetary economy itself, in that most economic contracts are expressed in terms of money of account.

7. The Theory of the Long-Run Phillips Curve

In reality, the inflexibility of money wages is *not* symmetric between upward and downward. As already pointed out, money wages in the modern capitalist economy are less flexible downward than upward. In our formal model of wage adjustment, this *downward* money wage inflexibility is translated into the assumption that the (detrended) cost of wage cut c_- is higher than the (detrended) cost of wage hike c_+. Now, this assumption of the downward inflexibility of money wage would bear a crucial implication for the long-run relation between the aggregate rate of involuntary unemployment and the rate of change in the general wage level. For we can immediately translate proposition 6–4, which established relations between the steady-state variance of the individual firm's subjective disequilibrium and the expectation and dispersion of the rate of change in the short-run optimal wage, into the following proposition pertaining to the aggregative nature of the long run of our Keynesian economy.

> Proposition 7–5. *In the Keynesian economy, even if it has settled into a macroscopic steady state, (a) if money wages are imperfectly flexible (or absolutely rigid) downward but perfectly flexible upward, the aggregate rate of involuntary unemployment is monotonically decreasing in the rate of change in the general wage level; and (b) if money wages are also inflexible upward but remain more flexible than downward, the aggregate rate of involuntary unemployment is still decreasing in the rate of change in the general wage level except when the value of the latter becomes very high. In either case, the stickier money wages are in the downward direction, the stronger is the inverse relation between the aggregate rate of involuntary unemployment and the steady-state rate of wage inflation. (c) Furthermore, under normal circumstances, the aggregate rate of involuntary unemployment tends to increase as the market conditions become more uncertain or firms' expectation-formation processes become more speculative. These relations are explained visually by figures 7–1 to 7–4.*

A set of curves in figures 7–1 and 7–2 were drawn first by exchanging the horizontal and vertical axes of figures 6–7 and 6–8, then by blowing up the resulting curves in the proportion of $u^{***}\psi^2$, and finally by shifting them to the right by the magnitude of u^*. Evidently, each one of them represents a "long-run Phillips curve"—the long-run trade-off between unemployment and inflation—of our Keynesian economy. As long as money wages are less flexible downward, the long-run Phillips curve is downward-sloping, at least for the relevant range of the values of the long-run rate of money wage inflation; and the more downwardly inflexible the money wage, the flatter the long-run Phillips curve and the worse the long-run trade-off between unemployment and inflation.

On the other hand, figures 7–3 and 7–4 are simple translations of figures 6–9 and 6–10. They now represent the long-run relation between the aggregate rate of involuntary unemployment and s—the measure of the volatility of the rate of change in the short-run optimal wage. They suggest that the stability of market conditions tends to reduce the aggregate rate of involuntary unem-

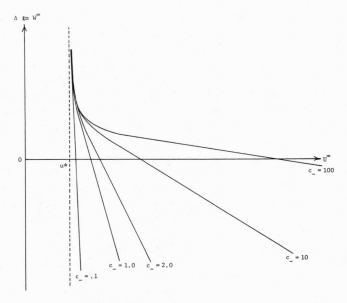

FIGURE 7–1. The Long-Run Phillips Curves in the Case of Complete Upward Money Wage Flexibility (i.e., $c_+ = 0 < c_-$)

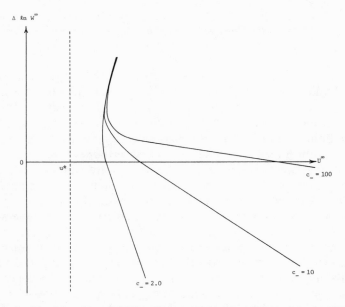

FIGURE 7–2. The Long-Run Phillips Curves in the Case Where Money Wages Are Relatively Inflexible Downward (i.e., $0 < c_+ = 1.0 < c_-$)

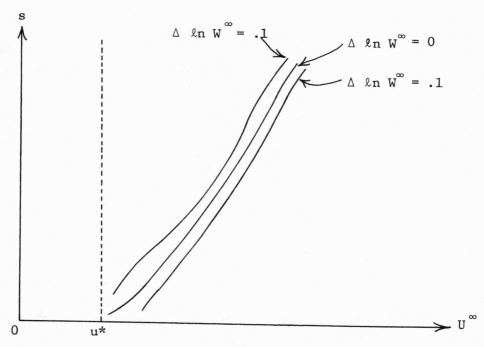

FIGURE 7–3. The Long-Run Relations between the Aggregate Rate of Involuntary
Unemployment and the Stochastic Volatility of the Economy in the
Case of Complete Upward Wage Flexibility (i.e., $c_+ = 0 < c_- = 1.0$)

ployment in the long run, even if the steady-state rate of wage inflation is kept
constant.

The course of economic changes is never uniform across firms. There are
always some firms that are contracting even during a boom, and some firms
that are expanding even during a slump. Contracting firms try to release some
workers into, and expanding firms try to lure some workers from, the labor
market. In a capitalist economy in which money wages are determined not by
a decree but by decentralized decisions of individual firms, such incessant
redistributions of workers, necessitated by the course of economic development,
have no other way but to be guided by the change in the structure of relative
wages, resulting from individual firms' wage adjustment activities. An expanding
firm that expects a supernormal excess demand for labor wishes to raise its
money wage relative to the general wage level (as well as to the general price
level); and a contracting firm that expects a subnormal excess demand for labor
wishes to lower its relative wage. But when money wages are more-or-less
rigid, this intended adjustment in the structure of relative wages tends to be

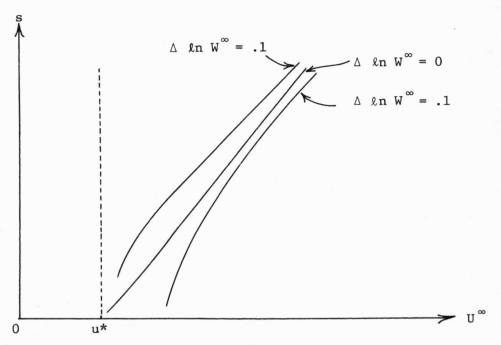

FIGURE 7-4. The Long-Run Relations between the Aggregate Rate of Involuntary Unemployment and the Stochastic Volatility of the Economy in the Case of Relative Downward Wage Rigidity (i.e., $c_+ = 0.5 < c_- = 1.0$)

delayed, and as a result, the involuntary unemployment of workers (and the unfilled vacancies of jobs) will never disappear from the labor market, even in the long run. If, furthermore, as is characteristic in the modern capitalistic economy, money wages are less flexible *downward*, such maladjustment of the structure of relative wages to ever-changing market climates can be made smoother, and hence the aggregate rate of involuntary unemployment can be lowered permanently if it is possible to raise the long-run rate of wage inflation without causing a cumulative inflation process. The reason is simple. If the rate of wage inflation is expected to be higher, firms anticipating excess labor supply are capable of lowering their relative wages not by lowering their own money wages and hence incurring expensive adjustment costs, but by merely sitting back and waiting for other firms to raise money wages! In other words, in the economy with downward inflexibility of money wages, the higher rate of money wage inflation works as a "lubricant" to the necessary adjustment of the structure of relative wages. And it is this lubrication mechanism that is responsible for the existence of a permanent trade-off between wage inflation and involuntary unemployment in our Keynesian economy, as asserted in proposition 7–5.[3]

Before leaving this section we must warn the reader that our downward-sloping long-run Phillips curve is drawn by tracing out the steady-state pairs of the aggregate rate of involuntary unemployment and the rate of change in the general wage level. Each point along the curve corresponds to one imaginary macroscopic steady state with a given rate of wage inflation. Therefore, the long-run Phillips curve itself represents only an *associative* relation between the aggregate rate of involuntary unemployment and the rate of wage inflation. It tells use nothing about the actual transition path of the economy from one macroscopic steady state to another, nor does it tell us whether such a transition is stable or even possible. To trace the actual development of our Keynesian economy out of the macroscopic steady state, we have to have recourse to the method of causal analysis developed in chapter 5.

The rationale for our derivation of the long-run Phillips curve should be found, therefore, not in its descriptive value but in its role as a benchmark for our description of the short-run behavior of the economy. The notion of the long run in our disequilibrium economic dynamics is not intended as an approximation of the reality, toward which the actual economy is supposed to be approaching, but is devised as an analytical norm by means of which we are able to scale the extent of disequilibrium of the actual economy and, if possible and necessary, provide a certain guide for the policy for its alleviation.

8. *The Inflexibility of Money Wages and the Stability of Monetary Economy, Once Again*

Perhaps the most important conclusion in part II was that it is not the Invisible Hand of the price mechanism but the inflexibility of money wages that empowers the monetary economy with rationality. Any attempt of fluidifying money wages, without any conscious coordination of firms' money wage determinations, would inject a violent instability into our monetary economy.

Of course, there is no "free lunch" in the sphere of economics. The inflexibility of money wages has enhanced the stability of the monetary economy only at a price. Indeed, we have learned in this chapter that an increase in the cost of wage adjustment would shift the long-run Phillips curve to the right

---

3. Similar points have been made by Schultz (1959), Lipsey (1960), Archibald (1970), Hansen (1970), Rees (1970), and Tobin (1972). It is also of some interest to point out that the disaggregative view of the phenomenon of unemployment expounded here has a certain similarity to that of Hayek in a 1958 article. There is, however, the fundamental difference between our view and Hayek's. It is that, whereas Hayek regards this as the primary explanation of unemployment both in the short and long runs, we regard this as complementary to the Wicksellian and Keynesian explanations of unemployment, discussed in chapter 3 to 5.

and worsen the "cruel dilemma" between inflation and unemployment in a macroscopic steady state. It is, however, quite wrong to translate the problem of the choice of a regime between a flexible wage economy and an inflexible wage economy into a simple trade-off between the favorable long-run Phillips curve and the stability of equilibrium. When the stability of equilibrium itself is at stake, it is absurd to judge the efficacy of alternative economic regimes by the performance of the equilibrium state alone. Only after we have solved the problem of how to get there should we face the problem of how to improve the performance of the equilibrium state. There is no simple trade-off, but a "hierarchy of problems," which we must attack one by one.

The foregoing consideration gives us a valuable insight into the nature of an incomes policy. By an "incomes policy" we mean a form of public policy that seeks to influence directly the wage-setting and/or price-setting behaviors of private institutions (such as firms and trade unions) to produce greater stability of prices and wages. Within the theoretical framework of part III, an incomes policy can be understood as a political devise for raising the cost of wage increases c_+. Then, if firms are convinced that the implementation of incomes policy is not temporary, they will start to raise the upper barrier of the satisfactory range in their wage adjustment rule, with the consequence of raising the barrier of inflationary hysteria of the equilibrium band in the labor market. It then follows that under an effective incomes policy, the danger of a large random shock's disrupting the conditions for Wicksellian equilibrium and triggering off a cumulative inflation process would recede. We can thus locate the primal raison d'être of incomes policy in its tendency to stabilize the monetary economy in the upward direction. It should not be regarded, as is often claimed, as a policy that seeks to obtain a favorable long-run Phillips curve. On the contrary, under incomes policy, as for any other policy that raises the cost of wage adjustment, the long-run Phillips curve will shift to the right and the economy must face a worsened trade-off between inflation and unemployment once it has reached a macroscopic steady state.

This is readily seen in figures 7–5 and 7–6 which depict the relationships between the steady-state rate of wage inflation and the equilibrium band of the aggregate rate of involuntary unemployment in the case where $c_+ = 0$ and $c_- = 10$ and in the case where $c_+ = 1$ and $c_- = 10$, respectively. They also show the long-run Phillips curves as benchmarks.[4] It is then clear from a comparison of these two diagrams that an increase in the cost of a wage hike c_+ from zero to 1 has enlarged the equilibrium band while shifting the long-

---

4. The equilibrium band of the aggregate rate of involuntary unemployment is given by (5–6) as $[u^* + u^{***}D_t - (u^{**}\psi\theta_+ - u^{***}\psi^2\theta_+^2), \ u^* + u^{***}D_t - (u^{**}\psi\theta_- - u^{***}\psi^2\theta_-^2)]$. Noting that $u^* + u^{***}D_t \underline{\Delta} U^\infty$, a simple substitution of the numerical relation between $\omega \underline{\Delta} \Delta \ln W^\infty$ and the satisfactory range $[\theta^*, \theta_+^*]$ obtained in section 10 of chapter 6 allows us to construct figures 7–5 and 7–6.

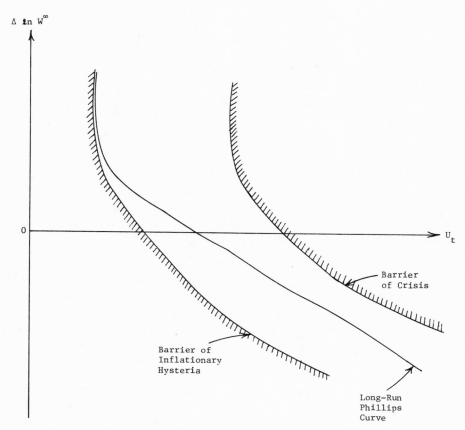

FIGURE 7–5. The Relation between the Equilibrium Band and the Steady-State
Rate of Wage Inflation in the Case Where $c_+ = 0$ and $c_- = 10$

run Phillips curve to the right (or more precisely, bending clockwise the upper
part of the long-run Phillips curve).

It goes without saying that this analysis can be applied not only to an
incomes policy, but also for any other institutional change whose effect is to
make money wages more inflexible.

9. Summary: On the Notion of Equilibrium in Economics

Equilibrium has been an indispensable notion in economic analysis. According
to the neoclassical economics, the static economy in which wants, resources,
and technologies are unchanging is said to be in a state of static equilibrium
"if every person is acting in such a way as to reach his most preferred position,

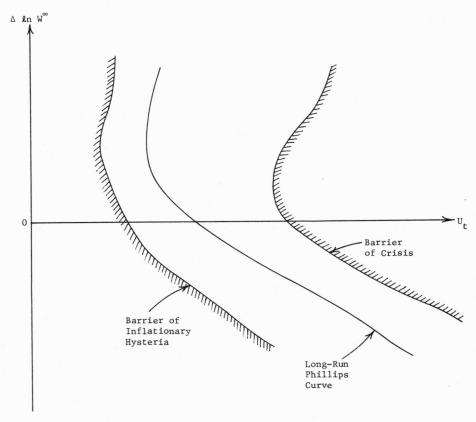

FIGURE 7–6. The Relation between the Equilibrium Band and the Steady-State
Rate of Wage Inflation in the Case Where $c_+ = 1.0$ and $c_- = 10$

subject to the opportunities open to him" (Hicks 1946, p. 58). In the case of
dynamic economy in which wants, resources, and technologies are changing
over time, expectations about the future play the central role in the notion of
equilibrium. Such a dynamic economy is said to be in equilibrium at a point
of time, or simply in temporary equilibrium, if every individual is reaching
the most preferred position, subject to the constraints by which he or she is
bound and with respect to the expectations that he or she has at that point in
time; and it is said to be in equilibrium over time if (a) it is in equilibrium in
every point of time, and (b) the expectations on which it is based, in each single
period, are consistent with one another and with what actually happens (Hicks
1946). Common to all these neoclassical equilibrium notions is the idea that
for the economy as a whole to be in equilibrium, *all* individuals must be in their
own equilibrium position *simultaneously*. In consequence, the whole edifice of

neoclassical equilibrium would collapse whenever any one of the individuals in it was displaced from his or her own subjective equilibrium point.[5]

In this chapter, however, we have demonstrated that even if the central authority succeeds in keeping a balance between total demand and total supply, and even if all the firms in the economy happen to have expectations that are consistent with what actually happens, the dynamic economy under the condition of money wage inflexibility has no tendency to approach the neoclassical equilibrium. It can only achieve, at best, a macroscopic steady state—a state of the economy as a whole which is maintained by offsetting motions of a large number of firms perpetually thrown out of their subjective equilibrium by incessant stochastic disturbances. This macroscopic steady state is, in other words, a macroscopic equilibrium of microscopic disequilibria. It differs fundamentally from the neoclassical notion of equilibrium, which can be simply characterized as a collection of mutually compatible microscopic equilibria.

Involuntary unemployment is, of course, a disequilibrium phenomenon in the labor market. Consequently, it has no place in neoclassical equilibrium. However, if the dynamic economy with wage inflexibility will never approach neoclassical equilibrium, the phenomenon of involuntary unemployment will never disappear, no matter how long the economy is run. The explanation of involuntary unemployment as a long-run phenomenon becomes possible only when we have freed ourselves from the rigid equilibrium notion of neoclassical economics. In fact, its careless import has been the source of much confusion in the conventional macroeconomics.

One of the fundamental attributes of neoclassical equilibrium is its money-neutrality property. The normal rate theory of unemployment, claiming the absence of any permanent trade-off between inflation and unemployment, is a restatement of this neoclassical theorem. However, if the neoclassical equilibrium is not even an asymptotic state of the dynamic economy, then the normal rate theory of unemployment loses its ability *even* to describe the economy's long run. In fact, we have shown here that the aggregate rate of involuntary unemployment in a macroscopic steady state is higher the more dispersively subjective disequilibria are scattered across firms; and we have also proved that under the condition of downward inflexibility of money wages, the subjective disequilibria in turn become more dispersed the lower the growth rate

---

5. This is a slight overstatement. There is a notion of approximate equilibrium in the neoclassical theory, which allows a certain degree of deviation from individual equilibria in a nonconvex environment. See Starr (1969) and Arrow and Hahn (1971, chap. 7). Note, however, that the whole point of this generalized equilibrium notion is to demonstrate that as the size of the economy gets larger, the degree of approximation approaches zero. So in the limit we again find ourselves in the old neoclassical equilibrium position. In contrast, our macroscopic steady state never approaches a neoclassical equilibrium position, no matter how large the size of the economy becomes. In fact, we have supposed from the start that the number of firms in the economy is very large.

of the general wage level. Having combined these two propositions, we have been able to derive an inverse relation between the aggregate rate of involuntary unemployment and the rate of wage inflation in a macroscopic steady state. This is nothing but the downward-sloping long-run Phillips curve, whose theoretical foundation macroeconomics has been looking for.

CHAPTER 8

A Model of Wage-Push Stagflation

1. Introduction: The Wage-Push Theory of Inflation

Economic theorists have adopted in the past a rather schizophrenic attitude toward the role played by trade unions in the aggregative performance of the economy. Some have dismissed trade unions as a highly visible but quite unimportant source of friction in the smoothly working market mechanism; others have been so overwhelmed by their significance that they have mistaken a few impressionistic observations for a legitimate analysis of their behavior. Whichever attitude has been taken, the place of trade unions in the main body of economic theories has been the same—they were simply left out of account. This is precisely why the wage-push theory of inflation has been regarded as either a statistical illusion or an almighty explanation of the explosion of inflation in postwar capitalist economies.

In this chapter we give some thought to the wage-push explanation of the phenomenon of inflation. It is an attempt to place trade unions at one of the central places in the macroeconomic theory and then study their activity's short- and long-run impact on the aggregate performance of the economy.

Admittedly, the analysis is fragmentary and tentative. But it is intended to be no more than a first step; I hope it is on the right track.

2. A Model of Trade-Union Strike Activity

The *strike* is the single most important weapon by which a trade union endeavors to materialize its demand for an advance in wages or resist a wage cut threatened by an employer. To examine the process of wage determination in the unionized labor market, we must therefore develop a comprehensive model of a union's strike activity.

The model of union strike activity we are about to construct follows closely that of Ashenfelter and Johnson (1969), which is in turn based on the view of the nature of trade unionism presented in the classic work of Arthur M. Ross (1948; see also Rees 1962, and 1973, pt. IV). According to this view, the trade union is not a homogeneous seller of labor attempting to maximize a well-defined object such as the total wage bill, but a complex political institution which participates in the establishment of wage rates. There are at least two types of members in the trade union, distinct in both their functions and objectives. One is the rank and file; the other is the union leadership. Although the formal objective of the union is the advancement of the economic welfare of its members and those of the rank and file in particular, it has a much more vital institutional objective—the survival and growth of the union as a political organization. Needless to say, for a union to survive and grow, the formal objective must be satisfied, to a greater or lesser extent; but when in conflict with the institutional objective, it is forced to give way.

In normal circumstances, the union leadership is able to identify their personal aims with the institutional objective. The growth of the union whose organization they lead is the springboard of their advancement as political leaders within the broad trade-union movement. Only in an unhealthy political atmosphere do the leader's personal ambitions clash with the union's institutional objective.

The wage policy of a trade union is the function of the leadership. In the process of collective bargaining the leadership must make decisions under pressures from both the rank and file and the employer. In fact, collective bargaining involves not two but *three* parties—the employer, the union leadership, and the union rank and file; and the function of the union leadership is first, to detect the true bargaining position of the employer, then to assess whether the rank and file's demand for wage increase is acceptable to the employer or not, and, if necessary, to find a way of compromise. If, however, the rank and file's demands are higher than those the employer would accept even at the last moment before contract expiration, the leadership must face two alternatives: either (a) to sign a contract whose terms will disappoint the expectations of the rank and file, thereby risking the possibility of rejection of the contract by the rank and file, and undermining their own long-term political power base; or (b) to provoke a strike, which is, from the purely economic standpoint, at odds with the welfare of the rank and file. Ashenfelter and Johnson maintain that the union leadership generally prefers the second alternative. Because "under strike conditions the leadership may at least appear as adversaries against management in a crusade which may even raise their political 'stock' and will unify the workers." They argue further that "the outbreak of a strike . . . has the effect of lowering the rank and file's expectations due to the shock effect of the firm's resistance and the resultant loss of normal income. After some passage of time the leadership feels that the minimum acceptable wage has fallen to a level at which it can safely sign with management, and the strike ends" (1969, p. 37).

Let $m_t(i)$ denote the minimum wage level in period t that the leadership can present to the rank and file of the ith firm as an acceptable offer from management without jeopardizing the leadership's political stock in the union organization. And let $\mu_t(i)$ denote $\ln m_t(i) - \ln w_{t-1}(i)$, which represents the minimum acceptable rate of wage increase in period t. This is the most crucial variable in our model of union strike activity. Many economic as well as noneconomic factors influence its determination.

The rank and file members tend to consider their wages in terms of *equity*, *justice*, and *fairness* (Ross 1948). Their concept of equitable or just or fair wages involves first and foremost the comparison of their wages with the wages received by workers in their own industry as well as in other industries whose skills, educations, and social background they feel to be comparable to their's. They feel it unjust if their wages lag behind the wages received by the comparable group of workers; and they are willing to strike to preserve the equitable structure of wages across firms and even across industries. The union leadership is also conscious of the comparison of wage increases across firms and across industries, because their performance as union leaders is most visibly measured by the accomplished wage increases in their union in comparison with the wage increases won by other unions. We can therefore expect $\mu_t(i)$, the minimum acceptable rate of wage increase, to be positively correlated with the rate of change in the general wage level (or some index of the wages of the "key group") and its recent history. Second, if their pay raises in the past have lagged behind the pace of price inflation, it is also considered by rank and file members as unjust to their working efforts. Thus, we can expect $\mu_t(i)$ to be positively correlated with past changes in the general price level as well. (Here, we do not distinguish between the consumer price index and the general price level.) The third factor that should influence $\mu_t(i)$ is the extent of the tightness of the labor market, which we might represent by the value of the labor market gap. This variable can be regarded as a proxy of the strength of the union's bargaining position. When the labor market is tight, it is easy for rank and file members to get part-time jobs during a strike and to find better jobs when they are dissatisfied with the settled wage and quit the current job. Thus, the union leadership is able to press for the higher wage increase without worrying too much about the cost of the resulting strike borne by the rank and file in the case of a breakdown in negotiations. In such circumstances their threat of strike would look more convincing to the employer. Although we can list many other variables (especially the rate of profit) as being strategically important for the labor union's bargaining position, it seems sufficient for our limited purposes here to single out these three variables.

All three factors can be regarded as economic determinants of the minimum acceptable rate of wage increases, for they are associated with visible changes in the economic situation. They do not, however, exhaust all the determinants. Union-militancy factors are no less important in determining the minimum acceptable rate of wage increase. In union-militancy factors we include all the noneconomic causes of the upheaval of the wage demands of the union, whose prime concerns are the expansion or the survival of the union organization, union politics, national politics, the advancement of humanitarian causes, and so on, all of which can be regarded as being independent of changes in the economic situation. Of course, in practice, it is almost impossible to draw a clear-cut line between economic factors and union-militancy factors, but at least for the theoretical analysis they provide us with a useful taxonomy.

As a very crude first-order approximation, let us assume that the minimum acceptable rate of wage increase is determined by the following linear equation:

$$(8-1) \qquad \mu_t(i) = \mu^{UM} + \sum_{s=2}^{\infty} \mu^W(s) \, \Delta \ln W_{t-s} + \sum_{s=2}^{\infty} \mu^P(s) \, \Delta \ln P_{t-s}$$

$$+ \sum_{s=2}^{\infty} \mu^F(s) \left(\frac{H_{t-s}}{L_{t-s}} - f^* \right) \bigg/ f^* + \textit{random disturbance},$$

where $\mu^W(s)$, $\mu^P(s)$, and $\mu^F(s)$ are nonnegative coefficients that represent the weights the union attaches to the lagged economic variables in forming its wage demand in period t; and the intercept μ^{UM} can be regarded as a parameter that measures the extent of the union's political militancy, formed independently of changes in economic climate. (Because of the assumed symmetry among firms, the functional form is assumed to be uniform across firms.)

3. The Rule of Money Wage Adjustment under Trade Unions

Let us assume that once a strike takes place, it is expected to inflict a lump-sum cost (equal to $v_t c_-$) on the employer. Although it would be very desirable to incorporate into our model the cost of a strike that is dependent upon the difference between the union demand and the agreed-upon wage level, we are unable to do so. This is an unfortunate simplification, for it is widely known that the length of a strike is positively correlated with the divergence of the positions taken by the union and the employer. However, there is little reason to expect that the theoretical conclusions of the present analysis would be weakened by the introduction of such non-lump-sum costs of a strike. Nor shall we discuss more basic economic, political, and sociological factors which help explain the magnitude of the cost of strike itself.[1]

At the point of contract expiration, the employer faces a choice. If it gives in to the last union demand and offers a level of wage equal to or higher than $m_t(i)$, the minimum acceptable wage level to the union, there will be no strike and the new contract will be made at the wage level offered. If, however, the level of the wage offered is lower than $m_t(i)$, the employer's action is tantamount

---

1. See Ashenfelter and Johnson (1969) for theoretical and empirical analysis of the determination of the duration of strike.

to "taking a strike." The strike will then be invoked and continue until the expectations of the rank and file are cooled down sufficiently.

Such a wage determination process by the employer at the point of contract expiration may be described by the following simple decision rule:

$$(8-2) \quad \ln w_t(i) = \begin{cases} \ln m_t(i) & \text{(the employer gives in)} \\ \quad \text{if } \theta_- \leqslant \ln w_t^*(i) - \ln m_t(i) \leqslant \theta_+, \\ \ln w_t^*(i) - \theta_0 & \text{(the employer takes a strike)} \\ \quad \text{if } \ln w_t^*(i) - \ln m_t < \theta_-, \\ \ln w_t^*(i) - \theta_0 & \text{(the employer lets wage drift)} \\ \quad \text{if } \ln w_t^*(i) - \ln m_t > \theta_+, \end{cases}$$

where $\theta_- \leqslant \theta_0 \leqslant \theta_+$. (Note that the length of the unit period in this model is taken to be the interval between wage negotiations or contract reviews.) The first situation in rule (8–2) says that when the proportionate difference between the short-run optimal wage and the level of money wage minimally acceptable to the union rank and file, $\ln w_t^*(i) - \ln m_t(i)$, lies within the satisfactory range $[\theta_-, \theta_+]$, the employer gives in and offers the minimum acceptable wage to the union. The second situation says that if the union's minimum acceptable wage level is intolerably high relative to the employer's short-run optimal wage, in the sense that $\ln w_t^*(i) - \ln m_t(i) < \theta_-$, the employer would rather incur the cost of strike and secure the low settlement equal to $\ln w_t^*(i) - \theta_0$ in log [which is lower than $\ln m_t(i)$ because of $\theta_0 \geqslant \theta_-$] after a certain cooling-off period. Finally, if the union's minimum acceptable wage is sufficiently low relatively to the firm's short-run optimal wage, in the sense that $\ln w_t^*(i) - \ln m_t(i) > \theta_+$, nothing would prevent the employer from securing the settlement equal to $\ln w_t^*(i) - \theta_0$ in log, which is a case of wage drift. Note that if the cost of wage drift, $v_t c_+$, is negligible, θ_+ should coincide with θ_0.

Let $z_t(i) \equiv \ln w_t^*(i) - \ln w_t(i)$ measure, as before, the firm's subjective disequilibrium in period t. Then, if we recall the definition $\mu_t(i) \equiv \ln m_t(i) - \ln w_{t-1}(i)$ and note an obvious identity $\ln w_t^*(i) - \ln m_t(i) \equiv z_{t-1}(i) + \Delta \ln w_{t-1}^*(i) - \mu_t(i)$, the money wage adjustment rule (8–2) can be easily transformed into the following more transparent form:

$$(8-3) \quad z_t(i) = \begin{cases} z_{t-1}(i) + [\Delta \ln w_{t-1}^*(i) - \mu_t(i)] & \text{(i.e., the employer gives in)} \\ \quad \text{if } \theta_- \leqslant z_{t-1}(i) + [\Delta \ln w_{t-1}^*(i) - \mu_t(i)] \leqslant \theta_+, \\ \theta_0 & \text{(i.e., the employer takes a strike)} \\ \quad \text{if } z_{t-1}(i) + [\Delta \ln w_{t-1}^*(i) - \mu_t(i)] < \theta_-, \\ \theta_0 & \text{(i.e., the employer lets wage drift)} \\ \quad \text{if } z_{t-1}(i) + [\Delta \ln w_{t-1}^*(i) - \mu_t(i)] > \theta_+. \end{cases}$$

Immediately, one can see the mathematical equivalence of rule (8–3) to rule (5–3) or (6–1) in the unorganized labor market, except for the fact that the rate of change in the short-run optimal wage $\Delta \ln w_{t-1}^*(i)$ in (5–3) or (6–1) is now replaced by the difference between that and the union's minimum acceptable wage increase, $\Delta \ln w_{t-1}^*(i) - \mu_t(i)$. Thus, all the propositions established in chapters 5 and 6 are directly applicable to this model of the organized labor market with a suitable translation. Indeed, we can claim that the model of wage adjustment activity in the unorganized labor market is a special case of the model of this section, with the minimum acceptable rate of wage increase $\mu_t(i)$ being assumed to be zero.

In this chapter it is supposed that all the firms in the labor market are unionized. This would appear to be an unrealistic assumption for the analysis of an economy such as that of the United States, in which only one fourth of the total labor force is unionized; but if employers of nonunionized sectors offer, out of the fear of unionization by their workers, wages that are systematically tied to unionized wages, our assumption of complete unionization of the labor market is not too wide of the mark.[2]

4. A Short-Run Theory of Wage-Push Stagflation

In this section we look at the short-run impact on the economy's aggregate performance of an upheaval of union wage demands.

To fix the starting point of our analysis, suppose that the economy had been in a happy state of Expectational equilibrium until for some reason the trade unions suddenly wake up and become militant. The parameter of union militancy, μ^{UM}, has thus increased uniformly across firms and hence unions' minimum acceptable rates of wage increase $\mu_t(i)$ on average increase.

Now, according to the rule of money wage adjustment in the unionized labor market, (8–3), such an upward jump in $\mu_t(i)$ will have the same quantitative effect as a downward jump in $\Delta \ln w_{t-1}^*(i)$ upon firms' wage determination. Indeed, the proportionate differences between the short-run optimal wage and the unions' minimum acceptable wage offer, $\ln w_t^*(i) - \ln m_t(i) \equiv z_{t-1}(i) + [\Delta \ln w_{t-1}^*(i) - \mu_t(i)]$, of a majority of firms have to decline. Then, those firms that were in prosperous conditions before [in the sense that their subjective disequilibrium in the previous period, $z_{t-1}(i)$, was relatively high] may find their $z_{t-1}(i) + [\Delta \ln w_{t-1}^*(i) - \mu_t(i)]$ lower than before but still above the lower barrier θ_- of the satisfactory range. They will give in to union demands and avoid a strike. Their new subjective disequilibria $z_t(i)$ will be automatically set equal to $z_{t-1}(i) + [\Delta \ln w_{t-1}^*(i) - \mu_t(i)]$, and at the same time the growth rates of their money wages will be tied to the new and higher minimum acceptable rates of money wage increase $\mu_t(i)$. On the other hand, most other firms whose subjective disequilibrium was already low even before the intensification of the union demands may learn that their $z_{t-1}(i) + [\Delta \ln w_{t-1}^*(i) - \mu_t(i)]$ has dropped below the lower barrier θ_-. The new subjective disequilibrium would be out of the

---

2. See Ashenfelter and Pencavel (1972) for analysis of the relation between nonunion and union wages.

satisfactory range unless they defy union demands. They will then "take a strike." They will push up their subjective disequilibrium to the return point θ_0 and secure the lower wage settlement equal to $\ln w_t^*(i) - \theta_0$ in log.

Strikes will spread through the economy, in proportion to the number of firms that have defied the union demands. The level of the general money wage will increase above the past trend level, in proportion to the number of firms that have given in to the union demands. (But the rise in the general money wage level will fall short of the rise that unions demanded, in proportion to the number of firms that have defied union demands.)

Such a union-induced wage hike will immediately give rise to a Keynesian disequilibrium in the labor market. First, the aggregate subjective disequilibrium Z_t, and hence the aggregate intended gap ψZ_t, will decline as long as a sufficiently large fraction of firms have given in to union demands and let their subjective disequilibria decline. Concurrently, the resulting wage increases will prompt firms to curtail their effective demands for labor. As a result, the value of the labor market gap $(H_t/L_t - f^*)/f^*$ will also decrease. However, as is suggested in the accompanying note, it is likely that the decline in the aggregate intended gap will exceed that of the actual market gap.[3] We will thus have a positive Keynesian disequilibrium in the labor market, in the sense that

$$(8\text{-}4) \qquad \left(\frac{H_t}{L_t} - f^*\right)\Big/ f^* > \psi Z_t,$$

in spite of the decline in the labor market gap.

It then follows from the generalized fundamental equation of the labor market (5–9) that a majority of firms will inevitably underestimate the tightness of the labor supply. They will then revise upward their expectations of the tightness of labor supply. Here, we can repeat the argument given in section 15 of chapter 5, with signs reversed, and assert that such upward revisions of the expectations will increase the aggregate intended gap, ψZ_t, more than the labor market gap. This will, of course, work to rectify the existing Keynesian disequilibrium in the labor market (8–4). Keynesian equilibrium will sooner or later be reestablished in the labor market, but the labor market gap will probably remain negative there.

Note, in passing, that the fact that the upheaval of the union militancy is likely to create a positive Keynesian disequilibrium in the labor market in spite of the induced decline of the value of labor market gap implies that the union militancy cannot itself be a cause of the crisis.

Let us look next at the product market. Here, a decline in the level of total

---

3. It is evident that a 1 percent increase of the level of money wage decreases the multiplied subjective disequilibrium $\psi z_t(i)$ by the factor $\psi \equiv [\eta + \varepsilon \eta(1 - \gamma) + \varepsilon \gamma]/[\eta - \gamma(\eta - 1)]$. It is also clear from the formula for the effective labor demand that the same 1 percentage point increment of money wage decreases it and thereby $[h_t(i)/l_t(i) - f^*]/f^*$, by the factor $\eta/[\eta - \gamma(\eta - 1)]$, which is, of course, lower than ψ.

labor demand, which resulted from the union-induced increase in money wages, will lower the level of total labor employment and then the scale of total product supply τ periods later. Moreover, the possible drop in effective working hours, caused by strikes, will further accentuate the decline of total product supply. A positive gap will emerge in the product market,

(8–5) $$\left(\frac{X_t}{Q_t} - g^*\right)\bigg/g^* > 0.$$

A cumulative price inflation process will start to evolve.

In the product market, however, we also have to take account of a possible induced change in the volume of total product demand. In the first place, the decline in the level of total labor employment will, through the familiar aggregate consumption function, lower the volume of total product demand in subsequent periods. Moreover, the loss of working hours during strikes may depress it further. On the other hand, such a declining tendency of total product demand will be at least partly offset by the rise of money wages won by wage negotiations. The net effect may go either way. It is therefore likely that even if the volume of total product demand declines, its effect will not be large enough to upset the existing positive gap in the product market. If this is the case, we experience a stagflation situation, in which the high aggregate rate of involuntary unemployment coexists with the wage-push inflation in terms of both money wages and product prices. This explanation of stagflation is different from the explanation given in section 24 of chapter 3, which sought its cause in a uniform decline of labor productivities across firms. Here we have found the upheaval of trade union militancy or the "wage-push" to be the original cause of the stagflation.

This is our short-run theory of wage-push stagflation.

5. Wage–Price and Wage–Wage Spirals

We shall first argue that if (and this is an important "if") unions' wage demands are sensitive to neither changes in fellow workers' money wages nor to changes in real wages, in the sense that neither $\mu^W(s)$'s nor $\mu^P(s)$'s in (8–1) are large, then the union-induced stagflation is, without a progressive intensification of the militancy, likely to be short-lived, for the pace of the cumulative price inflation will soon catch up with that of the union-pushed wage inflation and start stimulating the depressed effective demands for labor. In consequence, the level of total labor employment, and hence the level of total product supply, will begin to bounce back and eventually close the positive product market gap. The pace of cumulative inflation will then decelerate and in the meantime will settle down to the trend path that will sustain a stable relation with the growth rate of the general money wage level. (It is quite possible that the bouncing back of the level of total product supply may be excessive and give rise to a negative product market gap. But it will only invite the same equilibriating mechanism to do the opposite job.) We have thus shown that Keynesian disequilibrium in the product market has a self-correcting tendency even in the unionized economy, as long as the trade unions are insensitive to changes in economic conditions and do not react to the rising general price level. But as soon as it is admitted that the trade unions' wage demands are sensitive to changes in economic conditions, such an optimistic outlook as to the stability of Keynesian equilibrium has to be forsaken.

The primary mechanism that stabilizes the union-induced stagflation was seen to be the stimulating effect of the reduction of real wages (brought by the cumulative price inflation) on the effective demands for labor. Yet if the union members care about the erosion of the purchasing power of their wages, as is reflected in the high values of the weights $\mu^P(s)$'s in the equation (8-1), then, before such a stimulating effect prevails, the unions may start responding to the cumulative price inflation (caused by themselves), again pushing up their minimum acceptable rates of wage increase. A new round of wage-push stagflation will be triggered off, and the economy will be whirled in the upward spiral of wage *and* price inflation.

Next, if the union members are very sensitive to what their fellow workers have been getting, in the sense that the weights $\mu^W(s)$'s in (8-1) are large, it is easy to see that the rise in the general money wage, pushed by the unions, will feed back into their new and higher wage demands sooner or later and then start a spiral of wage pushes and induced wage inflations.

If, as an extreme case, the sum of the weights becomes close to unity, the economy will forever tread an upward random-walk path, never finding a stable point to converge. In this case, the entire advantage inherent in the inflexibility of wages, which has contributed to the stability of the monetary economy, disappears, and we are back to a system that is as prone to unstable cumulative processes as the flexible wage Wicksellian economy is. It should be noted here that the short-run behavior of an economy in which all wages are completely indexed is similar to that of the economy described above.

On the other hand, if the wage demands of the unions are influenced by the tightness of the labor market, in the sense that $\mu^F(s)$'s are large, then the decline of the labor market gap and the associated increase in the aggregate rate of involuntary unemployment, during the wage-push stagflation, may scare the rank and file and reduce their pushfulness. This will then work to shorten the life of wage-push stagflation.

6. The Long-Run Theory of Wage-Push Stagflation

Can trade unions push up inflation permanently? The immediate answer to this question would be negative. For, as was argued in appendix 7-b, the chief determinant of the rate of wage inflation in a macroscopic steady state, if the economy ever gets there, is the growth rate of the nominal value of total product demand per worker, over which trade-union activities appear to have little direct control in the long run. However, the aim of this section is to show that the trade unionism has an important channel through which it exerts a permanent influence upon the economy's aggregate performance.

To begin with, let us note that even in the unionized labor market, the rate of change in the general wage level in a macroscopic steady state, denoted by $\Delta \ln W^\infty$, is approximately equal to the expected rate of change in the short-run optimal wage, given by ω.[4]

Next, let μ^∞ be the expected value of the union's minimum acceptable increase in money wage in a macroscopic steady state. Noting that the labor market gap is approximately zero here, we can calculate it from (8–1) as

$$\mu^\infty \underline{\Delta} \mu^{UM} + \mu^W \Delta \ln W^\infty + \mu^P \Delta \ln P^\infty$$

or

$$(8\text{–}6) \qquad \mu^\infty \underline{\Delta} \mu^{UM} + (\mu^W + \mu^P) \Delta \ln W^\infty - \mu^P \Delta \ln (W^\infty/P^\infty),$$

where $\mu^W \equiv \Sigma_{s=2}^\infty \mu^W(s)$ and $\mu^P \equiv \Sigma_{s=2}^\infty \mu^P(s)$. That is, the minimum acceptable rate of wage increase in a macroscopic steady state is determined primarily by the long-run steady-state growth rate of the general wage level, $\Delta \ln W^\infty = \omega$, in addition to the long-run rate of change in the aggregate real wage, $\Delta \ln (W^\infty/P^\infty)$, and the index of union militancy, μ^{UM}.

We learned in section 3 of this chapter that the model of money wage adjustment under trade unionism can be formally transformed into the model of money wage adjustment with no wage bargaining, if the rate of change in the short-run optimal wage $\Delta \ln w_t^*(i)$ of the latter is replaced by its deviation from the union's minimum acceptable rate of wage increase [i.e., by $\Delta \ln w_t^*(i) - \mu_t(i)$]. Hence, the long-run Phillips curve of chapter 7—the inverse relationship between the aggregate rate of involuntary unemployment, U^∞, and the growth rate of the general money wage level, $\Delta \ln W^\infty \underline{\Delta} \omega$ in the macroscopic steady state—can be translated into an inverse relation between U^∞ and $\Delta \ln W^\infty - \mu^\infty$. Since μ^∞ also depends upon $\Delta \ln W^\infty$, this is not yet the long-run Phillips curve of the unionized labor market, but would become such after a straightforward translation. For, by virtue of (8–6), $\Delta \ln W^\infty - \mu^\infty$ can be expressed as

---

4. Even in the unionized labor market, we have $E[\Delta \ln w_t(i) : z_0(i)] = \omega - E[\Delta z_t(i) : z_0(i)]$, by definition of $z_t(i)$. Then, as $t \to \infty$, $E[\Delta z_t(i) : z_0(i)] \to 0$ if a stochastic steady state exists, so that $E^\infty[\Delta \ln w(i)] = \omega$, independently of $z_0(i)$. Applying the same argument as was used in proving proposition 7–2, even in the unionized labor market we have

$$\Delta \ln W^\infty \underline{\Delta} E^\infty(\Delta \ln w) = \omega.$$

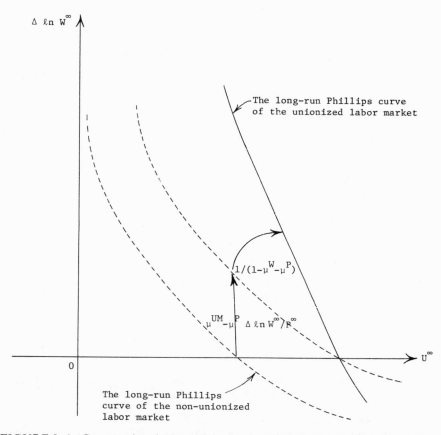

FIGURE 8–1. Constructing the Long-Run Phillips Curve of the Unionized Labor Market

$$(8\text{–}7) \qquad \Delta \ln W^\infty - \mu^\infty \triangleq (1 - \mu^W - \mu^P)\Delta \ln W^\infty - \mu^{UM} + \mu^P \Delta \ln (W^\infty/P^\infty).$$

Thus, if we shift the original long-run Phillips curve upward by a magnitude equal to $\mu^{UM} - \mu^P \Delta \ln (W^\infty/P^\infty)$ and then turn it clockwise by the angle equal to $1/(1 - \mu^W - \mu^P)$, we obtain the long-run Phillips curve of the unionized labor market. This construction is illustrated in figure 8–1.

It then follows that, *as long as the sum of the weights μ^W and μ^P is less than unity*, there still exists an *inverse* relation between the aggregate rate of involuntary unemployment and the long-run steady-state rate of wage inflation, even in the organized labor market. This is the downward-sloping long-run Phillips curve of the organized labor market. The general shape of this curve is determined by [in addition to such structural parameters as s, c_-, and $-\rho''(0)/2$] (a) the union-militancy factor μ^{UM}, (b) the long-run steady-state

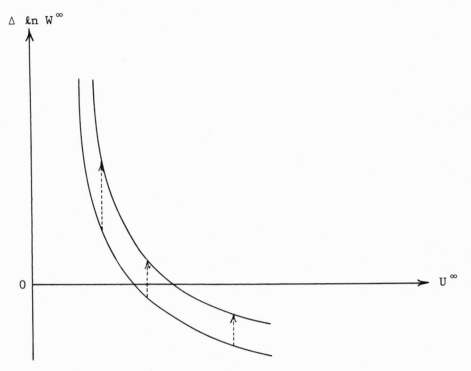

FIGURE 8–2. Shift of the Long-Run Phillips Curve of the Organized Labor Market
Caused by an Increase in Union Militancy

growth rate of real wage ($\Delta \ln W^\infty - \Delta \ln P^\infty$), and (c) the weights μ^M and μ^P,
which represent the responsiveness of the union to changes in economic situations. It is therefore of some interest to examine how the shape of this long-run
Phillips curve shifts as these parameters and variables change. This exercise
will tell us the possible long-run consequences of a change in unions' political
militancy, a change in the productivity growth, and a change in unions' sensitivity to economic climates.

     First, let us examine the long-run impact of the upheaval of unions'
political militancy, short-run aspects of which were studied in preceding sections.
It has, as is seen from (8–7), the effect of shifting the long-run Phillips curve
in the upward direction. This is illustrated by figure 8–2. The fiscal authority
and the central bank are thus left with a worsened long-run trade-off between
inflation and unemployment. If they stick to the previous target rate of inflation,
they must live with a higher aggregate rate of involuntary unemployment in
the long run. If, however, they give in to the public pressure for lowering the
rate of unemployment or for boosting sagging profit rates, they have no choice

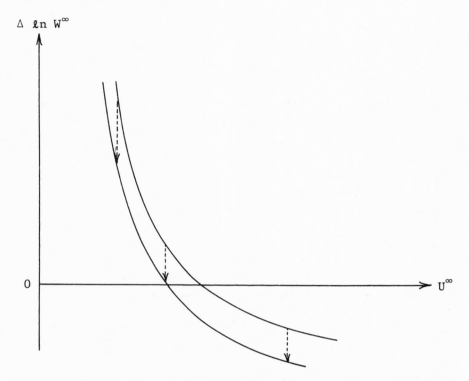

FIGURE 8–3. Shift of the Long-Run Phillips Curve of the Organized Labor Market
 Caused by an Increase in the Steady-State Growth Rate of Labor
 Productivity

but to inflate the economy and move up along the downward-sloping long-run
Phillips curve. In this manner, an increase in union militancy not only creates
a stagflation situation in the short run but is also capable of perpetuating it
through an accommodating change in long-run fiscal and monetary policy-
making.

This is our long-run theory of wage-push stagflation.

Figure 8–3, on the other hand, explains the long-run impact of the increase
in the growth rate of real wages. It shifts the long-run Phillips curve downward.
Since it is reasonable to suppose that the long-run growth rate of real wages
($\Delta \ln W^\infty - \Delta \ln P^\infty$) is determined chiefly by the long-run average growth rate
of labor productivity (here we ignore the long-run change in income distri-
bution), an increase in the long-run rate of labor productivity thus tends to shift
the long-run trade-off between unemployment and wage inflation favorably.
If a policymaker decides to keep the same rate of *wage* inflation as before, then
the aggregate rate of involuntary unemployment will be lower than before,

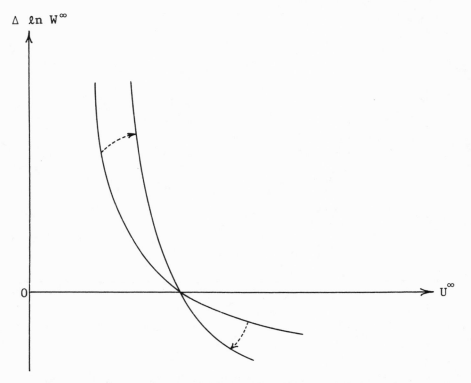

FIGURE 8–4. Shift of the Long-Run Phillips Curve of the Organized Labor Market
　　　　　　Caused by an Increase in Union Sensitivity to Other Union Wage
　　　　　　Settlements

even in the long run. If, instead, the policymaker decides to keep the same rate
of *price* inflation as before, then the rate of *wage* inflation consistent with an
improved growth rate of labor productivity has to be higher than before, and
the aggregate rate of involuntary unemployment will be lowered further by
virtue of their inverse relationship. In this sense the improvement in labor
productivity is *doubly* favorable to employment in the long run.

　　　As shown in figure 8–4, if trade unions become more sensitive to the performance of the other unions and as a result the value of μ^W increases, the slope
of the long-run Phillips curve becomes steeper. The long-run trade-off between
unemployment and wage inflation will then be worsened (as long as the rate
of wage inflation is positive). On the other hand, as trade unions become more
conscious of the real purchasing power of the receiving wage, and hence the
value of μ^P increases, the long-run Phillips curve shifts downward (as long
as the long-run average growth rate of real wage is positive), but its slope
becomes steeper than before. This is illustrated in figure 8–5. In this case, we

$\Delta \ \ell n \ W^{\infty}$

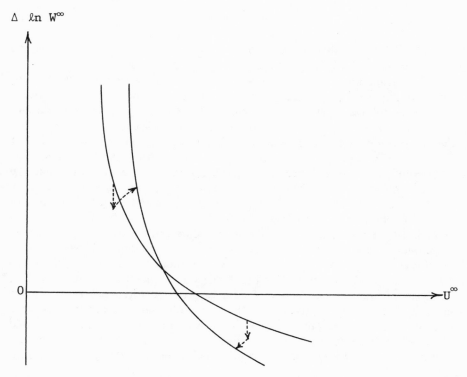

FIGURE 8–5. Shift of the Long-Run Phillips Curve of the Organized Labor Market Caused by an Increase in Union Sensitivity to a Change in the Cost of Living Index

cannot say a priori whether the long-run trade-off between unemployment and inflation has improved or deteriorated.

If, the weights μ^P and μ^W happen to add up to unity, the long-run Phillips curve becomes vertical. A very important special case of this situation is when the union wages are completely indexed, so that the weight μ^P is institutionally set to unity. Then, any kind of money illusion would disappear from the labor market and there remain no room for the trade-off between inflation and unemployment in the long run. However, it is also plain that in this case the economy would lose not only its money illusion but its stability as well. As argued in Section 5, the economy in such a case would forever float around capriciously without any place to set an anchor, rendering the notion of permanent trade-off itself irrelevant.

The analysis of the case where $\mu^W + \mu^P$ exceeds unity is left to the interested reader.

7. Summary

A model of wage-push stagflation in the short and long runs has been offered in this chapter. Since conventional macroeconomics has neglected the role played by trade unions in its theoretical framework, it was necessary for us to begin our analysis with a presentation of a simple model of union strike activity. Our model followed the classic work of A. M. Ross and started from the observation that wage negotiation involves not two but three parties: management, the union leadership, and the union rank and file, each having its own distinct objective. The rank and file members form their wage demands from the standpoint of fairness, justice, and equity. But it is the leaders who take the initiative on the side of the union in the process of wage negotiation; they have to decide at the time of constract expiration whether to sign a contract or to provoke a strike. However, the final decision as to the level of money wage is left to the action of management. Management has to decide on its wage offer by comparing the cost of giving in to union demands with the cost of taking a strike and securing a lower wage settlement. In this chapter it was shown that the formal model of the firm's wage adjustment constructed on the basis of the political theory of wage negotiation discussed above can be made mathematically equivalent to the model of wage adjustment developed in chapter 5, with a suitable translation of the variables. We then investigated the economy's short- and long-run responses to a change in trade unions' political militancy by applying the results of chapters 5 and 7 with little modification.

It has been argued that a sudden increase in union militancy increases the aggregate rate of involuntary unemployment simultaneously with rises in both money wages and prices, thereby producing stagflation in the short run. Such a wage-push stagflation is likely to be short-lived if union wage demands are insensitive to changing economic conditions. But if workers resist the erosion of the real purchasing power of their money wages or insist on catching up with the improvement of their fellow workers' money wages, a wage–price spiral or a wage–wage spiral will be triggered and the stagflation situation will continue.

In the long run, the impact of an increase in union militancy shifts the long-run Phillips curve upward and makes the dilemma between inflation and unemployment more cruel than before. It is likely to invite an inflationary policy on the part of the government and the central bank, which will perpetuate the stagflation situation, even in the long run.

If, as orthodox economists have believed, the decentralized market economy has a self-regulating nature, there is little raison d'être for "institutional economics" as a self-contained discipline. For, then, all social institutions could be regarded either as merely constitutive elements of the market system itself, or as obstacles to the otherwise smoothly working price mechanism of markets.

They are only to determine, along a unidimensional scale, the extent to which the actual market system deviates from the ideal form. If, however, it is not flexibility of prices and wages but rather some sort of rigidity in the process of wage determination (and/or the process of price formation) that stablizes an unstable monetary economy, the existence of social institutions, which interfere with the working of the price mechanism, becomes indispensable for the very survival of the market system itself. In consequence, the dynamic evolution of an economy in both the short and long runs can only be understood as a process of complex interactions between the price mechanism of markets and these social institutions, which have their own modes of existence. This, we believe, opens up a new perspective for institutional economics. The theory of wage-push stagflation, developed in this chapter on the basis of a model of a politicoeconomic institution called a trade union, might be considered as an attempt—albeit a meager one—to revive this almost extinct discipline in the science of economics.

Note for Future Research

It is time to break off our already lengthy exploration. There are, however, no definite conclusions to draw, for the present book is, after all, merely a progress report on the study of the dynamic workings of the capitalist economy. In their stead, we end by pointing toward two of the most important elements missing in our theoretical structure which need to be included in and analyzed by the authors of future studies.

1. The economy on which this book has focused is essentially a monetary one. The theory of cumulative process expounded in part I presupposes a form of economic system in which money is used as the most liquid store of value, that is, as "a subtle device for linking the present to the future" (Keynes 1936, p. 234). For it is this attribute of money that destroys Say's laws of markets and creates a precondition for the development of cumulative inflation or deflation. Moreover, the assumption of inflexibility of money wages introduced in parts II and III can have its raison d'être only in a full-fledged monetary economy in which a majority of economic contracts are fixed in terms of money of account. Indeed, it is precisely this inflexibility of money wages that is responsible for repression of the inherent instability of the value of money; and it is this consequent stability of the value of money that, in turn, works to buttress the institutional arrangement of fixing wages in terms of money of account, thereby strengthening the very inflexibility of money wages. However, in spite of the fact that money plays so essential a role in our disequilibrium dynamics, we have put all the details of the economy's monetary structure into the background and have restricted our attention to the study of general laws that govern the movement of a monetary economy from one disequilibrium position to another. If we wish to go beyond this and trace more closely the way in which the system evolves over time, it becomes necessary to develop a detailed model of financial markets and other monetary matters. For, as stated so cogently by Keynes, a monetary economy is one " in which money plays a part of its own and affects motives and decisions and is, in short, one of the operative factors in the situation, so that the course of events cannot be predicted, either in the long period or in the short, without a knowledge of the behaviour of money between the first state and the last"(1933).

2. This book has not analyzed the process of firms' investment decisions, which should run parallel to their short-run decisions on price, wage, output, and employment. There are at least two major roles that firms' investment in fixed capital plays in the dynamic working of the capitalist economy. First, firms' demand for capital goods makes up, together with households' consumption demand and the government's public expenditures, one of the chief components of total demand in the product market. Indeed, being based on firms' long-term expectations of future market conditions (as well as upon asset holders' bullish/bearish sentiments, which influence the determination of the rate of interest in financial markets), investment demand is subject to sudden, violent changes and thereby sets the pace and rhythm of the motion of total product demand in the short run. Second, since the act of fixed investment regulates the extent of capital deepening and works as a vehicle for technological progress, it exerts a decisive influence upon the long-run motion of total product supply. Firms' decisions on capital investment are therefore the main motive force that regulates the way in which a macroscopic imbalance between total demand and supply develops both in the short and long runs. "To understand . . . the genesis and the severity of the disequilibria," wrote Keynes, "it is chiefly necessary to consider what causes the rate of investment to fluctuate and to estimate the order of magnitude of such fluctuation"(1930, p. 95). The theoretical framework developed in this book thus consistutes only one half of the theory of economic disequilibria.

Mathematical Appendixes

Appendix to Chapter 1

(a) *Properties of the System of Product Demand Schedules*

First, we shall demonstrate that the system of product demand schedules $(1-5)$ is, with an appropriate definition of the general price level, consistent with the adding-up equation $(1-4)$. For this purpose, let us define the general price level P_t by the following (somewhat awkward) aggregation formula:

$$(A1-1) \qquad P_t \equiv \left\{ \sum_{i=1}^{I} \left[\alpha_t(i)(P_t X_t)^{\eta(i)-\bar{\eta}} \right] p_t(i)^{-\eta(i)+1} \right\}^{-1/(\bar{\eta}-1)},$$

and then define the total-demand elasticity $\xi(i)$ by

$$(A1-2) \qquad\qquad \xi(i) \equiv 1 + \eta(i) - \bar{\eta},$$

with

$$\bar{\eta} \equiv \sum_{i=1}^{I} \left\{ \frac{p_t(i)x_t(i)}{P_t X_t} \right\} \eta(i).$$

Then, we obtain

$$\sum_{i=1}^{I} p_t(i)x_t(i) = \sum p_t(i) \left[\frac{p_t(i)}{P_t} \right]^{-\eta(i)} X_t^{\xi(i)} \alpha_t(i)$$

$$= P_t X_t \sum P_t^{\bar{\eta}-1} \left[\alpha_t(i)(P_t X_t)^{\eta(i)-\bar{\eta}} p_t(i)^{-\eta(i)+1} \right]$$

$$= P_t X_t.$$

Note that the awkwardness of our definition of P_t is immaterial to our disequilibrium dynamics. Indeed, it is homogeneous of degree 1 with respect to the set of individual prices and homogeneous of degree zero with respect to total product demand, thereby satisfying all the necessary properties the general price level ought to have. It is also easy to show that the foregoing system of demand schedules is consistent with the minimization of an *addilog indirect utility function* $\Sigma[\alpha(i)/(\eta(i) - 1)][p(i)/PX]^{-\eta(i)+1}$, subject to an expenditure constraint $\Sigma p(i)x(i) = PX$. [Note that in this indirect utility minimization problem the control variables are $p(i)$'s and given data are $x(i)$'s and PX; see Houthakker (1960).]

This system of demand functions has several special properties. First, we can calculate gross cross-elasticity of demand for firm i's product with respect to the price of firm j's product as follows:

$$\frac{\partial x(i)/\partial p(j)}{x(i)/p(j)}\bigg|_{PX=\text{const.}} = [\eta(j) - 1]\frac{p(j)x(j)}{PX} > 0.$$

Therefore, (a) all products are gross substitutes, and (b) the degree of gross substitutability of product i in regard to product j is determined by the magnitude of price elasticity $\eta(j)$ and the value share of demand for product j. Second, since total demand elasticity $\xi(i)$ equals $1 + \eta(i) - \bar{\eta}$, all the products whose price elasticity is greater than average are luxuries and all the products whose price elasticity is smaller than average are necessities. Finally, the formula for total demand elasticity above immediately implies that the average total demand elasticity is equal to unity.

If we were heroic enough to assume that all the price elasticities, $\eta(i)$'s, are uniform across firms and equal to η, the specification of the demand system would become somewhat simpler. In this case, the general price level is represented by the following formula, known as the mean order $-(\eta - 1)$:

$$(A1\text{--}1') \qquad P_t \equiv \left[\sum_{i=1}^{I} \alpha_t(i)p_t(i)^{-(\eta-1)}\right]^{-1/(\eta-1)}$$

which is less awkward (although some readers may still so regard it); and the total-demand elasticity becomes constant and indeed equal to unity [i.e., $\xi(i) \equiv 1$ for all i]. In fact, this system of demand equations is consistent with the minimization of a special addilog indirect utility function $\Sigma \alpha(i)[p(i)/PX]^{-\eta+1}$. It is also consistent with the maximization of an addilog *direct* utility function $\Sigma \alpha(i)^{1/\eta}x(i)^{(\eta-1)/\eta}$, subject to an expenditure constraint $\Sigma p(i)x(i) = PX$. We shall *not*, however, limit ourselves to this convenient special case, at least at this stage of the investigation, although we will have to commit such a heroic act in part II. Here, the gain from the simplification seems to be far exceeded by the loss of generality.

(b) *Properties of the System of Labor Supply Schedules*

As in the case of product demand schedules (1–5), if we define (a) the general money wage level W_t by the equally awkward formula

$$(A1\text{--}3) \qquad W_t \equiv \left\{\sum_{i=1}^{I} [\beta_t(i)(W_tL_t)^{\bar{\varepsilon}-\varepsilon(i)}]w_t(i)^{\varepsilon(i)}\right\}^{1/\bar{\varepsilon}},$$

and (b) the total labor supply elasticity $\lambda(i)$ by

(A1–4) $$\lambda(i) \equiv 1 + \bar{\varepsilon} - \varepsilon(i),$$

with

$$\bar{\varepsilon} \equiv \sum_{i=1}^{I} \left[\frac{l_t(i)}{L_t}\right]\varepsilon(i),$$

then the system of labor supply schedules (1–7) satisfies the adding-up condition (1–6). Note that the level of general money wage is homogeneous of degree 1 with respect to individual wages and of degree zero with respect to total labor supply.

If we assume further that all the wage elasticities, $\varepsilon(i)$'s, are uniform and equal to ε, the foregoing specification of labor supply schedules would be somewhat simplified. Then the definition of the general money wage level would become

(A1–3′) $$W_t \equiv \left[\sum_{i=1}^{I} \beta_t(i)w_t(i)^{\varepsilon}\right]^{1/\varepsilon}$$

and the total-labor supply elasticity would become equal to unity:

(A1–4′) $$\lambda(i) \equiv 1.$$

(c) *Determination of the Optimal Pricing Policy*

The problem is to maximize the expected revenue with respect to product price. Wage cost is already a sunk cost at the beginning of the period. Let us first compute the expected revenue explicitly. (To lighten the typographical burden, we omit the time subscript t, the data set δ, and the carets indicating subjective parameters, unless otherwise indicated.) Let g denote $E(x/q)$; we then have

(A1–5)
$$\begin{aligned}
E(py) &= E(p\min(p^{-\eta}a, q)) \\
&= E(p^{-\eta+1}a : p^{-\eta}a \leqslant q) + E(pq : p^{-\eta}a > q) \\
&= pqE\left[\frac{p^{-\eta}a}{q} : \frac{a}{E(a)} \leqslant \frac{q}{p^{-\eta}E(a)}\right] + pqE\left[1 : \frac{a}{E(a)} > \frac{q}{p^{-\eta}E(a)}\right] \\
&= pqE\left[g\frac{a}{E(a)} : \frac{a}{E(a)} - 1 \leqslant \frac{1}{g} - 1\right] \\
&\quad + pqE\left[1 : \frac{a}{E(a)} - 1 > \frac{1}{g} - 1\right] \\
&= pq\left[\int_{-1}^{1/g-1} g(1 + z)\,dA(z) + 1 - A(1/g - 1)\right].
\end{aligned}$$

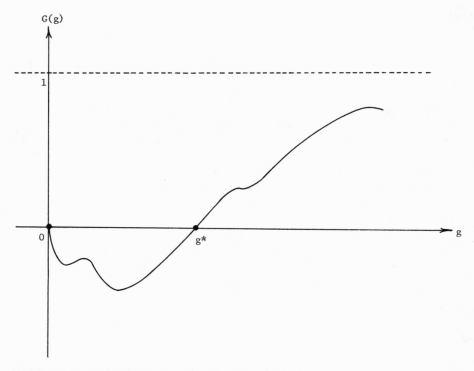

FIGURE A1–1. The Behavior of the Function $G(g)$

Differentiating this with respect to p, noting that $\partial g/\partial p \equiv \partial[p^{-\eta}E(a)/q]/\partial p = -\eta p^{-\eta-1}E(a)/q \equiv -\eta g/p$, equating the derivative to zero, and rearranging terms, we obtain the following first-order condition for a maximum:

$$(A1\text{–}6) \qquad 1 - A(1/g - 1) - (\eta - 1)g \int_{-1}^{1/g-1} (1 + z)\,dA(z) = 0.$$

The key observation about this first-order condition is that nowhere in it does the price p appear explicitly and that it can be regarded as an equation of g *only*! Consequently, if the maximum exists and is unique, the optimal pricing policy can be neatly characterized by an extremely simple condition that g be equal to a constant g^* that solves (A1–6). This constant is, of course, the sub-jective-normal ratio we defined by (1–10) in chapter 1, and we obtain the implicit formula for the optimal pricing policy (1–12).

Since this implicit formula $g^* = E(x/q)$ can be rearranged in the following manner:

$$(A1\text{–}7) \qquad g^* = E\left(\frac{x}{q}\right) = \frac{E(p^{-\eta}a)}{q} = \frac{p^{-\eta}E(a)}{q},$$

we can immediately obtain the explicit formula (1–11) for the optimal pricing policy by solving this with respect to p.

(d) *Existence, Uniqueness, and Comparative Statics in Regard to the Optimal Pricing Policy*

First, since $E(py) = 0$ for both $p = 0$ and $p = \infty$ and $E(py) > 0$ for some $0 < p < \infty$ if $q > 0$, the continuity of $E(py)$ in p [which is guaranteed by the fact that $A(\cdot)$ is a probability measure on $(-1, +\infty)$ and $p\min(p^{-\eta}a, q)$ is continuous in p] immediately implies the existence of at least one positive optimal price.

Next, in order to deduce the uniqueness condition, let $G(g)$ represent the left-hand side of the first-order condition (A1–6), defined over the interval $(0, \infty)$. Then it can easily be shown that $\lim_{g \to +0} G(g) \leqslant 0$ and $\lim_{g \to \infty} G(g) \geqslant 0$. It then follows that *if* we can show $G'(g) > 0$ around $g = g^*$, the subjective-normal ratio g^*, and thus the optimal price policy, must be unique. For, as figure A1–1 suggests, the curve $G(g)$ in this case can cut the horizontal axis only once from below.

When, for instance, $A(\cdot)$ is a uniform distribution, characterized by $A'(z) = \frac{1}{2}$ for $-1 \leqslant z \leqslant 1$ and $A'(z) = 0$ otherwise, the uniqueness condition can be easily proved. As a matter of fact, in this case we can directly solve the first-order condition (A1–6) and obtain $g^* = (\eta + 1)/4$. Similarly, when $A(\cdot)$ is characterized by an exponential distribution $A'(z) = e^{-(1+z)}$, $z \geqslant -1$, then g^* is determined uniquely by an equation $(e^{g^*} - 1)/g^* = \eta/(\eta - 1)$. Unfortunately, we have not been able to prove or disprove the uniqueness for the case of log-normal distribution, which possesses many attractive properties.

Finally, if we differentiate (A1–6) totally with respect to η at $g = g^*$ and rearrange terms, we obtain

$$(A1\text{–}8) \qquad \frac{dg^*}{d\eta} = g^* \int_{-1}^{1/g^* - 1} (1 + z)\,dA(z)/G'(g^*)$$

which is positive if $G'(g^*) > 0$. Namely, $dg^*/d\eta > 0$ if the optimal policy is unique.

(e) *Determination of the Optimal Employment Policy*

Let us first calculate the expected gross profit. If the firm adopts the optimal pricing policy $g_{t+\tau} = g^*$ in period $t + \tau$, it is easy to see from (A1–5) that

$$(A1\text{–}9) \qquad E(p_{t+\tau}y_{t+\tau} - w_t n_t : \delta_t \text{ and } w_t)$$

$$= E(p_{t+\tau}q_{t+\tau} : \delta_t) \left[\int_{-1}^{1/g^* - 1} g^*(1 + z)\,dA(z) + 1 - A(1/g^* - 1) \right]$$

$$- w_t n_t.$$

In view of formula (1–11) for the optimal price, $E(p_{t+\tau}q_{t+\tau} : \delta_t)$ in (A1–9) can be calculated as follows:

$$(A1\text{–}10) \qquad E(p_{t+\tau}q_{t+\tau} : \delta_t) = E\left\{\left[\frac{E(a_{t+\tau} : \delta_{t+\tau})}{g^*}\right]^{1/\eta} q_{t+\tau}^{(\eta-1)/\eta} : \delta_t\right\}$$

$$= \left[\frac{E(a_{t+\tau} : \delta_t)}{g^*}\right]^{1/\eta} q_{t+\tau}^{(\eta-1)/\eta} E\left\{\left[\frac{E(a_{t+\tau} : \delta_{t+\tau})}{E(a_{t+\tau} : \delta_t)}\right]^{1/\eta} : \delta_t\right\}.$$

Let ϕ and χ be constants defined by, respectively,

$$(A1\text{–}11) \qquad \phi \equiv E\left(\frac{y_t}{q_t} : \delta_t\right) = E\left[\min\left(\frac{x_t}{q_t}, 1\right) : \delta_t\right]$$

$$= \int_{-1}^{1/g^* - 1} g^*(1 + z)\,dA(z) + 1 - A(1/g^* - 1)$$

and

$$(A1\text{–}12) \qquad \chi \equiv E\left\{\left[\frac{E(a_{t+\tau} : \delta_{t+\tau})}{E(a_{t+\tau} : \delta_t)}\right]^{1/\eta} : \delta_t\right\}$$

$$= E\left\{\left[\frac{a_{t+\tau}}{E(a_{t+\tau} : \delta_{t+\tau})}\right]^{-1/\eta}\left[\frac{a_{t+\tau}}{E(a_{t+\tau} : \delta_t)}\right]^{1/\eta} : \delta_t\right\}$$

$$= \left[\int_{-1}^{\infty} (1 + z)^{-1/\eta}\,dA(z)\right]\left[\int_{-1}^{\infty} (1 + z)^{1/\eta}\,dA^{(\tau)}(z)\right].$$

The first constant, ϕ, represents the expected ratio of product sale to product supply, and the second constant, χ, represents the expected value of the ratio between the expectation of $a_{t+\tau}$ formed at the beginning of period $(t + \tau)$ (which is still an unknown variable at the beginning of period t) and the expectation of $a_{t+\tau}$ formed at the beginning of period t, both raised to the power of $1/\eta$. [In deducing the last line in (A1–12), we have assumed that the surprise $a_{t+\tau}/E(a_{t+\tau} : \delta_{t+\tau}) - 1$, and the surprise $a_{t+\tau}/E(a_{t+\tau} : \delta_t) - 1$, are mutually independent. It is, however, easy to drop this assumption.] In terms of these symbols, we can rewrite the firm's expected gross profit (A1–9) as follows:

$$(A1\text{–}13) \qquad E(p_{t+\tau}y_{t+\tau} - w_t n_t : \delta_t \text{ and } w_t)$$

$$= \phi\chi\left[\frac{E(a_{t+\tau} : \delta_t)}{g^*}\right]^{1/\eta} (j_t n_t^y)^{(\eta-1)/\eta} - w_t n_t.$$

Now, the problem of determining the optimal employment policy is to maximize the foregoing expected gross profit formula subject to the labor supply constraint $n_t \leqslant l_t$. This is one of the simplest constrained maximization problems.

The effective demand for labor h_t given by (1–16) is the optimal employment level when the labor supply constraint is not binding. Its value is thus determined by differentiating (A1–13) with respect to n_t and equating the derivative to zero:

$$\frac{\gamma(\eta - 1)}{\eta}\phi\chi\left[\frac{E(a_{t+\tau}:\delta_t)}{g^*}\right]^{1/\eta}j_t^{(\eta-1)/\eta}h_t^{\gamma(\eta-1)/\eta-1} - w_t = 0$$

or

(A1–14) $h_t = \left\{\left[\frac{\gamma(\eta-1)\phi\chi}{\hat{\eta}}\right]^{\eta}j_t^{(\eta-1)}\left[\frac{E(a_{t+\tau}:\delta_t)}{g^*}\right]w_t^{-\eta}\right\}^{1/[\eta-\gamma(\eta-1)]}.$

It is easy to see that h_t exists and is unique as long as $\gamma < \eta/(\eta - 1)$. On the other hand, it is self-evident that the optimal employment policy when the labor supply constraint is binding is the level of labor supply l_t itself. We can thus characterize the firm's optimal employment policy summarily as $n_t = \min(h_t, l_t)$, as in proposition 1–2.

(f) Derivation of the Ex Ante Markup Formulas

The purpose of this appendix is to derive formulas (1–18) and (1–19) explicitly. The expected price in period $t + \tau$ evaluated at the beginning of period t can be computed as follows:

(A1–15) $E(p_{t+\tau}:\delta_t) = E\left\{\left[\frac{E(a_{t+\tau}:\delta_{t+\tau})}{g^*q_{t+\tau}}\right]^{1/\eta}:\delta_t\right\}$ by (1–11)

$\qquad\qquad = \left[\frac{E(a_{t+\tau}:\delta_t)}{g^*q_{t+\tau}}\right]^{1/\eta}E\left\{\left[\frac{E(a_{t+\tau}:\delta_{t+\tau})}{E(a_{t+\tau}:\delta_t)}\right]^{1/\eta}:\delta_t\right\}$

$\qquad\qquad = \chi\left[\frac{E(a_{t+\tau}:\delta_t)}{g^*q_{t+\tau}}\right]^{1/\eta}$ by (A1–12).

When $n_t = h_t < l_t$, we can rewrite this further as

(A1–16) $E(p_{t+\tau}:\delta_t) = \chi\left[\frac{E(a_{t+\tau}:\delta_t)}{g^*j_th_t^{\gamma}}\right]^{1/\eta}$

$\qquad\qquad = \left[\frac{\eta}{\gamma(\eta-1)\phi}\right]\left(\frac{w_th_t}{j_th_t^{\gamma}}\right)$ by (1–16)

$\qquad\qquad = \left[\frac{\eta}{\gamma(\eta-1)\phi}\right]\left(\frac{w_tn_t}{q_{t+\tau}}\right).$

This is (1–18) of the text.

When $n_t = l_t \leqslant h_t$, on the other hand, (A1–15) can be rearranged as follows:

(A1–17) $E(p_{t+\tau}:\delta_t) = \chi\left[\frac{E(a_{t+\tau}:\delta_t)}{g^*j_th_t^{\gamma}}\right]^{1/\eta}\left(\frac{h_t}{n_t}\right)^{\gamma/\eta}$

$\qquad\qquad = \left[\frac{\eta}{\gamma(\eta-1)\phi}\right]\left(\frac{w_th_t}{j_th_t^{\gamma}}\right)\left(\frac{h_t}{n_t}\right)^{\gamma/\eta}$ by (A1–16)

$$= \left[\frac{\eta}{\gamma(\eta - 1)\phi}\right]\left(\frac{w_t n_t}{j_t n_t^{\gamma}}\right)\left(\frac{h_t}{n_t}\right)^{[\eta - \gamma(\eta - 1)]/\eta}$$

$$\geqslant \left[\frac{\eta}{\gamma(\eta - 1)\phi}\right]\left(\frac{w_t n_t}{q_{t+\tau}}\right)$$

for $n_t = l_t \leqslant h_t$. This is (1–19) of the text.

(g) *Determination of the Optimal Money Wage Policy*

The problem is to maximize the expected profit with respect to the money wage rate. To do this, let f represent $E(h/l)$ and then compute the expected profit explicitly as

(A–18) $$E(py - wn) = E\left\{\phi\chi\left[\frac{E(a)}{g^*}\right]^{1/\eta}(jn^{\gamma})^{(\eta - 1)/\eta} - wn\right\}$$

$$= E\left\{\frac{\eta}{\gamma(\eta - 1)}j^{-(\eta - 1)/\eta}wh^{[\eta - \gamma(\eta - 1)]/\eta}(jn^{\gamma})^{(\eta - 1)/\eta} - wn\right\}$$

by (1–16)

$$= whE\left[\frac{\eta}{\gamma(\hat{\eta} - 1)}\left(\frac{n}{h}\right)^{\gamma(\eta - 1)/\eta} - \left(\frac{n}{h}\right)\right]$$

$$= wh\left\{\left[\frac{\eta}{\gamma(\eta - 1)} - 1\right]E[1 : h \leqslant l]\right.$$

$$\left. + E\left[\frac{\eta}{\gamma(\hat{\eta} - 1)}\left(\frac{l}{h}\right)^{\gamma(\eta - 1)/\eta} - \frac{l}{h} : h > l\right]\right\}$$

$$= wh\left\{\frac{\eta - \gamma(\eta - 1)}{\gamma(\eta - 1)}E\left[1 : \frac{b}{E(b)} - 1 \leqslant \frac{1}{f} - 1\right]\right.$$

$$+ E\left[\frac{\eta}{\gamma(\eta - 1)}\left(\frac{fb}{E(b)}\right)^{-\gamma(\eta - 1)/\eta}\right.$$

$$\left. - \left(\frac{fb}{E(b)}\right)^{-1} : \frac{b}{E(b)} - 1 > \frac{1}{f} - 1\right]\right\}$$

$$= wh\left\{\frac{\eta - \gamma(\eta - 1)}{\gamma(\eta - 1)}B\left(\frac{1}{f} - 1\right)\right.$$

$$+ \frac{\eta}{\gamma(\eta - 1)}\int_{1/f - 1}^{\infty}[f(1 + z)]^{-\gamma(\eta - 1)/\eta}\,dB(z)$$

$$\left. - \int_{1/f - 1}^{\infty}[f(1 + z)]^{-1}\,dB(z)\right\}.$$

Differentiating this with respect to w, noting that $\partial(wh)/\partial w = -\gamma(\eta - 1)h/[\eta - \gamma(\eta - 1)]$ and $\partial f/\partial w = -[(1 + \varepsilon)\eta - \varepsilon\gamma(\eta - 1)]f/\{[\eta - \gamma(\eta - 1)]w\}$, and rearranging terms, we obtain the first-order condition for the optimal wage:

$$(A1-19) \qquad B\left(\frac{1}{f} - 1\right) - \varepsilon \int_{1/f-1}^{\infty} [f(1 + z)]^{-\gamma(\eta-1)/\eta} dB(z)$$

$$+ (1 + \varepsilon) \int_{1/f-1}^{\infty} [f(1 + z)]^{-1} dB(z) = 0.$$

This is, like (A1–6), an equation exclusively of f! In consequence, if the maximum exists and is unique, the optimal money wage policy can be characterized completely by a simple condition that f should be equal to the constant f^* that uniquely solves the above first-order equation. This f^* is nothing but the subjective-normal ratio of labor demand to supply we defined in (1–22), so that we have obtained the implicit formula (1–24).

Rewriting the implicit formula for the optimal policy (1–24) in the following manner:

$$(A1-20) \qquad f^* = E\left(\frac{h_t}{l_t} : \delta_t\right) = E\left(\frac{1}{w_t^\varepsilon b^{-1}} : \delta_t\right) h_t$$

$$= w_t^{-\varepsilon} E(b_t : \delta_t) \left\{\left[\frac{\gamma(\eta - 1)\phi\chi}{\eta}\right]^\eta j^{n-1} \frac{E(a_{t+\tau} : \delta_t)}{g^*} w_t^{-n}\right\}^{1/[\eta-\gamma(n-1)]}$$

and solving it with respect to w_t, we obtain the explicit formula (1–23) of the optimal wage policy.

(h) *Existence, Uniqueness, and Comparative Statics in Regard to the Optimal Money Wage Policy*

In the first place, since we can show that $E(p_{t+\tau}y_{t+\tau} - w_t n_t : \delta_t) = 0$ for both $w_t = 0$ and $w_t = \infty$ and > 0 for some w_t, its continuity with respect to w_t assures the existence of a positive optimal money wage w_t^*.

Second, in order to derive the uniqueness condition, let us denote the left-hand side of the first-order condition (A1–19) by $F(f)$ defined over $[0, \infty)$. Then we can show that $\lim_{f\to+0} F(f) \geqslant 0$ and $\lim_{f\to+\infty} F(f) \leqslant 0$. Therefore, if $F'(f^*) < 0$, then f^* and thereby the optimal money wage policy are unique. This is illustrated by figure A1–2. For example, when $B(\cdot)$ is a uniform distribution characterized by $B'(z) = \frac{1}{2}$ for $-1 \leqslant z \leqslant 1$ and $= 0$ for $z > 1$, we have

$$F(f) = \begin{cases} 1 & \text{for } f \leqslant 1/2 \\ \dfrac{1}{f}\left[1 + \dfrac{\varepsilon\eta}{\eta - \gamma(\eta - 1)} + (1 + \varepsilon)\ln(2f) - \dfrac{\varepsilon\eta}{\eta - \gamma(\eta - 1)}(2f)^{[\eta-\gamma(\eta-1)]/\eta}\right] \\ \text{for } f > 1/2. \end{cases}$$

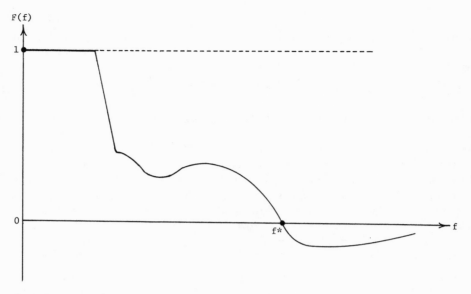

FIGURE A1–2. The Behavior of the Function $F(f)$

It is not hard to show that $F'(f^*) < 0$ in this case. Similarly, it is also possible to prove the uniqueness when $B(\cdot)$ is an exponential distribution characterized by $B'(z) = e^{-(1+z)}$ (see Iwai 1974).

Third, differentiating the first-order condition (A1–15) with respect to ε, we obtain

$$(A1–21) \qquad \frac{\partial f^*}{\partial \varepsilon} = \left\{ \int_{1/f^* - 1}^{\infty} [f^*(1+z)]^{-\gamma(\eta-1)/\eta} dB(z) \right.$$
$$\left. - \int_{1/f^* - 1}^{\infty} [f^*(1+z)]^{-1} dB(z) \right\} \Big/ F'(f^*).$$

The numerator is positive since the condition $\gamma(\eta - 1) < \eta$ or $-\gamma(\eta - 1)/\eta > -1$ guarantees that $[f^*(1+z)]^{-\gamma(\eta-1)/\eta} > [f^*(1+z)]^{-1}$ for $z > 1/f^* - 1$ or $f^*(1+z) > 0$. Thus, the whole expression is negative as long as $F'(f^*) < 0$ (i.e., as long as f^* is unique).

Finally, differentiating the first-order condition (A1–15) with respect to η and γ, we obtain

$$(A1–22) \qquad \frac{df^*}{d\eta} = -\frac{\gamma\varepsilon}{\eta^2} \int_{1/f^* - 1}^{\infty} \ln[f^*(1+z)][f^*(1+z)]^{-\gamma(\eta-1)/\eta} dB(z)$$
$$\Big/ F'(f^*)$$

and

(A1–23) $\quad \dfrac{df^*}{d\gamma} = -\dfrac{(\eta - 1)\varepsilon}{\eta} \displaystyle\int_{1/f^* - 1}^{\infty} \ln\left[f^*(1 + z)\right]\left[f^*(1 + z)\right]^{-\gamma(\eta-1)/\eta} dB(z)$

$\qquad\qquad /F'(f^*),$

where ln stands for natural logarithm. Therefore, as long as $F'(f^*) < 0$ (i.e., as long as f^* is unique), $\partial f^*/\partial\eta > 0$ and $\partial f^*/\partial\gamma > 0$.

(i) *Computation of the Expected Rate of Involuntary Unemployment*

$E(u)$ can be computed as follows:

(A1–24) $\qquad E(u) = E\left\{\max\left[1 - \dfrac{h}{l}, 0\right]\right\}$

$\qquad\qquad\quad = E\left\{\max\left[1 - \dfrac{h}{w^{\varepsilon}b^{-1}}, 0\right]\right\}$

$\qquad\qquad\quad = E\left\{\max\left[1 - f\dfrac{b}{E(b)}, 0\right]\right\}$

$\qquad\qquad\quad = E\left\{1 - f\dfrac{b}{E(b)} : 1 - f\dfrac{b}{E(b)} \geqslant 0\right\}$

$\qquad\qquad\quad = B\left(\dfrac{1}{f} - 1\right) - f\displaystyle\int_{-1}^{1/f - 1}(1 + z)dB(z) \geqslant 0.$

This is (1–28) of the text. Furthermore, we can easily show that

(A1–25) $\qquad\qquad\quad \dfrac{\partial E(u)}{\partial f} = -\displaystyle\int_{-1}^{1/f - 1}(1 + z)\,dB(z) \leqslant 0$

and

(A1–26) $\qquad\qquad\quad \dfrac{\partial^2 E(u)}{\partial f^2} = \dfrac{1}{f^3}B'\left(\dfrac{1}{f} - 1\right) \geqslant 0.$

Hence, $E(u)$ is a nonnegative, nonincreasing, and convex function of f.

Appendix to Chapter 2

(a) *Derivation of the Multiplicative Adaptive Expectation Formulas*

In this appendix we deduce formulas for the computation of the expected values of $a_t \equiv P_t^\eta X_t^\xi \alpha_t$, $b_t \equiv W_t^\varepsilon L_t^{-\lambda} \beta_t^{-1}$, and $a_{t+\tau} \equiv P_{t+\tau}^\eta X_{t+\tau}^\xi \alpha_{t+\tau}$. We examine first expectation formation regarding a_t. (In this appendix we again omit the carets that indicate subjective parameters.)

In the first place, $\ln P_t$ is assumed to be an observable random variable generated by the following random-walk model:

(A2–1) $$\ln P_{t+1} = \ln P_t + \ln(1 + \zeta_{P_t}).$$

Since $\ln P_t$ is observable, it is trivial to see that $\ln P_{t+1}$ at the beginning of period $(t + 1)$ is to the firm a normally distributed random variable with

(A2–2) $$E(\ln P_{t+1} : \delta_{t+1}) = \ln P_t + E[\ln(1 + \zeta_{P_t})]$$

and

(A2–3) $$\mathrm{Var}(\ln P_{t+1} : \delta_{t+1}) = \mathrm{Var}[\ln(1 + \zeta_{P_t})].$$

Second, $\ln X_t$ is assumed to be a random variable whose dynamic motion is described by the following random-walk model:

(A2–4) $$\ln X_{t+1} = \ln X_t + \ln(1 + \zeta_{X_t})$$

and whose observation is given by the following observational-error equation

(A2–5) $$\frac{1}{\xi}\ln(x_t p_t^\eta P_t^{-\eta}) = \ln X_t + \frac{1}{\xi}\ln \alpha_t.$$

Since ζ_X and α_t are log-normally distributed, independent random variables, both $\ln(1 + \zeta_X)$ and $(1/\xi)\ln \alpha_t$ become normally distributed, independent random variables.

Now, the system of a random-walk equation (A2–4) and an observational-error equation (A2–5), with normally distributed, independent random disturbances, is one of the most extensively discussed stochastic systems in econometrics, and the following result is well known:

Lemma A2–1. *If all the past data are available to the decision unit, the prior distribution of the unobservable variable* $\ln X_{t+1}$ *at the beginning of period* $(t + 1)$ *is characterized by a normal distribution, the mean of which is determined recursively by*

$$(A2–6) \qquad E(\ln X_{t+1} : \delta_{t+1}) = E(\ln X_t : \delta_t) + E[\ln(1 + \zeta_{X_t})]$$
$$+ \theta_X \left[\frac{1}{\xi} \ln(x_t p_t^\eta P_t^{-\eta}) - E(\ln X_t : \delta_t) \right],$$

the variance of which is a constant defined as a real positive solution to an equation:

$$(A2–7) \qquad \frac{\text{Var}(\ln X_{t+1})^2}{\text{Var}(\ln X_{t+1}) + \text{Var}((1/\xi)\ln \alpha_t)} \equiv \text{Var}[\ln(1 + \zeta_{X_t})],$$

with the adaptive coefficient θ_X *defined by*

$$(A2–8) \qquad \theta_X \equiv \frac{\text{Var}(\ln X_{t+1})}{\text{Var}(\ln X_{t+1}) + \text{Var}((1/\xi)\ln \alpha_t)} \qquad or$$

$$\equiv \frac{1}{2} \sqrt{\left[\frac{\text{Var}[\ln(1 + \zeta_{X_t})]}{\text{Var}((1/\xi)\ln \alpha_t)} \right]^2 + 4 \frac{\text{Var}[\ln(1 + \zeta_{X_t})]}{\text{Var}((1/\xi)\ln \alpha_t)}}$$

$$- \frac{1}{2} \frac{\text{Var}[\ln(1 + \zeta_{X_t})]}{\text{Var}((1/\xi)\ln \alpha_t)}.$$

This result can be found, for instance, in Nerlove (1967) and in a slightly different form in Muth (1960). [Although their model assumes that the means of both $\ln(1 + \zeta_X)$ and $(1/\xi)\ln \alpha_t$ are zero, this can be easily relaxed.] In fact, this result can be regarded as an elementary application of the well-known Kalman filter theory in information engineering (see Kalman 1960, Kushner 1971, or Aoki 1967 for its exposition).

Our next step is to combine the foregoing two results to obtain the expectation of $\ln a_{t+1} = \xi \ln X_{t+1} + \eta \ln P_{t+1} + \ln \alpha_{t+1}$. Since $\xi \ln X_{t+1}, \eta \ln P_{t+1}$, and $\ln \alpha_{t+1}$ are mutually independent normal random variables, their sum must also be a normally distributed random variable with mean equal to $\xi E(\ln X_{t+1} : \delta_{t+1}) + \eta E(\ln P_{t+1} : \delta_{t+1}) + E(\ln \alpha_{t+1})$ and variance equal to $\xi^2 \text{Var}(\ln X_{t+1}) + \eta^2 \text{Var}(\ln P_{t+1}) + \text{Var}(\ln \alpha_{t+1})$. In view of (A2–2) and (A2–6), its mean can be expressed more explicitly as

$$(A2–9) \qquad E(\ln a_{t+1} : \delta_t) = \xi \{ E(\ln X_t : \delta_t) + E[\ln(1 + \zeta_{X_t})]$$
$$+ \theta_X [(1/\xi)\ln(x_t p_t^\eta P_t^{-\eta}) - E(\ln X_t : \delta_t)] \}$$
$$+ \eta \{ \ln P_t + E[\ln(1 + \zeta_{P_t})] \} + E(\ln \alpha_{t+1})$$

$$
\begin{aligned}
&= \left[\xi E(\ln X_t : \delta_t) + \eta E(\ln P_t : \delta_t) + E(\ln \alpha_t)\right] \\
&\quad + \theta_X\{\ln(x_t p_t^\eta) - \left[\xi E(\ln X_t : \delta_t) + \eta E(\ln P_t : \delta_t)\right. \\
&\quad + \left.E(\ln \alpha_t)\right]\} + \eta(1 - \theta_X)\ln P_t - \eta(1 - \theta_X)E(\ln P_t : \delta_t) \\
&\quad + \eta E\left[\ln(1 + \zeta_{P_t})\right] + \xi E\left[\ln(1 + \zeta_{X_t})\right] + \theta_X E(\ln \alpha_t) \\
&\quad + E(\ln \alpha_{t+1}) - E(\ln \alpha_t) \\
&= E(\ln a_t : \delta_t) + \theta_X\left[\ln a_t - E(\ln a_t : \delta_t)\right] \\
&\quad + \{\eta(1 - \theta_X)(\ln P_t - \ln P_{t-1}) + \theta_X E\left[\ln(1 + \zeta_{P_t})^\eta\right]\} \\
&\quad + E\left[\ln(1 + \zeta_{X_t})^\xi\right] + \theta_X E(\ln \alpha_t).
\end{aligned}
$$

The final step is to translate formula (A2–9) for $E(\ln a_{t+1} : \delta_{t+1})$ into that of $\ln E(a_{t+t} : \delta_{t+1})$. [*Note*: $E(\ln a_{t+1} : \delta_{t+1})$ is *not* equal to $\ln E(\ln a_{t+1} : \delta_{t+1})$!] To this end, we have to recall the following well-known relationship between the mean and variance of a log-normal distribution and those of a normal distribution.

Lemma A2–2. *If a variable Z is a log-normally distributed random variable with mean $E(Z)$ and variance $\mathrm{Var}(Z)$, then $\ln Z$ is normally distributed with*

(A2–10) $$E(\ln Z) = \ln E(Z) - 1/2\,\mathrm{Var}(\ln Z)$$

and

(A2–11) $$\mathrm{Var}(\ln Z) = \ln\left[\frac{E(Z) + \mathrm{Var}(Z)}{E(Z)}\right],$$

and vice versa.

If we note the following relations:

$$
\begin{aligned}
\mathrm{Var}(\ln a_t) &= \eta^2\,\mathrm{Var}(\ln P_t) + \xi^2\,\mathrm{Var}(\ln X_t) + \mathrm{Var}(\ln \alpha_t), \\
\mathrm{Var}(\ln P_t) &= \mathrm{Var}\left[\ln(1 + \zeta_{P_t})\right] \quad \text{by (A2–3)}, \\
\mathrm{Var}(\ln X_t) &= \text{constant} \quad \text{by (A2–7)}, \\
\mathrm{Var}\left[\ln(1 + \zeta_{X_t})\right] &= \theta_X\,\mathrm{Var}(\ln X_t) \quad \text{by (A2–7) and (A2–8)},
\end{aligned}
$$

equation (A2–9) can be translated into

$$
\begin{aligned}
\Delta \ln E(a_t : \delta_t) &= \theta_X\left[\ln a_t - \ln E(a_t : \delta_t)\right] + \ln E(1 + \zeta_{X_t})^\xi \\
&\quad + \left[\eta(1 - \theta_X)\Delta \ln P_{t-1} + \theta_X E(1 + \zeta_{P_t})^\eta\right].
\end{aligned}
$$

If we approximate $\Delta \ln E(a_t : \delta_t)$, $\ln a_t - \ln E(a_t : \delta_t)$, $\Delta \ln P_{t-1}$, $\ln E(1 + \zeta_X)^\xi$, and $\ln E(1 + \zeta_P)^\eta$, respectively, by $\Delta E(a_t : \delta_t)/E(a_t : \delta_t)$, $a_t/E(a_t : \delta_t) - 1$, $\Delta P_{t-1}/P_{t-1}$, $\xi E(\zeta_X) \equiv \xi\mu_X$, and $\eta E(\zeta_P) \equiv \eta\mu_P$, then we obtain the adaptive expectation formula (2–7).

In the same manner, we can obtain the following formula for the computation of $E(b_t : \delta_t)$:

(A2–12) $$
\begin{aligned}
\Delta \ln E(b_t : \delta_t) &= \theta_L\left[\ln b_t - \ln E(b_t : \delta_t)\right] \\
&\quad + \ln E(1 + \zeta_{L_t})^{-\lambda} + \left[\varepsilon(1 - \theta_L)\Delta \ln W_{t-1}\right. \\
&\quad + \left.\theta_L E(1 + \zeta_{W_t})^\varepsilon\right],
\end{aligned}
$$

with

$$(A2\text{-}13) \quad \theta_L \equiv \frac{1}{2} \sqrt{\left[\frac{\mathrm{Var}\left[\ln\left(1 + \zeta_{L_t}\right)\right]}{\mathrm{Var}\left((1/\lambda)\ln \beta_t\right)}\right]^2 + 4\frac{\mathrm{Var}\left[\ln\left(1 + \zeta_{L_t}\right)\right]}{\mathrm{Var}\left((1/\lambda)\ln \beta_t\right)}}$$
$$-\frac{1}{2}\frac{\mathrm{Var}\left[\ln\left(1 + \zeta_{L_t}\right)\right]}{\mathrm{Var}\left((1/\lambda)\ln \beta_t\right)}$$

After a suitable approximation, we can obtain the adaptive-expectation equation (2–8).

Finally, if we note that the firm has no extra information for the expectation of a_{t+s} $(s > 1)$ other than the one used to compute $E(a_{t+1} : \delta_{t+1})$, (2–9) becomes evident.

Appendix to Chapter 3

(a) *On Strong Laws of Large Numbers*

Let $Z(1)$, $Z(2)$, ..., $Z(I)$ be random variables with mean equal to zero and defined over $i = 1, 2, \ldots, I$, and let $N(1) < N(2) < \cdots < N(I)$ be a monotonically increasing sequence of positive numbers with $N(I) \to \infty$ as $I \to \infty$. Our concern in this appendix is to state various conditions under which the "average," $\Sigma_{i=1}^{I} Z(i)/N(I)$, vanishes almost surely as $I \to \infty$; that is,

(A3–1)
$$\sum_{i=1}^{I} \frac{Z(i)}{N(I)} \to 0$$

with probability 1 as $I \to \infty$. Theorems that elucidate the conditions for this almost sure convergence are often called strong laws of large numbers.

Two random variables, $Z(i)$ and $Z(j)$ are said to be *uncorrelated* if and only if both have finite second moments and $E\{Z(i)Z(j)\} = E\{Z(i)\}E\{Z(j)\}$. They are said to be *orthogonal* if the equality above is replaced by $E\{Z(i)Z(j)\} = 0$. Obviously, if the expectation of either one of them is zero, the uncorrelatedness implies orthogonality. (Needless to say, if two random variables are independent, they are also uncorrelated, but not vice versa.) If $\{Z(i)\}$ is a sequence of orthogonal random variables, we have:

Theorem A3–1 (Strong Law of Large Number under Orthogonality). *Let the random variables $Z(i)$'s be orthogonal. If there exists a positive constant c such that for all i*

(A3–2) $$E\{Z(i)^2\} \leqslant c,$$

then as $I \to \infty$ [together with $N(I) \to \infty$], (A3–1) holds with probability 1.

A proof can be found in Chung (1968, pp. 97–98). The more general version of this theorem can be found, for instance, in Loève (1955, theorem 33.1.B).

The assumption of orthogonality (or uncorrelatedness) is often intolerably stringent in many applications, including our own. It is therefore desirable to state the following strong law of large numbers, which covers the correlated sequence of random variables. We have

Theorem A3–2 (Strong Law of Large Numbers for Second-Order Random Sequences). *Let* $\{Z(i)\}$ *be a sequence of possibly correlated random variables with zero mean and continuous covariance. Let* c, c', *and* γ *be finite positive constants. If*

(A3–3) $E\{Z(i)^2\} \leqslant c$

and for large I,

(A3–4) $\dfrac{1}{I^2} \displaystyle\sum_{i=1}^{I} \sum_{j=1}^{I} E\{Z(i)Z(j)\} \leqslant c' \left[\dfrac{N(I)}{(I)}\right]^2 I^{-\gamma},$

then, as $I \to \infty$ [*together with* $N(I) \to \infty$], (A3–1) *holds with probability* 1.

This is a trivial extension of theorem 33.7.A of Loève (1955).

(b) *Proof of Proposition 3–1′*

The purpose of this appendix is to prove proposition 3–1′. The proof of proposition 3–2′ is completely analogous.

To this end, let us imagine a hypothetical state in which *all* the firms are in expectational equilibrium with respect to the present state of the product market. Then, by the third set of conditions for expectational equilibrium (2–22) (other sets of conditions having been already satisfied), the fundamental equation of the product market (3–16) can be written as

(A3–5) $\displaystyle\sum_{i=1}^{I} \frac{1}{G^* P_t Q_t} \left\{ g^*(i) p_t(i) q_t(i) \left[\frac{a_t(i)}{E[a_t(i) : \delta_t(i)]} - 1 \right] \right\} = \left(\frac{X_t}{Q_t} - G^* \right) \Big/ G^*.$

It is then easy to show that

(A3–6) $E\left\{ g^*(i) p_t(i) q_t(i) \left[\dfrac{a_t(i)}{E(a_t(i) : \delta_t(i))} - 1 \right] \right\}$

$= E\left\{ g^*(i) p_t(i) q_t(i) E\left[\dfrac{a_t(i)}{E[a_t(i) : \delta_t(i)]} - 1 : \delta_t(i) \right] \right\} = 0.$

Here use was made of the fact that once $\delta_t(i)$ is given, $p_t(i)$ and $q_t(i)$ become known variables—for $p_t(i)$ is determined by the firm on the basis of $\delta_t(i)$ and $q_t(i)$ is the outcome of the firm's employment policy τ ($\geqslant 1$) periods earlier. Then, we can apply one of the strong laws of large numbers, established in appendix A2, to the left-hand side of (A3–5), by identifying $g^*(i) p_t(i) q_t(i) \{a_t(i)/ E[a_t(i) : \delta_t(i)] - 1\}$ with $Z(i)$ and $G^* P_t Q_t \equiv \Sigma_{i=1}^{I} g^*(i) p_t(i) q_t(i)$ with $N(I)$, and obtain under the conditions stipulated below:

(A3–7) $0 = \left(\dfrac{X_t}{Q_t} - G^* \right) \Big/ G^*$ with probability 1.

If it happens that all firms' objective surprises are uncorrelated with each other, then by theorem A3–1, we obtain the desired result under the very mild condition that the variances of the objective surprise are uniformly bounded. Of course, it is too much to ask for the uncorrelatedness of the objective surprises. And if the objective surprises are correlated with each other, the uniform boundedness of their variances is not sufficient to guarantee the validity of the strong law of large numbers. In such more general circumstances, therefore, some conditions on their covariances have to be imposed. Equation (A3–4) stipulates such conditions. Roughly speaking, it says that since there are I^2 covariance terms, a certain *average* of covariances should decrease, as I tends to infinity, at least as quickly as the decline of $[N(I)/I]^2 I^{-\gamma}$. This is likely to be satisfied if covariances are well dispersed between positive and negative and tend to cancel each other, or if there are very large numbers of firms whose objective surprises are correlated only negligibly with each other. These do not seem unreasonable assumptions to make.

We have therefore established that under reasonable assumptions, in order for all the firms to be simultaneously in expectational equilibrium (with respect to the present state of product demand), it is necessary that the product market gap be equal to zero, with probability 1. To put the matter in contrapositive, we have in fact shown that if the product market gap is nonzero, not all firms can be in expectational equilibrium with respect to the present state of product demand, with probability 1.   Q.E.D.

Appendix to Chapter 5

(a) *The Proportional Relation between the Subjective Disequilibrium and the Proportional Gap between the Expected Ratio and Normal Ratio of Labor Demand to Supply*

Let us substitute the explicit formula for w_t^*, given by (1–23), into the definition of z_t. We then obtain

(A5–1) $\quad z_t \equiv \ln w_t^* - \ln w_t$

$$= \frac{\eta}{\eta + \varepsilon\eta(1-\gamma) + \varepsilon\gamma}\left[\ln\frac{\gamma(\eta-1)\phi\chi}{\eta} + \frac{1}{\eta}\ln\frac{\hat{E}(a_{t+\tau}:\delta_t)}{g^*}\right.$$
$$\left. + \frac{\eta - \gamma(\eta-1)}{\eta}\ln\frac{\hat{E}(b_t:\delta_t)}{f^*} + \frac{\eta-1}{\eta}\ln j_t\right] - \ln w_t$$

$$= \frac{1}{\psi}\left\{-\ln f^* - [\varepsilon\ln w_t - \ln\hat{E}(b_t:\delta_t)]\right.$$
$$+ \frac{\eta}{\eta - \gamma(\eta-1)}\left[\ln\frac{\gamma(\eta-1)\phi\chi}{\eta} + \frac{\eta-1}{\eta}\ln j_t\right.$$
$$\left.\left. + \frac{1}{\eta}\ln\frac{\hat{E}(a_{t+\tau}:\delta_t)}{g^*} - \ln w_t\right]\right\}$$

$$= \frac{1}{\psi}[-\ln f^* - \ln\hat{E}(l_t:\delta_t) + \ln h_t],$$

or

(A5–2) $$\qquad\qquad\qquad \psi z_t = \ln\hat{E}(h_t/l_t:\delta_t) - \ln f^*,$$

where ψ is defined by

(A5–3) $$\qquad\qquad\qquad \psi \equiv \frac{\eta + \varepsilon\eta(1-\gamma) + \varepsilon\gamma}{\eta - \gamma(\eta-1)}.$$

(b) *Derivation of the Aggregate Unemployment Schedule*

In the text we approximated the aggregate rate of involuntary unemployment by the market-wide average of the expected values of individual rates of involuntary unemployment:

(A5–4)
$$U_t \equiv \sum_{i=1}^{I} \left[\frac{l_t(i)}{L_t} \right] u_t(i)$$

$$\underset{\Delta}{=} \sum_{i=1}^{I} \left[\frac{l_t(i)}{L_t} \right] E[u_t(i) : \delta_t(i)].$$

Consequently, we can determine U_t first by computing the expected value of individual rate of involuntary unemployment and then by aggregating it across firms.

The expected rate of involuntary unemployment can be given the following expression, if the method used in appendix 1–i is repeated:

(A5–5) $E[u_t(i) : \delta_t(i)] = B \left\{ \dfrac{1}{E[h_t(i)/l_t(i) : \delta_t(i)]} - 1 \right\}$

$$- E\left[\frac{h_t(i)}{l_t(i)} : \delta_t(i) \right] \int_{-1}^{1/E[h_t(i)/l_t(i) : \delta_t(i)] - 1} (1 + z) \, dB(z).$$

It is easy to show that the expected rate of involuntary unemployment thus calculated is a nonincreasing and convex function of the expected ratio of labor demand to supply. In fact, it will do little violence to our analysis, even if we approximate this relation by a quadratic function, ignoring third- and higher-order effects. In fact, a Taylor expansion of the foregoing relation around $E[h_t(i)/l_t(i) : \delta_t(i)] = f^*$ leads, with a suitable rearrangement of terms, to the following expression:

(A5–6) $E[u_t(i) : \delta_t(i)] \underset{\Delta}{=} u^* - u^{**} \left\{ E\left[\dfrac{h_t(i)}{l_t(i)} : \delta_t(i) \right] - f^* \right\} \Big/ f^*$

$$+ u^{***} \left\{ E\left[\frac{h_t(i)}{l_t(i)} : \delta_t(i) \right] - f^* \right\}^2 \Big/ f^{*2},$$

where $u^* > 0$ is the constant normal rate of involuntary unemployment, the definition of which we can rewrite here as

(A5–7) $u^* \equiv B\left(\dfrac{1}{f^*} - 1 \right) - \displaystyle\int_{-1}^{1/f^* - 1} f^*(1 + z) \, dB(z),$

and $u^{**} > 0$ and $u^{***} > 0$ are positive constants defined by, respectively,

(A5–8) $u^{**} \equiv \displaystyle\int_{-1}^{1/f^* - 1} f^*(1 + z) dB(z) \qquad (<1)$

and

(A5–9) $$u^{***} \equiv B'(1/f^* - 1)/2f^*.$$

Aggregating this expression across firms, we obtain

(A5–10) $$U_t \underset{\Delta}{=} u^* - u^{**} \sum_{i=1}^{I} \left[\frac{l_t(i)}{L_t} \right] \left\{ E\left[\frac{h_t(i)}{l_t(i)} : \delta_t(i) \right] - f^* \right\} \bigg/ f^*$$

$$+ u^{***} \sum_{i=1}^{I} \left(\frac{l_t(i)}{L_t} \right) \left\{ E\left[\frac{h_t(i)}{l_t(i)} : \delta_t(i) \right] - f^* \right\}^2 \bigg/ f^{*2}.$$

In view of the strong law of large numbers, the second term can be approximated as

(A5–11) $$\sum_{i=1}^{I} \left[\frac{l_t(i)}{L_t} \right] \left\{ E\left[\frac{h_t(i)}{l_t(i)} : \delta_t(i) \right] - f^* \right\} \bigg/ f^*$$

$$\underset{\Delta}{=} \sum_{i=1}^{I} \left[\frac{l_t(i)}{L_t} \right] \left[\frac{h_t(i)}{l_t(i)} - f^* \right] \bigg/ f^*,$$

which is by (5–7) equal to the value of labor market gap $(H_t/L_t - f^*)/f^*$. Substituting this approximation back into (A5–10), and rearranging terms, we have

(A5–12) $$U_t \underset{\Delta}{=} u^* - u^{**} \left(\frac{H_t}{L_t} - f^* \right) \bigg/ f^*$$

$$+ u^{***} \sum_{i=1}^{I} \left[\frac{l_t(i)}{L_t} \right] \left\{ E\left[\frac{h_t(i)}{l_t(i)} : \delta_t(i) \right] - f^* \right\}^2 \bigg/ f^{*2}$$

$$= u^* - u^{**} \left(\frac{H_t}{L_t} - f^* \right) \bigg/ f^*$$

$$+ u^{***} \sum_{i=1}^{I} \left[\frac{l_t(i)}{L_t} \right] \left[\left\{ E\left[\frac{h_t(i)}{l_t(i)} : \delta_t(i) \right] - f^* \right\} - \left(\frac{H_t}{L_t} - f^* \right) \right]^2 \bigg/ f^{*2}$$

$$+ 2u^{***} \left(\frac{H_t}{L_t} - f^* \right) \sum_{i=1}^{I} \left[\frac{l_t(i)}{L_t} \right] \left\{ E\left[\frac{h_t(i)}{l_t(i)} : \delta_t(i) \right] - f^* \right\} \bigg/ f^{*2}$$

$$- u^{***} \left(\frac{H_t}{L_t} - f^* \right)^2 \sum_{i=1}^{I} \left[\frac{l_t(i)}{L_t} \right] \bigg/ f^{*2}$$

$$\underset{\Delta}{=} u^* + u^{***} \sum_{i=1}^{I} \left[\frac{l_t(i)}{L_t} \right] \left\{ E\left[\frac{h_t(i)}{l_t(i)} : \delta_t(i) \right] - \frac{H_t}{L_t} \right\}^2 \bigg/ f^{*2}$$

$$- u^{**} \left(\frac{H_t}{L_t} - f^* \right) \bigg/ f^* + u^{***} \left(\frac{H_t}{L_t} - f^* \right)^2 \bigg/ f^{*2},$$

where in deducing the last line we have again used (A5–11). This is nothing but the aggregate unemployment schedule (5–13).

Appendix to Chapter 6

(a) *On the Goodness of the Simple Wage Adjustment Rule*

In the text it was supposed that our firm chooses a wage adjustment policy out of a restricted class of feasible rules, specified by (6–1). In this appendix it will be argued that this special form of adjustment rule is a "good" form and under certain assumptions may well be even the "optimal" form.

J.-P. Vial (1972) considered the following cash management problem (see also Richard 1977). Let the level of cash balance at time t be represented by x_t. The cost of keeping a positive or negative cash balance x_t is specified by a triangular function: max $(a_+ x_t, -a_- x_t)$, where $a_+ > 0$ and $a_- > 0$ are the constant rate of holding cost and the constant penalty rate of overdraft, respectively. There is also the cost of transferring resources into and from the cash balance; it has both lump-sum and proportional components. That is, if the cash balance is increased from x to x', the cost of transfer is $c_+ + C_+(x' - x)$; and if it is decreased from x to x', the cost of transfer is $c_- + C_-(x - x')$, where c_+, c_-, C_+, and C_- are nonnegative constants. It is further assumed that the cash level x_t is fluctuating according to the Wiener process, unless it is interrupted by the conscious transfer of resources in and out of the cash. Thus, unlike our model of wage adjustment, in this model the decision time is assumed to be continuous. Finally, it is supposed that the objective is to minimize the expected discounted sum of total cost. Vial was then able to show that, if an optimal policy exists in such a model, it is characterized by the simple rule that at any moment of time the cash level x_t should be transferred to $z_t = Z(x_t)$, where

(A6–1)
$$Z(x_t) = \begin{cases} \Theta_+ & \text{if } x_t > \theta_+, \\ \Theta_- & \text{if } x_t < \theta_-, \\ x_t & \text{if } \theta_- \leqslant x_t \leqslant \theta_+, \text{ and} \end{cases}$$
$$\theta_- \leqslant \Theta_- \leqslant \Theta_+ \leqslant \theta_+.$$

Several remarks are now in order on this result. First, if both C_+ and C_- are zero and hence the cost of transfer is all lump-sum, it is easy to show that

$\Theta_- = \Theta_+$ and the rule above becomes the continuous-time analog of our wage adjustment rule (6–1) with $\theta_0 = \Theta_+ = \Theta_-$. Second, although the objective function in Vial's model is the expected discounted sum of total loss, his result remains valid even if it is replaced by the long-run average total cost. Third, a careful examination of his proof has convinced us that his result holds true even if we substitute the quadratic cost function, $[-\rho''(0)/2]x_t^2$, for his triangular cost function. [The model of Richard (1977) does not assume this triangular form of the objective function.] Fourth, the Wiener process assumed there is the continuous-time, continuous-state analog of the Bernoulli-trial random-walk model and can be obtained from the latter by applying an appropriate limiting procedure (see, e.g., Cox and Miller 1965). In fact, it is possible to translate the partial differential equations in Vial's paper into the discrete-time, discrete-state, difference equations for the Bernoulli-trial random-walk model and reproduce most of his propositions. We can therefore claim that in the special case in which the random-walk distribution is a Bernoulli-trial distribution, the form of wage adjustment (6–1) is the *optimal* form, so that the best policy out of this class of simple rules is, in fact, the full-fledged optimal adjustment policy. Moreover, even if the random walk distribution is not Bernoulli, the assumed form of adjustment rule should be qualified at least as a *good* form.

(b) *The Recurrence Relation for the Transition Probability Distributions*

In this section we present a recurrence relation that is capable of determining all $\Pi_t(z:z_0)$'s for $t = 0, 1, 2, \ldots$, successively.

   Given the position z_{t-1} in period $(t-1)$, the conditional probability that $z_{t-1} + \Delta \ln w_{t-1}^* \leqslant z$ is equal to $\Omega(z - z_{t-1})$. Hence the conditional probability that $z_t \leqslant z$ in period t is, according to rule (6–1), equal to 0 for $z < \theta_-, \Omega(z - z_{t-1})$ $- \Omega(\theta_- - z_{t-1})$ for $\theta_- \leqslant z < \theta_0, \Omega(z - z_{t-1}) + 1 - \Omega(\theta_+ - z_{t-1})$ for $\theta_0 \leqslant z \leqslant \theta_+$, and 1 for $z > \theta_+$. From this consideration, it is easy to derive the following recurrence relation for $\Pi_t(z:z_0)$:

$$(\text{A6–2}) \quad \Pi_t(z:z_0) = \begin{cases} 0 & \text{for } z < \theta_-, \\[2mm] \displaystyle\int_{\theta_-}^{\theta_+} [\Omega(z-y) - \Omega(\theta_- - y)]\,d\Pi_{t-1}(y:z_0) \\ \quad \text{for } \theta_- \leqslant z < \theta_0, \\[2mm] \displaystyle\int_{\theta_-}^{\theta_+} [\Omega(z-y) + 1 - \Omega(\theta_+ - y)]\,d\Pi_{t-1}(y:z_0) \\ \quad \text{for } \theta_0 \leqslant z < \theta_+, \\[2mm] 1 & \text{for } z \geqslant \theta_+. \end{cases}$$

Using this relation, we can recursively determine the whole sequence of transition probability distributions $\{\Pi_t(z:z_0)\}$.

(c) *The Strong Law of Large Numbers for Markov Processes*

Let us first state the strong law of large numbers for Markov Processes.

Theorem A6–1 (Strong Law of Large Numbers for Markov Processes). *Let* $\Pi^\infty(z)$ *be the unique steady-state distribution of the sequence of Markov process random variables* z_t; *then for any function* $F(\cdot)$ *of* z_t *such that* $E\left|F(z_t)\right| < \infty$,

$$(A6–3) \qquad\qquad \lim_{T\to\infty} \frac{1}{T} \sum_{t=1}^{T} F(z_t) \to \int F(z)d\Pi^\infty(z)$$

with probability 1.

[See, for instance, Doob (1953, V–6), for the strong law of large numbers for Markov processes.] In particular, if we choose the function $F(\cdot)$ such that $F(z_t) = 1$ if $z_t \leqslant z$ and $= 0$ if $z_t > z$, theorem A6–1 can be interpreted as saying that

$$(A6–4) \qquad\qquad \{\text{The proportion of periods during which } z_t \leqslant z\}$$

$$\to \Pi^\infty(z) \qquad \text{with probability 1.}$$

Since the random-walk model with two return barriers is a Markov process, our steady-state theorem (theorem 6–1) guarantees the applicability of (A6–4) to that model.

(d) *Explicit Calculations of the Expected Rate of Money Wage Change as a Function of the Initial Subjective Disequilibrium*

In this section we calculate explicitly $E(\Delta \ln w_0 : z_0)$, obtained in (6–6), in two special cases—the case of Bernoulli-trial random walk and the case of mixexponential random walk.

In the case of Bernoulli-trial distribution with the probability of a positive jump s being equal to π and that of a negative jump $-s$ being equal to $(1 - \pi)$, we have

$$(A6–50) \qquad \begin{cases} E(\Delta \ln w_0 : z_0 = \theta_-) = (1 - \pi)(\theta_- - \theta_0)s < 0, \\ E(\Delta \ln w_0 : z_0) = 0 \qquad \text{for } \theta_- < z_0 < \theta_+, \\ E(\Delta \ln w_0 : z_0 = \theta_+) = \pi(\theta_+ - \theta_0)s > 0. \end{cases}$$

This is obviously a nondecreasing function of z_0. In the case of a mixed exponential distribution where $\Omega'(x) = e^{-x/\alpha}/(\alpha + \beta)$ for $x > 0$ and $\Omega'(x) = e^{x/\beta}/(\alpha + \beta)$ for $x < 0$, $\alpha > 0$, and $\beta > 0$, we have

$$(A6–5b) \qquad E(\Delta \ln w_0 : z_0) = \beta - \alpha + \frac{\alpha(\alpha + \theta_+ - \theta_0)}{\alpha + \beta}e^{z_0/\alpha}$$

$$- \frac{\beta(\beta - \theta_- + \theta_0)}{\alpha + \beta} e^{-z_0/\beta}.$$

This is a strictly increasing function of z_0.

(e) Representation of the Short-Run Expected Profit Function

In this section we represent explicitly the short-run expected gross profit function (6–13). (In what follows we once again omit the carets that indicate subjective parameters.) This can be done by substituting the definition (1–16) of h_t, the expression (1–23) of w_t^*, the definition (6–2) of z_t, and the relation (5–4) between z_t and $\ln \hat{E}(h_t/l_t : \delta_t) - \ln \hat{f}^*$ into the short-run expected profit (A1–13). Rearranging terms, we obtain

(A6–6) $$\hat{E}(r_{t+\tau} : \delta_t \text{ and } w_t) = \rho(z_t)v_t,$$

where

(A6–7) $$\rho(z) \equiv \exp\left[\frac{\gamma(\eta - 1)z}{\eta - \gamma(\eta - 1)} \right] \left\{ \frac{\eta - \gamma(\eta - 1)}{\gamma(\eta - 1)} B(e^{-\psi z}/f^* - 1) \right.$$

$$+ \frac{\eta}{\gamma(\eta - 1)} \int_{e^{-\psi z}/f^* - 1}^{\infty} [e^{-\psi z}(1 + z)/f^*]^{-\gamma(\eta - 1)/\eta} dB(z)$$

$$\left. - \int_{e^{-\psi z}/f^* - 1}^{\infty} [e^{-\psi z}(1 + z)/f^*]^{-1} dB(z) \right\}$$

and

(A6–8) $$v_t \equiv w_t h_t / \text{evaluated at } w_t = w_t^*$$

$$= w_t^*[w_t^{*\varepsilon} f^*/\hat{E}(b_t : \delta_t)] \qquad \text{by (1–23)}$$

$$= \left\{ \left[\frac{\gamma(\eta - 1)\phi\chi}{\eta} \right] \left[\frac{\hat{E}(a_{t+\tau} : \delta_t)}{g^*} \right]^{1/\eta} \right.$$

$$\left. \times \left[\frac{[\hat{E}(b_t : \delta_t)]}{f^*} \right]^{-\gamma(\eta - 1)/\eta(1 + \varepsilon)} j_t^{(\eta - 1)/\eta} \right\}^{(1 + \varepsilon)\eta/[\eta + \varepsilon\eta(1 - \gamma) + \varepsilon\gamma]}$$

(f) Proof of Proposition 6–3

In this section we prove proposition 6–3. For this purpose, let y_t, θ_+, and θ_- be defined by

(A6–9) $$y_t \equiv z_t - \theta_0,$$

(A6–10) $$\lambda_+ \equiv \theta_+ - \theta_0 (\geqslant 0),$$

(A6–11) $$\lambda_- \equiv \theta_- - \theta_0 (\leqslant 0).$$

They are nothing but the horizontal shift of z_t, θ_+, and θ_- to the left by the magnitude θ_0. Then the adjustment rule (6–1) of the subjective disequilibrium z_t can be rewritten in terms of y_t, λ_+, and λ_- as follows:

$$(A6-12) \qquad y_t = \begin{cases} y_{t-1} + \Delta \ln w_{t-1}^* & \text{when } \lambda_- \leqslant y_{t-1} + \Delta \ln w_{t-1}^* \leqslant \lambda_+, \\ 0 & \text{when } y_{t-1} + \Delta \ln w_{t-1}^* > \lambda_+ \text{ or } < \lambda_-. \end{cases}$$

It should be noted that this transformed adjustment rule does not involve θ_0 explicitly. Let $P(y)$, p_+^∞, and p_-^∞ represent, respectively, the steady-state distribution of the transformed variable y_t, the steady-state probability of a wage increase, and the steady-state probability of a wage cut. Then, obviously, they are functions only of λ_+, λ_-, and $\Omega(\cdot)$, without any explicit dependence on the value of θ_0.

It is clear from the construction of the transformed variable y_t that we have the following relationship between $P^\infty(y)$ and $\Pi^\infty(z)$:

$$(A6-13) \qquad\qquad \Pi^\infty(z) = P^\infty(z - \theta_0).$$

Moreover, since the probabilities of wage increase and decrease are invariant as to whether they are expressed in terms of y_t or z_t, we obtain

$$(A6-14) \qquad\qquad \pi_+^\infty = p_+^\infty$$

and

$$(A6-15) \qquad\qquad \pi_-^\infty = p_-^\infty.$$

As a result, the long-run average detrended total cost can be rewritten as

$$(A6-16) \qquad E^\infty(\Lambda) = -\frac{\rho''(0)}{2} \int_{\lambda_-}^{\lambda_+} (y + \theta_0)^2 \, dP^\infty(y) + c_+ p_+^\infty + c_- p_-^\infty.$$

Noting that $P^\infty(y)$, p_+^∞, and p_-^∞ are independent of θ_0, a differentiation of the expression above with respect to θ_0, while holding λ_+ and λ_- constant, leads to the following first-order condition for the minimum:

$$(A6-17) \qquad\qquad 0 = \int_{\lambda_-}^{\lambda_+} (y + \theta_0^*) \, dP^\infty(y) = E^\infty(y) + \theta_0^*,$$

which can be rewritten in terms of the original variables as

$$(A6-18) \qquad\qquad 0 = \int_{\theta_-}^{\theta_+} z \, d\Pi^\infty(z) = E^\infty(z).$$

The positive-definite quadratic form of the first term in (A6–16) guarantees the sufficiency of this condition for the global minimum. Hence, proposition 6–3, which maintains that at the optimum the long-run average value of the subjective disequilibrium, $E^\infty(z)$, equals zero, has been established.

(g) *The Expression of the Long-Run Average Detrended Total Cost in the Bernoulli-Trial Random-Walk Model*

In this section we give an explicit formula for the long-run average detrended total cost $E^\infty(\Lambda)$ in the case of Bernoulli-trial random walk.

In the first place, let us substitute (A6–17) into the expression of $E^\infty(\Lambda)$ given in (A6–16) and obtain

$$(A6–19) \qquad E^\infty(\Lambda)|_{\theta_0 = \theta_0^*} = -\frac{\rho''(0)}{2}\operatorname{Var}^\infty(y) + c_+ p_+^\infty + c_- p_-^\infty.$$

In the mathematical supplement to chapter 6 we are able to show that if the random-walk distribution $\Omega(\cdot)$ is a Bernoulli-trial distribution with unit step size equal to s, the probability of upward jump equal to $\hat{\pi}$ and the mean equal to $\omega = \pi s + (1 - \pi)(-s) = (2\pi - 1)s$, then $E^\infty(y)$, $\operatorname{Var}^\infty(y)$, p_+^∞, and p_-^∞ for the case of $\omega \neq 0$ are expressed as follows:

$$(A6–20) \qquad E^\infty(y) = \frac{1}{2}\left[\frac{(\lambda_+ + s)^2(\Psi^{\lambda_- - s} - 1) + (\lambda_- - s)^2(1 - \Psi^{\lambda_+ + s})}{(\lambda_+ + s)(\Psi^{\lambda_- - s} - 1) + (\lambda_- - s)(1 - \Psi^{\lambda_+ + s})} - \frac{s^2}{\omega}\right],$$

$$(A6–21) \qquad \operatorname{Var}^\infty(y) = \frac{1}{3}\left[\frac{(\lambda_+ + s)^2(\Psi^{\lambda_- - s} - 1) + (\lambda_- - s)^3(1 - \Psi^{\lambda_+ + s})}{(\lambda_+ + s)(\Psi^{\lambda_- - s} - 1) + (\lambda_- - s)(1 - \Psi^{\lambda_+ + s})} - s^2\right]$$
$$- \frac{1}{4}\left\{\left[\frac{(\lambda_+ + s)^2(\Psi^{\lambda_- - s} - 1) + (\lambda_- - s)^2(1 - \Psi^{\lambda_+ + s})}{(\lambda_+ + s)(\Psi^{\lambda_- - s} - 1) + (\lambda_- - s)(1 - \Psi^{\lambda_+ + s})}\right]^2\right.$$
$$\left. - \left(\frac{s^2}{\omega}\right)^2\right\},$$

$$(A6–22) \qquad p_+^\infty = \frac{\omega(\Psi^{\lambda_- - s} - 1)}{(\lambda_+ + s)(\Psi^{\lambda_- - s} - 1) + (\lambda_- - s)(1 - \Psi^{\lambda_+ + s})},$$

and

$$(A6–23) \qquad p_-^\infty = \frac{\omega(1 - \Psi^{\lambda_+ + s})}{(\lambda_+ + s)(\Psi^{\lambda_- - s} - 1) + (\lambda_- - s)(1 - \Psi^{\lambda_+ + s})},$$

where

$$\Psi \equiv \left[(1 - \pi)/\pi\right]^{1/s} = \left[(s - \omega)/(s + \omega)\right]^{1/s}.$$

Their expressions for the case $\omega = 0$ may be obtained by applying l'Hôpital's rule, or they can be found as (S–63′), (S–64′), (S–65′), and (S–66′) in the mathematical supplement to chapter 6.

A substitution into the long-run average detrended total cost (A6–19) leads to

(A6–24) $E^\infty(\Lambda)|_{\theta_0 = \theta_0^*} =$

$$-\frac{\rho''(0)}{6}\left[\frac{(\lambda_+ + s)^3(\Psi^{\lambda_- \; -s} - 1) + (\lambda_- - s)^3(1 - \Psi^{\lambda_+ \; +s})}{(\lambda_+ + s)(\Psi^{\lambda_- \; -s} - 1) + (\lambda_- - s)(1 - \Psi^{\lambda_+ \; +s})} - s^2\right]$$

$$+\frac{\rho''(0)}{8}\left\{\left[\frac{(\lambda_+ + s)^2(\Psi^{\lambda_- \; -s} - 1) + (\lambda_- - s)^2(1 - \Psi^{\lambda_+ \; +s})}{(\lambda_+ + s)(\Psi^{\lambda_- \; -s} - 1) + (\lambda_- - s)(1 - \Psi^{\lambda_+ \; +s})}\right]^2 - \left(\frac{s^2}{\omega}\right)^2\right\}$$

$$+\omega\left[\frac{c_+(\Psi^{\lambda_- \; -s} - 1) + c_-(1 - \Psi^{\lambda_+ \; +s})}{(\lambda_+ + s)(\Psi^{\lambda_- \; -s} - 1) + (\lambda_- - s)(1 - \Psi^{\lambda_+ \; +s})}\right].$$

If we minimize this with respect to $\lambda_+ \geq 0$ and $\lambda_- \leq 0$, we obtain their optimal values, λ_+^* and λ_-^*, as functions of the subjective parameters of the model, ω, s, c_+, c_-, and $-\rho''(0)/2$. Substituting them into the expression of $E^\infty(y)$, given by (A6–20), and solving the optimal condition (A6–17), we obtain the optimal return point θ_0^* as a function of the same set of structural parameters. Finally, the optimal upper and lower barriers, θ_+^* and θ_-^*, can be determined by the definitional equations (A6–10) and (A6–11) (i.e., by $\theta_+^* \equiv \theta_0^* + \lambda_+^*$ and $\theta_-^* \equiv \theta_0^* + \lambda_-^*$).

(h) *Determination of the Optimal Wage Adjustment Rule in the Case of Absolute Downward Wage Rigidity*

There is one case in which it is possible to obtain the formula for the optimal wage adjustment rule using pencil and paper. It is the case in which the downward wage adjustment cost c_- is infinite.

In this special case, it is evident that the firm never cuts the money wage, however low the position of subjective disequilibrium is. Hence, we have

(A6–25) $\theta_-^* = -\infty$ (and $\lambda_-^* = -\infty$).

But as long as the upward wage adjustment cost c_+ is not negligible, the value of λ_+^* (hence that of θ_+^*) is yet to be determined. Note that in this case if the expected rate of change in the short-run optimal wage ω is nonpositive, the subjective disequilibrium z_t will not approach any stochastic steady state but drift down toward minus infinity. Hence, to make the problem nontrivial, we have to assume that $\omega > 0$.

Now, if we let $\lambda_- \to -\infty$, we can simplify (A6–20) to (A6–23) as follows:

(A6–26) $E^\infty(y) = \frac{1}{2}\left(\lambda_+ + s - \frac{s^2}{\omega}\right),$

(A6–27) $\text{Var}^\infty(y) = \frac{1}{12}(\lambda_+ + s)^2 - \frac{1}{3}s^2 + \frac{1}{4}\left(\frac{s^2}{\omega}\right)^2,$

(A6–28) $p_+^\infty = \frac{\omega}{\lambda_+ + s},$

(A6–29) $$p_-^\infty = 0.$$

Then, the long-run average detrended total cost becomes

(A6–30) $$E^\infty(\Lambda)\Big|_{\theta_0=\theta_0^*} = \left[-\frac{\rho''(0)}{2}\right]\left[\frac{1}{12}(\lambda_+ + s)^2 - \frac{1}{3}s^2 + \frac{1}{4}\left(\frac{s^2}{\omega}\right)^2\right]$$
$$+ \frac{c_+\omega}{\lambda_+ + s}.$$

This is a strictly convex function of λ_+ (≥ 0) and hence has a unique minimum. For the sake of brevity, let us treat λ_+ as a nonnegative real number. Then, minimizing the expression above with respect to λ_+ (≥ 0) and making appropriate substitutions, we obtain the optimal return point and the optimal upper barrier as follows:

(A6–31) $$\theta_0^* = -E^\infty(y) = \begin{cases} \dfrac{1}{2}\left(\dfrac{s^2}{\omega} - s\right) \geq 0 \\[2mm] \text{when } 0 < \omega \leq \dfrac{-\rho''(0)s^3}{12c_+}, \\[4mm] \dfrac{1}{2}\left\{\dfrac{s^2}{\omega} - \left[\dfrac{12\omega c_+}{-\rho''(0)}\right]^{1/3}\right\} \geq 0 \\[2mm] \text{when } \dfrac{-\rho''(0)s^3}{12c_+} < \omega \,(\leq s), \end{cases}$$

(A6–32) $$\theta_+^* \equiv \lambda_+^* + \theta_0^* = \begin{cases} \theta_0^* = \dfrac{1}{2}\left(\dfrac{\hat{s}^2}{\hat{\omega}} - \hat{s}\right) \geq 0 \\[2mm] \text{when } 0 < \omega \leq \dfrac{-\rho''(0)s^3}{12c_+}, \\[4mm] \dfrac{1}{2}\left(\dfrac{s^2}{\omega} - s\right) + \dfrac{1}{2}\left\{\left[\dfrac{12\omega c_+}{-\rho''(0)}\right]^{1/3} - s\right\} \geq 0 \\[2mm] \text{when } \dfrac{-\rho''(0)s^3}{12c_+} < \omega \,(\leq s). \end{cases}$$

We have thus completely characterized the best money wage adjustment rule for our firm when the money wage is absolutely rigid downward. The solution above says that, when $0 < \omega \leq -\rho''(0)s^3/12c_+$, the optimal return point θ_0^* is decreasing in ω, increasing in s, but independent of $-\rho''(0)/2$ and c_+; and when $-\rho''(0)s^3/12c_+ < \omega$, it is decreasing in ω, increasing in s, increasing in $-\rho''(0)/2$, and decreasing in c_+. It also says that the optimal upper barrier θ_+^* coincides with the optimal return position θ_0^*, when $0 < \hat{\omega} \leq -\rho''(0)s^3/12c_+$; but when $-\rho''(0)s^3/12c_+ < \omega$, it becomes increasing in s, decreasing in $-\rho''(0)/2$, and increasing in c_+. The relationship between θ_+^* and ω is a bit more complicated.

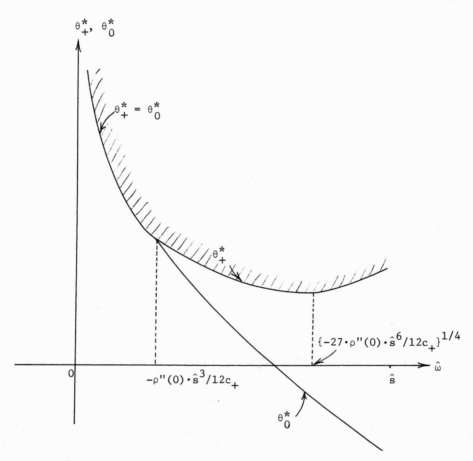

FIGURE A6–1. The Relation between Optimal Decision Parameters and the Expected Rate of Change in the Short-Run Optimal Wage in the Case of Absolute Downward Rigidity of the Money Wage (i.e., $c_- = \infty$).

The former is a decreasing function of the latter as long as $0 < \omega \leqslant [-27\rho''(0)s^6/12c_+]^{1/4}$ but becomes an increasing function after ω exceeds $[-27\rho''(0)s^6/12c_+]^{1/4}$. These relations are illustrated in figure A6–1.

(i) *The Explicit Formula for the Steady-State Variance of the Subjective Disequilibrium under the Best Wage Adjustment Rule in the Case of Absolute Downward Rigidity of the Money Wage*

The expression of the long-run average variance of the subjective disequilibrium induced by the best wage adjustment rule can be easily obtained by substituting the optimal parameters θ_+^* and θ_0^*, given by (A6–31) and (A6–32), into $\text{Var}^\infty(z)$, given by (A6–27). We have

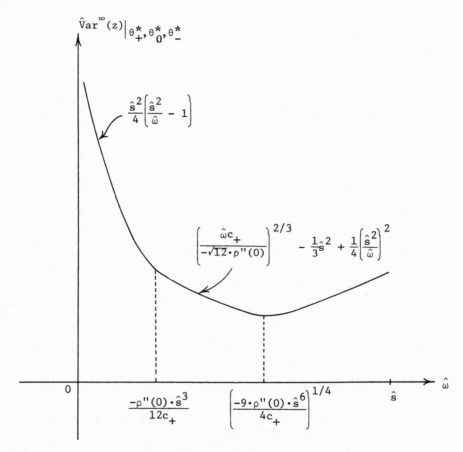

FIGURE A6–2. The Relation between the Steady-State Variance of Subjective Disequilibrium and the Expected Rate of Change in the Short-Run Optimal Wage in the Case of Absolute Downward Rigidity of the Money Wage (i.e., $c_- = \infty$)

$$(A6\text{–}33) \qquad \text{Var}^\infty(z)\big|_{\theta_0^*, \theta_+^*, \theta_-^*} = \begin{cases} \dfrac{s^2}{4}\left(\dfrac{s^2}{\omega} - 1\right) \\[2mm] \text{when } 0 < \omega \leqslant \dfrac{-\rho''(0)s^3}{12c_+}, \\[4mm] \left[\dfrac{\omega c_+}{-12^{1/2}\rho''(0)}\right]^{2/3} - \dfrac{1}{3}s^2 + \dfrac{1}{4}\left(\dfrac{s^2}{\omega}\right)^2 \\[2mm] \text{when } \dfrac{-\rho''(0)s^3}{12c_+} < \omega. \end{cases}$$

When $0 < \omega \leqslant -\rho''(0)s^3/12c_+$, $\text{Var}^\infty(z)$ is decreasing in ω, increasing in s, but

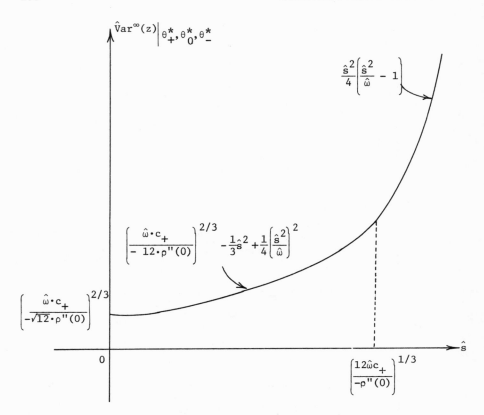

FIGURE A6–3. The Relation between the Steady-State Variance of Subjective
Disequilibrium and the Measure of the Volatility of the Rate of
Change in the Short-Run Optimal Wage in the Case of Absolute
Downward Rigidity of the Money Wage (i.e., $c_- = \infty$)

independent of $-\rho''(0)/2$ and c_+. When $-\rho''(0)\hat{s}^3/12c_+ < \omega$, it becomes increasing in s, decreasing in $-\rho''(0)/2$, and increasing in c_+. The relationship
between $\text{Var}^\infty(z)$ and ω is somewhat more intricate. The former is a decreasing
function of the latter as long as $0 < \omega \leqslant [-9\rho''(0)s^6/4c_+]^{1/4}$, but becomes an
increasing function once the latter exceeds $[-9\rho''(0)s^6/4c_+]^{1/4}$. Figure A6–2
illustrates this relationship between $\text{Var}^\infty(z)$ and ω. Figure A6–3, on the other
hand, illustrates the relationship between $\text{Var}^\infty(z)$ and s.

Some Steady-State Theorems for the Random-Walk Model with Two Return Barriers

(a) *Introduction*

This appendix is devoted to a study of the stochastic process called the random-walk model with two return barriers.

Let ξ_0, ξ_1, ξ_2, ..., be mutually independent random variables with a common probability distribution $\Omega(x) \equiv \Pr\{\xi_t \leqslant x\}$ whose mean equals ω, and let the sequence of random variables $\{z_t\}$ be generated by the rule:

(S–1) $\qquad z_{t+1} = \begin{cases} z_t + \xi_t & \text{when } \theta_- \leqslant z_t + \xi_t \leqslant \theta_+, \\ \theta_0 & \text{when } z_t + \xi_t > \theta_+ \quad \text{or} \quad z_t + \xi_t < \theta_-, \end{cases}$

where $\theta_- \leqslant \theta_0 \leqslant \theta_+$. If the system starts from a given initial position z_0, the position of z_t fluctuates along an interval $[\theta_-, \theta_+]$ as a partial sum of ξ_0, ξ_1, ..., ξ_{t-1}, and z_0. However, when $z_{t-1} + \xi_{t-1}$ passes one of the barriers, θ_+ or θ_-, the system returns instantaneously to the point θ_0, and the process starts anew from that point. The two parameters θ_+ and θ_- are then called return barriers, another parameter θ_0 a return point, and the sequence $\{z_t\}$ is said to constitute a random-walk model with two return barriers at θ_+ and θ_- and a return point at θ_0.

Let $\Pi_t(z:z_0)$ be the transition probability distribution of z_t if the system's starting point is z_0; that is, we put for $t = 1, 2, \ldots$,

(S–2) $\qquad\qquad \Pi_t(z:z_0) \equiv \Pr\{z_t = z : z_0\}.$

By convention we put $\Pi_t(z:z_0) = 0$ for $z < \theta_-$ and $\Pi_t(z:z_0) = 1$ for $z > \theta_+$. Our main concern in this supplement is first to demonstrate that under very weak conditions, as $t \to \infty$, z_t converges to a stochastic steady state in the sense that $\Pi_t(z:z_0)$ converges to a steady-state distribution $\Pi^\infty(z)$, independently of the initial condition z_0, and then to give a complete characterization of this steady-state distribution.

Let y_t, λ_+, and λ_- be defined by

(S–3) $\qquad\qquad y_t \equiv z_t - \theta_0$

281

(S–4) $\lambda_+ \equiv \theta_+ - \theta_0 \geqslant 0$ and $\lambda_- \equiv \theta_- - \theta_0 \leqslant 0.$

They are the horizontal shift of z_t, θ_+, and θ_-, respectively, by the magnitude of θ_0. Then the random-walk model above can easily be transformed into

(S–5) $y_{t+1} = \begin{cases} y_t + \xi_t & \text{when } \lambda_- \leqslant y_t + \xi_t \leqslant \lambda_+, \\ 0 & \text{when } y_t + \xi_t > \lambda_+ \quad \text{or} \quad y_t + \xi_t < \lambda_-. \end{cases}$

This is the random-walk model with two return barriers at λ_+ and λ_- and a return point at the origin.

Then let $P_t(y : y_0)$ be the transition probability distribution of y_t if the system (S–5) starts at y_0; that is, we put

(S–6) $P_t(y : y_0) \equiv \Pr\{y_t \leqslant y : y_0\},$

where by convention we have $P_t(y : y_0) = 0$ for $(y < \lambda_+)$ and $P_t(y : y_0) = 1$ for $(y > \lambda_-)$.

   In this appendix we consider only the transformed random-walk model (S–5) instead of dealing directly with the original model (S–1). Since it involves only two parameters (i.e., λ_+ and λ_-) rather than three (i.e., θ_0, θ_+, and θ_-), it will simplify the exposition considerably. Moreover, we can easily translate the results to be obtained in the present supplement into the propositions for the original random-walk model by means of the following obvious transformation of the two transitional probability distributions:

(S–7) $\Pi_t(z : z_0) \equiv P_t(z + \theta_0 : z_0 + \theta_0).$

(b) *The Random-Walk Model with Two Absorbing Barriers*

The study of the random walk with two return barriers introduced above is intimately connected with the study of the random walk model with two absorbing barriers. Before embarking upon our own investigation, we have to give a brief exposition of the theory of this well-studied random-walk model. This will make our study self-contained and at the same time facilitate understanding for the reader who is not familiar with the theory of random walk. Our exposition will follow closely that of Feller (1966).

   Let

(S–8) $S_0 = 0$ and $S_t = \xi_0 + \cdots + \xi_{t-1},$ $t = 1, 2, \ldots;$

then the sequence S_t constitutes the random-walk model generated by the probability distribution $\Omega(\cdot)$, which starts from the origin. However, if

(S–9) $\lambda_- \leqslant S_1 \leqslant \lambda_+, \ldots, \lambda_- \leqslant S_{t-1} \leqslant \lambda_+$ and $S_t = x$ where

$x > \lambda_+$ or $x < \lambda_-,$

then we say that either of the absorption barriers, λ_+ or λ_-, is passed through for the first time in period t and at the point x. The process terminates (or is absorbed) whenever the event (S–9) occurs. The absorption period T is then defined as the first period in which either of the absorption barriers is passed, and the absorption point is defined accordingly by S_T. That is, T is given by

(S–10) $T \equiv \{t$: The event (S–9) takes place for the first time in period $t\}$.

Clearly, both T and S_T are random variables. But if the event (S–9) does not take place at all, they become defective random variables. [A probability distribution $F(\cdot)$ is called defective if $F(+\infty) < 1$, whereas it is called proper if $F(+\infty) = 1$.] For the joint distribution of the pair (T, S_T), we write for $(x > \lambda_+)$ and $(x < \lambda_-)$,

(S–11) $H_t(x) \equiv \Pr\{T = t \text{ and } S_T \leqslant x\}$, $t = 1, 2, \ldots$.

By convention we put $H_t(x) = H_t(\lambda_-)$ for $\lambda_- \leqslant x \leqslant \lambda_+$. The marginal distributions of $H_t(x)$ are then given by

(S–12) $\Pr\{T = t\} = H_t(+\infty)$, $t = 1, 2, \ldots$,

and

(S–13) $\Pr\{S_T \leqslant x\} = \sum_{t=1}^{\infty} H_t(x) \equiv H(x)$.

$H(x)$ thus defined can be interpreted as the probability distribution of the event (S–9) taking place at all. The random variables T and S_T are proper if and only if $H(+\infty) = 1$.

Let $G_t(x)$ stand for the probability distribution of the event that in period t a point x, where $\lambda_- \leqslant x \leqslant \lambda_+$, is reached and up to period t no absorption at either λ_+ or λ_- took place; that is, for $\lambda_- \leqslant x \leqslant \lambda_+$ and $t = 1, 2, \ldots$, we put

(S–14) $G_t(x) \equiv \Pr\{\lambda_- \leqslant S_1 \leqslant \lambda_+, \ldots, \lambda_- \leqslant S_{t-1} \leqslant \lambda_+ \text{ and } S_t \leqslant x\}$.

We can extend this definition to any x by letting $dG_t(x) = 0$ for $x < \lambda_-$ and $x > \lambda_+$. As a convention we denote by $G_0(x)$ the atomic distribution with a unit jump at the origin; that is, we put

(S–15) $G_0(x) = 0$ for $x < 0$ and $G_0(x) = 1$ for $x \geqslant 0$.

Summing $G_t(x)$ over t, we obtain

(S–16) $G(x) \equiv \sum_{t=0}^{\infty} G_t(x)$

if the series converges. We can interpret $G(x)$ as the expected number that S_t will visit a point below or equal to x prior to the absorption.

Note that by definition, we have

(S–17) $G_t(\lambda_+) = G_t(\infty) = \Pr\{T > t\}$.

Summing over t we therefore obtain

(S–18) $G(\infty) \equiv \sum\limits_{t=0}^{\infty} G_t(\infty) = \sum\limits_{t=0}^{\infty} \Pr\{T > t\} = \sum\limits_{t=0}^{\infty} t\Pr\{T = t\} = E(T)$

if the series converges, where $E(T)$ is the expected absorption time.

Given the position y of ξ_t, the conditional probability that $S_{t+1} = S_t + \xi_t$ $\leqslant x$ is $G_t(x - y)$. It is then easy to derive the following recurrence relations for $H_t(x)$ and $G_t(x)$. We have for $t = 0, 1, 2, \ldots$,

(S–19) $H_{t+1}(x) = \displaystyle\int_{-\infty}^{\infty} G_t(x - y)\,d\Omega(y)$ if $x > \lambda_+$ or $x < \lambda_-$,

(S–20) $G_{t+1}(x) = \displaystyle\int_{-\infty}^{\infty} G_t(x - y)\,d\Omega(y)$ if $\lambda_+ \leqslant x \leqslant \lambda_-$.

If we sum these equations over t, we obtain the following representations of $H(x)$ and $G(x)$:

(S–21) $H(x) = \displaystyle\int_{-\infty}^{\infty} G(x - y)\,d\Omega(y)$ if $x > \lambda_+$ or $x < \lambda_-$,

(S–22) $G(x) - G_0(x) = \displaystyle\int_{-\infty}^{\infty} G(x - y)\,d\Omega(y)$ if $\lambda_- \leqslant x \leqslant \lambda_+$

if the series converge. These relations can be regarded as integral equations determining the unknown distributions $H(x)$ and $G(x)$.

One of the key results in the theory of random walk with two absorbing barriers is the following proposition, which spells out the conditions for the properness of the random variables T and S_T as well as for the existence of their moments.

Lemma S–1. (a) *If both λ_+ and λ_- are finite, both the random variables T and S_T are proper; T has finite moments of all orders; and S_T has a finite expectation. Furthermore, the following equation, which is called Wald's equation, holds if and only if $\Omega(\cdot)$ has a finite expectation ω.*

(S–23) $E(S_T) = \omega E(T).$

(b) *If λ_+ is finite but $\lambda_- = -\infty$, we then have three possibilities: (1) If ω is finite and positive, then T and S_T are proper, have finite expectations, and satisfy Wald's equation (S–23). (2) If $\omega = 0$, then T and S_T are proper, but $E(T) = \infty$. (3) Otherwise, either the random walk drifts to $-\infty$ (in which case T and S_T are defective), or else $E(S_T) = E(T) = \infty$. (c) The case where λ_- is finite but $\lambda_+ = \infty$ can be treated symmetrically to the case (b).*

A rigorous proof of this proposition can be found, for instance, in Feller (1966, pp. 380–381, 566–567). We shall prove it later as a by-product of theorem S–2.

Note in passing that if a system of random walk with absorbing barriers at λ_+ and λ_- starts at some arbitrary initial condition $S_0 = y_0$ ($\lambda_- \leqslant y_0 \leqslant \lambda_+$) instead of the origin, then it can be transformed into the system of the random walk with absorbing barriers at $(\lambda_+ - y_0)$ and $(\lambda_- - y_0)$, which starts from the origin. We can then apply all the results obtained above to this system without any modification.

(c) Recurrence Cycles and the Induced Renewal Process

Let us go back to the original random-walk model with return barriers, given by (S–5).

Starting at a given initial condition y_0 (which is not necessarily equal to zero), the system returns instantaneously to the origin in period t whenever

(S–24) $\qquad y_{t-1} + \xi_{t-1} > \lambda_+ \quad \text{or} \quad y_{t-1} + \xi_{t-1} < \lambda_-,$

and the process starts anew from the origin from then on. We define the kth return period T_k as the period of kth return to the origin; that is, we put for $k = 1, 2, \ldots,$

(S–25) $\qquad T_k \equiv \{t: \text{The event (S–24) takes place for the } k\text{th time in period } t\}.$

The characteristic feature of our random walk with two return barriers is that the section of the random walk following the kth return period T_k is a probabilistic replica of the random walk after the occurrence of the first return to the origin in period T_1. Therefore, the sequence of the numbers of periods between two successive returns to the origin, $(T_2 - T_1)$, $(T_3 - T_2)$, $\ldots$, are mutually independent, positive, and integer-valued random variables with a (possibly defective) common probability distribution. These random variables are called recurrence cycles. It is clear that the common recurrence cycle distribution, which we shall denote by $\Gamma(\cdot)$, is identical with the probability distribution of the absorption period T in the random-walk model with two absorbing barriers at λ_+ and λ_-, which starts at the origin. Hence, we have

$$
\begin{aligned}
\text{(S–26)} \qquad \Gamma(n) &\equiv \Pr\{T_k - T_{k-1} = n\} \\
&= \Pr\{T = n\} = H_n(\infty) \qquad \text{by (S–12).}
\end{aligned}
$$

It is also clear from the remark made at the end of the preceding section that the probability distribution of the first return period T_1, denoted by $\Gamma^1(\cdot)$, is identical with that of the absorption period in the random-walk model with absorbing barriers at $(\lambda_+ - y_0)$ and $(\lambda_- - y_0)$, which starts from the origin; that is, we have

$$
\begin{aligned}
\text{(S–27)} \qquad \Gamma^1(n) &\equiv \Pr\{T_1 = n\} \\
&= \Pr\{t = n: \lambda_- \leqslant S_1 + y_0 \leqslant \lambda_+, \ldots, \lambda_- \leqslant S_{t-1} + y_0 \leqslant \lambda_+ \\
&\quad \text{and } S_t + y_0 > \lambda_+ \text{ or } S_t + y_0 < \lambda_-\}, \\
&= \Pr\{t = n: \lambda_- - y_0 \leqslant S_1 \leqslant \lambda_+ - y_0, \ldots, \lambda_- - y_0 \leqslant S_{t-1} \\
&\quad \leqslant \lambda_+ - y_0 \text{ and } S_t > \lambda_+ - y_0 \text{ or } S_t < \lambda_- - y_0\}.
\end{aligned}
$$

If $S_0 = 0$, $\Gamma^1(\cdot)$ coincides with $\Gamma(\cdot)$.

Thus, the sequence of the return periods $\{T_k\}$ constitutes an integer-valued delayed renewal process generated by the common recurrence cycle distribution $\Gamma(\cdot)$ and the initial distribution $\Gamma^1(\cdot)$. [An excellent exposition of the integer-valued renewal theory can be found in Feller (1968, chap. 13).] A renewal process is said to be persistent if both $\Gamma(\cdot)$ and $\Gamma^1(\cdot)$ are proper. (If one of them is defective, it is said to be transient.) Lemma S–1, which states the conditions for the properness of the random variable T, turns out to be immediately applicable to the classification of our renewal process $\{T_k\}$. We have thus established:

Lemma S–2. (a) *If both λ_+ and λ_- are finite, $\{T_k\}$ is always persistent.* (b) *If λ_+ is finite but $\lambda_- = -\infty$, $\{T_k\}$ is persistent if and only if ω is finite and nonnegative.* (c) *If λ_- is finite but $\lambda_+ = \infty$, $\{T_k\}$ is persistent if and only if ω is finite and nonpositive.*

Let γ_t be the probability that the renewal event (S–24) takes place in period t; that is, we put

(S–28) $\gamma_t \equiv \Pr\{y_{t-1} + \xi_{t-1} > \lambda_+ \text{ or } y_{t-1} + \xi_{t-1} < \lambda_-\}.$

Then, the following proposition, often referred to as the renewal theorem, characterizes the long-run behavior of this probability.

Lemma S–3 (The Renewal Theorem). *Let $\{T_k\}$ be a persistent, integer-valued (delayed) renewal process. Then, as $t \to \infty$,*

(S–29) $\gamma_t \to \dfrac{1}{E(T)};$

if $E(T) = \infty$, then $\gamma_t \to 0$.

This is the basic ergodic result in the theory of renewal processes, and its proof can be found, for example, in Feller (1968, p. 318).

The theorem above justifies our interest in the conditions for the properness of the renewal process $\{T_k\}$ in lemma S–2.

(d) *The Steady-State Theorem*

We are now in a position to prove:

Theorem S–1 (The Steady-State Theorem). *If either (a) both λ_+ and λ_- are finite, or (b) λ_+ is finite, $\lambda_- = -\infty$ and $0 < \omega < \infty$, or (c) λ_- is finite, $\lambda_+ = \infty$ and $-\infty < \omega < 0$, then as $t \to \infty$ the random variable y_t, generated by (S–5), converges to a stochastic steady-state in the sense that*

(S–30) $P_t(y : y_0) \to P^\infty(y),$

independently of the initial condition y_0. *The steady-state distribution* $P^\infty(y)$
is characterized by the equation

(S–31) $$P^\infty(y) = \frac{G(y)}{E(T)} = \frac{G(y)}{G(\infty)},$$

where $G(y)$ *and* $E(T)$ *are given by* (S–16) *and* (S–18).

Proof. It is easy to see from (S–5) and (S–28) that for $\lambda_- \leqslant y < 0$, we have

$$P_t(y) = \Pr\{y_{t-1} + \xi_{t-1} \leqslant y\},$$

and for $0 \leqslant y \leqslant \lambda_+$, we have

$$\begin{aligned}
P_t(y) &= \Pr\{y_{t-1} + \xi_{t-1} \leqslant y\} + \Pr\{y_{t-1} + \xi_{t-1} < \lambda_- \text{ or } y_{t-1} + \xi_{t-1} > \lambda_+\} \\
&= \Pr\{y_{t-1} + \xi_{t-1} \leqslant y\} + \gamma_t \qquad \text{by (S–28).}
\end{aligned}$$

It is also easy to show that for $\lambda_- \leqslant y \leqslant \lambda_+$,

$$\begin{aligned}
\Pr\{y_{t-1} + \xi_{t-1} \leqslant y\} &= \Pr\{\lambda_- \leqslant y_0 + S_1 \leqslant \lambda_+, \ldots, y_0 + S_t \leqslant y\} \\
&\quad + \sum_{n=1}^{t-1} \Pr\{y_n + \xi_n > \lambda_+ \text{ or } y_n + \xi_n < \lambda_-\} \\
&\quad \times \Pr\{\lambda_- \leqslant S_1 \leqslant \lambda_+, \ldots, S_{t-n-1} \leqslant y\} \\
&= G_t^1(y) + \sum_{n=1}^{t-1} \gamma_n G_{t-n}(y),
\end{aligned}$$

where $G_t^1(y) \equiv \Pr\{\lambda_- \leqslant y_0 + S_1 \leqslant \lambda_+, \ldots, \lambda_- \leqslant y_0 + S_{t-1} \leqslant \lambda_+$, and $y_0 + S_t \leqslant y$, where $\lambda_- \leqslant y \leqslant \lambda_+\}$, just as $G_t(y)$ is defined by (S–14). Let $t' \leqslant t - 1$; then we can rewrite the expression above as

$$\begin{aligned}
\sum_{n=1}^{t-1} \gamma_n G_{t-n}(y) + G_t^1(y) &= \sum_{n=1}^{t-1} \gamma_{t-n} G_n(y) + G_t^1(y) \\
&= \sum_{n=1}^{t'} \gamma_{t-n} G_n(y) + \sum_{n=t'+1}^{t-1} \gamma_{t-n} G_n(y) + G_t^1(y).
\end{aligned}$$

Now, it follows from lemma S–2 that under the conditions stated in the steady-state theorem, the renewal process $\{T_k\}$ is persistent, so that we can apply lemma S–3 (the renewal theorem) and assert that as $t \to \infty$,

$$\gamma_t \to 1/E(T).$$

Thus, if we let $t \to \infty$ first and then let $t' \to \infty$, we obtain

$$\sum_{n=1}^{t'} \gamma_{t-n} G_n(y) \to \frac{1}{E(T)} \sum_{n=1}^{t'} G_n(y) \to \frac{G(y) - G_0(y)}{E(T)}.$$

Next, if we let $t \to \infty$, we obtain

$$0 \leqslant \sum_{n=t'+1}^{t-1} \gamma_{t-n} G_n(y) \leqslant \sum_{n=t'+1}^{t-1} G_n(y) \leqslant \sum_{n=t'+1}^{\infty} G_n(y) \leqslant \sum_{n=t'+1}^{\infty} G_n(\infty),$$

where the second inequality is assumed by the fact that γ_t is a probability so that $0 \leqslant \gamma_t \leqslant 1$. But the last series has to converge to zero as $t' \to \infty$, because by lemma S–1 the conditions stated in the theorem imply that $E(T) < \infty$, which is by (S–18) equivalent to the convergence of the series $\Sigma_{t=0}^{\infty} G_t(\infty)$. Finally, if we let $t \to \infty$, we also have

$$0 \leqslant G_t^1(y) \leqslant G_t^1(\infty) \to 0,$$

because again by lemma S–1 that the expected absorption period for the random walk with absorption barriers at $\lambda_+ - y_0$ and $\lambda_- - y_0$ is finite, so that the series $\Sigma_{t=0}^{\infty} G_t^1(\infty)$ is convergent.

Consequently, we can conclude that as $t \to \infty$ for $\lambda_- \leqslant y < 0$, we have

$$P_t(y) = \Pr\{y_{t-1} + \xi_{t-1} \leqslant y\} \to \frac{G(y) - G_0(y)}{E(T)} = \frac{G(y)}{E(T)},$$

and for $0 \leqslant y \leqslant \lambda_+$, we have

$$P_t(y) = \Pr\{y_{t-1} + \xi_{t-1} \leqslant y\} + \gamma_t \to \frac{G(y) - G_0(y)}{E(T)} + \frac{1}{E(T)} = \frac{G(y)}{E(T)},$$

where we have employed the definition of $G_0(y)$, given by (S–15), that $G_0(y) = 0$ for $y < 0$ and $G_0(y) = 1$ for $y \geqslant 0$. (Q.E.D.)

The proposition above is similar to the steady-state theorem for (S, s) inventory policy in the mathematical theory of inventory management. [See Karlin (1958a, 1958b) and Prabhu (1965). For the general reference, see, for example, Arrow et al. (1958), and Scarf et al. (1963).] In the mathematical inventory theory, however, one has only to consider the random-walk distribution $\Omega(\cdot)$, which is concentrated on the nonpositive half-line $(-\infty, 0]$ because the level of inventory is necessarily decumulating until it is restocked by an order. The proof of its steady-state theorem requires, therefore, only the twofold application of the renewal theory. Our steady-state theorem, on the other hand, has to deal with a completely general random-walk distribution $\Omega(\cdot)$ and consider not only the floor barrier ($s - S$ in the case of inventory model and λ_- in our model) but also the ceiling barrier (λ_+ in our model). It includes the former as a special case.

In (S–31) of the steady-state theorem, the steady-state distribution $P^\infty(y)$ is shown to be equal to the ratio between $G(y)$ and $E(T) = G(\infty)$. This result not only appeals to our intuition, but also is very useful to the actual computation of the steady-state distribution $P^\infty(y)$. In fact, $G(y)$ can be computed to any desired degree of accuracy by repeatedly applying the recurrence relation (S–20) and summing the resulting $G_t(y)$ over t. [If we are lucky enough, the integral equation (S–22) can be solved to obtain the explicit form of $G(y)$.]

In many special cases $E(T)$ can be easily computed or at least approximated to any desired degree of accuracy. In this sense, we can claim that the steady-state distribution $P^\infty(y)$ is completely characterized by equation (S–31).

(e) *A Corollary*

Let $p_{+,t}$ and $p_{-,t}$ be the probability that $y_{t-1} + \xi_{t-1}$ passes through the upper barrier λ_+ and the probability that $y_{t-1} + \xi_{t-1}$ passes through the lower barrier λ_-, respectively. They can be expressed as

(S–32)
$$p_{+,t} \equiv \Pr\{y_{t-1} + \xi_{t-1} > \lambda_+ : y_0\}$$
$$= \int_{-\infty}^{\infty} [1 - P_{t-1}(\lambda_+ - x : y_0)]\, d\Omega(x)$$

and

(S–33)
$$p_{-,t} \equiv \Pr\{y_{t-1} + \xi_{t-1} < \lambda_- : y_0\}$$
$$= \int_{-\infty}^{\infty} P_{t-1}(\lambda_- - x : y_0)\, d\Omega(x)$$

Thus, as an application of the steady-state theorem, we can establish:

Corollary S. *Under the same conditions as stated in theorem S–1, as $t \to \infty$, $p_{+,t}$ and $p_{-,t}$ converge to their corresponding steady-state probabilities, p_+^∞ and p_-^∞, where*

(S–34)
$$p_+^\infty = \frac{1 - H(\lambda_+)}{E(T)} = \frac{\Pr\{S_T > \lambda_+\}}{E(T)}$$

and

(S–35)
$$p_-^\infty = \frac{H(\lambda_-)}{E(T)} = \frac{\Pr\{S_T < \lambda_-\}}{E(T)}.$$

Proof. It follows from theorem S–1 that, as $t \to \infty$, we have

$$p_{+,t} \to p_+ \equiv \int_{-\infty}^{\infty} [1 - P^\infty(\lambda_+ - x)]\, d\Omega(x) = \int_{-\infty}^{\infty} \left[1 - \frac{G(\lambda_+ - x)}{E(T)}\right] d\Omega(x)$$

$$= \int_{-\infty}^{\infty} \frac{G(\infty) - G(\lambda_+ - x)}{E(T)}\, d\Omega(x) \qquad \text{by (S–18)}$$

$$= \frac{H(\infty) - H(\lambda_+)}{E(T)} = \frac{1 - H(\lambda_+)}{E(T)} \qquad \text{by (S–21)},$$

where we have also employed the fact that since T and S_T are proper under the stated conditions, $H(\infty) = 1$ [recall the remark given after (S–13)]. Similarly, we have as $t \to \infty$,

$$p^\infty_{-,t} \to p^\infty_- \equiv \int_{-\infty}^\infty P^\infty(\lambda_- - x)\,d\Omega(x) = \int_{-\infty}^\infty \frac{G(\lambda_- - x)}{E(T)}\,d\Omega(x)$$

$$= \frac{H(\lambda_-)}{E(T)}. \hspace{3cm} \text{(Q.E.D.)}$$

If we sum the two steady-state probabilities, p^∞_- and p^∞_+, we obtain

(S-36) $$p^\infty_+ + p^\infty_- = \frac{1 - H(\lambda_+) + H(\lambda_-)}{E(T)} = \frac{1}{E(T)},$$

because $H(\lambda_-) = H(\lambda_+)$, by definition. Thus, the long-run average probability of the return to the origin is equal to the reciprocal of the expected absorption time.

(f) *Calculations of the Steady-State Mean and Variance*

If we are only interested in the mean and variance (and higher moments) of the random variable y_t in the stochastic steady state, there is a method that enables us to calculate them directly without having recourse to the prior computation of the steady-state distribution $P^\infty(y)$. To this end, let us first define the joint expression of the generating function of T and the characteristic function of S_T in the random-walk model with absorbing barriers at λ_+ and λ_-:

(S-37) $$A(\zeta,u) \equiv E(u^T e^{i\zeta S_T}) = \sum_{t=1}^\infty u^t \left[\int_{-\infty}^{\lambda_-} e^{i\zeta y}\,dH_t(y) + \int_{\lambda_+}^\infty e^{i\zeta y}\,dH_t(y) \right],$$

where $i = \sqrt{-1}$ and e is the base of natural logarithm. Let us also define the characteristic function of $G_t(y)$ with respect to y over $\lambda_- \leqslant y \leqslant \lambda_+$ and with respect to $t = 0, 1, 2, \ldots$:

(S-38) $$B(\zeta,u) \equiv \sum_{t=0}^\infty u^t \int_{\lambda_-}^{\lambda_+} e^{i\zeta y}\,dG_t(y).$$

Finally, let us define the characteristic function of $\Omega(x)$ as

(S-39) $$C(\zeta) \equiv \int_{-\infty}^\infty e^{i\zeta x}\,d\Omega(x).$$

It then follows from the recurrence equations (S-19) and (S-20) that we obtain the following identity:

(S-40) $$A(\zeta,u) \equiv 1 - [1 - uC(\zeta)]B(\zeta,u),$$

for all ζ for which $C(\zeta)$ exists and for all u for which the two series (S-37) and (S-38) converge. This relation is called the generalized Wald's identity in the literature of the random-walk theory (see Cox and Miller 1965, Miller 1961, Kemperman 1961, and Feller 1968).

If we differentiate the generalized Wald's identity (S–40) repeatedly with respect to ζ, and evaluate the resulting derivatives at $\zeta = 0$ and $u = 1$, we obtain

(S–41) $A_\zeta^{(1)}(0, 1) = C^{(1)}(0)B(0, 1),$

(S–42) $A_\zeta^{(2)}(0, 1) = 2C^{(1)}(0)B_\zeta^{(1)}(0, 1) + C_\zeta^{(2)}(0)B(0, 1),$

(S–43) $A_\zeta^{(3)}(0, 1) = 3C^{(1)}(0)B_\zeta^{(2)}(0, 1) + 3C^{(2)}(0)B_\zeta^{(1)}(0, 1) + C^{(3)}(0)B(0, 1),$

(S–44) $A_\zeta^{(4)}(0, 1) = 4C^{(1)}(0)B_\zeta^{(3)}(0, 1) + 6C^{(2)}(0)B_\zeta^{(2)}(0, 1) + 4C^{(3)}(0)B_\zeta^{(1)}(0, 1)$
$+ C^{(4)}(0)B(0, 1),$

and so on, where $C^{(n)}(0) \equiv d^n C(\zeta)/d\zeta^n|\zeta = 0$, $A_\zeta^{(n)}(0, 1) \equiv \partial^n A(\zeta, u)/\partial\zeta^n|\zeta = 0$, and $u = 1$, and $B_\zeta^{(n)}(0, 1) \equiv \partial^n B(\zeta, u)/\partial\zeta^n|\zeta = 0$ and $u = 1$.

On the other hand, if we differentiate the characteristic functions (S–37), (S–38), and (S–39) with respect to ζ and evaluate the derivatives at $\zeta = 0$ and $u = 1$, we obtain

(S–45) $$E(S_T^n) = \int_{\lambda_-}^{\lambda_+} y^n \, dH(y) = i^n A_\zeta^{(n)}(0, 1),$$

(S–46) $$\int_{\lambda_-}^{\lambda_+} y^n \, dG(y) = i^n B_\zeta^{(n)}(0, 1),$$

and

(S–47) $$E(\omega_t^n) = \int_{\lambda_-}^{\lambda_+} x^n \, d\Omega(x) = i^n C^{(n)}(0).$$

We also have

(S–48) $$E(T) = G(\infty) = G(\lambda_+) = B(0, 1).$$

If we substitute these relations into (S–41), we obtain Wald's equation (S–23). If we substitute them into (S–42), (S–43), and (S–44), and rearrange terms, we can establish:

Theorem S–2 (Formulas for the Steady-State Mean and Variance). *If $\omega \equiv E(\xi_t) \neq 0$, the mean and the variance of y_t in the stochastic steady state can be expressed as*

(S–49) $$E^\infty(y) \equiv \int_{\lambda_-}^{\lambda_+} y \, dP^\infty(y) = \int_{\lambda_-}^{\lambda_+} y \frac{dG(y)}{E(T)} = \frac{1}{2}\left[\frac{E(S_T^2)}{E(S_T)} - \frac{E(\xi_t^2)}{E(\xi_t)}\right],$$

(S–50) $$\mathrm{Var}^\infty(y) \equiv \int_{\lambda_-}^{\lambda_+} y^2 \, dP^\infty(y) - E^\infty(y)^2 = \int_{\lambda_-}^{\lambda_+} y^2 \frac{dG(y)}{E(T)} - E^\infty(y)^2$$
$$= \frac{1}{3}\left[\frac{E(S_T^3)}{E(S_T)} - \frac{E(\xi_t^3)}{E(\xi_t)}\right] - \frac{1}{4}\left\{\left[\frac{E(S_T^2)}{E(S_T)}\right]^2 - \left[\frac{E(\xi_t^2)}{E(\xi_t)}\right]^2\right\}.$$

If $\omega = 0$ but $E(\xi_t^2) > 0$, they can be expressed as

(S–51)
$$E^\infty(y) = \frac{1}{3}\left[\frac{E(S_T^3)}{E(S_T)} - \frac{E(\xi_t^3)}{E(\xi_t)}\right]$$

and

(S–52) $$\mathrm{Var}^\infty(y) = \frac{1}{6}\left[\frac{E(S_T^4)}{E(S_T^2)} - \frac{E(\xi_t^4)}{E(\xi_t^2)}\right] - \frac{1}{9}\left\{\left[\frac{E(S_T^3)}{E(S_T)}\right]^2 - \left[\frac{E(\xi_t^3)}{E(\xi_t)}\right]^2\right\}.$$

The importance of this theorem lies in the fact that the moments of S_T are often very easy to calculate, or at least easy to approximate.

(g) *A Special Example: The Bernoulli-Trial Random-Walk Model*

In this section we consider a special example in which the random-walk distribution $\Omega(\cdot)$ is a Bernoulli-trial distribution; that is, we assume that

(S–53) $$d\Omega(s) = \mathrm{Pr}\{\xi_t = s\} = \pi, \qquad d\Omega(-s) = \mathrm{Pr}\{\xi_t = -s\} = 1 - \pi,$$

where $s > 0$ is a unit step size and $0 < \pi < 1$ is the probability of a positive jump. The mean ω and the second moment of ξ_t are given by

(S–54) $$\omega \equiv E(\xi_t) = s\pi + s(1 - \pi) = (2\pi - 1)s$$

and

(S–55) $$E(\xi_t^2) = s^2\pi + s^2(1 - \pi) = s^2.$$

Let $g(x) \equiv dG(x)$ for $x = 0, \pm s, \pm 2s, \ldots$, where $G(x)$ is defined by (S–16) in the random-walk model with two absorbing barriers at λ_+ and λ_-. The term $g(x)$ can be interpreted as the expected number that S_t visits the position x prior to the absorption. By convention we have $g(x) = 0$ for $x = \lambda_+ + s$, $\lambda_+ + 2s, \ldots$, and for $x = \lambda_- - s, \lambda_- - 2s, \ldots$. Then equation (S–22) can be transformed into

(S–56) $$g(x) = \pi g(x - s) + (1 - \pi)g(x + s),$$

for $x = \lambda_-, \lambda_- + s, \ldots$, and $-s$, and $= s, \ldots, \lambda_+ - s$ and λ_+, and into

(S–57) $$g(0) - 1 = \pi g(-s) + (1 - \pi)g(s).$$

Employing the boundary conditions, $g(\lambda_+ + s) = g(\lambda_- - s) = 0$, this difference equation can be easily solved. Then, if $\omega \neq 0$, we obtain

(S–58) $$g(x) = \begin{cases} \dfrac{s(1 - \Psi^{\lambda_+ + s})(\Psi^{\lambda_- - s - x} - 1)}{\omega(\Psi^{\lambda_- - s} - \Psi^{\lambda_+ + s})} & \text{for } x = \lambda_-, \lambda_- + s, \ldots, 0, \\[4mm] \dfrac{s(\Psi^{\lambda_- - s} - 1)(1 - \Psi^{\lambda_+ + s - x})}{\omega(\Psi^{\lambda_- - s} - \Psi^{\lambda_+ + s})} & \text{for } x = 0, s, \ldots, \lambda_+, \end{cases}$$

where $\Psi \equiv [(1 - \pi)/\pi]^{1/s}$, and if $\omega = 0$, we obtain

$$(S\text{-}58') \qquad g(x) = \begin{cases} 2\left(\dfrac{x - \lambda_- + s}{\lambda_+ - \lambda_- + 2s}\right) & \text{for } x = \lambda_- + s, \ldots, 0, \\[2ex] 2\left(\dfrac{\lambda_+ + s - x}{\lambda_+ - \lambda_- + 2s}\right) & \text{for } x = 0, s, \ldots, \lambda_+. \end{cases}$$

In the Bernoulli-trial random-walk model, an absorption can take place only at $\lambda_+ + s$ or $\lambda_- - s$. Let us then denote by $h(\lambda_+ + s)$ the probability of $S_T = \lambda_+ + s$ and by $h(\lambda_- - s)$ the probability of $S_T = \lambda_+ - s$. By construction, $h(\lambda_- - s) \equiv dH(\lambda_- - s) = H(\lambda_-)$ and $h(\lambda_+ + s) \equiv dH(\lambda_+ + s) = 1 - H(\lambda_+) = 1 - H(\lambda_-)$. It is easy to see that if $\omega \neq 0$, these two probabilities are given by

$$(S\text{-}59) \qquad h(\lambda_+ + s) = \pi g(\lambda_+) = \frac{\Psi^{\lambda_- -s} - 1}{\Psi^{\lambda_- -s} - \Psi^{\lambda_+ +s}},$$

$$h(\lambda_- - s) = (1 - \pi)g(\lambda_-) = \frac{1 - \Psi^{\lambda_+ +s}}{\Psi^{\lambda_- -s} - \Psi^{\lambda_+ +s}}.$$

If $\omega = 0$, they are given by

$$(S\text{-}59') \qquad h(\lambda_+ + s) = \frac{-\lambda_- + s}{\lambda_+ - \lambda_- + 2s}, \qquad h(\lambda_- - s) = \frac{\lambda_+ + s}{\lambda_+ - \lambda_- + 2s}.$$

Employing these expressions, we can calculate the moments of the absorption point S_T as follows. If $\omega \neq 0$, for $n = 1, 2, \ldots$,

$$(S\text{-}60) \qquad \begin{aligned} E(S_T^n) &= (\lambda_+ + s)^n h(\lambda_+ + s) + (\lambda_- - s)^n h(\lambda_- - s) \\[1ex] &= \frac{(\lambda_+ + s)^n(\Psi^{\lambda_- -s} - 1) + (\lambda_- - s)^n(1 - \Psi^{\lambda_+ +s})}{\Psi^{\lambda_- -s} - \Psi^{\lambda_+ +s}}, \end{aligned}$$

and if $\omega = 0$ and $s^2 \neq 0$, for $n = 1, 2, \ldots$,

$$(S\text{-}60') \qquad E(S_T^n) = \frac{(\lambda_+ + s)^n(-\lambda_- + s) + (\lambda_- - s)^n(\lambda_+ + s)}{\lambda_+ - \lambda_- + 2s}.$$

If $\omega \neq 0$, then the expression of the expected absorption period $E(T)$ can be obtained from Wald's equation (S–23):

$$(S\text{-}61) \qquad E(T) = \frac{E(S_T)}{\omega} = \frac{(\lambda_+ + s)(\Psi^{\lambda_- -s} - 1) + (\lambda_- - s)(1 - \Psi^{\lambda_+ +s})}{\omega(\Psi^{\lambda_- -s} - \Psi^{\lambda_+ +s})},$$

and if $\omega = 0$ but $s^2 \neq 0$, it can be obtained from (S–42), (S–45), and (S–47):

$$(S\text{-}61') \qquad E(T) = \frac{E(S_T^2)}{E(\xi_t^2)} = \frac{(\lambda_+ + s)(-\lambda_- + s)}{s^2}.$$

Now, let $p^\infty(y) \equiv dP^\infty(y)$ be the steady-state probability of $y_t = y$, where

$y = \lambda_-,\ \lambda_- + s,\ \ldots,\ \lambda_+ - s$, and λ_+, in the random-walk model with two *return* barriers at λ_+ and λ_-. Since we have obtained the expressions for both $g(x) \equiv dG(x)$ and $E(T)$, its explicit formula can be deduced from (S–31) of the steady-state theorem. Thus, if $\omega \neq 0$, we have

$$(\text{S–62}) \qquad p^\infty(y) = \frac{g(y)}{E(T)} = \begin{cases} \dfrac{s(1 - \Psi^{\lambda_+ + s})(\Psi^{\lambda_- - s - y} - 1)}{(\lambda_+ + s)(\Psi^{\lambda_- - s} - 1) + (\lambda_- - s)(1 - \Psi^{\lambda_+ + s})} \\[2mm] \text{for } y = \lambda_-,\ \lambda_- + s,\ \ldots,\ 0, \\[3mm] \dfrac{s(\Psi^{\lambda_- - s} - 1)(1 - \Psi^{\lambda_+ - s - y})}{(\lambda_+ + s)(\Psi^{\lambda_- - s} - 1) + (\lambda_- - s)(1 - \Psi^{\lambda_+ + s})} \\[2mm] \text{for } y = 0,\ s,\ \ldots,\ \lambda_+. \end{cases}$$

If $\omega = 0$ but $s^2 \neq 0$, then we have

$$(\text{S–62}') \qquad p^\infty(y) = \begin{cases} \dfrac{2s^2(y - \lambda_- + s)}{(\lambda_+ + s)(-\lambda_- + s)(\lambda_+ - \lambda_- + 2s)} \\[2mm] \text{for } y = \lambda_-,\ \lambda_- + s,\ \ldots,\ 0, \\[3mm] \dfrac{2s^2(\lambda_+ + s - y)}{(\lambda_+ + s)(-\lambda_- + s)(\lambda_+ - \lambda_- + 2s)} \\[2mm] \text{for } y = 0,\ s,\ \ldots,\ \lambda_+. \end{cases}$$

Furthermore, since we have also obtained the expressions for $E(S_T^n)$, the explicit formulas for the steady-state mean and variance can be deduced from equations (S–49) to (S–52) of theorem S–2. If $\omega \neq 0$, we have

$$(\text{S–63}) \qquad E^\infty(y) = \frac{1}{2}\left[\frac{(\lambda_+ + s)^2(\Psi^{\lambda_- - s} - 1) + (\lambda_- - s)^2(1 - \Psi^{\lambda_+ + s})}{(\lambda_+ + s)(\Psi^{\lambda_- - s} - 1) + (\lambda_- - s)(1 - \Psi^{\lambda_+ + s})} - \frac{s^2}{\omega} \right]$$

and

$$(\text{S–64}) \qquad \text{Var}^\infty(y) = \frac{1}{3}\left[\frac{(\lambda_+ + s)^3(\Psi^{\lambda_- - s} - 1) + (\lambda_- - s)^3(1 - \Psi^{\lambda_+ + s})}{(\lambda_+ + s)(\Psi^{\lambda_- - s} - 1) + (\lambda_- - s)(1 - \Psi^{\lambda_+ + s})} - s^2 \right]$$
$$- \frac{1}{4}\left\{ \left[\frac{(\lambda_+ + s)^2(\Psi^{\lambda_- - s} - 1) + (\lambda_- - s)^2(1 - \Psi^{\lambda_+ + s})}{(\lambda_+ + s)(\Psi^{\lambda_- - s} - 1) + (\lambda_- - s)(1 - \Psi^{\lambda_+ + s})} \right]^2 \right.$$
$$\left. - \left(\frac{s^2}{\omega}\right)^2 \right\},$$

and if $\omega = 0$ but $s^2 \neq 0$, we have

$$(\text{S–63}') \qquad\qquad E^\infty(y) = (1/3)(\lambda_+ + \lambda_-)$$

and

$$(\text{S–64}') \quad \text{Var}^\infty(y) = (1/18)\left[(\lambda_+ + s)^2 - (\lambda_+ + s)(\lambda_- - s) + (\lambda_- - s)^2 \right] - (1/6)s^2.$$

Finally, the explicit expressions for the steady-state probabilities of wage increase and wage decrease, p_+^∞ and p_-^∞, can be obtained by substituting the expressions of $h(\lambda_+ + s)$ and $h(\lambda_- - s)$, given in (S–59) or (S–59'), into (S–34) and (S–35) of corollary S. Thus, if $\omega \neq 0$, we have

$$(\text{S–65}) \qquad p_+^\infty = \frac{1 - H(\lambda_+)}{E(T)} = \frac{h(\lambda_+ + s)}{E(T)}$$

$$= \frac{\omega(\Psi^{\lambda_- - s} - 1)}{(\lambda_+ + s)(\Psi^{\lambda_- - s} - 1) + (\lambda_- - s)(1 - \Psi^{\lambda_+ + s})}$$

and

$$(\text{S–66}) \qquad p_-^\infty = \frac{H(\lambda_-)}{E(T)} = \frac{h(\lambda_- - s)}{E(T)}$$

$$= \frac{\omega(1 - \Psi^{\lambda_+ + s})}{(\lambda_+ + s)(\Psi^{\lambda_- - s} - 1) + (\lambda_- - s)(1 - \Psi^{\lambda_+ + s})},$$

and if $\omega = 0$ but $s^2 \neq 0$, we have

$$(\text{S–65'}) \qquad\qquad p_+^\infty = \frac{s^2}{(\lambda_+ + s)(\lambda_+ - \lambda_- + 2s)}$$

and

$$(\text{S–66'}) \qquad\qquad p_-^\infty = \frac{s^2}{(-\lambda_- + s)(\lambda_+ - \lambda_- + 2s)}.$$

There is another special example in which we can readily apply the method developed in this supplement to the calculation of the explicit formulas for the steady-state mean, variance, and other relevant statistics. It is the case in which the random-walk distribution $\Omega(\cdot)$ can be characterized by the following mixed-exponential distribution:

$$d\Omega(x) \equiv \{\text{probability density of } \xi_t = x\}$$

$$= \frac{1}{\alpha + \beta} e^{-x/\alpha} \qquad \text{for } x > 0,$$

$$= \frac{1}{\alpha + \beta} e^{x/\beta} \qquad \text{for } x < 0,$$

where $\alpha > 0$ and $\beta > 0$. The random-walk model with this density function is a discrete-time analog of the so-called birth-and-death process. In order not to lengthen this already long mathematical excursion, however, we leave the analysis of this second example for the interested reader.

Appendix to Chapter 7

(a) *The Rate of Change in the General Wage Level*

When firms are assumed to be symmetric, the definition of the general money wage level W_t given by (1–10) can be simplified as the mean of order ε:

$$(A7-1) \qquad W_t \equiv \left[\sum_{i=1}^{I} \beta_t(i) w_t(i)^\varepsilon \right]^{1/\varepsilon}.$$

Then, the labor supply function corresponding to (1–5) is now given by

$$(A7-2) \qquad l_t(i) = \left[\frac{w_t(i)}{W_t} \right]^\varepsilon \beta_t(i) L_t.$$

From this we can readily deduce that

$$(A7-3) \qquad \ln W_t = \ln w_t(i) - \frac{1}{\varepsilon} \ln \left[\frac{l_t(i)}{\beta_t(i) L_t} \right]$$

or

$$(A7-3') \qquad \Delta \ln W_t = \Delta \ln w_t(i) - \frac{1}{\varepsilon} \Delta \ln \left[\frac{l_t(i)}{\beta_t(i) L_t} \right].$$

If this is multiplied by the weight,

$$(A7-4) \qquad \sigma_t(i) \equiv \frac{\Delta[l_t(i)/L_t]/\Delta \ln [l_t(i)/\beta_t(i) L_t]}{\sum_{j=1}^{I} \Delta[l_t(j)/L_t]/\Delta \ln [l_t(j)/\beta_t(j) L_t]},$$

summed over i from 1 to I, and substituted for by the adding-up condition $\sum_{i=1}^{I} l_t(i) = L_t$, we obtain

$$(A7-5) \qquad \Delta \ln W_t = \sum_{i=1}^{I} \sigma_t(i) \Delta \ln w_t(i).$$

This *exact* aggregation formula is a trivial extension of the so-called ideal log-change index number recently discovered by Kazuo Sato (1976).

(b) *Determination of the Rate of Change in the General Money Wage Level in the Macroscopic Steady State*

In this section we show that in the macroscopic steady state, $\omega \triangleq \Delta \ln W^\infty$ is roughly equal to $\Delta \ln (PX/L)^\infty$. For this purpose, let us recall the formula for the short-run optimal wage (1–23). From this, the rate of change in the short-run optimal wage is given by

$$(A7\text{–}6) \qquad \Delta \ln w_t^* \triangleq \frac{1}{\eta + \varepsilon\eta(1 - \gamma) + \varepsilon\gamma} \{\Delta \ln \hat{E}(P_{t+\tau}^\eta X_{t+\tau}\alpha_{t+\tau} : \delta_t)$$

$$+ [\eta - \gamma(\eta - 1)] \Delta \ln \hat{E}(W_t^\varepsilon L_t^{-1} \beta_t^{-1} : \delta_t)$$

$$+ (\eta - 1)\Delta \ln j_t\}.$$

In the macroscopic steady state, its expected value (i.e., ω) becomes roughly equal to

$$\frac{1}{\eta + \varepsilon\eta(1 - \gamma) + \varepsilon\gamma} \{\eta \Delta \ln P^\infty + \Delta \ln X^\infty$$

$$+ [\eta - \gamma(\eta - 1)](\varepsilon \Delta \ln W^\infty - \Delta \ln L^\infty) + (\eta - 1)\Delta \ln j^\infty\}.$$

But, since $\omega \triangleq \Delta \ln W^\infty$, we can simplify this equation as

$$(A7\text{–}7) \qquad \omega \triangleq \Delta \ln P^\infty + \frac{1}{\eta}\Delta \ln X^\infty - \frac{\eta - \gamma(\eta - 1)}{\eta}\Delta \ln L^\infty + \frac{\eta - 1}{\eta}\Delta \ln j^\infty,$$

which can be further rewritten as

$$(A7\text{–}8) \qquad \hat{\omega} \triangleq (\Delta \ln P^\infty + \Delta \ln X^\infty - \Delta \ln L^\infty) - \frac{\eta - 1}{\eta}(\Delta \ln X^\infty - \gamma \Delta \ln N^\infty$$

$$- \Delta \ln j^\infty) + \frac{(\eta - 1)\gamma}{\eta}(\Delta \ln L^\infty - \Delta \ln N^\infty),$$

where N_t represents the level of total labor employment. Now, in the macroscopic steady state, X_t must grow at the same rate as Q_t in order to keep the product market gap closed. But Q_t grows roughly at the rate equal to $\gamma \Delta \ln N_t + \Delta \ln j_t$. Hence, the second term of (A7–8) has to vanish there. Also, in the macroscopic steady state, in order to have a constant rate of involuntary unemployment, L_t must grow at the same rate as N_t. Hence, the third term of (A7–8) vanishes as well. In consequence, in the macroscopic steady state, we have

$$(A7\text{–}9) \qquad\qquad \hat{\omega} \triangleq \Delta \ln (PX/L)^\infty. \qquad\qquad \text{Q.E.D.}$$

References

Akerlof, George A. 1969. Relative wages and the rate of inflation. *Quarterly Journal of Economics* 83(3), pp. 353–74.

———. 1976. Inflationary tales told by static models: the case of price setters. *American Economic Review* (Papers and Proceedings) 66(2), pp. 72–76.

———. 1980. The economics of social customs, of which unemployment may be one consequence. *Quarterly Journal of Economics* 94(4), pp. 749–75.

———, and Miyazaki, Hajime. 1980. The implicit contract theory of unemployment meets the wage bill argument. *Review of Economic Studies* 47(2), pp. 321–38.

Aoki, Masanao. 1967. *Optimization of Stochastic Systems.* New York: Academic Press.

Archibald, G. C. 1970. Structure of excess demand for labor. In Edmund S. Phelps et al., eds., *Microeconomic Foundations of Employment and Inflation Theory.* New York: Norton, pp. 212–23.

Arrow, Kenneth J. 1959. Towards a theory of price adjustment. In M. Abramovitz, ed., *The Allocation of Economic Resources.* Stanford; Calif.: Stanford University Press.

———, and Hahn, F. H. 1971. *General Competitive Analysis.* San Francisco: Holden-Day.

———, Karlin, S., and Scarf, H. 1958. *Studies in the Mathematical Theory of Inventory and Production.* Stanford; Calif.: Stanford University Press.

Ashenfelter, Orley, and Johnson, George E. 1969. Bargaining theory, trade unions, and industrial strike activity. *American Economic Review* 59(1), pp. 35–49.

———, and Pencavel, John H. 1972. Trade unions and the rate of change of money wage rates in United States manufacturing industry. *Review of Economic Studies* 39(1), pp. 27–54.

Azariadis, Costas. 1975. Implicit contracts and unemployment equilibria. *Journal of Political Economy* 83(6), pp. 1183–1202.

Baily, Martin N. 1974. Wages and employment under uncertain demand. *Review of Economic Studies* 41(1), pp. 37–50.

299

Barro, Robert J. 1972. A theory of monopolistic price adjustment. *Review of Economic Studies* 39(1), pp. 17–26.

———, and Grossman, Herschel I. 1971. A general disequilibrium model of income and employment. *American Economic Review* 61(1), pp. 82–93.

Bellman, Richard. 1957. *Dynamic Programming*. Princeton; N.J.: Princeton University Press.

Benassy, Jean-Pascal. 1975. Neo-Keynesian disequilibrium theory in a monetary economy. *Review of Economic Studies* 42(4), pp. 503–23.

Bodkin, R. G. 1969. Real wages and cyclical variations in employment. *Canadian Journal of Economics* 2(2), pp. 353–74.

Chamberlin, Edward H. 1933. *The Theory of Monopolistic Competition*. Cambridge; Mass.: Harvard University Press.

Champernowne, David G. 1953. A model of income distribution. *Economic Journal* 63(250), pp. 318–51.

Chung, Kai-Lai. 1968. *A Course in Probability Theory*. New York: Academic Press.

Clark, K. B., and Summers, L. H. 1979. Labor market dynamics and unemployment: a reconsideration. *Brookings Papers on Economic Activity* 1979(1), pp. 13–60.

Clower, Robert W. 1965. The Keynesian counter-revolution: a theoretical appraisal. In F. H. Hahn, and F. P. R. Brechling, eds., *The Theory of Interest Rates*. London: Macmillan, pp. 103–25.

———, and Leijonhufvud, Axel. 1975. The coordination of economic activities: a Keynesian perspective. *American Economic Review* 65(2), pp. 182–88.

Cournot, Augustin A. 1897. *Researches into the Mathematical Principle of the Theory of Wealth*. London: Macmillan. (English translation by N. T. Bacon of the French original, published in 1838.)

Cox, D. R., and Miller, H. D. 1965. *The Theory of Stochastic Process*. New York: Wiley.

Cyert, Richart M., and March, James G., eds. 1963. *A Behavioral Theory of the Firm*. Englewood Cliffs, N. J.: Prentice-Hall.

Davidson, P. A. 1972. *Money and the Real World*. New York: Wiley.

———. 1980. The dual-faceted nature of the Keynesian revolution. *Journal of Post Keynesian Economics* 2(3), pp. 291–307.

Doob, J. L. 1953. *Stochastic Processes*. New York: Wiley.

Dow, J. C., and Dicks-Mireaux, L. A. 1959. Excess demand for labor. *Oxford Economic Papers*, N. S.10(1), pp. 1–33.

Drèze, Jacques H. 1975. Existence of an exchange equilibrium under price rigidities. *International Economic Review* 16(2), pp. 301–20.

Dunlop, John T. 1938. The movement of real and money wage rates. *Economic Journal* 48(191), pp. 413–34.

———. 1944. *Wage Determination under Trade Unions*. New York: A. M. Kelley.

Eckstein, Otto, and Wyss, David. 1972. Industry price equations. In O., Eckstein, ed., *The Econometrics of Price Determination: Conference, October 30–31, 1970, Washington, D.C.* Washington, D.C.: Board of Governors of the Federal Reserve System and Social Research Council, pp. 133–65.

Fair, Ray C. 1969. *The Short-Run Demand for Workers and Hours.* Amsterdam: North-Holland.

Feller, William. 1966. *An Introduction to Probability Theory and Its Application,* vol. 2, 2nd ed. New York: Wiley.

———. 1968. *An Introduction to Probability Theory and Its Applications,* vol. 1, 3rd ed. New York: Wiley.

Fisher, Irving. 1926. A statistical relation between unemployment and price changes. *International Labor Review* 13(6), pp. 185–92. (Reprinted in 1973 as: I discovered the Phillips curve. *Journal of Political Economy* 81(2), part 1, pp. 495–502.)

———. 1933. The debt-deflation theory of great depressions. *Econometrica* 1(3), pp. 337–57.

Friedman, Milton. 1968. The role of monetary policy. *American Economic Review* 58(1), pp. 1–17.

———. 1970. *The Counter-revolution in Monetary Theory.* London: IEA (for the Wincott Foundation) Occasional Paper 33.

———. 1975. *Unemployment versus Inflation? An Evaluation of the Phillips Curve.* London: IEA (for the Wincott Foundation) Occasional Paper 44.

Godley, Wynne A. H., and Nordhaus, William D. 1972. Pricing in the trade cycle. *Economic Journal* 82(327), pp. 853–82.

Gombrich, E. H. 1960. *Art and Illusion.* New York: Pantheon Books.

Gordon, Donald F. 1975. A neo-classical theory for Keynesian unemployment. *Economic Inquiry* 12(4), pp. 431–59.

Grandmont, Jean M., and Laroque, Guy. 1976. On temporary Keynesian equilibria. *Review of Economic Studies* 43(1), pp. 53–67.

Hansen, Alvin H. 1953. *A Guide to Keynes.* New York: McGraw-Hill.

Hansen, Bent. 1951. *A Study in the Theory of Inflation.* London: Macmillan.

———. 1970. Excess demand, unemployment, vacancies and wages. *Quarterly Journal of Economics* 84(1), pp. 1–23.

Hayek, Friedrich A. von. 1931. *Prices and Production.* London: Routledge & Kegan Paul.

———. 1933. *Monetary Theory and the Trade Cycle.* London: Jonathan Cape. (The German original was published in 1929.)

———. 1937. Economics and knowledge. *Economica* (New Series) 4(1), pp. 33–54 (also in Hayek, 1948).

———. 1945. The use of knowledge in society. *American Economic Review* 35(4), pp. 519–30 (also in Hayek, 1948).

———. 1948. *Individualism and Economic Order.* Chicago: University of Chicago Press.

————. 1958. Inflation resulting from the downward inflexibility of wages. Reprinted in *Studies in Philosophy, Politics and Economics*. Chicago: University of Chicago Press, 1969, pp. 295–99.

Hicks, John R. 1937. Mr. Keynes and the "classics": A suggested interpretation. *Econometrica* 5(2), pp. 147–59.

————. 1946. *Value and Capital*, 2nd ed. Oxford: Clarendon Press.

————. 1965. *Capital and Growth*. Oxford: Clarendon Press.

————. 1975. Revival of political economy, the old and the new. *Economic Record* 51(4), pp. 365–67.

————. 1976. Some questions of time in economic. In A. M. Tang, F. M. Westfield, and J. S. Worley, eds., *Evolution, Welfare and Time in Economics*. Lexington, Mass.: Heath, pp. 135–51.

Houthakker, H. S. 1960. Additive preferences. *Econometrica* 28(2), pp. 244–57.

Hurwicz, Leonid. 1960. Optimality and informational efficiency in resource allocation processes. In K. J. Arrow, S. Karlin, and P. Suppes, eds., *Mathematical Methods in the Social Sciences*. Stanford; Calif.: Stanford University Press, pp. 27–46.

————. 1972. On informationally decentralized system. In C. B. McGuire and R. Radner, eds., *Decision and Organization*. Amsterdam: North-Holland, pp. 297–336.

Iwai, Katsuhito. 1974. The firm in uncertain markets and its price, wage, and employment adjustments. *Review of Economic Studies* 41(2), pp. 257–76.

Jackman, R. 1974. Keynes and Leijonhufvud. *Oxford Economic Papers* 26(2), pp. 259–71.

Johnson, Harry. 1958. Monetary theory and Keynesian economics. *Pakistan Economic Review* 8(2), pp. 56–70.

Johnston, J. 1960. *Statistical Cost Analysis*. New York: McGraw-Hill.

Kaldor, Nicholas. 1956. Alternative theories of distribution. *Review of Economic Studies* 23(1), pp. 83–100.

————. 1961. Capital accumulation and economic growth. In F. A. Lutz and D. C. Hague, eds., *The Theory of Capital*. London: Macmillan, pp. 177–222.

Kalecki, Michal. 1938. The determinations of distribution of the national income. *Econometrica* 6(2), pp. 97–112.

————. 1939. *Essays in the Theory of Economic Fluctuations*. London: Allen & Unwin.

————. 1954. *Theory of Economic Dynamic: An Essay on Cyclical and Long-Run Changes in Capitalist Economy*. London: Allen & Unwin.

Kalman, R. E. 1960. A new approach to linear filtering and prediction problems. *Journal of Basic Engineering* (ASME translation) 82D, pp. 35–44.

Karlin, S. 1958. Steady-state solutions. In K. J. Arrow, S. Karlin, and H. Scarf, eds., *Studies in the Mathematical Theory of Inventory and Production*. Stanford, Calif.: Stanford University Press, pp. 223–69. (a)

————. 1958. The application of renewal theory to the study of inventory policies. In K.J. Arrow, S. Karlin, and H. Scarf, eds., *Studies in the Mathematical Theory of Inventory and Production*. Stanford; Calif.: Stanford University Press, pp. 270–97. (b)

Kemperman, J. H. B. 1961. *The Passage Problems for a Stationary Markov Chain*. Chicago: University of Chicago Press.

Keynes, John M. 1930. *A Treatise on Money*, vol. 1: *The Pure Theory of Money*. (Reprinted in Keynes's *Collected Writings*, vol. 5.)

————. 1933. A monetary theory of production. In *Festschrift für Arthur Spiethoff*. (Reprinted in Keynes's *Collected Writings*, vol. 13.)

————. 1936. *The General Theory of Employment, Interest, and Money*. (Reprinted in Keynes's *Collected Writings*, vol. 3.)

————. 1937a. The general theory of employment. (Reprinted in Keynes's *Collected Writings*, vol. 14.) (a)

————. 1937b. Ex post and ex ante. Note from his 1937 Lectures. (In Keynes's *Collected Writings*, vol. 14.) (b)

————. 1939. Relative movements of real wages and output. (Reprinted in Keynes's *Collected Writings*, vol. 7.)

————. 1940. *How to Pay for the War: A Radical Plan for the Chancellor of the Exchequer*. (Reprinted in Keynes's *Collected Writings*, vol. 9.)

————. 1971–. *The Collected Writings of John Maynard Keynes*. London: Macmillan (for the Royal Economic Society).

Koopmans, Tjalling C. 1957. *Three Essays on the State of Economic Science*. New York: McGraw-Hill.

Kornai, Janos. 1971. *Anti-equilibrium*. Amsterdam: North-Holland.

Kregel, J. A. 1976. Economic methodology in the face of uncertainty: the modelling methods of Keynes and the post-Keynesians. *Economic Journal* 86(342), pp. 209–25.

Kuh, Edwin. 1965. Cyclical and secular labor productivity in United States manufacturing. *Review of Economics and Statistics* 47(1), pp. 1–12.

Kushner, Harold. 1971. *Introduction to Stochastic Control*. New York: Holt, Rinehart and Winston.

Lange, Oskar. 1952. Say's law: a restatement and criticism. In O. Lange, F. McIntyre, and T. O. Yntema, eds., *Studies in Mathematical Economics and Econometrics*. Chicago: University of Chicago Press, pp. 40–68.

Leijonhufvud, Axel. 1968. *On Keynesian Economics and the Economics of Keynes*. London: Oxford University Press.

————. 1969. *Keynes and the Classics*. London: IEA (for the Wincott Foundation) Occasional Paper 30.

Lerner, Abba. 1952. The essential properties of interest and money. *Quarterly Journal of Economics* 66(1), pp. 172–93.

Lindahl, Erik. 1939. *Studies in the Theory of Money and Capital*. London: Allen & Unwin. (The Swedish original was published in 1929–1930).

Lipsey, Richard G. 1960. The relationship between unemployment and the rate of change of money wage rates in the United Kingdom, 1862–1957: a further analysis. *Economica* 27(105), pp. 1–31.

Loève, M. 1955. *Probability Theory*. New York: Van Nostrand Reinhold.

Lucas, Robert E., Jr. 1972. Expectations and the neutrality of money. *Journal of Economic Theory* 4(2), pp. 103–24. (a)

———. 1972. Econometric testing of the natural rate hypothesis. In *The Econometrics of Price Determination: Conference, October 30–31, 1970, Washington, D.C.* Washington, D.C.: Board of Governors of the Federal Reserve System and Social Research Council, pp. 50–59. (b)

———. 1975. An equilibrium model of the business cycle. *Journal of Political Economy* 83(6), pp. 1113–44.

Malinvaud, Edmond. 1977. *The Theory of Unemployment Reconsidered*. New York: Wiley.

March, J. G., and Simon, H. A. 1958. *Organizations*. New York: Wiley.

Miller, H. D. 1961. A generalization of Wald's identity with applications to random walks. *Annals of Mathematical Statistics* 32, pp. 549–60.

Minsky, Hyman P. 1975. *John Maynard Keynes*. New York: Columbia University Press.

Mises, Ludwig von. 1934. *The Theory of Money and Credit*, translated by H. E. Baton. London: Jonathan Cape. (The German original was published in 1912.)

Modigliani, Franco. 1944. Liquidity preference and the theory of interest and money. *Econometrica* 12(1), pp. 45–88.

———. 1963. The monetary mechanism and its interaction with real phenomena. *Review of Economics and Statistics* 45(1), pp. 79–107.

Muth, John F. 1960. Optimal properties of exponentially weighted forecasts. *Journal of the American Statistical Association* 55(290) pp. 299–306.

———. 1961. Rational expectations and the theory of price movements. *Econometrica* 29(9), pp. 315–335.

Myrdal, Gunnar. 1939. *Monetary Equilibrium*. London: W. Hodge. (The Swedish original was published in 1931.)

Nash, John F., Jr. 1950. Equilibrium points in N-person games. *Proceedings of the National Academy of Sciences* 36, pp. 48–49.

Negishi, Takashi. 1961. Monopolistic competition and general equilibrium. *Review of Economic Studies* 28(3), pp. 196–201.

———. 1962. The stability of a competitive economy: a survey article. *Econometrica* 30(4), pp. 635–69.

Neild, R. R. 1963. *Pricing and Employment in the Trade Cycle*. Cambridge: Cambridge University Press.

Nelson, Richard R., and Winter, Sidney G. 1974. Neoclassical vs. evolutionary theory of economic growth: critique and prospectus. *Economic Journal* 84(336), pp. 886–905.

———, and Winter, Sidney G. 1975. Factor price changes and factor substitution in an evolutionary model. *Bell Journal of Economics* 6(2), pp. 466–86.

Nerlove, Marc. 1967. Distributed lags and unobserved components in economic time series. In W. J. Fellner et al., eds., *Ten Economic Studies in the Tradition of Irving Fisher*. New York: Wiley, pp. 127–69.

Ohlin, Bertil. 1937. Some notes on the Stockholm theory of saving and investment: I and II. *Economic Journal* 47(185, 186), pp. 53–69, 221–40.

Otani, Ichiro. 1978. Real wages and business cycles revisted. *Review of Economics and Statistics* 60(2), pp. 301–04.

Patinkin, Don. 1965. *Money, Interest, and Prices*, 2nd ed. New York: Harper & Row.

Phelps, Edmund S. 1970. Money wage dynamics and labor market equilibrium. in E. S. Phelps, et al., eds., *The Microeconomic Foundations of Employment and Inflation Theory*. New York: Norton, pp. 124–66.

———, et al., eds. 1970. *The Microeconomic Foundations of Employment and Inflation Theory*. New York: Norton.

Phillips, A. W. 1958. The relations between unemployment and the rate of change of money wage rates in the United Kingdom, 1861–1957. *Economica* 25(100), pp. 283–99.

Piaget, Jean. 1957. *The Origin of Intelligence in the Child*. London: Routledge & Kegan Paul. (English translation of *La Naissance de l'intelligence chez l'enfant*, 1936.)

———. 1967. *Six Psychological Studies*. New York: Random House. (English translation of *Six études de psychologie*, 1964.)

———, and Inhelder, B. 1972. *Psychology of the Child*. New York: Harper & Row.

Pigou, A. C. 1943. The classical stationary state. *Economic Journal* 53(212), pp. 343–51.

Prabhu, N. U. 1965. *Queues and Inventories*. New York: Wiley.

Rees, Albert. 1962. *The Economics of Trade Unions*. Chicago: University of Chicago Press.

———. 1970. The Phillips curve as a menu for policy choice. *Economica* 27(147), pp. 227–38.

———. 1973. *The Economics of Work and Pay*. New York: Harper & Row.

Richard, Scott F. 1977. Optimal impulse control of a diffusion process with both fixed and proportional costs of control. *SIAM Journal of Control and Optimization* 15(1), pp. 79–91.

Robertson, D. H. 1940. *Essays in Monetary Theory*. London: Staple Press.

Robinson, Joan. 1933. *The Economics of Imperfect Competition*. London: Macmillan.

———. 1962. *Essays in the Theory of Economic Growth*. London: Macmillan.

Ross, A. M. 1948. *Trade Union Wage Policy*. Berkeley; Calif.: University of California Press.

Rothschild, Michael. 1975. Models of market organization with imperfect information: a survey. *Journal of Political Economy* 81(6), pp. 1283–1308.

Samuelson, Paul A. 1949. *Foundations of Economic Analysis*. Cambridge; Mass.: Harvard University Press.

———. 1964. A brief survey of post-Keynesian developments. In Robert, Lekachman, ed., *Keynes' General Theory: Reports of Three Decades*. New York: St. Martin's Press, pp. 331–47.

———. 1976. *Economics*, 10th ed. New York: McGraw-Hill.

Sargent, Thomas J. 1973. Rational expectations, the real rate of interest and the natural rate of unemployment. *Brookings Papers on Economic Activity*, No. 2, pp. 429–79.

———, and Wallace, N. 1975. "Rational" expectations, the optimal monetary instrument, and the optimal money supply rate. *Journal of Political Economy* 83(2), pp. 241–54.

———, and Wallace, N. 1976. A classical macroeconometric model for the United States. *Journal of Political Economy* 84(2), pp. 207–37.

Sato, Kazuo. 1976. The ideal log-change index number. *Review Economics and Statistics* 58(2), pp. 223–28.

Say, Jean-Baptiste. 1921. *A Treatise of Political Economy*, princeps ed., Boston. (English translation of *Traité d'economice politique*, 1st ed., 1803.)

Scarf, H., Gilford, D., and Shelly, M. 1963. *Multistage Inventory Models and Techniques*. Stanford; Calif.: Stanford University Press.

Scherer, Frederic M. 1970. *Industrial Market Structure and Economic Performance*. Chicago: Rand McNally.

Schultz, Charles L. 1959. Recent inflation in the United States. In *Employment, Growth and Price Levels* (Hearings before the Joint Economic Committee, 86th Congress, 1st Session). Washington, D.C.: U.S. Government Printing Office, pp. 4–10.

Simon, Herbert A. 1955. A behavioral model of rational choice. *Quarterly Journal of Economics* 58(1), pp. 99–118.

———. 1959. Theories of decision making in economics and social sciences. *American Economic Review* 49(3), pp. 253–83.

———. 1972. The theories of bounded rationality. In C. B. McGuire and Roy, Radner, eds., *Decision and Organization: A Volume in Honour of Jacob Marschak*. Amsterdam: North-Holland, pp. 161–76.

———, and Bonini, Charles P. 1958. The size distribution of business firms. *American Economic Review* 48(4), pp. 607–17.

Solow, Robert M. 1968. Short-run adjustment of employment and output. In J. N. Wolfe, ed., *Value, Capital and Growth: Essays in Honour of Sir John R. Hicks*. Edinburgh: University of Edinburgh Press.

Sraffa, Piero. 1926. Laws of returns under competitive conditions. *Economic Journal* 36, pp. 535–50.

Starr, Ross. 1969. Quasi-equilibria in markets with non-convex preferences. *Econometrica* 37(1), pp. 25–38.

Stigler, George J. 1961. The economics of information. *Journal of Political Economy* 69(3), pp. 213–25.

Tarshis, Lorie. 1939. Changes in real money wages. *Economic Journal* 49(193), pp. 150–54.

Theil, Henri. 1971. *Principles of Econometrics*. New York: Wiley.

Tobin, James. 1965. Money and economic growth. *Econometrica* 33(4), pp. 671–84.

———. 1972. Inflation and unemployment. *American Economic Review* 62(1), pp. 1–18.

———. 1975. Keynesian models of recession and depression. *American Economic Review* (Papers and Proceedings) 65(2), pp. 195–202.

Triffin, Robert, 1940. *Monopolistic Competition and General Equilibrium Theory*. Cambridge; Mass.: Harvard University Press.

Vial, Jean-Phillipe. 1972. A continuous time model for the cash balance problem. In G. P. Szegö and K. Shell, eds., *Mathematical Methods in Investment and Finance*. Amsterdam: North-Holland, pp. 244–91.

Walras, Leon. 1954. *Elements of Pure Economics*. Homewood, Ill.: Irwin. (English translation of *Eléments d'économie pure*, Lausanne, 1874 and 1877, by W. Jaffe.)

Weintraub, Sidney. 1959. *A General Theory of the Price Level, Output, Income Distribution and Economic Growth*. Philadelphia: Chilton.

Wicksell, Knut. 1907. The influence of the rate of interest on prices. *Economic Journal* 17(27), pp. 213–19.

———. 1935. *Lectures on Political Economy:* vol. 2: *Money*. London: Routledge & Kegan Paul. (English translation of *Vorlesungen über Nationalökonomie*, vol. 2, 1906, by E. Classen.)

———. 1936. *Interest and Prices*. London: Macmillan. (English translation of *Geldzins und Güterpreise*, 1898, by R. F. Kahn.)

———. 1958. The influence of the rate of interest on commodity prices. In *Selected Papers on Economic Theory*. Cambridge; Mass.: Harvard University Press. (The original article was published in 1898.)

Younes, Y. 1976. On the role of money in the process of exchange and existence of non-Walrasian equilibrium. *Review of Economic Studies* 42(4), pp. 489–501.

Index

Cowles Foundation Monographs

1. Charles F. Roos, *Dynamic Economics* (out of print)
2. Charles F. Roos, *NRA Economic Planning* (out of print)
3. Alfred Cowles and Associates, *Common-Stock Indexes* (2nd edition) (out of print)
4. Dickson H. Leavens, *Silver Money* (out of print)
5. Gerhard Tintner, *The Variate Difference Method* (out of print)
6. Harold T. Davis, *The Analysis of Economic Time Series* (out of print)
7. Jacob L. Mosak, *General-Equilibrium Theory in International Trade* (out of print)
8. Oscar Lange, *Price Flexibility and Employment* (out of print)
9. George Katona, *Price Control and Business* (out of print)
10. Tjalling C. Koopmans, ed., *Statistical Inference in Dynamic Economic Models* (out of print)
11. Lawrence R. Klein, *Economic Fluctuations in the United States, 1921–1941* (out of print)
12. Kenneth J. Arrow, *Social Choice and Individual Values* (2nd edition)
13. Tjalling C. Koopmans, ed., *Activity Analysis of Production and Allocation*
14. William C. Hood and Tjalling C. Koopmans, eds., *Studies in Econometric Method* (out of print)
15. Clifford Hildreth and F. G. Jarrett, *A Statistical Study of Livestock Production and Marketing*
16. Harry M. Markowitz, *Portfolio Selection: Efficient Diversification of Investments*
17. Gerald Debreu, *Theory of Value: An Axiomatic Analysis of Economic Equilibrium*
18. Alan S. Manne and Harry M. Markowitz, eds., *Studies in Process Analysis: Economy-Wide Production Capabilities* (out of print)

(over)

19. Donald D. Hester and James Tobin, eds., *Risk Aversion and Portfolio Choice* (out of print)
20. Donald D. Hester and James Tobin, eds., *Studies of Portfolio Behavior* (out of print)
21. Donald D. Hester and James Tobin, eds., *Financial Markets and Economic Activity*
22. Jacob Marschak and Roy Radner, *Economic Theory of Teams*
23. Thomas J. Rothenberg, *Efficient Estimation with A Priori Information*
24. Herbert Scarf, *The Computation of Economic Equilibria*
25. Donald D. Hester and James L. Pierce, *Bank Management and Portfolio Behavior*
26. William D. Nordhaus, *The Efficient Use of Energy Resources*
27. Katsuhito Iwai, *Disequilibrium Dynamics: A Theoretical Analysis of Inflation and Unemployment*

Orders for Monographs 12, 13, 16, 17, 22, 23, 24, 25, 26, and 27 should be sent to Yale University Press, 92A Yale Station, New Haven, Conn. 06520, or 13 Bedford Square, London WC1 B3JF, England.

Orders for Monograph 15 should be sent to John Wiley & Sons, Inc., 605 Third Avenue, New York, N.Y. 10016.

Orders for Monographs 14 and 21 should be sent to University Microfilms, 300 North Zeeb Road, Ann Arbor, Michigan 48106.